NEVER SLEEP AGAIN

NEVER SLEEP AGAIN

THE ELM STREET LEGACY

THE MAKING OF WES CRAVEN'S

A NIGHTMARE ON ELM STREET

THOMMY HUTSON

Foreword by WES CRAVEN

First Published by: Red Rover Books, 2016

DESIGN
Cover designed by—Tara Vermette at Tru Blu Grafix
Frontispiece Art—Nathan Milliner
Art Direction & Layout—Peter M. Bracke

ISBN: 978-1-958842-42-3
Library of Congress Control Number: 2024941312

Published by Dark Ink, 2024,
Southwick, MA.
www.DarkInkBooks.com
Dark Ink and its logo are trademarked by AM Ink Publishing.

www.elmstreetbook.com

For Wes

"The wicked spirits...injured men in their sleep...and men called them the nightmare."
– St. Michael

"To die to sleep, to sleep, perchance to dream; Ay, there's the rub."
– William Shakespeare

"Whatever you do, don't fall asleep."
– Nancy Thompson

Table of Contents

Preface by Robert Shaye

You think making this film would have been easy. It was not.

The gestation was long and arduous. Wes had a great idea. Extremely marketable. Unique. But he couldn't get an accomplished producer interested. So, he deigned to show it to us. Somewhat less accomplished.

Five grand for an option. Wes would do re-writes that resonated based on our discussions and notes. Though both of us were stridently opinionated, we got along reasonably well. The script evolved nicely. As did casting and creative personnel. All that was required was the finance. Kind of what producers principally do. There again, we were less than accomplished.

Deals appeared, and deals disappeared. We had hired a cast and crew, and I had to start paying them, personally. I've been warned about that. Two weeks before we were supposed to "start" shooting, I was asked to give an important speech at an investment conference entitled, "How to Finance Independent Productions." This was the same week that the crew was quitting and I had been advised that New Line was about to go bust.

Anyhow, as sometimes does happen, the whole thing worked. And one of the greatest thrills a producer can experience is to see lines around the block opening night. The scary prelude definitely added to the thrill.

As the cliché goes, the rest is history. But never to be forgotten is my gratitude to Wes, Robert, Johnny, Heather, and the entire team. More of a labor of love for some than others, but the result reflected much talent, originality, inspiration, and guts. The film speaks for itself.

Your interest in this very special production is greatly appreciated.

(Also a shout out to Thommy for a hell of a job that was clearly a labor of love. This book is personally much appreciated.)

Foreword by Wes Craven

Author's note: The below text first appeared in the limited-edition, hardcover version of this book. Sadly, Wes Craven passed away on August 30th, 2015. His foreword is reprinted here as he originally wrote it.

I had nightmares as a kid, and after a particularly scary night, I asked my mother if she could come with me into my dreams to keep the boogey man away. She answered as gently as she could that sleep was the one place we all had to go alone.

I was appalled.

But that realization became the cornerstone of *A Nightmare on Elm Street*.

Freddy began as a real-life man who woke me when I was around ten. We lived in a second-story apartment in Cleveland, and my bedroom window overlooked the street. There was a muttering and shuffling out there, so I went to the window. An old man dressed in a long overcoat and felt hat was approaching, and when he got under my window, he stopped dead in his tracks and looked straight towards my window. I jumped back into the shadows and waited for him to go. After what seemed like an eternity, I looked again. He was still there, and thrust his head forward with an I-can-see-you leer, looking directly into my eyes. Then he started for the entrance of our building, looking over his shoulder at me the whole while.

I ran to our apartment door and listened. The door to the street opened. I woke my big brother and he ran out with a baseball bat. And the man was gone.

But he stayed with me, too.

Studying psychology in college, I was fascinated by Freud and Jung's exploration of dreams, and I began keeping dream journals. It wasn't long before dreams were as much a part of my reality as waking life. After years of this I began to be aware I was dreaming while still in the dream. And with that I began writing my own dreams. My life soon doubled in scope.

Just as it did years later for Nancy.

After college and now a filmmaker, I was exploring Eastern Mysticism and ran across the writings of a Russian mystic name Gurdjieff. He wrote about how consciousness was a spectrum that stretched from where most of us are, basically sleep-walking through life, to a rarely visited peak of absolute consciousness, where one was in total mindfulness. Few went there, the mystic wrote, because of the pain involved with

seeing things so bluntly. Most people would have "gone out a door" by that time, back into the sleep of food, sex, intoxication, job, or any of a thousand other distractions. But that rare person that could bear to keep his or her eyes open, looking straight at the nitty-gritty: that we all die, are violent to each other and, as parents, often hide dark secrets that will later cost our children dearly; that hardy person could make a difference in the world. These are the heroes. Spiritual warriors.

Like Nancy.

About four films into my career as a maker of scary movies, I happened across a newspaper story of a young man in Los Angeles who had suffered from nightmares in which he was pursued by a monstrous man intent on killing him. So real were the dreams that this kid decided to stop sleeping. He stayed awake a day, two days, three, four—until his family worried for his very sanity. His father, a physician, gave him sleeping pills, and finally, one evening while watching TV with his family, he at last fell asleep. His father carried him to his bedroom and tucked him in. The family went to bed thinking the crisis was finally over. Then in the middle of the night they heard him screaming. They rushed to his room to see him thrashing on his bed. Before they got to him, he fell still and was dead. An autopsy found no physical harm. His father discovered the uningested sleeping pills. His mother found a long extension cord that led to a coffee maker in the boy's closet, full of hot black coffee.

That was all I needed. I sat down and began to write.

There would be a girl, Nancy. Ordinary on the surface, but heroic to the bone. She would know what everyone else was denying: that there was a monstrous human, like in a horror film. But this man wasn't masked behind leather or plastic, but by his own scarred face—the evidence of what Nancy's parents and their friends did to him. His wardrobe? As seen from a Cleveland window. His weapon? A combination of the most miraculous thing: the human hand, and the most nightmarish: the primal claws of the eternal predator.

As for his name? The name of the worst bully I knew in grade school was Freddy. "Hmm," I thought, "that'll do just fine."

And *A Nightmare on Elm Street* was born.

It was a movie that was almost unmade before it was finally made. The process was one that took its toll in a number of ways, and I look back and recall how it was difficult, strenuous and, at times, exasperating. Conversely, making the film also had its rewards: it was as fun as it was challenging, and it was more than just another horror film. New friendships were made and filmmaking boundaries were encountered and, mostly out of necessity and ingenuity, breached.

Always hoping I might say something interesting with my films, this was a project that allowed me to do just that in a way that could, if I did my job well, give viewers a new way to see terror—even when they closed their eyes.

Creating what some have called a genre icon was just icing on the cake.

Ultimately, one could say everything about *Elm Street* worked in the way it was supposed to. For better or worse, in good times and bad.

This is that story.

Wes Craven on the set of *A Nightmare on Elm Street*.

Introduction

As I write these words, I frequently pause to take in the mountain view outside the window of my home office. The sun is shining, birds are chirping, and yes, there is even the occasional sighting of a slinking bobcat searching for the rabbit that ducked into the brush near a set of evergreens.

Strange a sight as that may be, what keeps my attention most is that even though I am crafting a tome about a film starring a particular razor-gloved dream demon, the recurring, almost unbelievable, thought that jolts me back to the task at hand is this: can it really be that I first encountered the inimitable Freddy Krueger four decades ago?

They say you always remember your first time and, let me tell you, they (whomever "they" are) weren't lying.

Looking back, I didn't see an inordinate amount of movies in the theater as a child (that would eventually change), but I seemed to devour films on television as fast as they would air. Many of those early experiences have stayed with me through the years:

Superman (1978) – A film I gazed upon with wondrous eyes. An unforgettable hero, a whip-smart leading lady, and a diabolical villain. And Christopher Reeve really made me believe a man can fly.

Grease (1978) – For years to come I would firmly believe breaking into song at any moment to express my feelings was not only appropriate, but also necessary.

The Muppet Movie (1979) – The lessons in that film about friendship and staying true to one's self are as real and important today as the first time I learned them.

E.T.: the Extra-Terrestrial (1982) – I was certain I had my very own alien waiting for me in the barn.

And of course, the *Star Wars* trilogy (1977–1983) – For a time, which was admittedly far too long, I thought I was Luke Skywalker; and I don't mind the Ewoks, so everybody stop judging me.

Simply put, I loved movies.

I sought out adventure, romance, musicals, drama, science-fiction, and animation. Movies, movies, movies. Strangely enough to me now, especially at this moment, what I did not seek out was horror. It was a genre of film that I did not see, nor barely knew existed until it was, quite literally, thrust upon me.

It was the early eighties and it all started with—as who is now arguably the most famous "mama's boy" in history, Norman Bates, would say—Mother. Well, my grandmother to be exact. Yes, that maternal nurturer on my mother's side, the one my parents entrusted to care for me, keep me safe, and ensure I grow up big and strong and stable—

Made me watch *Salem's Lot* (1979) with her.

Yes, *made* me. My cousin had brought over this thing called a VCR, Grandma popped in this thing called a videocassette, and the terror, somehow recorded from a television broadcast, unfolded. I was scared. And I firmly believe that when the vampiric Glick boy floated on the screen with fangs bared, enshrouded in fog, and scratched on the bedroom window, I was scarred as well. In any case, it was a defining moment for me, because although I was terrified and tried not to watch, I did watch.

Then I wanted to watch. Then I stayed home from grade school, pretending to be sick, so I could absorb the overabundance of fright fare that pay cable was offering. (Sorry for playing hooky, Dad, to catch *Motel Hell* [1980] on HBO, but thanks for bringing me the *Jedi* coloring book to cheer me up when I was, ahem, "sick.")

After all that, still many more cover-my-eyes moments would happen at home with family and friends. I longed to obtain the thrill of feeling terrified, dreading what lurked around every corner, but all the while knowing that by the end of the movie, I'd be safe.

It was at this time I somehow became entranced with the idea of seeing a horror film in a movie theater; it couldn't possibly be more terrifying than watching one in the safety of my living room, under my favorite blanket, surrounded by family, right?

I learned the answer very quickly when my older brother and his friends (it's at this point I should have placed a lot of blame for my taste in movies on my family) made a trek to the timeworn movie house on the corner of Titus and Broadway streets in Buffalo, New York to see some werewolf movie. This was 1981. I was still a little kid and the film was, of course, John Landis' classic horror comedy *An American Werewolf in London*.

"You can't come with us," my brother scolded, ticking off a list of reasons even my child-eyes could see through: I was too little (that didn't stop anyone before), I would never get past the ticket lady (everyone got past the ticket lady) and, the topper, that the movie was just too scary (please).

Really?

I remember looking him in the eye and telling him, with every bit of seriousness and big kid bluster I could exhibit, "Believe me, I can handle a scary movie!" So in we went.

I can't remember a time when I ever felt more terrified.

Barely a frame of the film was viewed by my little eyes after the moment the first howl rang across the moors, a sound filtered through the theater's stereo speakers before sinking deep into my soul. I closed my eyes as tight as I could. I plugged my ears. It was more than I could endure. Every once in a while I would look at my brother and his friends and see them laughing. Laughing! I wasn't sure what they were seeing, but it wasn't funny to me. (Years later, it would be.)

I decided I would stick to terrors on the tube, thank you very much.

And so it went, me catching whatever fright fare I could find—WPIX out of New York City, and WWOR out of Secaucus, New Jersey were particularly good at quenching my genre thirst. A *Friday the 13th* (1980) sequel here, a *Halloween* (1978) movie there, until one night, while watching the series *V* (1984–1985), it came on the television: a commercial for a horror film that did more to scare me than anything my grandmother, my cousin, my brother, or television had shown me before. My heart raced as I watched the images flicker across the screen. How could a face be pressing through a wall? Was that a claw? Who is the man with the arms that keep stretching out!? I ran out of the room, not even knowing what the title of such terror was, but I was sure of two things: I had never felt such fear, and I *had* to see that movie.

The one-screen Lincoln Theater in Buffalo, New York. For a single dollar I was scared out of my mind "watching" *An American Werewolf in London*. Sadly, the building was destroyed by fire in the nineties.

I knew I was finally ready for the big time.

Days went by where I was simultaneously enraptured and terrified by the notion that the preview might come on again. And then I finally worked up the courage to ask my father if he would take me to see this film. Politics aside, he rightly said I was too young.

I was also persistent.

I kept at him, angling to see this phantasmagoric concoction of terror, mystery, and blood. And he kept saying "no." But my time would come when he spied me looking through the Friday newspaper entertainment section. I happened to be cutting out the small ad for the film, which I had now come to know as 1984's *A Nightmare on Elm Street* (oh, that title! So scary. So real!), ready to tape it to my bedroom wall, when he came over, defeated.

"You really want to see this thing?" he asked, almost certainly against his better judgment. Judgment be damned, my small self thought; this is what adults call a breakthrough!

"Yes, please, let's go, it will be great, you'll like it!" I exclaimed. Whether it was my pathetic attempt to convince him it was a good idea for him to see the film and have me tag along, or just that I probably looked pitiful, he agreed. We went that afternoon, driving into the city to the General Cinema.

What happened next would be ingrained in my memory forever.

From almost the first moment, I was petrified. I resolved myself to watch, even though I feared my heart would burst from beating so fast. And when that man, that monster, popped up behind that pretty, young, blonde girl in the boiler room nightmare, I was literally paralyzed with fear. The audience screamed.

I started to cry.

Maybe I wasn't ready after all.

And when I begged and begged to go home, my father did what every responsible parent would have done to teach their movie-obsessed child a lesson. He turned to me and said, "You wanted to watch this thing, so we're staying!" And that's exactly what we did.

I can't blame him. He was right: I did want to watch it. So for the next ninety-one minutes I stared through squinted, covered eyes at a screen filled with screams, mayhem, and murder. And though I didn't watch it all, I did catch more than my previous horror-movie-in-a-theater excursion, and I saw the things that would be forever etched into the minds and memories of every moviegoer with me.

A dirty brown hat. A filthy red and green sweater. A horribly burned man. And what would become a trademark as iconic as a shower in *Psycho* (1960) or a machete in *Friday the 13th*, I saw knives for fingers. Sharpened, pointed steel that glistened in light and shrieked against metal.

I saw Freddy Krueger. And my life was never going to be the same. Fortunately for me, I wasn't alone.

Freddy Krueger and *A Nightmare on Elm Street* have since become a big part of not only my life, or the lives of countless fans, but part of popular culture around the globe. What started out as a film that no one wanted, and one that saw writer and director Wes Craven desperate for money as he tried to sell the project, has turned into a veritable cornucopia of entertainment. Through eight original films, a television series, a remake, and more consumer products than one could count, Freddy Krueger became a fixture of the times.

The lingering question on the minds of many is, simply, "Why?" What is it about a child-murdering, burnt maniac who kills people in their dreams that is so fascinating, so compelling? The answer may lie in the question. Dreams. Nightmares. It was a brilliant conceit that gripped moviegoers; the idea that in this film there is a villain who can break the tenuous boundary between reality and illusion. A villain that can eradicate the hoped-for line between what is safe and what is not. How can you possibly survive when the evil after you is, in essence, within your own mind?

What's more, the first line of defense for many is to jump into bed, pull the covers over their head, close their eyes,

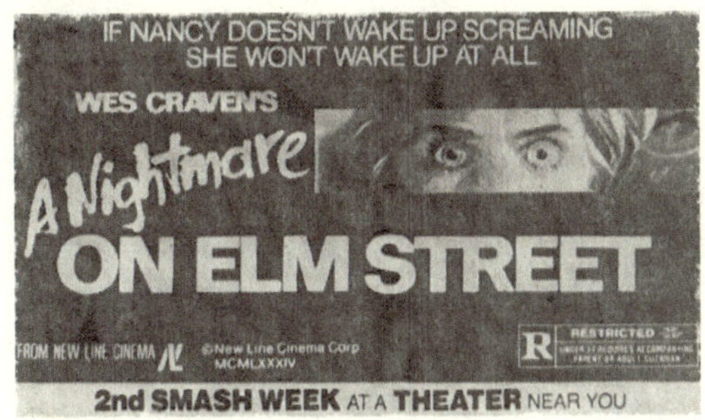

The clipping I'll never forget. When my father saw me cutting with such precision, he relented. (I'm sure I threw in a look that said, "Don't worry, Dad. I'll just make do with this. I bet the movie isn't very good, anyway.")

and wait the terror out. But on Elm Street, that good night's sleep may very well be your last.

That notion was also something attractive to horror film aficionados. In a time when most genre films were hacking limbs and spilling guts in far-off, woodsy retreats, Freddy Krueger literally got us where we lived. *A Nightmare on Elm Street* was proving the point that neighborhoods could be just as scary as campgrounds, and that the chaste girl next door was just as vulnerable as the loose one on the corner. The film gave audiences a chance to take a break from mindless, masked killers out to destroy sex-starved teenagers.

But Freddy Krueger, who would evolve from an in-the-shadows terror to the wisecracking bastard son of a hundred maniacs, needed no mask. His modus operandi was to show you his face, hoping to look each victim in the eye as he absorbed the one thing that fueled his rage: fear. Fear of death. Fear of abandonment. And for some, fear of life itself.

What makes *Elm Street* so compelling is that Freddy Krueger is not about mindlessly slicing up any who cross his path. Instead, he creates a symphony of terror—psychological as well as visceral—rooted in one of the oldest human concepts: revenge.

It's a motif that proves Freddy Kruger has a plan. Freddy Krueger has a reason. The fact that this unabashed vengeance is generated by the sins of the parents leads the on-screen, teenaged victims to feel already defeated by a world that was supposed to protect them. Consequently, their deaths become a mockery of their lives: Tina Gray, the young girl looked upon as easy, dies half naked in bed. Rod Lane, the troublemaking bad boy, dies in a jail cell. Glen, the jock, fades into slumber instead of helping his girlfriend and literally disappears in a fountain of blood.

But then there is Nancy Thompson, representing all the good that young people can do and be. A singular point of hope, she finally understands a way to undo the evil that had been thrust upon her. It's this notion of taking charge, fighting back, and facing your fear that brings the nightmare full circle, for even though the sins of the past may never be forgiven, they might, in some small way, be rectified. And the bogeyman can finally be put in his place.

At least until the sequel.

The film and its villain opened up to me the idea that movies on the big screen were oftentimes scarier and more powerful than those I saw on our small, living room television. That when I left the cinema, the larger-than-life images stayed deep in my mind far longer than when I simply got up and left the living room. As I grew up, the *Nightmare* films and Freddy Krueger grew up with me and, I must admit, wound up being a bigger part of my life, in one way or another, than I would ever have imagined as a little boy.

The very powerful memory of seeing the film for the first time helped me land my job as a Universal Studios Tour Guide when I first arrived in Los Angeles to follow my dreams. (We were given a minute to speak extemporaneously, and I was

Thommy Hutson (center), Heather Langenkamp, and Robert Englund pay a visit to a location well-known to every *Nightmare* fan: Nancy Thompson's *Elm Street* home in Los Angeles, California.

asked to describe a movie that impacted me; boy, did I luck out.)

Wes Craven's imagination, and creation, gave me the power to believe I, too, could one day make my mark in the ever-evolving business of entertainment when I thought of packing it in and going back home. Believe it or not, I asked for a sign if I should stay or go, and one day, I got it: while taking a route home I normally wouldn't have, I noticed the marquee at the now long gone Galaxy Theater on Hollywood Boulevard showcasing the director's latest, *Wes Craven's New Nightmare* (1994). I hopped off, saw the film and, well, I suppose you know.

So here I now sit, the sky a little darker, the birds silent and, yes, a rabbit now pushing daisies, looking back on four decades of history for the movie that started it all. I'm reminded of the hard work, dedication, and creativity of every single person associated with the film. Of the movie magic that was imagined and realized. Of the launched careers of many who have gone on to make their own indelible mark in Hollywood. And most personal of all, how I have been lucky to meet so many of them, and luckier to say that more than a few are now my good friends.

As many travelers know, every town seems to have an Elm Street, and though it was a long, winding road getting to the one that Wes Craven dreamed up, it's a place all involved have, in some way, come of age.

And now, the creator, cast, and crew of the seminal, original film have come together to tell their *Elm Street* story. Dramatic, sweeping, funny, poignant, and always honest, these are the tales told by those who lived it. And like them, I stepped into the darkened theater, survived the nightmare, and emerged into the light of day a little different. Someone stronger, more resourceful, and wiser. Ready to tackle my nightmares and achieve my dreams.

So turn out the lights, pull the covers up close, and get ready for a bedtime story like none other. It's the saga of a little movie that could, and did. *A Nightmare on Elm Street*, in all its ingenious terror, and Freddy Krueger, in all his wicked glory, will be revealed in a way that shows how both have enraptured a generation of moviegoers, and then some.

Sweet dreams...

1

Dream Weaver

Elm Street Creator Wes Craven

Nineteen seventy-two.

Atari kicked off the first generation of video games with the arcade release of *Pong*. Incumbent president Richard Nixon won re-election in a landslide vote. The last U.S. ground units began leaving Vietnam. The Goodyear Blimp set to the skies for its very first flight. The FBI started admitting female officers. The world of movies saw *The Godfather*, *The Poseidon Adventure*, and *What's Up, Doc?* leading the box office. And within the context of Coordinated Universal Time, it was the longest year ever, as two leap seconds were added during this 366-day calendar, an event that has not since been repeated.

By all accounts it was a remarkable year of firsts and milestones. But there was another event, unmarked in the lives of many everyday citizens, heralded by rabid fans of the horror movie genre: the release of *The Last House on the Left*, a hypnotically brutal rape and revenge film which marked the auspicious debut of then thirty-three-year-old writer and director Wes Craven.

Born on August 2, 1939 in Cleveland, Ohio, Craven was brought up in what now might be looked upon as a fire and brimstone Baptist household. The tenets of his upbringing were as

HNSON
BARGAIN ST
NEWS
WILLKIE RETURNS & TESTIF
BRITISH MOP-UP
NEW U.S. DEFENSE PLAN
CLEVELAND PLAIN DEA
8th YEAR—NO. 295
CLEVELAND, SATURDAY MORNING, OCTOBER 21, 1939

powerfully enforced as they might seem cliché: no movies, no smoking, no drinking, no card playing.

Though this "protection" from the horrors of the world may have worked for some, shadows lurked around many corners of Craven's life: his parents separated when he was just four years old and, on the eve of his sixth birthday, Craven had heard his father died of a heart attack. Admitting to not sharing the religious views of those around him, he states, "I failed to find Jesus, find redemption. I felt I was at fault. [I] had a very dark view of myself."

Even with such early darkness, which he admits has had a lasting impact on his life and art, Craven never dreamed he would one day be referred to as a master of horror and suspense. "I didn't see a great many films when I was young, because I was restricted from seeing them by my family," he says. "With the exception of Walt Disney films, which were consistently, you know, kind of safe, Hollywood and its product was considered to be kind of the work of the devil."

But when Craven was young, just after his father had passed, he did get to experience real life on the screen in the form of newsreels shown to him by his best friend's father. "This man would take us to Telenews at the end of World War II, and we'd watch all these newsreels," he recalls. "So I had seen film, but I'd seen real stuff. That kind of stuck in my mind."

Though the real world on screen was buried deep in his mind, it wasn't until Craven was far away at college that he started to really experience, and ultimately fall in love with, the cinema. "The films of Buñuel, Fellini, Bergman, Cocteau. I was immediately drawn to these sort of fantastic visions of dreamlike things," he says.

While Craven discovered something about which he was passionate, real life could not be ignored.

By the mid to late sixties, while the rest of America was caught up in a whirlwind of free love, radical change, and recreational drugs, Craven was immersed in the complexities of family life and career. With a new wife, Bonnie, two children, Jonathan and Jessica, and equipped with a background in education and a master's degree in writing and philosophy from Johns Hopkins University, Craven found himself trading the creative for the collegiate, teaching humanities at Clarkson College in Potsdam, New

This page: Wes Craven, the man who would create one of horror cinema's biggest icons, poses for his high school photo.

Opposite page (counterclockwise from bottom right): A page from the May 8, 1968 Clarkson College newspaper, *The Integrator*, sits alongside the school's old main building, a college-aged Craven playing guitar, and Craven as a professor. The cost for audiences to see Craven's first project, billed as the "ultimate movie experience?" Fifty cents.

The INTEGRATOR, Wednesday, May 8, 1968, Page 5

The Potsdam Underground Surfaces With Pandora Experimentia

On Friday and Saturday nights, May 10 and 11, The Clarkson Drama Club prepares to hoist itself out of the depths of oblivion with its cinematographic presentation of "Pandora Experimentia." This ultimate movie experience, written and directed by John F. Heneage and Kenneth D. Lyon, and photographed by Wes Craven, will be shown along with several short experimental films in Damon Hall, Room 101, at 7, 8, and 9 o'clock.

Shot on location in Potsdam with the cooperation of many local businesses, "Pandora Experimentia" hopes to attain an equal rating with such great films as "The Dragon Lilies of Kazunga" and "Gidget Goes Berserk." With a cast of over sixty, Ondo Mustner, underground movie guru without whom the entire movie could not have been possible, is able to conquer the wide screen in naked color, Ultra-Vision, and Vision-Vision. Interviewed at his Spring retreat in the Bahamas, Mustner was quoted as saying, "Not once did my directors use any common knowledge or sense of decency, therefore I will be using them for all my films in the near future."

While filming, the entire technical crew was arrested, fourteen belly dancers disappeared from Raja Maja's harem, and the two directors appeared on the F. B. I.'s missing persons list.

Hundreds of people were unaware that they were being filmed by hidden cameras as the "Pandora Experimentia" crew swept over Potsdam like a case of acute ingrown toenail. Even innocent little children fell under the great cogwheels of the budding Clarkson film industry. Everyone was amazed how the directors could cram so much excitement, suspense, sex, mystery, intrigue, sex, and spaghetti into forty minutes of film.

To encourage a big turnout this weekend for the chance of a lifetime to view an experimental film in which "you might be one of the cast," an award will be given to the film critic who can determine beforehand the exact number of splices that will break in the film during the two days of showing.

The Potsdam police finally exposed.

Body transplants were interrupted.

The directors being booked for Censored

Party Director.

York. Still, the erstwhile professor could not ignore the itch to scratch the burgeoning filmmaker in his own mind.

Armed with a sixteen-millimeter camera (a Revere, which he had purchased) and a handful of eager students from the drama club, Craven took part in creating a forty-five minute film entitled *Pandora Experimentia* (1968), a spoof on the immensely popular television show *Mission: Impossible* (1966–1973). Shot by Craven, and made for the meager sum of three hundred dollars, he recalls, "None of us knew about sound, none of us knew about editing, none of us knew about cinema. It was more like, 'Let's make as many mistakes as possible and see what happens.'"

The project, which had club members placing bets on whether the film would come apart during its two showings, might not have made an enormous impact on the general public, but it did have an effect on Craven. He quickly understood that while he may have had a thing or two to learn about the true craft of making movies, he was bound and determined to find his way out of the respectable teaching profession and into the tumultuous cinematic world. "I just realized I was profoundly bored and out of place," the writer and director admits.

That ennui was something quite tangible, too, when Craven's department chairman confronted him with the notion he stop playing around with a movie camera. Before long, the emerging moviemaker remembered being given an ultimatum when his superior stated, "I want you to either get your Ph.D., or you're fired."

Clearly understanding his options, Craven knew what he had to do: he quit on the spot. "It just wasn't me, so I made one of those big leaps," he recalls. "I said, 'I'm gonna take a shot at doing something I would really enjoy,' so I quit and went to New York [City]."

That leap of faith would change Craven's life—for worse and for better. In between having to drive a cab for half-a-year to make ends meet (a job in which he was robbed twice), his indoctrination into the world of professional filmmaking started with him being a messenger for filmmaker-turned-musician Harry Chapin.

Of his time working with and observing Chapin and his team, whose documentary detailing the exploits of American boxers, *Legendary Champions* (1968), was nominated for an Academy Award, Craven says, "It was a unique opportunity, because it was within a very wide-open structure of people that were making documentaries, little feature films, industrials, everything. So I got exposed to a great amount of technique."

Though Craven learned to edit film, it wasn't the place he ultimately imagined himself, so he pushed onward and made as many connections in the New York film community as he could; as well as taking as many jobs as he could find. "I worked all around the clock, just going from one job to another," he remembers.

This intense period of work, although creatively interesting and more satisfying than teaching, took its toll. Craven ran himself physically and emotionally ragged, dropping down to one hundred thirty-five pounds and seeing the end of his nuptials. "My marriage collapsed. I had virtually nothing," he remembers. "It was a real watershed in my life. I was dropping out, doing drugs, getting into filmmaking."

IT'S ONLY A MOVIE

It was that getting-into-filmmaking process that led to a chance meeting with hopeful film producer and director Sean S. Cunningham. In a matter of weeks, Craven happily realized his earlier editing skills would come into play when he was tasked with syncing dailies for Cunningham's second feature film, *Together* (1971).

"This was, I guess 1970, 1971, right in there, and we were at a point in time where anything seemed possible," Cunningham recalls. "Wes and I were two guys that really didn't know how to make movies, but were gonna try to figure out how to do it outside of the system."

Wes Craven on the set of *The Last House on the Left* with children Jonathan and Jessica.

The film was the very first feature on which Craven worked. "I came in to synch up dailies from a two-day shoot, so it was supposed to be a very short job," he says.

That brief work led Craven to stay on as assistant editor to Roger Murphy, who ultimately left the film, giving Craven the ability to expand his duties. "It left Sean and I together and we were pretty much the same age. We had kids about the same ages," he states. "We kind of related to each other very easily and that ended with my becoming the editor, pretty much, and taking the film through the mix with Sean. We really bonded, staying up all hours and everything."

The experience kept Craven at the forefront of Cunningham's mind when the latter was offered the chance to produce a new, and scary, film. This time, Craven would take part in the project from the very beginning. "It was a huge step for me," he admits. "In the course of one year I went from just some guy synching up dailies to a guy who had a feature film about to be put in his lap."

Craven was eventually given the chance to finally do what he had set out to do. "Sean had been offered ninety thousand dollars as the whole budget for a scary movie as a result of *Together*," he remembers. "He asked me if I wanted to write it and direct it and cut it. I said, 'Sure,' even though I never thought of writing a scary movie before. So I said, 'Okay, what's a horror film?'"

The answer was a gritty revenge picture based loosely on an Ingmar Bergman film classic. Originally titled *Sex Crime of the Century*, and later re-titled *Night of Vengeance*, the film would soon be known to an unsuspecting world as *The Last House on the Left*. "When I saw [Bergman's] *The Virgin Spring* (1960) I thought, 'What an incredible story.' I just thought it would be great to update into something completely bizarre," Craven muses.

Left to right: Mari Collingwood (Sandra Cassell) rebuffs Junior Stillo (Marc Sheffler); Craven works to prepare actress Lucy Grantham (playing Phyllis) for a chase scene. "The reason why people still talk about the film is it was the first of its kind," states Sheffler. "It was exactly what Wes had in mind: take film violence from the background, where people get shot and then just fall over and you wouldn't really see anything, and throw it up into the front."

The cinéma vérité, documentary approach to the powerful violence in the story of two young girls who are captured, raped, and killed, then later avenged by the parents of one of them, was as successful as it was polarizing. The synergy of Craven's sheltered upbringing, professorial past, and many styles of filmmaking came together in a way that took audiences to what seemed to be the edge of madness. Years later, Craven waxes philosophical about the venture. "My feeling as an academic, and I did approach it in some ways academically, was that until you, sort of, disembowel a human and, sort of, see the messiness of the inside, you haven't come to the essence of the matter, which is the complete mortality and the kind of unglamorousness of our bodies exempt from our minds and spirits," he reveals. "And so I felt it was important to go to that level."

David Hess, who portrayed the terrifying and terrorizing lead villain, Krug, agreed. "It wasn't an Earth-driven movie, it was created by some other kind of force. It was like we were tools of something else," he recalled. "There has never been another movie like it, nor will there be."

And if Craven, as a first-time writer and director, set out to make a statement about society, he succeeded in spades. "I see [*Last House*] as a protest film," he says. "It had, among other things, as well as attempting to be a popular film and a controversial film, been an attempt to show violence the way I and the producer thought it really was."

And violence was, at the time, something at the forefront of America, very much being displayed for all to see in the horrors of the Vietnam War. "Not to put too fine a point on it, but I very much was influenced—and I think the whole country was kind of in a state of shock—for the first time seeing the horror and cruelty of war," Craven states. "Recently shot sixteen-millimeter footage was coming back and appearing on television immediately, so there was little censorship of what you saw, and it was just appalling."

Understanding those ideas and influences was none other than one of the film's women-in-jeopardy, Lucy Grantham, whose character shared more than a few horrific, cringe-inducing moments before a final, almost-too-realistic gutting at the hands of her attackers. "When you put *Last House* in its correct timeframe, it's remarkable, it's gutsy, and it has a wonderful combination of humor and horror," the actress says. "I know Wes prides himself on being able to do that, and a lot of people have tried and failed."

Fellow cast member Marc Sheffler, in his first film role playing the less-than-enthused-about-violence Junior Stillo, believes that the mix of horror and humor not only worked, but was necessary. "If you analyze the film or take it apart, what you'll see is that after every horrific, violent scene, there's a letdown. There's levity," he says. "In a film that's so intensely violent and so intensely emotional, what you have to do is give the audience a chance to catch its breath."

And while it may seem unbelievable now, critic Roger Ebert, somewhat known for his condemnation of almost everything genre, agreed. In his original review, he gave high marks to the writer and director: "Wes Craven's direction never lets us out from under almost unbearable dramatic tension." The stalwart reviewer then went another, unexpected step further to praise what many had found unredeemable, writing, "*Last House on the Left* is a tough, bitter little sleeper of a movie that's about four times as good as you'd expect...[*Last House*] is a powerful narrative, told so directly and strongly that the audience (mostly in the mood for just another good old exploitation film) was rocked back on its psychic heels."

It was reviews such as Ebert's, coupled with an incredibly simple, but memorable ad campaign ("To avoid fainting, keep repeating: it's only a movie...only a movie...")

Sex Crime of the Century, the original title of *The Last House on the Left*, is shown on a script cover page and advertisement. Its final moniker is showcased in a poster that asks, "Can a movie go too far?"

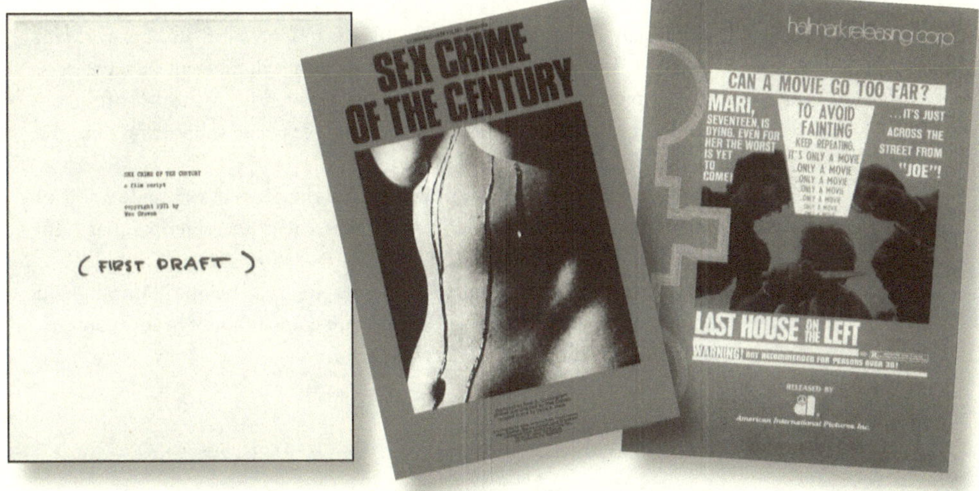

that had audiences lining up for what quickly became one of the most notorious movies of all time. "The reason why people still talk about the film is it was the first of its kind," offers Sheffler. "It was exactly what Wes had in mind: take film violence from the background, where people get shot and then just fall over and you wouldn't really see anything, and throw it up into the front."

Infamous as the film may be for its savage violence, Sheffler makes it known that the on-screen antics were nowhere near the behind-the-scenes activities. "The space between the brutality on the screen and the frivolity off the screen was as wide as the Grand Canyon. We were a bunch of goofy, young people running around the woods in Connecticut with a camera and special effects that were, on the day, very crude and primitive special effects," he says. "But they obviously worked."

Even as recently as 2009, the film was finding new viewers and analyses within the Hollywood ranks when writer and producer James Schamus screened the movie for *Brokeback Mountain* (2005) director and Academy Award-winner Ang Lee. Schamus reportedly told Lee that *Last House* was one of the greatest films ever, to which Lee responded, "You're right, James, it's one of the greatest films ever. And now that I've seen it, it should be banned."

Such a visceral reaction to the film was not uncommon and, says Sheffler, "It allowed people to connect with that really, really dark side and not just watch it from the distance, but actually feel it. It has become a pivotal movie in that particular arena."

Not bad for Craven's writing and directing debut and a film that, at the time, had producer Cunningham wondering, "Could this ever be shot and cut into something that looks like a movie?"

Indeed, it was, and the power of *The Last House on the Left* is something that seems undeniable. It's a film simultaneously admired and abhorred, respected and reviled. Understanding the many points of view, Craven looks back and states, "It is still an assaultive film, it is still a film that just is completely uncompromising and does not make you comfortable." He went on, adding, "In that sense, it had a real purpose to it, and I think it has a legitimate artistic power."

MOVING FORWARD

Having made what many considered an indelible first impression in the world of filmmaking, Craven tried to parlay that artistic power into a number of new projects, tackling ideas from American atrocities in Vietnam to a redux of the horrific fable *Hansel & Gretel*. But even with the financial success of *Last House* supporting him, the projects couldn't land financing.

"[*Hansel & Gretel*] was with Sean Cunningham, and the concept was to do a sort of adult version that was really scary," says Craven. "It was one of many scripts that I did with Sean that we couldn't find financing on."

Other projects that Craven wrote at the time, hoping that he and Cunningham could get them to the screen, included *American Beauty*, a comedy about beauty contests. "We couldn't get money for that, either," Craven recounts.

Another unproduced script of his was *Mustang*, which told the tale of Colonel Anthony Herbert, who is best known for his claims that he observed Vietnam war crimes, though his commanding officer refused to investigate. "Nobody wanted to hear about that either, so those were at least three that I can remember going all the way through a script with Sean where nothing happened," Craven states. "There's been a lot of scripts over the years that I've worked on that must just be in drawers someplace."

With work coming to a standstill, Craven found himself toiling once again in the trenches introduced to him on *Together*: namely, more adult-oriented film fare. This time he would be under the tutelage of director and producer Peter Locke.

"I met Wes at 56 West 45th Street where we were both working on films," recalls Locke. "I was doing something called *You Gotta Walk It Like You Talk It [Or You'll Lose That Beat]* (1971), which was my first film. I'm not quite sure exactly what he was doing but, come to pass, he made *Last House on the Left* and that was all done at the same place. So we knew each other from that area."

A newspaper advertisement for It *Happened in Hollywood* (top), Locke's second feature. Craven also went on to edit Locke's third feature, *The Carhops*, an R-rated sex comedy.

Helming his second feature, *It Happened in Hollywood* (1973), Locke decided to enlist Craven (who traveled to California even as his own *Last House* was just hitting theaters) to help tell the story of a woman, Felicity Split, who hopes to achieve Tinseltown superstardom—the spin on the tale is that she does so in the world of adult films. The project, which subversively caricatured the cliché of chasing Hollywood fame and fortune, was seemingly for "mature audiences only," boasting crude humor and some sexual encounters. It also saw Craven credited thrice as editor, assistant director, and actor. (He was an impossible-to-spot, masked litter-bearer. He wasn't alone; Locke also had an appearance in the film.)

The partnership proved a fine enough experience for Craven to edit Locke's next feature film, the 1975 sex comedy *Kitty Can't Help It* (aka *The Carhops*). The film showcased the sexual proclivities of roller skating waitresses, particularly one named Kitty who is finding it difficult to lose her virginity. "That was an R-rated comedy and we shot it in California, in and around Hollywood," recalls Locke.

"It was a very short phase where there was work, and it was interesting, but it certainly wasn't what I wanted to do," Craven sportingly says of his time on the aforementioned films. "I moved through it, and out, very quickly."

As he exited from his brief foray into sex comedies of the seventies, Craven next landed in the director's chair for a segment of a horror anthology. It was the brainchild of independent filmmaker Roy Frumkes (*Document of the Dead* [1979–2012], *Street Trash* [1987]), who struck up a friendship with Craven after viewing his inaugural film.

"I went to Manhattan to see *Last House on the Left*, knowing nothing about it. But then, who did? And I went with two good friends, a fellow named Bob Winston, who I used to write screenplays with, and also Robert A. Harris, the world's leading restoration man who restored *Vertigo* (1958), *Spartacus* (1960), and *Lawrence of Arabia* (1962)," says Frumkes. "Harris walked out; he couldn't take it. Bob stayed for the whole film, but felt it was the only film he'd ever seen that made a case for censorship."

"Wes was delighted to just walk in on it, think about the script and direct this thing."

Roy Frumkes on *Tales That Will Tear Your Heart Out*

As for Frumkes? "Me, I loved it," he admits. "I was the odd man out and I sensed, while I was watching it, that it was shot in sixteen millimeter, and I really felt it was the director's first film. I was really impressed at what a great job he had done."

Frumkes took down the name of the company behind the film and wrote Craven a letter. "I said, 'If this was your first film, I thought you just did a great job and I wish you lots of luck in the future.' And two weeks later, this large box arrives with all the outtakes and all the various versions of the scripts with the different titles, and a note saying, 'If you like it so much, you can have it,'" he recalls. "The note also said, 'My crew at the screening, they spit at me as they walked out.' And a nice relationship developed from there."

That rapport led to Frumkes, who was teaching film courses at SUNY Purchase, asking Craven to be a part of his project, entitled *Tales That Will Tear Your Heart Out* (1976). "I think there were seven stories. All I did was give each director or writer one little guideline: that this all happened in one night, and these corpses came up and they would try to complete what they were doing when they died," Frumkes explains. "But what they were trying to do when they died, all that was left up to the filmmakers."

Approaching writers and directors who weren't working much at the time, Frumkes was able to get interesting names to participate, such as Ernest Tidyman, writer of *The*

French Connection (1971), Al Kilgore, creator of the *Bullwinkle* comic strip, and DeWitt Bodeen, writer of *Cat People* (1942).

And of course, Craven.

"Wes and I were friends by then and I asked him if he would like to direct one. He didn't want to write it, but he wanted to direct it," remembers Frumkes. "A friend of mine named Allen Pasternak wrote it, and it was a western set about a hundred years ago. Wes was delighted to just walk in on it, think about the script, and direct this thing."

Unfortunately, lack of finances saw the project collapse.

"That was my mistake," Frumkes confesses. "I was producing it and everybody wanted to start simultaneously and I just couldn't say no. So they all grabbed whatever equipment there was at the school, ran off and all the money got used up in the first few weeks. And really, the sequences that had the gore, the ones that were the real ones that would've sold the film, didn't get finished. So I was left with forty or forty-five minutes of unsellable footage."

Craven, however, did finish his segment, utilizing whatever was left to the best of his abilities, something for which Frumkes gives the director high praise. "When everyone came to grab the equipment they just all ran away and Wes was kind of standing there scratching his head," he says. "There were three lights left and he's supposed to shoot a western. We'd arranged barns and all these big sets, and he just nonchalantly took the stuff and he designed these cathedral-like cross lights; lights that would go up diagonally and hit so that there was some design in the darkness. And he made it work. And I think he had a lot of fun doing it, too."

This page and **opposite**: In the director's chair for a zombie western starring Allen Pasternak as an undead cowboy, Craven worked with Roy Frumkes on the anthology *Tales That Will Tear Your Heart Out*. Though Craven (who also had a cameo) finished his segment, the film in its entirety remains incomplete. "I thought that it might be fun to see if we could accumulate enough money to actually shoot a film in sixteen millimeter," Frumkes says. "And it began to work. It was just unbelievable. And more is the pity because it didn't get finished."

Domestic one-sheet poster for Craven's *The Hills Have Eyes*; Janus Blythe, in costume as Ruby, is all smiles behind the scenes with Craven.

BLOOD RELATIONS

With time passing, and no new writing or directing assignments pressing, Craven once again joined forces with Locke, this time on something more mainstream.

Quite familiar with Craven's work, Locke repeatedly asked him to craft something akin to *Last House*. "His film was very scary. And I had certain success with my first film, and I had some money, and I said, 'Let's do another terror movie,'" he says. "I didn't know anything about terror movies, I just knew how strong Wes' was."

Still, as a fledgling writer and director who clearly had an eye for the shocking, Craven wished to venture into non-horror territory, hoping to escape what he saw as a limiting genre. It was then he again came face-to-face with the harsh realities of moviemaking: when no other potential projects seemed forthcoming, and money issues resurfaced, he relented, but with one thought. "I wanted something more sophisticated than *Last House on the Left*. I didn't want to feel uncomfortable again about making a statement about human depravity," he says.

In crafting what he hoped would be a refined version of a previously explored theme, Craven found himself in the New York Public Library. "He looked up terrible things, and we came down to a choice between two terrible things," remembers Locke. "And we chose something from old Scottish history."

Craven was quickly engrossed in a book that told a gruesome tale. "There was a chapter on a sixteenth century, feral tribe known as the Sawney Bean Family," he recalls. "They had gone wild several generations ago, lived in a sea cave, and attacked and ate travelers between London and Edinburgh. They were undiscovered for many years, and the area they hunted in was thought to be haunted, since travelers would enter and then never be seen again."

Eventually, the fabled family was caught, tried, and convicted, with deadly punishments such as being broken on the wheel, hanging, and dismembering.

While the veracity of the existence of the Bean clan and their comeuppance has since been questioned, it was enough fodder for Craven to conceive a new take on sheer violence and terror. "I was struck by how on one hand you have this feral family that's killing people and eating them," he muses, "but, if you look at it, they weren't doing anything that much worse than what civilization did to them when they caught them."

It was this violent irony, not lost on Craven, that prompted him and Locke to cinematically explore how the most civilized can become the most savage and the most savage can become the most civilized. "That," Locke recalls, "was the basis for *The Hills Have Eyes* (1977)."

Armed with a budget of three hundred twenty-five thousand dollars, and shot on sixteen-millimeter film, Craven and his crew traveled to the desert where his latest scenario would play out. It would tell the tale of the prototypically happy Carter family, out for an RV vacation, breaking down and facing atrocities at the hands of a gang of inbred, desert-dwelling cannibals.

"Wes took an all-American family who go the wrong way through a shortcut in the desert where the hard-headed father says, 'I know best,' and they wind up in trouble," explains Locke. "He created a great story, with great characters that are extremely compelling, and made terrifying moments happen throughout the picture."

Originally titled *Blood Relations*, in true Craven fashion, when the going gets tough, the victims get going. Of the prey turning the tables on their attackers, committing what many have viewed as acts just as horrible (or more so) than their antagonists, the writer and director states, "I set out to have the two families in *The Hills Have Eyes* be mirror images of each other, so I could explore the different sides of the human personality."

This time out, however, Craven made conscious decisions about what he would—and would not—shoot. He jokes, "There was a phrase that went around the cast and crew, 'If you kill the baby, we're leaving!'"

Looking back, it might seem amusing, but it was certainly a sentiment that had validity. Michael Berryman, who played mutant family member Pluto, recalls, "You couldn't kill the baby. I don't think that would have been a wise choice at all."

Dee Wallace, playing a Carter family member not lucky enough to survive, concurs. "Well, especially back then, that's a line you didn't step over. You didn't hurt kids and animals. It was an unspoken rule," she states. "So I said, 'Guys, you cannot ask people to sit through what we're gonna put them through with no win at the end. They'll hate you.'"

A script page from *The Hills Have Eyes*. Of the shoot, Craven recalls, "We couldn't afford a union crew and we were paying minimum to the actors. We shot in Victorville, outside Los Angeles, where it was alternately burning and freezing."

SC 1 EXT. DESERT. LATE MORNING.

CLOSE ON A HAND-PAINTED SIGN ATOP A RUSTED PILLAR:

LAST CHANCE GAS
(No-Mo for 200 miles)

WIND RUNS THROUGH THE RUSTED BULLET HOLES RIDDLING THE 'O'S.

CRANE DOWN AND OVER AN ENDLESS SWEEP OF DESERT BISECTED BY TWO-LANE BLACKTOP TO AN ANCIENT STATION, DUST-WHITE, ITS WOOD FRAME DRIED AND BOWED BY THE FURNACE SUN. A SCREEN SLAPS OUT BACK AND FRED, AN OLD DESERT RAT, LUGS A HEAVY CARTON INTO THE SUN. HE SLIDES IT INTO THE BACK OF HIS PICKUP AGAINST OTHERS ALREADY THERE. ALL ARE SEALED.

THERE'S A SMALL PIG ALREADY LOADED ABOARD AS WELL, LOCKED IN A WIRE CAGE.

Fred
(to the pig)

Get out while th gettins good --
no tellin what happens next --
Aww!

THE WHISKEY HE'S PULLED FROM HIS BACK POCKET IS DISAPPOINTINGLY LOW. HE SWALLOWS WHAT'S LEFT AND HANGS THE BOTTLE ON A NEARBY BRANCH. THE LOW TREE ALREADY HAS A DOZEN OR SO OTHERS ON IT, BLEACHING IN THE SUN. ALL AROUND THE OLD MAN IS AN INCREDIBLE COLLECTION OF BONES, JUNK, RUSTED TREASURES AND BROKEN FURNITURE, ARRANGED IN GARDENS, ON FENCE POSTS, IN HEAPS AND ROWS. HE SCANS IT ALL LIKE A DEPOSED KING REVIEWING HIS DOMAIN FOR THE LAST TIME.

THEN HE LOOKS BEYOND, TO THE DESERT ITSELF, AND HIS FACE ALTERS.

The actress, who lobbied for the baby to live (spoiler: she does), admits that it's sometimes difficult to truly prepare for living out the movie on the page. "It's one thing to read something on paper, it's a whole other thing when you get there with the dirt and the grime and the sweat and the blood," Wallace says. "We really didn't know what we were getting into energetically or creatively until we got there."

"We couldn't afford a union crew and we were paying minimum to the actors," reveals Craven. "We shot in Victorville, outside Los Angeles, where it was alternately burning and freezing."

When all was said and done, however, Wallace was pleased with the outcome of the cast and crew's efforts. "I was horrified!" she laughs. "In a good way. It was beyond creepy to me. I went, 'Oh my God! I can't let my mom see this!' Of course I did, ultimately."

Even Janus Blythe, who played the savage-cum-savior, Ruby, had to wonder about her scholarly director and his seemingly odd ability to craft a film with such impact and imagery. "I loved it, but I said to Wes, 'You're so quiet and reserved. How do you make these violent films?'" she remembers. "And he said, 'I've gotta make a living.'"

"I wanted something more sophisticated. I didn't want to feel uncomfortable again about making a statement about human depravity."

Wes Craven on *The Hills Have Eyes*

How audiences would react to Craven's living on a film such as this, however, was the more important question. And when it was time to release the project, the mutant desert movie seemed to find its way. "We set records in a lot of the places that we opened," Craven remembers. "It did extraordinarily well."

In his second critical nod, Hollywood trade paper *Variety* reported favorably on the film and Craven, saying, "Gratifying aspects are Craven's businesslike plotting and pacy cutting, and a script which takes more trouble over the stock characters than it needs."

Such notices were welcome news. Still, in what could be seen as a nod to the movie business of today, the opening numbers needed to be strong, for Craven and Locke's little film was about to go head-to-head with a major star when, the following week, *The Hills Have Eyes* saw its box office fall at the hands of Burt Reynolds' *Smokey and the Bandit* (1977).

Ultimately, the film performed fine for Craven's second outing as writer and director, much to the pleasure of producer Locke. "It wasn't a breakout hit, but it wasn't a bust. It did okay," he says.

"It's a cult classic," says Wallace. "How many films like that last as long as *The Hills Have Eyes*? I certainly thought Wes did the job."

Happy with the picture, Locke agrees. "We had a great cast, Wes was a great director, and things fell together," he says, going on to lavish more praise on Craven.

"He has a great knack for scaring the shit out of people. He understands exactly how to do it. He's really brilliant about it, and he understands where the pieces are and what he needs to have to make something come together to be terribly frightening."

Craven also looks back on his experience in the desert as a good one. "It got me a lot of attention," he says. "I think somehow people saw after that there was a filmmaker there. It wasn't just, 'Oh, let's slash a million throats and therefore it will be a really good horror film.' We were talking about something."

TELEVISION TERROR

Getting attention as a filmmaker and talking about issues were two things Craven had going for him. Luckily, the dry spell in work he saw between *Last House* and *Hills* didn't last nearly as long the next time out. Next up was a very short stint on Cunningham's sixth film, *Here Come the Tigers* (1978), a youth sports comedy. The experience of making that film was, says Cunningham, "Good and bad, frustrating and exciting. I loved it."

Craven's participation was small, but decidedly more action-oriented than previous collaborations with his *Last House* producer. "I went to the set one day and I think I did something like falling out of a car or something silly like that, because I don't think Sean had a stunt coordinator," he says. "So that was it."

Even with that small detour, Craven still seemed to be indelibly connected to the horror genre since the start of his career. It might not have been something with which he was particularly thrilled, but it certainly was not an impediment: he was, at least, being seen as a director with skill. It was that recognition which helped him land his next assignment, this time dipping his toe into television and taking the director's reins for the NBC project *Stranger in Our House* (1978).

Based on the novel *Summer of Fear* by Lois Duncan (who would see another of her teen-in-peril thrillers, *I Know What You Did Last Summer* [1997], turned into a film nearly twenty years later, written by *Scream* [1996] scribe Kevin Williamson), Craven was in familiar territory with the theme of a threatened family. The film saw a cast-against-type Linda Blair have her life turned upside down when her character suspects that the cousin sent to live with her family might be a witch. It was Blair's third outing in a horror film, after her Oscar-nominated role as Regan in *The Exorcist* (1973) and her reprisal in *Exorcist II: The Heretic* (1977). Playing Blair's mother was well-known stage and television actress Carol Lawrence, and working with higher-caliber talent was just one of the reasons Craven was interested in the job.

"*Stranger in Our House* was my first television movie. I had come out to California to do some work on minor stuff and got invited in to do that," says Craven. "I think that was the first time working with a Hollywood star of sorts, Linda Blair. First time working in thirty-five millimeter, first time using a crane, a dolly, so it was a great education for me. And we had a good shoot."

In the role of Blair's nemesis, Julia, was actress Lee Purcell, a young woman who had already racked up dozens of television and movie credits. During what could be called a golden Hollywood moment in her career, where she was receiving multiple offers, the actress decided to accept her first television movie role. "I had wanted to do a thriller for a while, because I thought it was a really fun genre and one that I didn't feel like I had thoroughly explored or experienced," she says. "And this was like three different roles in the script."

Those portrayals included the Ozark teenager whose parents died, a sexy witch in a black negligee and, finally, a nanny for a new household. "There was supposed to be a sequel. Everybody thinks that's she's dead but, of course, she's a witch and she lives forever," offers Purcell, adding, "Playing the villain is the most fun you can have in anything. Wearing the black negligee, trying to cut off Linda's head with the paper cutter was all a lot of fun. What's not to like?" laughs Purcell.

In addition to her enjoying the different characterizations, Purcell recalls the joys of working under Craven's direction. "He does stand out for several reasons: he was very witty, he was modest, he was real soft-spoken, and he was humble," lists the actress. "He was very specific in what he needed for the film, which was great. And since he was working with primarily very experienced actors, he didn't get in our way, which some directors do. But if we veered from what he wanted, then he would get us back on track. And that, to me, is kind of a perfect director."

Foreign home video artwork for Craven's television film of Lois Duncan's novel, *Summer of Fear.*

The actress also remembers Craven for a very specific occurrence, one that would impact her personally and could be labeled apropos to a film that involved the supernatural. "It was late on Friday, we were supposed to start shooting Monday morning, I was in the first shot the first day, and I had this strange, psychic experience," recalls Purcell. "It was about a family member of mine and then, when I left wardrobe, I got word that that family member had died. And it was devastating."

Having to fly out of state immediately, arrange everything, go to the funeral in one weekend, and be back that next Monday to start shooting definitely took its toll. "That was really hard. I remember the first scene was a scene where I was sobbing. And I'll always remember that Wes, who I guess had been told what had happened, was so kind and he was so compassionate," reveals Purcell. "He gave me a hug, and he wanted to know what she was like and he was just really wonderful. And he didn't have to do that. He could've just said, 'Gee, I'm sorry for your loss. Next shot.' And he didn't. And I always remember that."

The shoot also contained its fair share of stunts, something that made an impact on the director, particularly when they involved a stuntwoman in her late seventies, a horse, and an embankment. "She was just tough as nails, and a very sweet lady," Craven recalls. "The stunt was for the horse to rear on Linda's character and fall down an

Carol Lawrence (famed for playing Maria in the original Broadway production of *West Side Story*) is Leslie, the concerned mother of Rachel, played by Linda Blair (well-known for her role in *The Exorcist*) in *Stranger in our House*; Lee Purcell (right) relished the chance to play wicked cousin Julia, who is out to destroy Rachel's family. "Playing the villain is the most fun you can have in anything. Wearing the black negligee, trying to cut off Linda's head with the paper cutter was all a lot of fun. What's not to like?" laughs Purcell.

"The red contact lenses that I wore were like seashells in my eyes. They were horrible!"

Lee Purcell on *Summer of Fear*

---

embankment, but I kept saying, 'What are you going to do with the horse? I don't see how you're going to avoid the horse if you're going to roll the horse.' And she says, 'Ahh, don't worry about it.'"

Craven and crew went forward and, "Sure enough, the horse rolled right over her on the way down the embankment. She just stood up and brushed herself off and said, 'I've had worse than this on the ranch,'" he recalls with a laugh.

It wasn't the only equine-related memory, as Purcell recalls the moment her character is accosted by a horse that can sense the evil within her. "They couldn't use the real horse to do this because the real horse would've injured me, so the prop man came over with these fake horse legs," she says. "And he was pumping those horse's legs like milking a cow at me. I was trying so hard not to laugh and I was supposed to be terrified out of my mind."

The film aired as an NBC Halloween event on October 31, 1978 (ironically, the date the terrifying, though fictional, events take place in John Carpenter's influential shocker, *Halloween*) and performed remarkably well with audiences and critics, with *TV Guide* stating the film is a "fast-paced, made-for-TV mix of horror and teen angst."

"As I remember, it got very high numbers and, for the genre, I thought it was absolutely great," says Purcell.

In addition to new techniques, good ratings, and positive reviews, the telefilm gave Craven membership into the Directors Guild of America and something else he might not have had access to before: millions of viewers seeing him work outside the realm of blood, guts, and what many deemed exploitation. "I wasn't allowed to have any violence," states Craven, "but the story didn't need it anyway."

The writer and director looked back somewhat coolly on his trek into television, saying, "It was a great entrée into working with great stars. We had a good time and that eventually led to another movie of the week."

THE WRITE STUFF

With newfound filmmaking respectability, Craven was approached by a young, Italian documentarian named Alessandro Fracassi, who specialized in films about Grand Prix racing. He commissioned two screenplays from Craven, one being on the drug trade between Columbia and the United States. That project was *Marimba*, referring to the word for marijuana in that culture.

"One of the most exciting things about that was, we went to Columbia three times. That film went all the way up to pre-production," Craven says. "And we were in Rome doing our final pre-production business when the Italian government changed entirely."

That altered everything, as half of the financing was from the former regime. Craven adds, "The new government didn't want to finance it. So we had the script and we had everything else and I was basically sent home. Steve Miner had been hired on that, too. It was a good script."

Another project he was asked to write was centered on a hot topic at the time: the mass murder-suicide of the Reverend James Warren "Jim" Jones' Peoples Temple cult on November 18, 1978 in Jonestown, Guyana.

The event had immortalized the now oft-spoken phrase "drink the Kool-Aid" as the charismatic (some would later say paranoid and insane) Jones commanded his desperate followers to ingest a mixture of the soft drink Flavor Aid laced with cyanide. Though some followers refused and later escaped, more than nine hundred people were found dead. The result was the greatest single loss of American civilian life in a deliberate act until the September 11, 2001 attacks. Jones, too, was found dead from a gunshot wound to the head. To this day, it is unknown if his death was a suicide or murder.

Unfortunately, "Nothing happened with it," says Craven.

It was a time that simultaneously shattered Craven's faith in the producers, but also made the writer and director believe it might not have necessarily been a bad thing. Although both projects kept him busy, working, and paid for a short time, Craven came to terms with the creeping reservations he felt while drafting the Jones film. "I wrote it thinking, 'My God, I'm going from being a director of horror films to a director of horrifying true incidents,'" he states.

MIXED BLESSINGS

Leaving those darker projects behind, the year was now 1981 and Craven, who hadn't directed a feature film since *The Hills Have Eyes* four years earlier, was itching to work. It was at this time that the writers of *Stranger in Our House* approached Craven to rewrite a script with which they had been involved. In accepting the assignment, Craven knew he had his work cut out for him, going so far to begin a trend for which he would later find great use: basing scenes of the film on his very own dreams and nightmares.

"To my mind it was not a very good story, but the money was there," Craven says. "The film would have a good distributor, and it was a chance to work with some interesting people, so I did it."

The movie, a complex story of religion, repression and murder, was titled *Deadly Blessing*. It followed the widow of a former member of an Amish-like sect who had died mysteriously, and explored her fear that the remaining cult members may have evil designs for her. The film gave Craven his second chance to work with name talent, this time in front of, and behind, the camera.

In addition to being produced by Jon Peters and Peter Guber, later known for such megahits as *Flashdance* (1983) and *Batman* (1989), Craven would be directing screen legend Ernest Borgnine and, in her first speaking role, future star Sharon Stone.

"Ernest was a pro, but many of us were in our infancy. Sharon Stone was not Sharon Stone as she is today. I had second billing!" jokes Susan

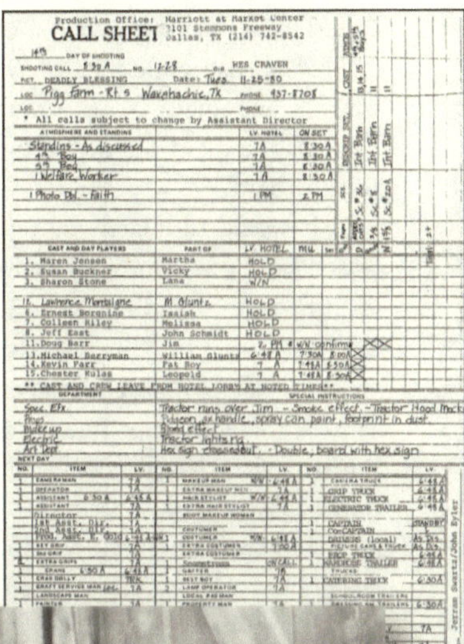

CALL SHEET

Production Office: Marriott at Market Center
2101 Stemmons Freeway
Dallas, TX (214) 742-8542

14th DAY OF SHOOTING
SHOOTING CALL 8:30 A NO. 12-28 DIR WES CRAVEN
PICT. DEADLY BLESSING Date: Tues. 11-25-80
LOC Pigg Farm - Rt 5 Waxahachie, TX PHONE 937-8708

* All calls subject to change by Assistant Director

ATMOSPHERE AND STANDINS		LV HOTEL	ON SET
Standins - As discussed		7A	8:30A
4th Boy		7A	8:30A
5th Boy		7A	8:30A
1 Welfare Worker		7A	8:30A
1 Photo Dbl. - Faith		1PM	2PM

CAST AND DAY PLAYERS	PART OF	LV HOTEL	MU	SET
1. Maren Jensen	Martha	HOLD		
2. Susan Buckner	Vicky	HOLD		
3. Sharon Stone	Lana	W/N		
12. Lawrence Montaigne	M. Gluntz	HOLD		
6. Ernest Borgnine	Isaiah	HOLD		
7. Colleen Riley	Melissa	HOLD		
8. Jeff East	John Schmidt	HOLD		
11. Doug Barr	Jim	2 PM # W/N confirm		
13. Michael Berryman	William Gluntz	6:45A	7:30A	8:00A
14. Kevin Farr	Fat Boy	7 A	7:45A	8:30A
15. Chester Kulas	Leopold	7 A	7:45A	8:30A

** CAST AND CREW LEAVE FROM HOTEL LOBBY AT NOTED TIMES**

DEPARTMENT	SPECIAL INSTRUCTIONS
Spec. Efx	Tractor runs over Jim - Smoke effect, - Tractor Hood Mock
Props	Pigeon, ax handle, spray can paint, footprint in dust
Makeup	Blood effect
Electric	Tractor lights rig
Art Dept	Hex sign [illegible] - Double, board with hex sign

NEXT DAY

Call sheet for a day's shooting on *Deadly Blessing*; Roy Frumkes visits Wes Craven on the set; Domestic one-sheet poster for the film.

Buckner, co-star of the film whose character meets an untimely end in an exploding Camaro. "But it was a wonderful time. Wes was really exploring his creativity, and he was so allowing of anything."

Looking back, Craven states, "I finally felt I had absorbed enough to consider myself somewhat of a professional."

It was also interesting for Craven to be tackling a subject that was most certainly closer to home than any previous project: religious fanaticism and oppression. Of such aspects, Buckner states, "I respect that it does provide the glue, for the people it touches, to keep them together. I didn't give the religious aspect much thought at the time, that people lived like that. It was extreme."

The film showcased not one, but two killers (one being a hermaphrodite), and the reveal that while religion was a common thread, it was not the overt cause of the murder and madness. On the topic, Craven says, "It was an intriguing notion, to first of all look at the hypocrisy of the religion and then at the very end to say that it wasn't them."

It would ultimately be revealed that an incubus, a demon in male form that is feared by the religious community, was the murderous puppet master. Fully showing itself in a shock ending, the creature explodes from the floorboards in an array of light and fog to seize the film's surviving leading lady (played by Maren Jensen), dragging her to the depths of hell. This coda, requested by the producers who felt the original ending needed something spectacular, was not favored by Craven; in fact, he didn't even helm the material. (It was shot back in Hollywood and credited to Everett Alson and Ira Anderson, who did effects on the film.)

The new dénouement was, to some, a complete surprise. "I saw it with everyone else!" Buckner says. "You mean the whole time there is some superbeing underneath everything? I mean, now the mystery is completely gone. I was disappointed. I think it would have been nicer to just end it with everyone saying goodbye and moving on."

Generally grounded in reality, tackling subject matter that was decidedly more complex, and showcasing maturity in his approach to the genre, Craven, though less than thrilled with the final picture, was pleased with what he had accomplished. "Interestingly enough, a lot of people really, really like that film. I have to take a step back from it and say there were certainly some things in it that were very successful," he says. "A lot of the scenes and images, just the sequences, were very powerful."

Critics generally agreed, with the *Los Angeles Times* saying, "Wes Craven knows how to manipulate and sustain tension. He keeps your juices flowing."

Going a step further, and perhaps voicing something more prophetic, *The Village Voice* wrote, "Wes Craven might be the man to bring horror films out of the dark ages."

COMIC AMBITION

Whether he was rescuing the horror film or not would remain to be seen, but one thing was clear: even with his artistic strengths, greater passion for the material, more time, and more money, Craven's next project would be an uphill battle for success. This time, he'd be fighting on soggy ground in the swamps of Louisiana with a live-action adaptation of Bernie Wrightson and Len Wein's popular DC comic book, *Swamp Thing*.

It gave Craven another opportunity to leave bloody, gut-wrenching horror behind and focus on science, creation and, for the first time, romance. "It was a very popular comic book. It was one I wasn't particularly familiar with, because that was another thing that was forbidden by the church," he recalls.

While he may not have had a great deal of knowledge about the comic, Craven understood that as both writer and director, he had a responsibility to not just craft a good movie, but a movie that fans of the source material would find acceptable. Of the challenge, he says, "I certainly felt that once I'd taken it on I had the responsibility to do as best I could, because by the time I had absorbed it all and realized what a following it had, and how important it was to people, I wanted to capture the spirit of the comic."

It would become a task easier said than done. After reading and analyzing the comic books, Craven formulated a story that was to be an amalgam of all the characters and scenarios. "It was sort of an adaptation, if you will," he says.

The writer and director's film version of *Swamp Thing* (1982) focused on Dr. Alec Holland (Ray Wise), a brilliant scientist hiding away in the depths of the swamps as he creates a formula to stimulate plant growth and, potentially, end world hunger. But when the evil madman Arcane (Louis Jourdan) tries to take it for his own, a lab accident transforms Holland into the title character (Dick Durock), now bent on bringing Arcane to justice and protecting government agent Cable (Adrienne Barbeau).

Fans of the source material will have noticed the gender switch of the character Cable from a man in the comic to a woman in the movie. Craven thought long and hard about this and made the change for a very pointed reason. "I changed the character of Cable, who is obsessed with finding out who the Swamp Thing is, into a woman, so I could have a more romantic element," he confesses. "I was intrigued by making it into a *Beauty and the Beast* tale."

Barbeau was excited by the concept and the script. "I loved the script. Absolutely loved it," she says, while also acknowledging, "I didn't know the comic book at all; in fact, I'm not sure I knew it was based on a comic book. I certainly didn't run out to buy it. I just thought this was a wonderful *Beauty and the Beast* story and it should be really well-received." In addition to that, she believed the script was also very funny and it "was really delightful as well as being action-adventure, which I hadn't done too much of, so I looked forward to it immensely."

Unfortunately, many of Craven's creative ideas and ambitions for the film were never fully realized, due to a number of circumstances beyond his control. In retrospect, he saw the flaws. "It was under-budgeted from the get go," he states. "A lot of what was in the script was thrown out, and it was made under incredible duress."

"The biggest issue was having the completion guarantor on the set slashing the budget on a daily basis. At least, that's how it seemed to me," explains Barbeau. "Wes had to lose entire scenes because the studio pulled the money out from under him. I felt it most personally in terms of the cheap, crappy costumes I had to wear; purchased, if I remember correctly, at Woolworth's downtown. And then there was the day we showed up to find the makeup trailer missing because the rent on it hadn't been paid."

All that said, however, the actress has high praise for her director, about whom she admittedly didn't know much before accepting the role. "I knew nothing about Wes or his work prior to my receiving the script. I'd only seen one horror film in my life and I really wasn't planning on seeing anymore," Barbeau admits.

Being married at the time to horror icon John Carpenter, who spoke highly of Craven and his work, was enough to convince Barbeau. "I loved working with Wes," she happily admits. "He started with a silk purse, the studio budgeted for a sow's ear, and he managed to deliver that silk purse just a little tattered around the edges, with enough artistry to keep it well-loved all these many years later."

"Wes started with a silk purse, the studio budgeted for a sow's ear, and he managed to deliver that silk purse just a little tattered around the edges."

Adrienne Barbeau on the budget battles of *Swamp Thing*

Co-star Wise also had fond, though not overly romanticized, memories. "We had a wonderful time doing it, but we did shoot in the swamps for about six weeks," he says. "We were surrounded by alligators, water moccasins, and deer flies. And everything bit and stung."

"That made it quite challenging for us," concurs effects artist William Munns, who was tasked with the creation of both the title character and the Arcane creature. "In terms of the makeup effects, the most challenging thing was that the swamp water is heavy in tannic acid. That led to some tremendous problems in maintaining both the adhesives to hold the costumes together as well as the paint jobs. And that was something that absolutely nobody expected. So we had a lot of the usual challenges, but that was definitely the most unusual."

Reminiscing on what was more than a tough time for cast and crew, Craven agrees with all of the above sentiments and more. "It was one of the most arduous shoots I've ever had."

Unfortunately, his hard work would not be rewarded at the box office upon the film's release, although the movie has since become a cult favorite among many. Roger Ebert, in his original review for the film, saw that potential when he wrote it was "one of those movies that fall somewhere between buried treasures and guilty pleasures."

Perhaps more pointedly, and hitting closer to the feelings that have helped the film achieve its cult status, is Vincent Canby's review from *The New York Times*, which states, "When, near the end, the two creatures slug it out in the swamp, it looks as if two guests at a costume party were fighting over the last hors d'oeuvre, which, of course, is Miss Barbeau."

Behind the scenes of *Swamp Thing*. Though it was a difficult shoot, Craven states that he felt the comic-to-screen adaptation was "aesthetically successful."

For a comic book movie, one could argue it simply doesn't get any better than that. Unless, perhaps, you are Miss Barbeau who, in response to the review, quips, "Not a high-class costume party obviously, from the looks of the costumes."

Still, the success of the film at the time of its release was what mattered to Craven—and the Hollywood town watching him. Sadly, due to its lackluster performance, the writer and director found his promising career again put in somewhat of a holding pattern. "After *Swamp Thing*, I had a difficult time finding another job, quite frankly," he admits. "It was the first of my films that really didn't make its money back right away."

Never one to waste time, Craven kept busy by writing a new, original script. It was to be a dark, scary, psychological horror film about a malicious figure that murders people in their nightmares. It was a project remembered by someone who not only played the role of Arcane's secretary in *Swamp Thing*, but was personally familiar with Craven: Mimi Meyer.

The woman who would one day become Mimi Meyer-Craven (she and Craven married in 1982 and would divorce in 1987) had a chance meeting with the writer and director while she was a flight attendant on a flight that saw Craven and *Swamp Thing* producer Michael Uslan on board. "I was working back in B zone or C zone and Wes and Michael were in first class," she recalls. "I kept running back and forth grabbing things from first class and, on one of my trips back, Wes stopped me and said these exact words, which are amazing to me: 'You are the most beautiful woman I have ever seen, and will you come be in my movie?'"

Just twenty-two years old, and not having been out of her home state of Indiana much at the time, Meyer-Craven took the compliment, and was polite, even if she wasn't sure she believed him "I just said, 'That's nice. Thank you very much, but no.'" After the flight she didn't think too much more of it—until a telegram arrived for her a week later. "I don't remember who asked for my contact information and it was the only telegram I have ever gotten. I didn't even realize they still existed at that time," she laughs.

The message was from Uslan. "It said, 'My director can't eat, can't sleep, please reconsider and do the part in *Swamp Thing*. It will change your life.' So I did," recalls Meyer-Craven. Spending a week on the set, Meyer-Craven states that Craven was "the smartest, funniest man I ever met. And that's still true."

It was also at this time that Meyer-Craven read the early drafts of the script on which Craven was working, even after *Swamp Thing* wrapped and they were both back in Los Angeles. (Interestingly, another project she had seen and commented on was Craven's jettisoned *Hansel & Gretel*.) "Every night I would read, and tell him what I thought, and correct things that I thought needed correcting," she remembers. "He basically taught me how to edit the written word."

What Meyer-Craven was so steadfastly looking at was the material that would become the screenplay for *A Nightmare on Elm Street*. The project was not, however, the easy sell Craven had hoped it would be, as he found himself flooded with rejection after rejection for his dream-killer movie.

With the dog-eared script getting passed on by every major studio, it was time to move on to something else.

WILTED FLOWERS

In addition to shopping his newest script around, Craven also took the time to develop material, write treatments, fix other films' problematic screenplays, and even tried his hand at adapting V.C. Andrews' chilling, incestuous novel *Flowers in the Attic* for the big screen. The latter proved to be an interesting exercise for the writer and director.

"I would not classify *Flowers in the Attic* as a horror film," Craven states of the script he crafted. Instead, he talked about how it was more of "a good old-fashioned escape story" and a slight homage to the classic fable of *Hansel & Gretel* on a grand scale.

In his adaptation, Craven went a step further by utilizing elements from the second volume in the controversial book series, *Petals on the Wind*. Realizing he needed a grand comeuppance for both the villainous mother and grandmother, his take was certainly darker, didn't shy away from the incest and, unlike the novels, gave the film a more visual, rather than cerebral, feel.

His work, however, would be all for naught. The script was rejected, not by author V.C. Andrews, who had screenplay approval, but by the producers, who deemed it too expensive to make, that it would invariably garner an R rating and, subsequently, not have the mass appeal for which they were hoping. "There was a market survey or something, and they canceled out. They were also very afraid of the novel's theme of incest," Craven states of his version being rejected.

Years later, in 1987, a film version was released, and though Craven was frequently mentioned as being a part of the project, none of his material was used. The final, released product was written and directed by Jeffrey Bloom.

Craven harbors no lost love over the project, believing that the people involved never truly had a handle on the material. Thinking back on his seeing the final version of the film, he states, "I was right. It came out as a TV-movie-type thing, much too cheap and bland."

HISTORY REPEATS ITSELF

With yet another potential project gone, and almost two years where he wasn't working steadily, Craven found himself answering the call from Locke to revisit a former property of his. The project? *The Hills Have Eyes Part II* (1984).

The domestic one-sheet poster for *The Hills Have Eyes Part II*; What did lucky crew members on the film receive as a parting gift? A bandana, to remember their time in the desert sun.

Having seen the success of the first film, the producer deemed that a sequel was in order. Although Craven was reluctant, feeling he had done everything he set out to do with the film and its characters the first time out, the money was there, he was available and, ultimately, decided to go back to the desert. "We had a budget of one million dollars, which was really marginal, but it got me working again," he recalls.

The film, originally titled *The Night of Jupiter*, saw Craven wrestle with the notion that the main villains of the first film, Pluto and Jupiter, had been killed off, while trying to bring back two survivors, family member Bobby and cannibal clan sister Ruby. Craven found his answer by marrying Bobby to a rehabilitated Ruby and giving them ownership of a Yamaha dealership. While on a trip to test a powerful new racing fuel, Ruby and a busload of motocross racers find themselves stranded in the former desert domain of Papa Jupe, inhabited with a new set of cannibal mutants.

In addition, the film saw the return of original villain Pluto, once again played by Berryman. Of his unlikely return, he states, "I've had eight years to heal and I still have a limp."

The reappearance of original cast members, a more action-oriented plot, and the tribe of new cannibals wasn't enough to elevate the sequel beyond what many had feared it could only be: a lesser rehash of the original.

"I think it had too much going on with all the other characters. The blind girl, the motorcycles, the races," says

Blythe. "To me, it should've stuck to the original format. It should've been just about the families and not so much about adding all these other characters. I think that took away from it."

Craven, however, understood that doing the film meant something more than simply returning to ground on which he had already tread; it kept the idea alive that he was a writer and director who was working. "It was an important film for me to do, just to get the momentum going," he states. But the film's flaws did not escape him. "The movie was originally budgeted on the first draft of the script. And the producers thought it should be expanded, so I wrote a much better and bigger script, but the budget stayed the same. It was a real nightmare to shoot."

Locke doesn't shy away from taking his share of the responsibility. "That was a picture that didn't have enough money to be completed properly and I'm the producer, so I take the blame for that," he candidly states. "Wes wrote it, he had a great idea for it, but

Clockwise from top left: John Bloom, as new mutant villain Reaper, talks to crew; Kevin Spirtas takes a break between takes; Blythe, returning as Ruby, tries to comfort Bobby, once again played by Robert Houston; Behind-the-scenes for an effect where a bus explodes. Blythe worried the film had "too much going on," while Craven joked that the seven-foot-two-inch Bloom sitting atop a motorcycle "made it look like a tricycle."

we just didn't have the finances to finish it properly, the way it needed to be finished. I'm sure he would've made a very, very successful film had he gotten the money he needed."

Reception to the movie didn't fare much better, with audiences and critics agreeing it was not the director's best work. *Variety* summed it up when they wrote that the film was a lesser follow up to the original, filled with "dull, formula terror pic clichés, with one attractive teenager after another picked off by the surviving cannibals."

Ever the consummate, honest professional, Craven understood the reaction. "I'm sorry about *The Hills Have Eyes II*," he admits. "I was dead broke and needed to do any film. I would have done *Godzilla Goes to Paris*."

TO THE DEVIL

Fortunately for Craven, it wouldn't come to that. Despite his mixed feelings on *The Hills Have Eyes Part II*, and the fact that the film sat on the shelf for nearly two years before finally being released, Craven did land another job. This time, he would be working with a character as old as time: the devil himself.

Or in the case of the television movie of the week entitled *Invitation to Hell* (1984), herself.

Susan Lucci (best known for her four-decade-long stint as Erica Kane on *All My Children* [1970-2011]) plays Old Scratch as she lures high-level executives to hell through a portal in an exclusive health spa. The convoluted plot thickens when the new-in-town scientist, Matt Winslow (Robert Urich, who was well-known for the television series *Vega$* [1978-1981]), finds his family drawn into the she-devil's machinations, forcing him to don his experimental space suit, face the fires of the underworld, and rescue their souls.

Award-winning television and film actress Joanna Cassidy (famous for her turn as the replicant Zhora in Ridley Scott's *Blade Runner* [1982]) played Urich's wife, Patricia, who succumbs to Lucci's power. "I thought, 'My gosh, the devil's going to reside in this cute, little woman? This is really interesting. I'm interested to see what Susan's got,'" says the actress. "And she pulled it off. She was good. She was really good."

Good enough to lure Cassidy's character into her web of evil. The actress recalls, "Her power overcame me and I suddenly went from being the sweet little girl next door to this sexual powerhouse kind of deviant. I remember Wes got a big kick out of that."

Craven, in addition to enjoying the performances, also used the film to experiment.

"On this show we used a thankfully forgotten system called Introvision," remembers first assistant director John Poer. "You could put a graphic image in the camera and shoot action against that slide."

It was an expensive technique on a limited budget, but proved somewhat beneficial for the scene in which Urich's character is facing down Lucci in the bowels of hell.

Even then, it had its drawbacks.

"You couldn't move the camera at all and it took so long for every shot," Poer reveals. "We had let Susan and Robert go home as the crew worked to get the shot ready. Everyone kept saying, 'We're an hour away.' But they just kept saying that every hour. It was crazy."

1011 N. Fuller Avenue · Hollywood, California 90046 · (213) 851-9262

SCHEDULE A

SHOT LIST - THE CLUB

SCENE: 213

1. MATT'S POINT OF VIEW - 35mm. film without visor and without steam that will have to put optical effects in.

2. PLATE #1 - Start tight on plate top left of frame. Steam Effects needed on stage. Matt walks out of steam and down ramp in cavern. Pull back to reveal scope of cave to full plate.

. . . .

SCENE: 215

1. PLATE #1 - Tight on Plate #1 top left same seam effects needed as above. Miss Jones moves out of bank of steam.

. . . .

SCENE: 216

3. MEDIUM WIDE ON PLATE #1 - Prop stalagmite behind Miss Jones on Stage. (Possible smoke or steam effects as desired.) Miss Jones at center of Plate #1, Matt at right of Plate #1 foreground. Matt fires "laser gun" (post production optical over Introvision composite). "Laser passes through" Miss Jones hitting prop stalagmite behing her. (Squib explosion effect supplied by Production Company.) (Optical effect supplied by Production Company.)

5. TIGHT ON INTROVISION PLATE #1 - Featuring Matt, pan with him as he exits running frame right.

. . . .

"THE CLUB"

by

Richard Rothstein

Producers:
Frank von Zerneck
Robert M. Sertner

Director:
Wes Craven

MOONLIGHT PRODUCTIONS

SHOOTING DRAFT

February 15, 1984

Clockwise from bottom right: The script cover page for Craven's second TV movie (released as *Invitation to Hell*, the film started off with the less sensational title *The Club*); Stuntman Anthony Cecere dons the spacesuit for an effects shot; A memo regarding the complicated Introvision technology; Craven prepares Susan Lucci for her fiery scene.

It was a big movie for Craven technically, with stunts, effects, children, soundstage work, location shoots, and animals. But in the minds of more than a few critics, the May 24, 1984 ABC-TV movie was not the director's best. The film, which some saw as a strange, Reagan-era amalgamation of *The Stepford Wives* (1975) and *Invasion of the Body Snatchers* (1956) had *TV Guide* stating, "This made-for-TV thriller's towering 1980s hairdos are far more frightening than its limp story about satanic possession."

Decidedly mixed reviews were not something that surprised Cassidy. "It wasn't a great movie. It was a little on the silly side in terms of the idea, but for all intents and purposes, you couldn't help but like the people. You certainly liked the family," says the

> **"I learned a great deal from the crew, cameraman, gaffers and the electricians, of what the basics were of making a film on a solid budget."**
>
> Wes Craven on working in television

actress. "The devil stuff was a little out there, but I don't think they had a huge budget at the time, and with what we had we did the best we could."

It's a sentiment Craven neither echoed nor denied, fully aware of where his television projects fell. "They were jobs. They were obviously in the genre, but at that time there was no real adventurous spirit in network TV," he states.

They were also advantageous in another regard: understanding the methods of making a film. "When I first started doing those television movies of the week, I didn't really know anything about the technique of making a film," admits Craven, offering that *Last House* and *Hills* were done in a more documentary-style manner. "I didn't know what the basic shots were, like a master. I didn't know the term, I didn't know the concept. I knew very little about continuity, screen direction, all that stuff. I learned a great deal from the crew, the cameramen, the gaffers, the electricians, of just what the basics were of making a film on a solid budget as opposed to on ten cents."

Admitting that the telefilms were, at least in a technical capacity, important to him, Craven resolutely says, "But there's nothing in there that I would say really represents something I would call people's attention to."

THE DREAM IS STILL ALIVE

Despite downtime between projects, financial struggles, and creative rejections, Craven did amass quite a respectable body of work. It would seem that the writer and director who created sadistic killers, cannibal mutants, swamp creatures, and terrifying teen angst had run the gamut of the horrors he would cinematically birth. But there was one more Craven movie monster that was yearning to be set free. It was the horrifying, original brainchild to which everyone kept saying, "no."

It remained a project seemingly placed in the recesses of Craven's mind, until the day he received a call that there was someone interested in his dream-killer screenplay, known as *A Nightmare on Elm Street*.

Craven's tale of Fred Krueger, a vengeful dream demon with knives for fingers, had found a champion with independent producer Robert Shaye, and a home with his upstart production company, New Line Cinema.

With this development, Craven would be focused on rewrites and pre-production for a film that, unknown to him at the time, would change his life and career forever.

2

Prudent Aggression

Robert K. Shaye and the Birth of New Line Cinema

Groceries. The Museum of Modern Art. Czechoslovakia. Marijuana.

As incongruent as the above-mentioned items might seem, they do, in fact, have a common bond. And though it could prove tempting to imagine their relationship as being something fantastically worldly, politically provocative, or even magically epic, the link is much simpler and, paradoxically, far more interesting.

FAMILY MATTERS

The connective tissue belongs to one man: Robert Shaye.

He was born in 1939 to Max Mendel Shaye, who studied to be a Rabbi until the day he put his books down on the Sabbath to help his own father and brothers salvage bags of sugar during a rainstorm. Having reconsidered his religious quest, Max decided to go into the family trade, a dry goods wholesaler named Grosse Pointe Quality Foods that, with his law degree, he helped build into a solid business.

FAIRFIELD AV
WALKER & Co.
WELCOME
to DETROIT
and MICHIGAN
rosse Pointe
QUALI
ANNED FOODS
AFETY MATCHE
ADE IN THE UNITED STATE
R. SCHAYOWITZ & SONS-DET
ROSSE POINTE
G.P.O.

"My dad was kind of the creative guy in the wholesale grocery business. He used to take me to work with him on Saturdays, because this was a time when industrious people worked half a day on Saturday as well as the regular workweek," Shaye says. "He put me as an apprentice filling orders for cigarettes and candies and stuff like that. But that was the distribution business, and even though it didn't particularly interest me, I was immersed in the mechanics of distribution."

It was also a place where ingenuity and ambition—two traits that Max lived by—were passed down to son Robert and firmly took root. The demonstration of those qualities was made clear to the young Shaye when Max finally pooled enough money for their first delivery vehicle.

"They painted it real shiny red, so it looked brand-new and, though I'm not sure of the exact number, they put something like 'Truck No. 26' on it, as if it was a fleet of twenty-six trucks," laughs Shaye's younger sister, Linda ("Lin"). "I guess you could say that has to do with ingenuity and ambition."

And the will to succeed was not something relegated to just the family patriarch.

Shaye's mother, Dorothy, may have been a housewife who loved flowers and gardens, but she also proved her mettle when arriving in the United States from Russia at the age of thirteen, unable to speak a word of English. Even though she was placed in the first grade with six-year-olds (where, as a teenager, she was too tall for the children's desks), she managed to graduate high school on time and speaking her new homeland's native language perfectly.

"She was very much 'the lady' and prided herself on being an American woman," Lin says.

The upper-middle-class family of Max, Dorothy, Robert, and Lin lived in a nice Tudor home on Fairfield Avenue in Detroit, Michigan. The close-knit household had dinner at the table every night, lit candles every Friday, and was active in their community. It must also be said that the parents were incredibly supportive of their children's endeavors, taking an active, participatory role in helping them achieve their goals.

PICTURING THE FUTURE

One of those enterprises for the young Shaye, one that would become an important and inseparable part of the rest of his life, was an attraction to the photographic image. "What's very profound for me," he admits, "is to find something you love."

Seeing and understanding this affinity, and to stoke their son's creative fires, Max and Dorothy went so far as to build a darkroom in the basement of their home.

"I was making money taking pictures at dances and at weddings and things like that when I was in high school," recalls Shaye. "So I became the go-to photographer of more adventuresome people in the northwest side of Detroit, where I lived."

The ability for Shaye to produce pictures in his own home was something that would, in the not-too-distant future, turn into a passion for the moving image. In fact, his first taste of being behind the camera came at age fifteen, when he produced a training film for the bag boys at his father's supermarket.

But Shaye's interest in making movies didn't stop there.

"When I was young, first I wanted to be an actor, and then I wanted to be a director, and then I wanted to be a photographer," Shaye admits. "I tried all of those things and I tried them diligently, actually. And one of the film ideas, a short that I came up with, was this goofy, sort of Dada-esque idea called *Will Fondue Do?* because I liked making fondue."

The narrative project, about a Machiavellian magician who tries to seduce a girl using "a particularly exotic and erotic version of fondue," explains Shaye, was filmed at the house with his girlfriend and high school friends. The black-and-white, no sound, sixteen-millimeter film, which he says was "true cinema of the underground sort," gave him a taste for what could be done when you invest in something about which you are enthusiastic.

Taking a notice in his son's ability to balance his passion for creative endeavors with an eye for the logistics of business, Max strongly suggested his son go to law school. The reasoning wasn't so much based on his own experiences, but simple logic: a degree in law would serve Shaye well no matter what he pursued.

"I didn't want to go to law school," asserts Shaye. "My dad was not only an artist, but an extremely effective salesman both in the way he conducted his life and in the way he co-opted other people into doing things that he felt were the right things to do."

Robert Kenneth Shaye, graduate of the class of 1956 from Samuel C. Mumford High School in Detroit, MI. One of the first schools built in Detroit after World War II, it gained fame in the 1984 comedy *Beverly Hills Cop* when Eddie Murphy's character, Axel Foley, wore a Mumford Phys. Ed. Dept. shirt. The building was demolished in 2012 and subsequently rebuilt.

At first, Shaye thought he had enough confidence in himself to make a living of his own volition, but then realized, "It's kind of hard to go against your parents when you respect their very fervent wishes," he says. "And I had no clear idea what I was really going to do, so I thought that having a little foundation was not such a bad thing."

Heeding his father's advice, Shaye graduated from high school and went on to the University of Michigan, where he earned his degree in business in 1961. From there, he kept his word, doing post-graduate studies at Paris' Sorbonne and continuing on to Columbia University in New York.

Looking back on his time there, Shaye admits that, while there were fascinating subjects and incredible teachers, it wasn't necessarily a place one might call creatively energizing. "I was daydreaming about making movies all the time in lectures," he admits. Still, he does concede, "Every so often, something really grabbed my imagination. Like the copyright seminar. When I found out we were studying a case where Superman sued Captain Marvel, I saw that the law could even be fun."

Perhaps deciding fun was close enough to creative, Shaye specialized in copyright law, even though he confesses, "I wasn't keen on my familial destiny to become a lawyer. I really wanted to be in the film business. An actor or director, maybe."

AWARDS AND WITCHES

Now twenty-four-years-old, Shaye was about to receive information that would further propel him in his future career field, even though he had not yet specifically chosen it.

A friend told him that someone they went to high school with had just won a prize in the Society of Cinematologists' prestigious Rosenthal Competition, which happened to be based at Columbia University where Shaye was going to law school. "I had been dethroned as the de facto photographer in the community. So I took that as a stimulus to determine to make *Image* (1963), and also with the objective of winning the prize," he says.

Working out the story of the film while in lectures, Shaye admits, "I didn't do well in Trusts and Estates, but I made a film that I liked a lot."

The eleven-minute venture still impresses him. "If you can excuse the highfalutin theories behind it, it's an epistemological parable about what is real and what is not real, and the phenomena of movie making and how movies emulate reality," explains Shaye.

Having completed the film, Shaye submitted the project two days before the deadline, which was just shy of his quarter-century birthday. Timing was on his side: any later and he would have been rendered ineligible, as the competition was for filmmakers under the age of twenty-five. "I then sort of forgot about it," he says. "And one day, I received a phone call from a Columbia University professor whom I didn't know who said, 'Congratulations, you've won the first prize for this competition,' which, of course, I was extremely excited about."

Then came the caveat.

Shaye found out he would be splitting the first prize with another young filmmaker, though he would be in good company. "It happened to be one of the first

Shaye was the recipient of the ASCAP/Nathan Burkan Memorial Competition Award for academic papers on copyright law; Shaye on the streets of New York City, the place where he would begin his journey into film distribution and, eventually, film production.

shorts Marty Scorsese made," he reveals. "He and I split the prize that year, which was a thousand bucks."

In addition to accolades and prize money, Shaye received the honor of having his project purchased by the Museum of Modern Art for its permanent archives (where it still resides today).

Achieving the cachet of being a young, award-winning filmmaker who saw one of his first efforts immortalized in a celebrated archive was just the beginning. Shaye also found himself the well-deserved recipient of two non-cinematic awards, having won the ASCAP/Nathan Burkan Memorial Competition for academic papers on copyright law, and receiving a Fulbright Scholarship, one of the most prestigious award programs in the world. Fortuitously, that invitation arrived the very same day Shaye was drafted into the U.S. Army for duty in Vietnam.

"I sent my draft board my very official-looking Fulbright acceptance letter, and two months later found myself most wonderfully ensconced at the University of Stockholm, instead of on the front lines of the Ho Chi Minh trail," says Shaye.

It could be said, at least at that moment, following his father's "safe" career advice paid off. "Boy, was I glad I went to law school," Shaye adds.

Through the Fulbright program, he spent two years continuing his education in copyright law. And though case studies and exams might have taken up much of his time, his interest in film did not wane under the weight of studying law. "In the back of my mind was being a filmmaker, but in the broadest sense of the word," Shaye states.

That wide-ranging sense was proved when Shaye branched out in terms of the filmic projects in which he was interested, taking a turn from narrative film to pointing the camera at subjects that had a story to tell. The result was *On Fighting Witches* (1965), a short documentary about students in Stockholm who ventured out on the celebrated Walpurgis Night (Valborgsmässoafton in Sweden), a traditional spring festival celebrated exactly six months after All Hallow's Eve.

"I actually was very anxious to continue as I wanted to make movies," says Shaye. "I got through law school and the only courses I did well in had something to do with entertainment law. I wanted to join an entertainment law firm. I just wanted to be in the movie business."

A driven individual who was aware at a young age what he was after, Shaye is adamant that passion is paramount. "I knew what my passion was when I was five years old, which is a point to make, because as soon as you discover what your passion is, you're so ahead of the game because you're motivated by yourself and the same energy," he says. "It's almost like sexual energy when you have a passion. And it's an extremely effective motivator."

It was an important ideal that would one day pay off for the promising cineaste.

NEW YORK CINEMA

With Shaye's education complete (and his Fulbright experience coming to an end), it became apparent that both his schooling and travels had served him well, even if in ways he most likely hadn't anticipated.

With award-winning films under his belt and a degree in copyright law at his fingertips, Shaye decided to relocate back to American soil, but not to his home state of Michigan. Essentially moving on from Detroit after high school, his return to the states would find him looking to begin his career in the Big Apple.

Making the move from Stockholm to New York City, Shaye settled on a small, fifth-floor apartment in Greenwich Village for his living quarters. It wasn't much, but the tiny dwelling on 14th Street and Second Avenue was all that he needed to prove necessity was truly the mother of invention.

And Shaye planned to do a lot of inventing.

It was during one of his first jobs in New York, working in the Museum of Modern Art's film archives, that Shaye began meeting other filmmakers. These encounters, and his own consuming interest in movies, would coalesce into a leap that would forever alter his career path and his life.

The year was 1967 and Shaye, a bright twenty-eight-year-old who was very much the entrepreneur, started a then little-known distribution company called New Line Cinema with one thousand dollars. Like many small businesses, its beginnings were humble, with the up-and-coming film executive working at a small desk in his apartment.

Lin remembers the modest early stages well, as she happened to be staying with him at the time. "I was living in what we called the 'mole hole' in the back," she says.

"The very inception in the back of my mind was to distribute two short films I had made."

Robert Shaye on the start of New Line Cinema

"It was a room that college kids had put cork on the walls and stuff," confirms Shaye. "And it was all kind of funky off the kitchen, and she slept on the floors for a while. So she decided it was a 'mole hole.'"

Not only was it a place to live for the siblings, but, as Lin recalls, "It's where New Line started, literally, at the desk in the living room. It became the New Line Cinema desk."

Ever the master of self-promotion, Shaye's first order of business was not to make real the hopes of other moviemakers. Instead, he had designs on fulfilling his own dreams after they had been dashed. "The very inception in the back of my mind was to distribute two short films that I had made," he admits, but then realized the difficulty in finding viable buyers for less-than-feature-length material. "I got turned down by a couple of people because short films weren't very attractive economically, so I decided I'm gonna go out and distribute them myself."

Of her brother's resourcefulness and drive to achieve his goals, clearly reminiscent of their father, Lin states, "Bob likes to translate that into 'prudent aggression.' You've gotta be aggressive about what you want, but you have to do it with prudence."

"I had to summarize in some way what our personal business philosophy was that somehow explained that I want to make movies that people wanted to see; what differentiated us from the other people, whether true or not," Shaye states. "So I came up with this idea that we sit poised, but we don't go after everything. And when the really big thing comes along, that's when we pull out all the stops to aggressively acquire it and distribute it or make it. I just coined a phrase for the sake of familiarity. Prudent aggression. And it sort of stuck."

The philosophy allowed Shaye to take the knowledge he had gained in getting his own works out into the world and then move into the acquisition of material from others. "I was working in the film stills department in the Museum of Modern Art," he remembers, "and I went to one of the parties for New Czech Cinema. And some guy came up to me and said, 'You know, there's a great market for distributing movies on college campuses if you know how to find movies to distribute.'"

Armed with that advice, Shaye's first thought was that he knew how to find films to distribute. Off and running, he struck his first deal: a fifty-fifty profit-sharing agreement to distribute two Czechoslovakian films that first appeared courtesy of the Museum of Modern Art. "I put together a program of movies and then I decided that I had to put myself on the line to get these films, which didn't cost me anything except fifty percent of whatever came in," he states. "And so I just decided to start distributing."

The first film, *Konec srpna v Hotelu Ozon* (*Late August at the Hotel Ozone* [1967]), received generally favorable reviews, with *The New York Times* critic Bosley Crowther focusing not just on a critique of the film, but the distribution possibilities of films like it. "How many of these pictures will be released here commercially remains to be seen," he wrote.

The Museum of Modern Art where Shaye not only once worked, but today has his award-winning film *Image* in its archives.

The second release, entitled *Mucedníci lásky* (*Martyrs of Love* [1967]), saw Vincent Canby (also of *The New York Times*) asking an analogous question—this time directly calling out New Line Cinema—and writing that Shaye's business was "a small, independent company whose aim is to handle movies that other distributors wouldn't touch with a pole of any imaginable length."

It seemed to some critics and moviegoers that Shaye was the answer to finding movies of that ilk. But the deal for the films was more than just a matter of understanding a business model, the convenience of seeing the films bow at the Museum of Modern Art, or (whether tepid or not) audience interest.

This page: A poster for New Line Cinema's first release, the 1967 film *Konec srpna v Hotelu Ozon* (aka *Late August at the Hotel Ozone*). The film was a bleak portrait of life after simultaneous nuclear attacks by the East and West. The hotel of the title is a home for a lonely old man holding on to remnants of the destroyed civilization; Early New Line Cinema logo.

Opposite page: Letter from Shaye detailing a proposal to distribute the documentary *Confrontation at Kent State*.

While all of those things played a part, a prevailing reason for New Line Cinema to begin with those Czech films came down to what it often does come down to: financial necessity for the fledging company.

"We got involved with European movies because that was all we could buy," Shaye recalls, not as a negative, but something from which he and the company had learned a valuable lesson. "[It] brought the other side of the equation, which was the values and bootstrapping and learning the business by practicing it without having a lot of money to squander."

NEW GENERATION

Becoming skilled at the lesson of outlaying as little as possible while trying to reap maximum rewards, Shaye began to glimpse modest success. With a tagline that read "Film Distribution for the New Generation," he and his growing company seemed to mean it, filling the void for, and listening to the voice of, that new generation.

Independent producer Mark Ordesky, a former executive and producer at New Line Cinema, agrees that Shaye understood the needs and wants of moviegoers. "Bob's father was in the grocery business, and Bob always had a really keen appreciation of the customer," he states. "And he meant that term in a really cherished way. The customer and the fan, I think, were sort of in Bob's DNA."

It was this ingrained sense that had Shaye and his New Line Cinema striking profit-sharing deals with films such as Jean-Luc Godard's documentary on Western counter-culture, *Sympathy for the Devil* (1968). And with what one might deem melancholy, he remembers, "Nobody liked the movie. Well, I wouldn't say nobody. It did have good provenance; it was Jean-Luc Godard. The movie has some virtue. And it had the Stones."

If virtue was something New Line Cinema was interested in offering, then another film, this time put out as a public service message, fit the bill. *Confrontation at Kent State* (1970), a forty-one-minute, black-and-white documentary, chronicled the violent conflict at the University on May 4th, 1970.

July 10, 1970

Mr. Richard Myers
1224 N. Mantua
Kent, Ohio

Dear Richard,

Thanks for sending the Kent State Confrontation film to us. In spite of its limitations, we found it a moving and illuminating document.

As I told Carla Ruff in our recent telephone conversation, we are certainly interested in distribution for the film, and we are confident that we could provide a wide, effective, and orderly dissemination that would get the film to a broad cross-section of American students.

We have tried to structure a proposal that would be as equitable as possible for everyone concerned. In result I suggest an agreement based on the following:

1) A 60/40 division of gross receipts, 60% for your group and 40% for New Line. New Line would be exclusive North American distributor for five years.

2) You provide your six prints. We pay for the next six if necessary, and any additional prints are paid for by us with that cost reimbursable from gross receipts. We pay for all sales promotion, and materials from our 40%.

3) We would take 10% of our 40% and establish a "movement film competition" which, over the next year, would award that 10% to the best politically oriented film made by an American independent filmmaker. There would be no strings attached to the award.

4) Rental for the film would tentatively be pegged at $100 vs. 50% and $150 flat rental. Print sales at $300 would be split 70/30 in your group's favor, your group providing the prints.

5) Groups unable to pay these rentals would not be denied the use of the film because of inability to pay the rental alone. Rates would, in special circumstances, be flexible.

I hope we can work something out. Let me hear your feelings about the proposal as soon as possible.

Sincerely,

Robert Shaye

P.S. Got your packet on AKRAN today. I'll get the stills back as soon as we can. The film went out two days ago.

RS/cem

New Line Cinema Corporation 121 University Place, New York, N.Y. 10003 Telephone (212) 674-7460 Film Distribution of the New Generation

Poster for *Reefer Madness*. The tale originally meant to warn against the dangers of marijuana later proved to be a minor hit for New Line Cinema; One-sheets for other 1930s cautionary tales that sensationalized the evils of drugs: *Sex Madness* and *Cocaine Fiends*.

"It was a very political idea, a very political documentary, and it fit within the marketplace that we were catering to, which was other colleges," says Shaye. "And frankly, it was showable, so we always needed product that we could fit into our program. So in a nutshell that's why we distributed it."

In his world of eclectic distribution, Shaye continued to release foreign films, branching out to German (two films from celebrated director Werner Herzog), Italian (from controversial Renaissance man Pier Paolo Pasolini), and Brazilian (a surreal allegory on the military by "cinema novo" member Joaquim Pedro de Andrade) offerings.

Shaye also dabbled in the world of Cuban cinema when, for a short time, he was a co-lessee of the Olympia Theater in New York City's Upper West Side. That foray may be better remembered not for what was on screen (Humberto Solás' *Lucia* [1968]), but for the mêlée that ensued when a throng of white mice, released by anti-Castro protestors, interrupted the film.

"White mice and snakes and a lot of things that were released," Shaye recalls. "And guys were coming in chains and chaining themselves to the front door. It was funny, we leased the theater and we did the programming and we showed film programs, and we actually came to the theater one day and found our sixteen-millimeter projector was stolen."

That wasn't all, as Shaye also recounts a business partner of his being mugged in one of the bathrooms, in addition to troubles with a women's film festival they had scheduled. "It was quite a scene. All the avant-garde women in the community picketed the theaters with mops and brooms," he says.

Protests and programming troubles aside, when taken together with the earlier projects released by New Line Cinema, the company was indeed sporting an impressive, eclectic and, it could be said, intellectual repertoire. Seeing this, and perhaps deciding to broaden the company's commercial horizons, Shaye released a group of youth-targeted "underground" films on the college circuit.

One of these films proved to be an unexpected, minor hit for Shaye and the company.

Originally financed by a church group in 1936, *Tell Your Children* was a morality tale to showcase the dangers of cannabis to young people. The idea failed in execution, however, until exploitation filmmaker Dwain Esper purchased the film, added salacious content, and rechristened it the more titillating *Reefer Madness*. In doing so, he took what was purported to be a serious anti-drug message and turned it into something howlingly funny.

Enter Shaye and New Line Cinema.

"There is a certain quality in merchandising subversive material to youth. And when I heard that *Reefer Madness* was around and was doing great business, I was tremendously jealous," Shaye admits.

That feeling fueled an opportunity for Shaye to utilize his legal acumen. "My one strength in law school was copyright law, and I had a feeling that *Reefer Madness* couldn't be under copyright," he states.

Attending a screening of the film at the Bleecker Street Cinema, Shaye soon learned he was right, astutely noticing the film did not contain a proper copyright notice and had fallen into the public domain. "It's impossible to recount the times my legal training has served me. Hooray for my copyright seminar," he jokes.

With one hurdle jumped, the next would be to avoid any property law issues and obtain a copy of the film legally. And in what might seem like a modern miracle for a fledgling company, Shaye did.

While at the Lincoln Center museum, Shaye happened upon a collection of photos from the film, all donated by a woman who simply loved one of its actors. Knowing only her name and the city in which she lived—Philadelphia—allowed Shaye to do what he did best: work. He picked up the phone and dialed as many names as he needed to in the City of Brotherly Love until he found her.

"I told her that I had a little distribution company and asked her if she would come and show me what she had," Shaye remembers. "She came down to New York on the train, and I saw that she had a pristine print of *Reefer Madness*. She was gracious in loaning it to me for twenty-four hours. And that's how the film began."

As did the inklings of New Line Cinema's success when *Reefer Madness* was a hit at midnight showings and on college campuses, ultimately grossing over two million dollars.

Rachel Talalay, who began her career at New Line Cinema as a production assistant, and who would rise through the ranks to produce and direct for the company, recalls, "Bob started his little independent distribution business through picking up films that didn't have copyrights and distributing them to colleges."

In a move that might be seen as prophetic, Shaye realized there was more where that came from, subsequently releasing other cautionary tales from the 1930s, such as *Cocaine Fiends* (1935) and *Sex Madness* (1938).

Of Shaye's ideas and vision, Ordesky says, "Bob, he saw things. The whole conceit of midnight movies and all that stuff about driving *Reefer Madness* prints around in his car to college campuses. Because he could read the MCLXV at the end of the thing, and see that it'd gone to the public domain, he was a real pioneer."

And the woman who helped make this happen with her print of *Reefer Madness?* Shaye was eventually able to write her a check for fifty thousand dollars, to which the appreciative woman simply said, "Thank God, I can pay my mortgage."

Looking back, Shaye reflects, "There's sometimes an opportunity to be gracious and kind."

NEW WATERS

Throughout the 1970s, New Line Cinema continued its run at distributing films to college campuses, but Shaye did more than bet on eager students who were hungry to relinquish their studies and catch a flick. Instead, he capitalized on the very tangible notion that this new, free-thinking generation wanted something edgier, left-of-center, and out of the mainstream.

"I remember my father taking Bob Dylan off my record player because he thought it was just a bunch of noise," Shaye says.

With that in mind, Shaye kept up his search for material that would satiate the appetites of his younger, campus audiences. And at the time, it seemed that no one could better serve up the goods than filmmaker John Waters.

"Then I saw Divine eating dog poop and I said, 'This is our kind of movie.'"

Robert Shaye on *Pink Flamingos*

Born in Baltimore, Waters' first feature film, *Eat Your Makeup* (1968), told the story of a deranged nanny who kidnaps young girls and forces them to "model themselves to death." Never released commercially, he followed it with what many would deem the equally bizarre *Multiple Maniacs* (1970). Though Shaye was looking for new material, he was acutely aware of the line he wished to toe: edgy, but accessible. And for his money, Waters' earlier efforts seemed a bit too "out there."

However, two years later Waters would make a film that seemed the perfect amalgamation of what Shaye had envisioned.

Pink Flamingos (1972), starring the inimitable Divine, became a fantastic, gross-out success for New Line Cinema and Waters. Sara Risher, who joined the company and would later rise to become its chairman of production, recalls, "When I came to the company, Bob had just gotten [the film] and it proved to be a big hit."

Shaye admits New Line Cinema never shied away from films that were outrageous or controversial. "That was kind of part of our bread and butter. We never distributed

John Waters behind the camera on the set of *Desperate Living*.

outright porno, and I suppose I'm a better man for it, but we did have things like *The Best of the New York Erotic Film Festival* (1974), *Pigsty* (1969), and *120 Days of Sodom* (1975)," he says. "So we've had some pretty racy and controversial stuff, but when I looked at *Pink Flamingos* the first time on our sixteen-millimeter projector, I saw one scene I couldn't believe existed, so I stopped the projector and ran it back to see what it was."

The moment that had Shaye take a second glance was when a beautiful woman (Elizabeth Coffey) turns the tables on a flasher (David Lochary).

"She lifts up her skirt and she's got a cock," Shaye says, deciding at the time to run the film again, this time the whole way through. "Then I saw Divine eating dog poop and I said, 'This is our kind of movie.'"

The film did quite well at its premiere theater, The Elgin, and then New Line Cinema broadened its release. Waters, the director sometimes labeled the "Pope of Trash," happily adds, "I've seen it in theaters where the first three rows repeat every word of dialogue and mimic the actors' voices." He goes on to say, "That's the most satisfying part of making a film, hearing a good audience react to it."

Not one to ignore the wants of moviegoers, Shaye soon thereafter made a deal to distribute Waters' next four films, including the camp classics *Female Trouble* (1974) and *Desperate Living* (1977). "I'm not complaining," says Waters. "I haven't had to get a regular job ever since."

Including successful bad-taste movies to an already diverse slate, Shaye and New Line Cinema added other genres in the mid and late seventies. *Mimí metallurgico ferito nell'onore*

Night of the Living Dead, one of the most successful independent horror films, made George Romero and John Russo well-known genre names. New Line Cinema re-released the film in 1978.

(1972), released by the company as *The Seduction of Mimi*, was a film by Italian director Lina Wertmüller that deftly mixed politics and sexuality. It was another art house hit.

There was also *A Very Natural Thing* (1974), about a gay man who defects from a monastery, becomes a teacher, and searches for true love in a gay bar. While it wasn't the most commercially successful film, it was of note for being one of the first gay relationship films intended for the mainstream.

In addition to sex and politics, New Line Cinema opened the door to horror—a genre with which the company would have a long-standing relationship going forward—when they re-released classics like Tobe Hooper's *The Texas Chain Saw Massacre* (1974) and *Night of the Living Dead* (1968).

George A. Romero's seminal film about a horde of flesh-eating, walking corpses is today considered a national cinematic treasure that permanently resides in the Library of Congress. The choice for New Line Cinema to distribute what many consider the progenitor of zombie films and television may have been based on more than just its popularity. In fact, it could look like a case of history repeating itself: the picture, much to Romero and company's dismay, was originally let loose upon unsuspecting audiences sans copyright information.

"Our title was *Night of the Flesh Eaters*," Romero explains. "And we put the copyright right on the title card, so when the distributor changed the title to *Night of the Living Dead*, they just never thought about it. So when the copyright thing came off, it became a public film."

"It was really just a question of timing and circumstance. We would've done more horror films if there were more horror films around."

Robert Shaye on acquiring genre cinema

It also created another opportunity for Shaye (and countless others) to take the film to the masses and turn a profit.

"Our whole thing always was date movies, because that was the market that wanted to leave the house and just get away from their families, and we wanted to be the guys to entertain them," Shaye states. "Horror was definitely within that category, but it was really just a question of timing and circumstance. We would've done more horror films if there were more horror films around."

Seeing the appeal of foreign and genre films, Shaye had a moment of foresight when he realized combining the two cinematic variables could spell big box office. Enter martial arts expert Bruce Lee, a talent Shaye believed could provide a serious boost to his bottom line, both creatively and financially.

"I saw the first Bruce Lee movies and I said, 'This guy's fantastic,' so I ran out and found the guy who was the sales agent for the films and made a deal for the first two Bruce Lee movies, *The Big Boss* (1971) and *Fist of Fury* (1972)," Shaye recalls. "And I thought that was so fantastic."

The excitement was short-lived.

Just as the negatives were being ordered, a letter was received from the sales agent that they changed their mind and would not license the films to Shaye unless he paid fifty thousand dollars for each. "So end of story. We didn't have the money, we couldn't get it," he recounts. "They sold to someone else and Bruce Lee movies speak for themselves. So I was always looking for some way to get back."

Shaye did, moving on to what one could consider the next best thing after seeing the success of the Lee films. "We'd been doing some business dealings with [distributor]

Toei and we said, 'Do you have any Kung Fu movies?' And they said, 'Yes, come to Tokyo, we have a bunch of Kung Fu movies,'" he remembers.

Shaye and his team did just that, and it was while in Tokyo they took note of a performer deemed a standout in the films they were shown: Shin'ichi Chiba. It prompted them to make a deal for his 1974 film *Gekitotsu! Satsujin ken*.

"We brought it to the United States and retitled it *The Street Fighter*, which pissed off Paramount tremendously because they had a Charles Bronson movie that they were gonna call *Street Fighter*," Shaye says. (Paramount's movie was released in 1975 as *Hard Times*, directed by future *Alien* [1979] producer and *48 Hours* [1982] director Walter Hill.)

Under New Line Cinema, the film became a smash at midnight screenings and was effectively the company's first "tent pole" release, with Shaye releasing the sequel, *The Streetfighter's Last Revenge* (1974), a few years later.

"I personally call myself Sonny's godfather because I renamed him 'Sonny Chiba, the Street Fighter,' and he actually adopted the name and started calling himself Sonny Chiba in Japan," says Shaye. "But he called himself Sony Chiba, S-O-N-Y, for obvious reasons."

Now replete with its artful, popular (and sometimes controversial) releases, New Line Cinema was profiting. Still, financial gain, though important, was not the only thing Shaye was to focus on and achieve for his upstart company.

In the late 1970s, New Line Cinema would also begin receiving accolades from the entertainment industry's highest office when the Gérard Depardieu starrer *Get Out Your Handkerchiefs* (1978), a French-Belgian comedy, won the Academy Award for Best Foreign Language Film. "That was an amazing story. We got it in a tax shelter deal and we really loved [director] Bertrand Blier. We were very proud to have the movie," Shaye says.

But even moderate success and an Oscar weren't enough to convince everyone of Shaye's triumphs.

"I got really excited and got a little drunk, or maybe more than a little drunk, and kept hopping around saying, 'We won the Academy Award, we won the Academy Award!'" recalls Shaye. "And there was a big party at Studio 54 afterwards."

Ready to enter the groundbreaking and, some would say, iniquitous nightclub co-owned by Steve Rubell, the doorman revealed Shaye was not on the list.

"I said to him, 'Well, I'm probably the only guy in the whole place that just won an Academy Award. You can't do this,'" Shaye remembers. "And the guy turns around, looks at me and says, 'You know what, buster? I don't care if you're the King of England. You're not getting in the club tonight.' So my alcoholic high went down very quickly. I grabbed my wife, we jumped into a taxi cab, and went to bed extremely early."

LIGHTS, CAMERA, ACTION!

Filled with the taste of success in many forms, Shaye had decided that, in addition to his rapidly increasing distribution business, he would go further back into his roots: producing.

"Ultimately it was about being an entertainer and being a purveyor of entertainment," Shaye says of his goals. "I had once said at an investor's conference, 'We are distributors of diversion,' and I still get a kick out of that."

Behind the scenes of *Stunts*, with director Mark L. Lester and stars Joanna Cassidy and Richard Lynch.

It was in 1977 when that kick jump-started New Line Cinema as a production company, as they bankrolled their first feature film, *Stunts*.

The action-thriller focused on the mystery of a maniac who is killing all the stuntmen on a particular production. Directed by Mark L. Lester (later known for *Firestarter* [1984] and *Commando* [1985]), Shaye, in addition to producing, received story credit for the film, which was generally well-received by critics.

"Oh, it was actually great fun. It was my idea and I got it from going to Cannes a few years before the movie," says Shaye. "They used to do all these incredibly outlandish things to get press attention and to get the buyers' attention. So I met a guy who was a stuntman there, sat down with him, and learned a lot about what the business of stunts really was."

Working with his head of international sales to get storyboards made up of the six best action sequences in the story, Shaye and his team headed to Cannes to presell the movie. "We had a stuntman run down the Croisette on fire and jump into a boat," reveals Shaye, "and he speeds off to a yacht, and he jumps off the yacht. It was just for nonsense."

Maybe so, but it worked.

"It got a lot of press coverage and we presold the film just about for everything the film cost to make," says Shaye.

Ultimately, the movie had a modest release and grossed a respectable two million dollars on its six hundred thousand dollar budget. Reviews were kind as well, with *Variety*

Jack Sholder outside a 42nd Street theater in New York City showing his directorial debut; Cast and crew behind the scenes of *Alone in the Dark*: Shaye, Erland van Lidth, Martin Landau, Sholder, and Jack Palance.

praising Robert Forster's performance and writing, "There is much emphasis on expertise, emotional control, and the details of the craft, which are shown in docu-like style."

Shaye, it would seem, was now more than a distribution mini-mogul, he was a legitimate feature film producer. "I chose this profession because I love entertaining and I love turning the world on," he admits.

It could be said that Shaye was mirroring another independent entity—New World Pictures—headed by Roger Corman, a man who ran the gamut when it came to the distribution and production of films across many genres.

"I think Roger Corman was someone he admired a great deal," Risher states as she looks back at the many different avenues New Line Cinema had crossed. "New Line was patterned after New World Pictures to some extent, because we did some exploitation films, some horror films, raucous comedies, and things like that."

NEW DECADE

Shaye and his company welcomed the 1980s by focusing on the old and bringing in the new. On the side of tried and true, the company continued its distribution of foreign-language films, such as Ettore Scola's *Ugly, Dirty and Bad* (1976), and *Stay as You Are* (1978) starring Nastassja Kinski. But adding to the company was its eventual co-chairman and co-CEO, Michael Lynne, who joined New Line Cinema in 1980 as outside counsel and advisor.

"He joined us in the middle of these maelstroms that were going on," Shaye recalls. "We didn't have any money. I never was smart enough to go out and raise money from the get-go."

Of his becoming part of the company and his success as Shaye's eventual partner, Lynne states, "I think the important thing about the alchemy of our relationship is that it really didn't begin as a business relationship." He goes on to say, "We met, we were friendly in law school, and we reconnected as friends some thirteen years later, fourteen years later."

In addition to new faces, the company debuted its first logo, a stylized "NL," which went out with all promotional material. Production was also ramped up when Shaye executive produced *Polyester* (1981), a John Waters project that, at the time, was considered his most mainstream. Janet Maslin of *The New York Times* stated the film had "a hip, stylized humor that extends beyond the usual limitations of his outlook."

It fit New Line Cinema well, with the film having the added gimmick of something Waters dubbed "Odorama": a special card that audiences could scratch and sniff as the film went along. The publicity stunt was something that coincided with the company's "make it work" philosophy, and one that seemed to come right out of the playbook of ambitiously promotional producer William Castle (*House on Haunted Hill* [1959], *The Tingler* [1959], and *13 Ghosts* [1960], among many others).

Risher explains that the marketing tactics were part and parcel of the New Line Cinema way of thinking. "It was fun. In those days, you were flying by the seat of your pants. Because we didn't have money, we had to be innovative."

It was clear to many that Shaye recognized ways to do that in spades. "Bob is really creative and smart," Risher adds. "He always said, 'Lateral thinking. Never say something can't be done.'"

It was that philosophy which, in 1982, had New Line Cinema looking to capitalize on (and monetize) the growing horror movie boom. Shaye and the small-but-growing group at the company were more than aware of the runaway success of movies like *Halloween* and *Friday the 13th*, finally deciding to move forward with their own horror film production.

Jack Sholder, who began his career as an editor for the company (after his own short films were rejected for distribution by Shaye), remembers, "We were all sitting around one night, after work, and one of the guys said, 'If we could come up with a low-budget horror film, we could really make money.'"

That was all that Sholder needed to press forward in the hopes he could parlay his skills as an editor into that of a director. "So a couple weeks went by and they called me and they said, 'Where's the treatment?'" Sholder recalls. "And I said 'Oh, you were serious!?'"

New Line Cinema was, so Sholder went off and wrote a draft. The resulting script, in which Sholder and Shaye share story credit, turned into the feature *Alone in the Dark* (1982). The film tells the tale of four escaped psychopaths who, with murderous intentions, pay their doctor a revenge-filled, bloody house call. Starring Jack Palance, Donald Pleasence, Martin Landau, and featuring the first-ever appearance of Shaye's younger sister, Lin, in a New Line Cinema film, Sholder's directorial debut fared well enough.

Says Sholder, "A lot of people sort of compare it to *Straw Dogs* (1971), in a certain sense. It was a lot funnier." Such was a sentiment that reviewers felt as well, with *The New York Times*' Janet Maslin writing, "The genre [Sholder is] sending up is more than ready for parody. [The film] is unobjectionable even when it doesn't work, and certainly amusing when it does."

With the release of its second production, and the first independent film from the United States screening at Cannes (*Smithereens* [1982], the directorial debut of Susan Seidelman, who would go on to direct Madonna in the popular *Desperately Seeking Susan* [1985]), New Line Cinema moved into larger offices, located at 38th Street and Eighth Avenue.

It was a move for the better, according to former employee and screenwriter David Chaskin, who vividly recalls the offices from when he first started with the company in 1978 as a film inspector. "We were down on Union Square, 14th Street and Broadway. This really dumpy office on the fourteenth floor there," he says.

A promotional button for the release of *The Evil Dead.* New Line Cinema's marketing department had the idea to run a Times Square blood drive: give a pint of blood and get a button and a ticket to the movie. "Ultimately," remembers David Chaskin, "the blood people got cold feet and pulled out a few days before the premiere."

And though the company was moving and growing in new directions, it still remained focused on its foundation of distribution. One title in the growing catalog was Sam Raimi's cult classic *The Evil Dead* (1981), which became another of the company's successes.

They also tried to make a minor hit of *Big Meat Eater* (1982), a deranged Canadian horror science-fiction musical that seemed tailor-made for the midnight movie circuit. While the film was not a breakout financial smash, it did find an audience, even garnering a nomination for best screenplay at the fourth annual Genie Awards, the Canadian equivalent to the Oscars.

Having found solid footing in the distribution arena, and certainly looking forward to ramping up more original productions, New Line Cinema continued to grow. Even Lynne, who began as an advisor looking in, took a step toward being a bigger part of the company when he joined the board of directors in 1983. He acknowledged an understanding of the vision Shaye had, including the perception that both the man and the business were mavericks with a truly independent spirit.

"It was something that I related to when we reconnected in 1980," Lynne says, "and it was very clear to me then that if we could imbue the spirit that began the company in the people who were going to take the company to the next stage, that we would have something very special that didn't exist anywhere else."

That notion of a permeating ideal amongst its people and projects, should it come to fruition, was one that could propel them into a fresh atmosphere of creativity and

A behind-the-scenes still from the production of *Big Meat Eater*, the Canadian horror sci-fi musical released in the United States by New Line Cinema. Combining murder, aliens, musical numbers, and a futuristic theme park, the film seemed made-to-order for midnight movie audiences in search of campy, wacky fun; The domestic one-sheet poster.

financial success. The question then became: what would take New Line Cinema to the next level?

It was now 1984 and the answer was a project Shaye had acquired in script form two years earlier from writer and director Wes Craven. Having optioned the rights for approximately five thousand dollars, Shaye and his team worked to develop the material, entitled *A Nightmare on Elm Street*, into a film that could be made—and made well—for less than two million dollars. It was a creative and financial gamble that Shaye hoped could be pulled off.

His enthusiasm for Craven's script was clearly blooming, creating an almost myopic focus on the film and how best to make it happen. That intensity of purpose brought to mind Shaye's past at summer camp when, as Lin states, "Everybody else was out playing baseball and Bob was at the rifle range. He was on his stomach, on a cold slab of something, practicing target practice."

Though all the other young kids might have been otherwise engaged in some rough-and-tumble sport, Shaye was focused on the singular goal in front of him: to hit the bull's-eye.

Little would he realize that producing Wes Craven's *A Nightmare on Elm Street* would have him doing just that.

3

Pre-Production

One, Two, Freddy's Comin' for You...

Wes Craven, the man who had spent the better part of a decade writing and directing projects at the request of others, had ostensibly come to terms with the notion that his status as a filmmaker, and an architect of more than one "cult" movie, had its ups and downs. Though he unquestionably carved out a nascent career in the film industry, he still longed to do more and, some might say, better.

Surviving the desert of *The Hills Have Eyes* and the close-to-home topics in *Deadly Blessing*, but not yet suffering the grueling shoot of *Swamp Thing*, Craven decided to take matters into his own hands. Instead of waiting for someone to bestow upon him yet another idea that he would craft into a workable screenplay (and eventual movie), he set out to capture the lightning from his own bottle, finding what he hoped would be a silver lining in the cloudy arena of work-for-hire employment.

"I had an idea already," recalls Craven. "And when those two films [*Blessing* and *Eyes*] finished and everybody was saying, 'Oh man, you're on your way up,' I went and I took six months off and I wrote."

The question was, what to write?

Third Draft

A NIGHTMARE ON ELM STREET

by

Wes Craven

MAKE 2ND
COVER SHEET
W/ DREAMSKILL

Registered
Writers Guild
of America West
1982

CORRECTION GALLEY

"During that period I wrote about twelve different full-length treatments for various projects," Craven remembers. "Rewrites for people, script doctoring, and several things of my own." Being entrenched in a genre full of blood and terror, he knew very well in what Hollywood proper was, and was not, interested. At that time, Craven had noted, "a terrible backswing against horror in Hollywood," and he, with his fair share of notoriety in the genre, and as a writer and director in general, paid attention to the whims of those with the decision-making power in Tinseltown.

Craven recalls learning that studios were particular about their needs, looking for "films about ordinary people doing interesting things, in stories about love, wacky couples in strange, quirky situations." He was also quick to point out the memory that they were, without hesitation, not interested in horror.

Still, Craven was. "The world of genre pictures is very easy to sort of sneer at and say, 'This isn't art,' but at the same time it's incredibly vital," he says, hoping others might see his fascination and expertise in terror as something other than wicked. "A horror film shouldn't be there just for the amusement of seeing people diced and sliced, but you have to admit there's been a hell of a lot of slicing and dicing in the course of human history. Certainly there's an eternal evil there."

CRAVEN IMAGES

Even with the knowledge of horror's current, lowly place in the minds of many with pockets to back a new project, Craven still pursued the genre he knew well, and for good reason, aside from his philosophical musings. "Horror films are unique," he offers, "even more than, say, westerns used to be. [They] are a very inexpensive way to make a film."

Like successful genre fare such as *The Texas Chain Saw Massacre* and *Halloween*, Craven knew that "all you need is a great idea and a lot of vision, and you go out there and make something that scares the pants off people." It was something Craven not only understood, but at which he proved to be very good.

"The basis of any movie is take your hero and chase him up a tree and then chop down the tree, and a horror picture does that in spades," Craven states. He knew that horror films, even in their simplest form, could engage an audience member quickly. All he needed now was a fresh take on the old genre. So, as he usually did, Craven looked within.

"The idea of alternate realities, particularly dream reality, has always interested me," Craven admits. This curiosity in the ethereal realm of the subconscious and the dream state started for the writer and director in college, while he wrote a research paper on the subject. When a directive of the assignment deemed it necessary to pay close attention to and record his own dreams, Craven found it was a talent at which he was quite proficient. Of the unusual ability, he says, "I was recalling four to five to six dreams a night. I would spend a lot of time during the day just writing them down. By the end of that semester I stopped, but I retained the facility to recall my dreams."

It was this aptitude, coupled with the desire to craft a project for himself, that guided Craven in the direction he would ultimately take when he decided to sit down

This page: Steve Miner (below) is seen on the set of *Friday the 13th Part 2*, which he directed. His association with Craven (right) began with *The Last House on the Left*.

Previous page: Original title page from the third draft of Craven's *Elm Street*, written in 1982. Note the handwritten text referencing a possible alternate title: *Dreamskill*.

at the typewriter. "I had done two pictures back to back and had some money in the bank," he says.

Realizing that he could afford to take time off even as he supported his two children, Craven looked forward to the prospect of working totally for himself. The idea of spending upwards of six months writing was "completely experimental," he states. But that was, in many ways, the point: a project by him, for him, and based on a subject in which he had a personal expertise.

The synergy and timing seemed perfect when Craven sat down to craft his original screenplay, which happened to deal with dreams and, more importantly, nightmares. "The dream world premise had interested me for a very long time," he says. "I found that the idea intrigued me so much that I wanted to build a whole film around it."

TRUTH IS STRANGER THAN FICTION

When discussing the formulation of the script idea on a conceptual level, Craven quickly points out that his utilization of the dream state was not new territory for him. He had toyed with dreams and nightmares in earlier films like *The Last House on the Left* and *Deadly Blessing*, where the characters on screen (and the audience watching them) are unsure of what is real and what is not.

"Just about all of my films have had dream sequences," admits Craven, going a step further to acknowledge his own nightmares as inspiration for moments in *The Hills Have Eyes*. "The cinema lends itself to dreaming. It is, in a sense, a dream itself. People go into a dark room very much like a bedroom. They see phantasmic images on a screen that aren't really there. It's part and parcel of dreams."

And though Craven had used his own dreams to help him write in the past, this new project would focus less on what horrific situations he had dreamed for himself and explore something deeper.

The story of the film would ultimately play with the perception of dreams (and the darkness they can sometimes harbor) in a more profound and terrifying way, with the role of nightmares as inspiration not too far behind. This time, though, the source of the bad dream was something external to Craven.

"The dream world premise had interested me for a very long time. The idea intrigued me so much I wanted to create a whole film around it."

Wes Craven

The origins of his story, entitled *A Nightmare on Elm Street*, actually began over small talk with someone who was a production assistant on *Last House*. That man, Steve Miner, eventually carved out his own directing career with films such as *Friday the 13th Part 2* (1981), *Forever Young* (1992), and *Halloween H2O: Twenty Years Later* (1998), among others. The pair had apparently met at a coffee shop on Los Angeles' bustling Santa Monica Boulevard and, in the course of their get-together, discussed something Craven had uncovered and found interesting.

It may come as no surprise that what Craven brought up, and what became the genesis of his screenplay, began with something learned and, due to the nature of its location, cultural. "The beginning of *A Nightmare on Elm Street* really came to me with a series of articles in the *L.A. Times* about young men who were dying in the middle of nightmares," he states. "They were specifically from the Asian Rim and from a particular area of Cambodia, if I'm not mistaken, where historically it happens there, too."

What was happening involved the case of a young man experiencing severe, debilitating nightmares, to the point that he had told his parents he simply could not, and would not, go back to sleep. He believed with certainty that if he slept, death would befall him. Digging deeper into the story, Craven remembers reading that the family "had come out of relocation camps in the war zone." Because of this, the father, who was a physician, told his charge that the fears he was experiencing are normal after a trauma.

The simplest solution was to give the young man sleeping pills, which the father did, but for the next two evenings his son still would not go to sleep. "It became clear," Craven says, "that he was trying to stay awake despite everything, and this went on for a long time." The notion struck the writer and director, because "it was an extraordinarily long time for anyone to go without sleep."

Eventually, despite his fighting slumber, the young man succumbed to the inevitable and, while he and his family were in the living room watching television, fell asleep. "They took him upstairs and put him to bed, thinking, 'Thank God that little crisis is over,'" recalls Craven.

But it wasn't.

In the silence of the middle of the night, the family was roused to the terrible sounds of their son screaming wildly in his room. Rushing over, they entered to the dreadful sight of him thrashing horribly on the bed and, before the father could get to him, the young man fell still and died. And in what might seem like proof of the young man's will to stay awake, the family next found all of the sleeping pills hidden in the bed, which their son had only pretended to take. A deeper search also found something that lingered with Craven. "He had a Mr. Coffee machine in his closet with a hidden extension cord that went to the nearest plug, with black coffee that he used to try to stay awake," he remembers reading.

To Craven, it proved the point that the young man had clarity of vision: he knew what was looming if he fell asleep and it had, sadly, come to pass. An autopsy was performed and it was discovered there was nothing wrong with him physically.

"I just thought, 'Wow.' It moved me. It literally brought tears to my eyes," Craven says, "because here's a guy who has a vision that's accurate, but it's so unusual that it seems like it's part of some sort of madness."

Dr. Robert Kirschner, a physician who has an understanding of the bizarre phenomenon, states, "In the Philippines, it's called 'bangungot,' in Japan 'pokkuri,' in Thailand, something else."

Still, no matter the name, the translation is roughly the same: "nightmare death."

The concept of something that seems so inexplicable—staying awake for fear of death—versus the seemingly easier alternative—go to sleep and you'll be fine—spoke to Craven. "It appealed to me also as a symbol for our culture," he states. "And to me that felt socially like, 'It's never gonna happen,' until it finally

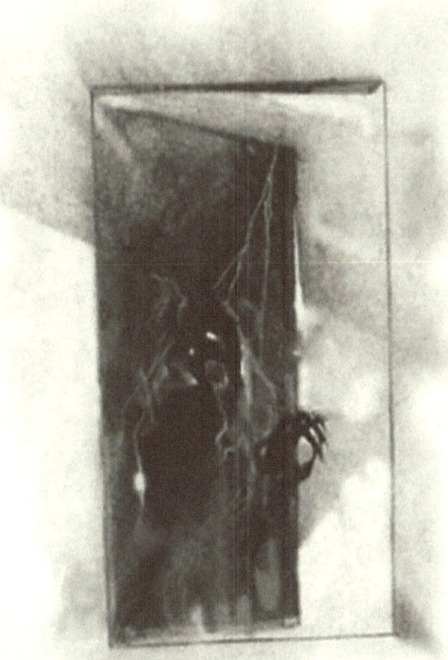

Artist rendering of the dream creature believed to suffocate one while sleeping. Sudden Unexpected Nocturnal Death Syndrome (SUNDS) was first noted in the Philippines in 1977.

The Nightmare (left) is a 1781 oil painting by Anglo-Swiss artist Henry Fuseli (1741–1825). It had its first exhibition in 1782 at the Royal Academy of London and remains Fuseli's best-known work. Seemingly portraying a dreaming woman and the images in her nightmare, critics and theorists have long discussed its meaning; *Satan Devouring His Son* is the name given to the painting by Spanish artist Francisco Goya. It depicts the Greek myth of the Titan Cronus, who, fearing that he would be overthrown by one of his children, ate each one upon their birth. The work is from c. 1819-1823.

comes and bites you on the butt, because you just haven't been able to comprehend it's possible that it's true."

FEAR IS A PERSON

With a moving, scary account rooted in fact, and in a milieu that Craven had already personally and professorially explored, his next step was to unearth the movie within the story. That pursuit led the writer and director to ask himself the one question that would cement the structural basis of the film: what if someone in the boy's dream had killed him? It was an intriguing notion that he sought to explore further, leading him to ask more interesting questions and discover, much to his delight, exciting answers.

Craven recalls, "I said, 'Okay, what if it's a guy?'" And with that one notion he had, though unknown to him at the time, struck upon the beginnings of a character now firmly rooted in the annals of horror–and pop culture–history. But first he had to create a three-dimensional persona to fit the concept that someone, or something, had murdered a boy in his sleep.

That guise, Craven decided, would be named Freddy Krueger (early drafts of the screenplay saw the character's name spelled Freddie), once again for reasons in which he had firsthand experience. "There was a kid named Freddy who was kind of my nemesis in elementary school," he says. "He was a big kid and he would beat me up with some regularity."

With such a negative memory attached to the name Freddy, it may come as no surprise that Craven bestowed upon his film's antagonist such a moniker. Coming up with the last name Krueger was a bit less painful, but no less personal. "It was an extension of the name 'Krug,' who was the lead character in *The Last House on the Left*," he says.

But it wasn't just the murderous, flesh-and-blood villain from his first film that presented Craven with inspiration. "Krueger sounded very German to me," he says, the scholar in him almost certainly not naïve to the existence of a Nazi official, and high-ranking member of the SA and SS, named Friedrich-Wilhelm Krüger.

Craven also knew his bad guy was more than just a name, recognizing the need for his creation to not just be truly, believably evil, but also whole. Once again, he did not have to go much farther than his own memory to start crafting, and recounting, the (now almost famous) childhood incident that inspired his dream killer's personage.

"I remember myself as a child, sixth grade-ish, I'm guessing, because we moved a lot," Craven recalls. "I know my family was in a particular apartment building in Cleveland, in the city, on the second floor, and my bedroom looked down onto the sidewalk outside."

It was that bedroom view that would give the young Craven the fright of his life and, as he would only come to realize decades later, necessary and wonderful inspiration.

The events that transpired began when, lying in bed one night, Craven heard feet shuffling and a voice mumbling. Ever curious, he crept over to the window and took a look outside. What he saw stayed with him forever. "It was a man in an overcoat and a sort of fedora hat, and somehow he sensed that someone was watching and he looked right up and into my eyes," he remembers.

Afraid, the young Craven quickly jumped back from the window, literally sitting on the edge of his bed, hoping that the man would just go away. With no more noise coming from outside, he assumed it was safe to take another look.

He was wrong.

"I went back and he was still there, and then he started walking and looking over his shoulder at me," says Craven.

It didn't seem that the moment could have been more unsettling, until something unexpected and even more worrisome occurred: the strange man made it clear he was about to enter the young boy's building. "He turned the corner where I knew the entrance to our building was, and I ran to our front door and I heard the door downstairs leading to the street open. I was more terrified than I can ever remember being," Craven admits.

Craven recalls it was an unfortunate time when his father was long dead and he lived with his mother, sister, and older brother, Paul, who "went downstairs with a baseball bat, literally with a baseball bat, but the guy was already gone. They weren't even sure I had seen it."

Friedrich-Wilhelm Krüger, a high-ranking member of the SA and SS, organized and supervised numerous war crimes and played a major role in the Holocaust. Like Hitler, he committed suicide by shooting himself.

Looking back, Craven was certain. "I know I saw that guy."

The event affected Craven for a number of reasons, but one in particular. "The thing that struck me most about that man, probably a drunk or something, was that he had a lot of malice in his face," he explains. "And he also had this sort of sick sense of humor about how delightful it was to terrify a child."

The identity of the teasing, creepy man would forever remain unknown, yet he would gain infamy in his anonymity—as the inspiration for the villain who would be Freddy Krueger.

Craven further examined what it was that moved him to include the idea of this seemingly wicked stranger into his fictional character, saying, "Extrapolating that and taking that to the 'nth' degree, I think you have the kind of mentality of older men that can send young men off to war. Or a generation that always hates the music of a young generation because it's threatening to them, because they are the ones inheriting new life, you know, whereas the older people are the ones inheriting old age. So that became the essence of Freddy."

Navigating a far more personal arena, Craven had another answer for his character's origins. "I sometimes jokingly say, 'Dad.' I was very afraid of my father and I only have two or three memories, and they're all fear-based," he admits. "That idea of the father figure that is threatening as opposed to protective is a very powerful figure to me, and that's in a lot of my films."

Ever Craven, he was also quick to point out the historical significance behind such sentiment. "There's a great Goya painting of [the Greek god] Cronus devouring his children, just ripping the head off one of his sons because he had betrayed him or something like that," he says.

Past experience, familial underpinnings, and mythological intervention aside, it was more than just the idea of who the man was and what he might have wanted that went into Craven's creation. Also taking a cue from the outsider's physical appearance, the writer and director imagined that his Freddy could more than resemble the man who terrified him so many years ago. "That man wore a hat like Freddy, so that's the origin of that hat," he reveals.

Though the hat may have shielded the stranger's visage from young Craven's eyes, he continued to contemplate what his movie villain would look like. Starting with a general notion of hiding his creation under a mask, the idea was quickly jettisoned; not only had it been done so often before in horror films, Craven wanted something not entirely standard for the genre. "After going through a series of masks and saying, 'Well, what if he has a mask that looks like this or that,' I said, 'Well, but I want him to be able to talk,'" he muses.

More important than just having a voice for his antagonist, Craven went further. "I wanted to have a sense of a personality in there, so somehow I had the great idea to have his face covered in scar tissue."

The concept of imbuing the character with a frightening countenance in addition to a type of dark vocal eloquence was more than just a passing notion. Craven knew that, particularly in America, heroes and villains tend to be easily identifiable. "In

President John F. Kennedy with wife Jacqueline Kennedy Onassis, in the vehicle where he would be assassinated on November 22, 1963; A newspaper headline announcing the tragedy that would devastate America.

Western slang, you have a guy in a white hat and a guy in a black hat," he says. "One's the good guy, one's the bad guy."

But Craven wanted more from his film's nemesis, taking the duality of hero and villain a step further than many other cinematic monsters at the time, creating a memorable amalgamation. "Freddy is vicious, but he has a sense of humor," he states.

Though that humor would be dark, it would also be used sparingly, punctuating the evil that Craven had always imagined for Krueger. "I just felt that Freddy was the paradigm of the threatening adult. Freddy stood for the savage side of male adulthood. He was the ultimate bad father," says the writer and director. "It's a sickness where youth is hated. Childhood and innocence is hated. And it's attacked and exploited, and he tries to snuff it out. From the very beginning, that's how I saw him."

FEAR IS A PLACE

Satisfied with who his villain would be, Craven turned his attention to the setting for his horror movie. As was usual for one of his films, the location wouldn't be a far-off place that nobody could understand, but instead something to which many viewers could relate: a suburban, tree-lined street. In this case "Elm" was the very specific name where the nightmares would be centered. For a long while, many have speculated why that was.

"The school I taught at before I jumped ship out of academic teaching was Clarkson College of Technology in Potsdam, New York. And the main street of Potsdam is Elm Street," says Craven.

That could explain why many claim it must be the reason for the name and there is, perhaps, a small amount of ego involved from those in that area. "Everybody up there is convinced that I based it on that," adds Craven. (Locals might be disappointed to hear that the writer and director stated that isn't the case.)

There are also viewers and critics who paint a much grander, politically charged motivation behind it. "And then, of course, Elm Street was the street that Kennedy was shot on," mentions Craven. "So people thought maybe that was it."

Craven, though, has gone on record with a reason that is much simpler and, at the same time, psychologically deeper. "The reason Elm Street was used, the actual reason, is that I wanted to have an idea of a place that was just pure Americana," he admits about bringing the idea to life. "And to me, the elm tree was kind of the symbol of that primordial tree that we all took shelter under as early humans. To my memory it was just a symbol of Americana."

Tapping into that nostalgia was an important aspect of the story, as Craven didn't seem to just be after the juxtaposition that terror might happen in a place which is normally viewed as a safe haven. Instead, he looked at amping up the real dread that can build as a result of one's own upbringing. "To me, the most poignant and powerful area of our memory is childhood. And that, almost exclusively, takes place in regular, residential houses," he states. "In fact, for the first five years of our lives, we don't get away very much from the house and yard."

Seemingly innocuous, Craven explained it is where many of our fears take root. "That's where you encounter most of the really primal events of your experience, and that's why you're afraid of the attic, the basement, the dark, everything else," he says. Going a step further, he offered his thoughts on why the idea of terror being in hard-to-reach locales is sometimes more tepid than the fears of home. "Films set in those locations are able to evoke those memories more easily than films set in a castle or even outer space, where we don't have personal memories."

Thus, the nightmare would begin on Elm Street.

FEAR IS A THING

The next question Craven asked himself would prove to be something as important then as it is iconic now: what implement would his murderer utilize to dispatch victims? He understood that his choice of weapon could very well prove to be a point of success or failure, if for no other reason than genre audiences remember a villain's trademark method of death dealing.

At the time, films such as *The Texas Chain Saw Massacre* (effectively metamorphosing a tree-trimming implement into one of terror), *Halloween* (forever changing one's view of the butcher knife) and more than one *Friday the 13th* (a machete, an axe, a spear, and the list goes on) had seemingly cornered the market on ways to kill effectively, lest one repeat the past. Craven wanted to do no such thing, deciding instead to drum up a new way to slay victims.

In essence, he looked to the past as he contemplated the future.

"There were a lot of killers with masks and with some sort of an edged weapon," notes Craven. After going through lists of would-be implements, including knives and even a sickle, he realized he could put his years of study to good use. "I said, 'Okay, you used to be a professor. Put your academic mind on. What's the earliest weapon that mankind might've been afraid of?'"

It was an interesting way to approach the issue, and one that paid off as Craven explored his options. One of his initial realizations was the weapon of an animal, something that "can reach around the corner with these big, giant claws," he says. "You know, saber-tooth tigers and incisors and claws and talons and everything else."

Pleased with the notion, Craven continued to take it further, recalling in scientific journals that one of the many reasons human development was spectacular was because people were gifted with an opposable thumb. "So I said, 'Okay, let's take a combination of the human hand, which is the epitome of mankind—the dexterity of the human hand—and combine that with the claw.'"

It was the all-important thumb that allowed humanity to do complex motor activities that most animals could not. It also freed Craven to extrapolate and devise a powerful, memorable killing apparatus for an "animal" with a larger brain and human motivation. "The two fed off of each other and got better and better. The claws were the sort of piéce de résistance," he says.

Craven finished his creation by placing him in a type of forbidden lair: a boiler room. To him, it was like putting Krueger "in a labyrinth in the Hades and the hell," he says. But more than that, he felt it reinforced the idea that it placed the villain "in that kind of mysterious, dark place that's underneath what society gives to kids at his school."

NOW I LAY ME DOWN TO SLEEP

The basics of his killer, setting, and weapon taking shape allowed Craven to flesh out his story, yet the foundation of the piece was still not set in stone. A talking villain with a scarred countenance and unforgettable killing mechanism was one thing, but it still had him wondering: "Okay, where'd that come from?"

That answer would, as it had in the past, spring from aspects of Craven's upbringing that were ripe for exploration. This time he utilized his biblical studies with the age-old concept that the sins of the parents shall be visited on the children. "I said, 'Perfect. It's something the parents did to him,'" he recalls. It was this revelation, as important as it was intriguing, that laid the groundwork for his screenplay.

Craven would write the script for *A Nightmare on Elm Street* following teenager Nancy Thompson, her boyfriend, Glen, her best friend, Tina, and Tina's boyfriend, Rod. All seems quiet in their suburban dwelling until an evil begins rising to the surface in the form of a nightmare the four friends all share. It's a terrifying vision of a horribly burned man with a glove of razor-sharp knives on his right hand. "He appears first to all four of these kids and scares the hell out of them," Craven says.

It quickly becomes apparent to Nancy that this frightening apparition is more than something in their minds when it brutally murders her friends in their dreams—and they die in real life.

Craven wanted more than just another blood and guts fest, so he laced his screenplay with a little mystery. "[Freddy kills] in a way that suggests that someone in waking life might have done it," allowing the idea that there may be real world explanations for each death.

But Nancy knows there is more to uncover, confronting her alcoholic mother who reluctantly shares the tale of Fred Krueger. Known years before as the "Springwood

Slasher," he was a murderous child molester arrested by Nancy's father and tried in court, but subsequently freed on a legal technicality. Unable to cope with terror in their midst, the angry parents of Elm Street tracked Krueger down to his boiler room hideaway and burned him alive.

Armed with the truth, the resourceful Nancy formulates a plan to pull the monster out from her nightmare, bring him into the real world, and destroy him.

But, as she finds out, evil never really dies.

THE COST OF DREAMS

Now finished with a piece of material Craven felt was interesting, intriguing, and powerful, not to mention something that was, as he stated, "one from the heart," he was ready to let his newest work loose upon a town looking for something original, even if what he had to offer was in a genre that many had frowned upon. Craven's friend and first producer, Sean Cunningham, was quick to point out his concerns when he was first introduced to the concept.

"Wes had, for three or four years, been nursing this notion of trying to do a horror film that involved dreams reacting with real life," recalls Cunningham. "I remember telling him, 'Wes, I don't think anybody's ever going to buy into that.'" Cunningham's worry for his friend's material aside, Craven was convinced it could succeed, believing it was a project worth exploring and a gamble worth taking.

Before unleashing his latest effort to a wide audience, Craven felt comfortable first showing the finished script to the creator and director of the wildly successful *Friday the 13th*, hoping his friend would finally understand. Unfortunately, Cunningham's reaction was, as Craven feared, lukewarm at best.

"Sean gave it a read and simply said, 'Meh,'" recalls Craven. Cunningham went on to explain his lackluster reaction, saying once again that, even in final screenplay

Original *Variety* ad for Sean Cunningham's wildly successful *Friday the 13th*. The film went on to gross nearly forty million dollars and spawn a franchise; Cunningham on the set of *Friday the 13th*.

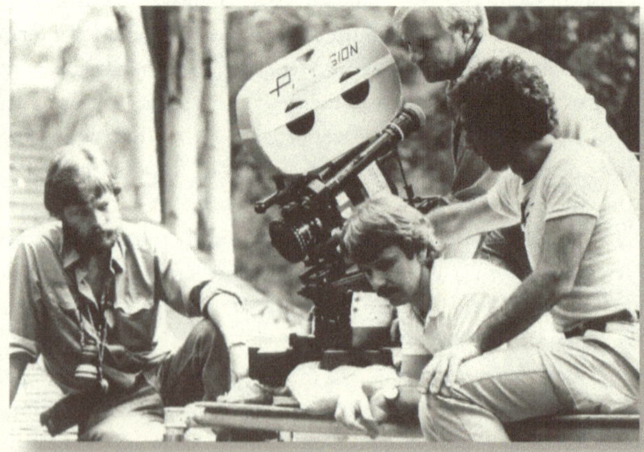

The domestic one-sheet poster from *Dreamscape*, the film that Craven felt could be his creation's undoing.

form, he "didn't feel anybody would be afraid of the film or the villain because it's a dream."

Certainly not what Craven hoped to hear, but he still held on to the notion it was one person's opinion. "I thought everyone would see that it was a fine script and it would be snapped up," he says. But that wasn't the case as seemingly everyone he showed the script to passed on it. "I thought that it would have been a quick sale. I had done three or four horror films and everyone would just jump on it, but actually *Deadly Blessing* and *Swamp Thing* both didn't do that well at the box office, and *Friday the 13ths* were starting to get old. There was this notion around Hollywood that horror was dead."

It was a powerful view surfacing through Hollywood: genre films were bad, or could corrupt, and nobody was interested in seeing them.

Many in the studio system ultimately rejected the script for the very reasons Craven had feared. What's more, to many who read it, the script was difficult to label. It combined elements of slasher, monster, and mystery movies, with touches of the fantastic in an otherwise realistic, everyday setting. "I collected a huge stack of rejection letters," he recalls, "saying 'Thank you very much, but we don't think it's for us and we don't think it's scary.'"

Confirming that the script was sent to a lot of studios, Craven even detailed a rejection letter from Universal Pictures, which he kept through the years. "It reads, 'We have reviewed the script you have submitted, *A Nightmare on Elm Street*. Unfortunately, the script did not receive an enthusiastic enough response from us to go forward at this time. However, when you have a finished print, please get in touch and we would be delighted to screen it for a possible negative pick up,'" he says. "That's from December 14th, 1982. So I had a whole drawer full of rejection slips like that."

Craven realized people seemed to like the writing, just not enough to buy what was written, which was certainly not the news he wanted to hear, either creatively or financially. Having worked so hard, and having heard numerous rejections, he admits to going through an interesting process where he worried, "I'm losing it. I'm losing it, and I'll never work again. I'll have to go back to teaching."

That was not in Craven's future, but it was certainly a rough time, as his dream of creating something for himself had practically destroyed him financially. Even taking the occasional job of rewriting others' material while he crafted *Elm Street* did not prevent all of his savings from being eaten up. Ultimately, he was forced to sell his house at a loss as he tried to make ends meet. "It's a long, sad story ending with me not being able to pay any bills," he remembers of the time.

One of those bills was a five thousand dollar tax payment and, not knowing where to get the money, he turned to Cunningham, flush with profits from his *Friday the 13th* successes. He was generous to loan his friend the money, but, Craven recalls, "He said, 'That's all I can give you.'"

At the same time Craven worried about his finances, he continued to work at selling the script. Surprisingly, it has been rumored he came close with one unlikely buyer: Disney. Although a deal was never made, it might have been for the best as that version was said to have been toned down to make the film more palatable for a younger set, a sort of Halloween season film that could be played again and again, which was certainly not his intended vision. When asked about the potential for this kind of deal, Craven matter-of-factly states, "It doesn't ring a bell."

After that fell through, he received another dose of bad news when studio 20th Century Fox rejected the project. Somewhat used to a negative response at this point, Craven felt more dismayed not because they passed, but why they did so: executives deemed his script too similar to a film they would soon be distributing.

Dreamscape (1984), starring Dennis Quaid, Kate Capshaw, and Max von Sydow, told the story of a psychic who is brought aboard a government project to help the President of the United States overcome terrifying nightmares of nuclear war. Soon after, people begin dying while in the dream state, and a plot to murder the chief executive while he sleeps is uncovered.

It did not take a scholar to see the similarities between that film and Craven's script. "When I first heard about *Dreamscape*, I bit my tongue about a thousand times for having spoken rather freely about *Nightmare on Elm Street* in interviews so long before we were ready to do it," he says.

In no way did Craven accuse them of stealing the idea, though he declared his concept had been around for years before. "Maybe if I'd kept my mouth closed, no one would have thought of it," he offers. And while at the time there was an upsurge in the concept of dreams and nightmares, he adds, "The basic premise was suspiciously coincidental."

When Craven finally saw the film, and what was done with that similar dream death concept, the experience stirred within him feelings of dread for his own project. "It had things in it including somebody with claws on their fingers and everything," he recalls. "I remember sitting in the theater and my heart just sank through the bottom of my shoes. I thought, 'It's taken the essence of the idea and we'll never be able to get my film made.'"

Even with the dark specter of a project that was in the same milieu as his, Craven tried to find a bright spot, looking at what set his script apart from that project: there were no creatures in *Elm Street*, just a killer of children.

Hoping that the power of his concept and its execution would prevail, Craven admitted to being "aghast," and that *Dreamscape* might hurt him. "Sometimes that kind of thing can just wipe your film out and sometimes it doesn't matter," he says.

Luckily for Craven, due to *Dreamscape* being less-than-stellar at the box office, it would be the latter.

NEW OPPORTUNITIES

Determined to find a home for his screenplay, Craven jettisoned the studio system. The script always garnered compliments, but, as he remembers, "I think everybody got a look at it. I couldn't get anyone to put their money where their mouths were."

Robert Shaye, the visionary behind New Line Cinema and the one who believed in *Elm Street*; Sara Risher (posing with John Waters), who also worked diligently to ensure the film reached its full potential.

Craven next looked to private, independent financing, a decision which offered him the break he'd been waiting for with the script on which he had worked so hard. "So about that time, the one guy who thought the script was interesting was Bob Shaye," he says. "It was an interesting thing that really only Bob saw the potential of it."

With his New Line Cinema having already distributed over one hundred films, including Academy-Award winners as well as horror projects, Shaye seemed the perfect person in the autonomous film sector to propel *Elm Street*. "Bob is many different things, but he has an extraordinary intelligence," offers Craven. "And he was able to see how [the script] could grab an audience in a way that other people weren't."

Shaye understanding and liking the general idea actually began when he was in the market to meet new directing talent. "The original *Elm Street* script came to me because I had gone to Los Angeles to meet some young directors like Joe Dante, and Wes, and Tobe Hooper," he recalls. "I didn't meet Wes, but I spoke to him on the phone and he was telling me about this great idea that he had for *Nightmare on Elm Street*."

Craven described the film to Shaye as "a nightmare that you don't wake up from" and that there was a group of kids that were being killed by the bogeyman in their nightmares. From that, New Line Cinema's founder was intrigued.

"I thought it was incredibly inspired because it had this great marketing hook that was a familiarity to the entire world," Shaye states. "We've all had nightmares."

He was also impressed with Craven's villain. "His character of Freddy Krueger, with a domain in the vulnerable underbelly of our nightmares, where we have no control, was profoundly disturbing," Shaye states, adding, "and a whole lot of fun."

Concluding what seemed to be an interesting conversation, with Shaye expressing interest in the material and Craven trying to find it a home, the producer ran into one small problem. "Wes wouldn't send me the script!" he says. "I think I probably kept calling him every few months. And in the interim, he or his agent had taken it to everybody else who possibly had the wherewithal to make a movie."

NE3 CORRECTION GALLEY 2

NOTE:

This was prepared 8/15/82 for final consideration by Bob Shaye and New Line Cinema. The Second Draft, with Nancy's Father the villain in the end, remains on disc 114 sides A & B, and Disc 113 side A.

The Third Draft, on discs 112, 106, 115 and 111, has the following major changes: (1) Lt Marks is Nancy's father, divorced from Marge (2) subtitles for each day (3) addition of the legend of Fred Krueger, (with a discussion in Civics Class with Maxell there), to lay the foundation (4) return of Krueger as killer (simplification of backstory) (5) deletion of: the knife as prime weapon; the scenes with Mr Maxell as homeroom teacher/friend; the punching of Rod by Krueger; the library scene; the Mexican fisherman; Nancy jumping down into grave (6) suggestion of a possible alternative or new title -- DREAMSKILL * (7) inclusion of a new weapon -- the steel talons.

(Dreamskill has both the notion that dreams can kill, and that one can possess a dreamskill, an arcane but real ability to manipulate dreams for good or evil.)

CORRECTION GALLEY

A page tdetailing changes made to an early version of the *Elm Street* script for consideration by Bob Shaye and New Line Cinema. "We flew Wes out to New York several times over the spring and summer of 1983 and often stayed with Bob [and his wife] at their house on a lake in upstate New York," recalls Risher. "I remember the marathon sessions Bob and I would have with Wes on the script."

It would turn out the reasons for waiting seemed to be nothing more than who could make the best deal and the best movie, and the humble beginnings of Shaye's company were no secret.

"New Line, at that time, was a small, tiny, tiny company; I think a couple of people out of a store front on the lower East Side," Craven says. The writer and director was more than aware of Shaye acquiring the rights to films like *Reefer Madness* and *Pink Flamingos*, and his methods of distribution. "They would distribute them to army bases, and prisons, and colleges. Those were their three venues. So I figured, 'This guy is never gonna raise the money.'"

When no one else was biting, however, Craven went back to Shaye with the script, not knowing he was half right about the financial possibilities of New Line Cinema. Shaye reveals, "And then Wes came back to us. I didn't have the wherewithal to make the movie, either, but I didn't exactly tell Wes that at the time."

Risher, who co-produced the film, remembers well Shaye's receiving the script. "He read it and liked it very much. He immediately knew there was a premise there that was strong and original," she says, with Shaye adding, "*A Nightmare on Elm Street* was not read that night. It was consumed." The producer liked the archetypal concept and the fact that it wasn't a slasher film filled with "gore for gore's sake."

With someone finally interested in making the movie happen, Craven recalls his first discussions regarding the money required to make the film. "I had it budgeted and it came out to about two million dollars. Bob wanted to do it, I remember, for fifty thousand." Craven looked back, laughed, and joked at the time that he "could go to eighty!"

But as reality set in, Shaye knew he wanted the picture and figured out a way to get things started. "I think we gave Wes a small amount of money for an option and began to work on polishing the script," he says. "I think the option was around five thousand dollars."

"Ultimately, it was about getting the money together," Risher admits. "We had to piece it together because we weren't that well known as a production company."

With New Line Cinema the proud owner of Craven's *A Nightmare on Elm Street* Shaye wasted no time and went right into development on the material, feeling that with the strongest script possible he could raise the necessary funds.

"During that time the thing was constantly being worked on, changed, and altered," says Craven. "Bob gave me a lot of notes."

"Bob felt that it needed work on the story. It was a first draft, and it did," Risher recalls. Working with Wes to develop and strengthen the script over a period just shy of a year, and for very little money, Risher says, "Wes was a trooper to be working with us. He and Bob really clicked creatively. They had great ideas."

To get to the core of those ideas, and implement them, New Line would fly Craven out to New York several times over the spring and summer of 1983, where the writer and director would often stay with Shaye and his wife at their house on a lake in upstate New York. Risher recalls the marathon script development sessions that took place. "I think we ultimately went through four to five drafts," she says. "Bob had very specific ideas on what would work and what wasn't working. He believed strongly in verisimilitude, as he would say: the logic of the dream world had to be consistent, and he wouldn't let Wes cheat it or take the easy route. We all got along really well, I remember, and Bob and Wes developed a great deal of mutual respect."

At least one of the fictional ideas of Craven's original script would be altered due to events in real life, as one of the longest trials in United States history was playing out, ultimately changing the course of *Elm Street* in a small way. "During the time that I was writing, the McMartin trial was going on endlessly," Craven recalls.

By some accounts, the McMartin trial has been called America's twentieth century witch hunt. It concerned allegations of child abuse by staff members at an otherwise well-regarded daycare facility, owned by the McMartin family, in the sleepy seaside community of Manhattan Beach, California. Rumors of Satanism, animal cruelty, and sexual abuse caused parents to become hysterical, feeding into a trial that was laden with difficult-to-prove allegations, coercion, and a lack of credible expert witnesses.

"The children had accused the teachers of molesting them in a very systematic way and over a period of many years," Craven says. As the trial went on, and with hard evidence lacking, it was deemed the entire thing was "some sort of psychological fabrication on the part of the children," he adds. "At least most people think that now."

Ultimately, after years of investigation and a lengthy and expensive trial, no convictions were obtained and all charges were dropped in 1990. Still, it was a time of extreme sensitivity to the issue of hurting children in any way, particularly sexually.

"That was part of the reason why Freddy was described as a harmer of children. And there were many, many drafts of it," admits Craven. Thus, his pedophilic murderer was soft-pedaled into "simply" a child murderer. "I think he was always going to be despicable and a murderer somehow. And in my mind, the killer of children is about the most despicable thing you can think of."

GIVING AWAY THE FARM

As work on the script continued, Shaye was diligently trying to secure funding for the project, a process that ultimately took a couple of years from the time he started. "Bob had actually been trying to raise money for it, and finally found enough money for us to start," Craven remembered. "He finally raised, I think, a little over the two million dollars."

With that hurdle seemingly conquered, the time had come for Craven and Shaye to enter the not-so-subtle dance of negotiating fees. It became clear to both parties that something was going to have to give in order to move forward. The question was: who would give, and what?

"Unfortunately, there was a point where Bob said, 'This picture's not gonna get made if we keep fooling around with your agent,'" Craven remembers. Shaye had gently reminded Craven that they were friends and there was no reason they couldn't just sign.

"And I did," says Craven, recalling the fee for his writing and directing to be around seventy thousand dollars." But included in that number, he lamented, "Bob got everything."

Craven was broke and, worse, in debt by the time Shaye had wrangled the finances to make the film. "I was in no position to make a good deal," he remembers. It was one of more than a few issues—some minor, some not—that caused a rift between Shaye and his writer and director.

When pressed for an explanation on that perceived discord, at least back when things were beginning, Shaye offers, "I don't know, and frankly it's been a bone of contention which I hope has been buried between Wes and I."

Only time would tell.

THE DREAM TEAM

Although Craven might have felt the deal he had struck for *Elm Street* was one made quickly in order to sustain him through a financial crisis, what mattered was that the movie was on its way to being made.

Because the film was going to be an ambitious project on a limited budget, it was crucial that those chosen to take part in making the movie a reality be ready to handle whatever might come their way. With that in mind, one important position sought out was that of accountant. However, in what would become true New Line Cinema fashion, Shaye looked within to find someone who could get the job done. And then some.

Initially meeting Shaye when she was a production assistant on the John Waters film *Polyester*, Baltimore native Rachel Talalay ("She's a good friend of John's," states Shaye) remembers her unorthodox indoctrination to *Elm Street*, which started with reading the script.

"It scared me so much, I actually didn't sleep the night after I read it," Talalay recalls. "It was so effective in terms of being just sheer plain-ahead terrifying." What might have added to the fear was her lack of familiarity with Craven and his work. "I was never a horror film fan at that point. I was so sensitive, and so frightened, that I was too scared of his early films to watch them."

Eventually, Talalay did watch them and has since become "a serious, obsessive horror film fan," she reveals, realizing that Craven knew well how to tap into the base emotion of fear and successfully exploit it.

On board with the script, Talalay found herself starting out once again as a production assistant; that is, until she was quickly and unexpectedly promoted. "They hired me for one hundred fifty dollars a week," she recalls. "And then they said, 'Oh my God, no one knows how to do the accounts, and you were a math major, so you can do the accounts.'"

A nice sentiment, but Talalay admits she "knew nothing about accounting," so she did her best to fit in with Shaye and New Line Cinema's can-do attitude. "I went, 'Okay fine,' and quickly learned what I needed to learn. It's a lesson for the film business, which is, unless you're really going to get in trouble, if you think you can figure out how to do something, you should say, 'Yes' to be promoted," she says. "But not if you tell them you can do something you think you're really going to fail at."

She didn't fail and, working closely with Shaye, learned to crunch the numbers, which worked out perfectly since both she and the film would be in Los Angeles.

But her rise through the ranks wouldn't end there, as worrying about the books was not the only unforeseen thing with which she would be tasked. "I remember getting the call," says Talalay, "when they said, 'And by the way, we also need people to double up in jobs.'"

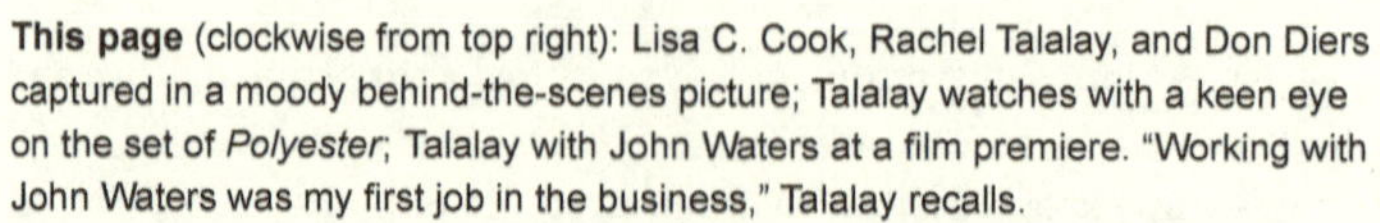

This page (clockwise from top right): Lisa C. Cook, Rachel Talalay, and Don Diers captured in a moody behind-the-scenes picture; Talalay watches with a keen eye on the set of *Polyester*; Talalay with John Waters at a film premiere. "Working with John Waters was my first job in the business," Talalay recalls.

Opposite page (clockwise from top right): Anne Huntley; Cook on the backlot; Diers with set dresser Dorree Cooper and a friend; Behind-the-scenes fun with the art department—and a very special prop; Greg Fonseca backstage and hard at work.

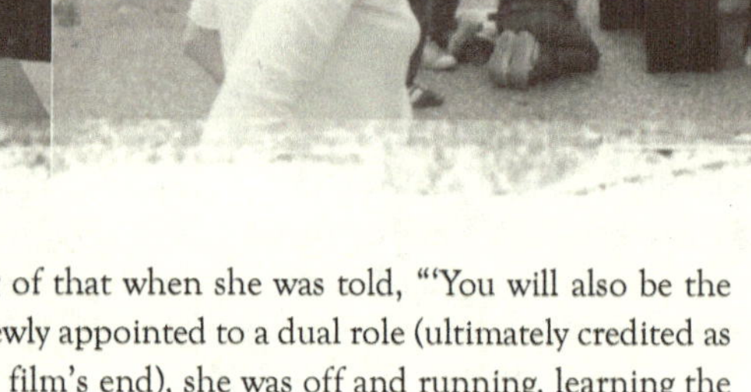

Talalay found out the meaning of that when she was told, "'You will also be the location manager,'" she recounts. Newly appointed to a dual role (ultimately credited as assistant production manager by the film's end), she was off and running, learning the intricacies of her positions.

As she did that, more behind-the-scenes crew were added, including production designer Greg Fonseca. Having attended the University of Southern California's well-regarded School of Film and Television, *Elm Street* was only his third feature (and second as production designer), but his work, and work ethic, was in full effect, on set and off.

"I remember Greg very well. He was a wonderful guy to work with. He was full of ideas, and he had the ability to do really good things on a very limited budget," says Craven, who quickly recalled a vivid encounter of Fonseca and the key grip at odds.

"The grip was always saying that the sets weren't made right for taking down walls or whatever he had to do for lighting, and there was one moment when he needed to get a light through a wall and there was no way to take it apart, and he said, 'That's all right, I got a solution for it, Greg,'" Craven remembers. "And he literally went out to his truck and came back with a chainsaw and chainsawed through the wall. There was this huge screaming fight between them and I threw both of them off of the set."

Talalay also recalls the squabble. "That caused a huge rift between the shooting department and the art department," she says. "Talk about putting yourself in a position where the production designer hates you."

Crew arguments aside, Craven appreciated that Fonseca fought for what he thought was best on the film, calling him "a great guy." And he wasn't alone in that assessment.

"Greg was so wonderful and so much his own character," Talalay says. "He had a very strong vision for the film and worked incredibly well with Wes to bring that to the screen."

Praise also comes from set decorator Anne Huntley, who reported to Fonseca and handled "purchasing, renting, styling all the furniture, carpeting, the light fixtures, lamps, accessories, everything but the walls in a show," she says. "I create, shop, rent, or have them installed."

Huntley's employment was a direct result of her relationship with Fonseca. "I'd done *Hardbodies* (1984) with Greg and I'd gone to graduate school with him. He was a fantastic production designer," she says. "He was so full of wonderful ideas and sort of pushed the envelope for the look and style of the show. And also had lots of fun. Greg got in there, got his hands dirty, and he was really a team player. He was a sweetheart and really inspired us all."

Sadly, after utilizing his innumerable talents on two dozen projects across multiple genres, including well-known hits such as *House* (1986), *Honey, I Shrunk the Kids* (1989), and *Wayne's World* (1992), Fonseca passed away due to complications from HIV.

"He was a great guy and that's one of the many, many tragic deaths from the AIDS plague," states Craven. "I couldn't say enough about him. He was wonderful."

Huntley agrees. "We lost him too early. He's greatly missed."

As the film continued with their designer who, at the time, Huntley adds, "really thought about the style and how the style could be real, but also look like a movie," the project picked up its newest team member.

Production coordinator Lisa C. Cook was brought onto the film by production manager Gerald Olson (*The Sword and the Sorcerer* [1982]), with whom she had previously worked. As she would learn, it would quickly be an opportunity to shine on her own.

"About a month in, I think, Gerald left *Nightmare* to work for HBO, and John Burrows came on board," Cook says. "So I'm very grateful that John kept me on, because usually production managers and coordinators are a team. You don't normally come on board without your person."

"Bob and Sara hired me to produce the film, but they had no money," admits Olson, who ultimately rejoined the New Line Cinema family as an executive. "I was running the production out of my living room when HBO offered me a solid job. Since New Line didn't have the film financed at the time, I took that job."

With the film needing to replace Olson, Burrows, who was out of work at the time *Elm Street* came his way, was on the roster of available production managers and was asked if he might be able to work on the film with Craven. "I said, 'Of course I can. I had heard about him, but I didn't know him,'" recalls Burrows. "They said, 'Well, why don't you meet him?'"

Craven and Burrows met at the writer and director's home, which happened to be near the Santa Monica Airport, a fact well-remembered by Burrows. "As I was talking to him there were planes coming in and landing. I said, 'Gee, Wes, I don't know how you write anything or do any thinking here with these planes going over every twenty minutes.' And he said, 'We don't seem to be hassled by it, we just allow it. Anyway, John, keep talking because I'll listen.'"

As requested, Burrows talked, Craven listened, and the out-of-work Burrows landed the job, becoming Cook's new boss. "She was very educated and trying to learn the film business," he says of his production coordinator. "She got very close to Wes

The crew, a close-knit group, found the time to work hard and still have fun. "I think the most fun was just the movie magic of it to me," admits Jensen. "And everybody's job and how they did it. It seemed like we were all doing it pretty much close to the stage and close to each other. Everybody was just out there doing whatever they could to make it work. It was great."

and he enjoyed telling her why he was doing certain things when she asked pertinent questions. He took patience with her and he did tell her a lot."

Moving to Los Angeles in 1980, Cook recalls her response to a colleague stating they wanted to make their living working only on horror films. "I said, 'Well, that's ridiculous. Nobody can do that. Who wants to do that?' And of course, I went on to make lots of horror movies."

Glad to be a part of Craven's horror film, Cook describes her job as "kind of like an office manager. I remember that Rachel had her office behind me, John had an office, and Wes had an office. So for the first few weeks it was just us and I feel like I got to know Wes as well as anybody does."

One of Cook's many tasks on the film came directly from Craven, who sent her to the Writer's Guild of America. "The WGA has a service where if you're doing research on some kind of script, they will set you up with a professional in that field so you can kind of ghost what they're doing and shadow them," she says. "He wanted one where someone was doing sleep research, so I remember going through that process for him."

Like many others, it was the production coordinator's first time meeting and working with the writer and director, and she came away with nothing but high praise. "Working on *Elm Street* was my introduction to Wes and I knew nothing about his horror legacy," admits Cook. "I was very gratefully surprised at what a pleasure he was to work with. He was just a great guy and super smart. The crew loved him and were very devoted to him, so that was a real lucky break."

Through a relationship with Cook, the film also found a production assistant for the front office. "My duties were to answer phones, run off scripts, do errands, do runs, and things like that," says Don Diers, who would, in what seemed to be de rigueur at New Line Cinema, quickly segue into another position.

"I find that it always illustrates how Hollywood works and, in a funny way, how we all end up in the right place in Hollywood as well," says Diers. "I was working in the studio and there was this cute cat that would just be friendly. The cat's name was Debbie and, for some reason, this thing came out called the 'Flat Cat,' which was the idea of a run-over cat. And so I started making cardboard cat Xerox art because I was bored in the office between phone calls and running scripts. The art department and the production designer got hold of some of my art and thought I was better suited for the art department."

Plucked from one position into another, which began the start of a thirty-year career in art direction and set decorating, Diers also had nothing but kind words to say about his new boss, Fonseca. "If he had an idea, or thought something was right, he would pursue it," he says. "Greg wasn't afraid of things. He had a lot of courage to try things, and experiment, and had a certain amount of confidence that what he was doing would be the right decision."

The film found its makeup artist in Kathy Logan, who had feature film and television credits in multiple genres prior to coming on board, such as the horror spoof *Saturday the 14th* (1981) and the Roger Corman-produced thriller *Love Letters* (1983). Getting the job through her connection with Talalay's boyfriend, *Elm Street* would be her first foray into true horror.

"I thought it was a pretty good script; maybe a little far-fetched, to say the least, but I thought it could be a good project," admits Logan. Even with that, she was nothing but happy with her director. "I think Wes is absolutely brilliant. It was very pleasant working with him."

Logan also enjoyed time with her counterpart, key hair stylist RaMona Fleetwood. "She is a character unto herself," laughs Logan. "She was a hoot to work with, a lot of fun. She was a personal friend of Wes', which is how she got the job."

It was, indeed, when some producers Fleetwood knew asked if she would give a haircut to a friend of theirs. "I said, 'Sure,'" she recalls. "So we sat at a football game, and this man shows up, and I cut his hair and I find out it's Wes Craven. He liked the way I did his hair and we sort of bonded."

That first good meeting led Craven to hire Fleetwood for *The Hills Have Eyes* and, subsequently, *Elm Street*. "I just ended up being his hairdresser and friend," she admits.

The relationship was strong enough that, when Fleetwood was hospitalized at one point and her insurance ran out, Craven picked her up and let her live in his house. It just so happened that, at the same time, the writer and director was hard at work on a new script that would be the portent of future employment for his houseguest.

"He was writing *Nightmare on Elm Street*. I was at his house the whole time he created Freddy," Fleetwood laughs. "And the script was phenomenal. I loved it. I loved the whole character of it."

As for her job on the show, Fleetwood flatly states it's more than meets the eye. After reading the script and breaking it down, she says, "A third of my job is paperwork, a third is psychology, and a third I actually get to do hair. I also follow through with continuity on all the hairstyles and created a few of them."

Another position to be filled was that of costume supervisor, which would go to a woman with just a few credits to her name. "It was fairly soon after moving from New York where I'd only worked in theater and very rarely went to the movies," says Lisa Jensen, whose path to *Elm Street*, like others, was informal. "I had somehow been introduced to the costume designer on a picture that she was doing called *Breakin'* (1984), and worked on that for maybe only a few days. We got along. I really didn't have any experience in wardrobe supervising, but kind of winged it. Then, she asked me to do *Nightmare*."

While the designer sets the look of the show, Jensen, as supervisor, "kind of worked with her on the breakdowns of what was worn in what scene," she states.

Though it was still early in her career, Jensen was about to find that she would be steering the wardrobe ship after the designer left the film to work on another project. "She left me with all the notes, and what was to be worn where, and I gaffed it, essentially. I made it work while it was being shot on set," she says. "All the looks were set, and she was good with the multiples for all the goo, and the gore, and the blood, and the water, and the fire, and everything. I just made sure that it all worked out within those parameters."

"Wes understood what he needed to make the story move along, which made him a pleasure to work with. He didn't require the effects to carry the scene."

Jim Doyle

Things were continuing to advance on other fronts as well, with Craven setting his sights on finding the craftsmen who would help make the terrors of his *Nightmare* a reality. Near the top of the list were people who would form the necessary special and mechanical effects teams, two important groups in a film that would rely heavily on creating the specter and illusion of nightmares and death.

One of the first to be brought on was mechanical special effects designer Jim Doyle, later known for his work on such projects as *The Stand* (1994), *Showgirls* (1995), and *The Nutty Professor* (1996). As he recalls, he ended up on the film when the production was casting around for somebody "young and nuts."

Originally, the film had made overtures to another special effects crewman, Robbie Knott (then known for work on *The Muppet Movie*), who was deemed too expensive, so they asked him for a recommendation. "And Robbie said, 'Call Jim Doyle, because he is young and will kill to do this movie,'" remembers Doyle.

Knott was right. "I read Wes' script and I had a great immediate relationship with it," Doyle reveals. "It had a killer story."

After getting the seal of approval from the producers, Doyle next sat down with the writer and director who was not only eager to be up and running, but clear about what he wanted. "Wes understood what he needed to make the story move along, which made him a pleasure to work with. He didn't require the effects to carry the scene," he says.

Doyle was also pleased to hear that Craven was interested in his perspective on what could realistically be accomplished. "Wes and I got to sit down and spend some time talking about the dreams and the different sequences," he says. "And that's when I think he decided he could work with me."

Also brought on at the beginning was special effects assistant Lou Carlucci, who would go on to work on such films as *Blade* (1998), *Hatchet* (2006), and *Real Steel* (2011). Coming on board *Elm Street*, he quickly realized ingenuity would be the prevailing notion.

Two of the crew who would help *Elm Street*'s effects come to life: Christina Rideout and Charles Belardinelli (left); Anthony Cecere (center), who would bring the heat to the film's fiery finale, among other stunts, was entrusted by Craven to make sure no one got hurt; Director of Photography and crew behind the scenes (right). "I loved it," Haitkin says. "I knew it was a commercial piece that on the surface of it would thrill and scare audiences. But I knew it went deeper than that. To this day, look how successful and popular horror films are: the appeal behind horror films is fear."

"Jim Doyle handed me the script," Carlucci recalls, "and there were gags that were very unique, and it took a lot of creative thought with very little money."

With the seemingly ever-present issue of big ideas and small funds, it was important to find a way to keep things moving. "Bob had a determination to make things work," says Risher. "Even if we didn't have the money to do it right, he would find a way to do it anyway."

Carlucci agrees, adding, "We tried to create a look with the mechanical effects that just kept getting better in creativity."

In the end, it would be the culmination of the entire team putting their heads together and figuring out a way to create things that had never been done before. "It just kept growing in terms of how much we can make it better," says Carlucci. "How much spookier, different, weird can we make what we're trying to do?"

Still, there would be more help needed to develop and craft the things that would go bump in the *Nightmare*. Enter special effects technician Charles Belardinelli, who had already known Carlucci. "Lou and I were working together as carpenters prior to the movie," recalls Belardinelli.

After Carlucci landed his position, Belardinelli remembers being asked to join the film. "Lou had said, 'Hey, I got this guy who needs some carpenters, and he's working on a movie doing special effects. You want a job?'" With an affirmative answer, Belardinelli quickly found himself meeting Doyle and getting ready to start.

Another member of the team was Christina Rideout, who ended up on the film because she was, quite literally, in the right place at the right time. Graduating from the University of Southern California with a Bachelor of Fine Arts, Rideout found herself the recipient of a job offer from Doyle in a way that humorously could make her seem like "the other woman."

Doyle was renting shop space at the university's scene dock and happened to be dating a good friend of Rideout's at the time. "Jim wanted his girlfriend, Jean, to stay in town and work on the movie with him," Rideout recalls. "But she wanted to go to the Santa Fe Opera, where she'd been the past couple of summers."

Seeing Doyle's apprehension at losing a technician he trusted ("Jean was a techie with a BFA in technical design in theater," Rideout recalls), Jean looked at Doyle and suggested he ask Rideout. Doyle did just that, hiring her as his assistant. Ecstatic at the post-university offer, she thought, "'Sweet! A movie for graduation. I'm in!'"

It wasn't long before Doyle had the team he needed to move forward on the creative, complicated effects and set pieces that demanded his attention. While he toiled away, Craven worked on readying his screenplay for production and finding a director of photography with whom he could work to bring it to life.

"Normally, directors have a DP, and Wes didn't have one, so we brought in a lot of DPs for him to meet," recalls Cook. "He ended up selecting Jacques Haitkin."

The cinematographer was coming off the Judd Nelson comedy *Making the Grade* (1984) and already had lower-budgeted horror experience with *Galaxy of Terror* (1981), produced by Roger Corman. (The film featured Robert Englund, and also had a young James Cameron as its production designer and second unit director.)

Cook wasn't present for Haitkin's interview with Craven, but clearly believes that "Jacques told him what he wanted to hear, and he had a very good handle on the script and the way Wes wanted it done."

Haitkin did. "Wes was trolling for cinematographers and I read the script and loved it," he says. "I knew it was a commercial piece that on the surface of it would thrill and scare audiences." He also knew the film Craven wanted to make would go deeper than that, touching upon something that was, he adds, "societally and culturally relevant to people's fears."

Describing Craven as a visionary for finding a way to take a moralistic concept and fit it within a commercial framework, Haitkin made sure to demonstrate he could handle the technical side of things—even as he showed an understanding and appreciation of the philosophical. "I was definitely a content-oriented person, always speaking in terms of the content," he says. "I was always careful to make sure I was resonant with what the material was doing."

It was something Craven noticed, admitting that Haitkin was "an absolute perfectionist," a quality the cinematographer believes got him the job.

"I was so committed to asking him questions about the material, characters, intent, all of that, rather than just the technical side," Haitkin says. "We were both so into it."

Understanding and analyzing the depths to which Craven wanted his film to go, in addition to looking for the truths in any film on which he was employed, Haitkin admits that his approach to work is not exactly typical. It was this that caused at least one challenge for the crew.

"He was a little tough," Cook admits. "I remember we used Arriflex cameras and I was calling them to get details about the package for Jacques. That's my job, right? He'd given me a camera list, I was calling around, and I was on the phone with them when Jacques came up to my desk. I said, 'Okay, just a minute.'"

Apparently, Haitkin was looking for a quicker response. "He literally hung up the phone," Cook recalls. "He just put his hand on the button and clicked it off. I said, 'Jacques, I was talking about your camera.' And he goes, 'Well, I need your attention right now.'"

With film productions usually being high stress and, in the case of *Elm Street* for New Line Cinema, high stakes, it was easy to recognize why tensions might have been present. Cook understands, ultimately giving Haitkin praise for his work. "It's a well-shot movie. And it was very challenging, at the time, with the level of special effects in there and everything," she admits. "It took somebody who had a real handle on that, and that was Jacques."

One of the last, but not least, important aspects of the crew for a film so full of special effects and dazzling (some would later say precarious) set pieces was the stunt coordinator. The job, in which someone reads the script to figure out all of the stunts in the film and the safest way they can be handled, would go to a man who not only had stunt experience in the genre, but with whom Craven had a firsthand relationship.

Casting director Annette Benson.

Prior to *Elm Street*, Anthony Cecere worked for the director on *Invitation to Hell* and *The Hills Have Eyes Part II*, but it was actually his first job with Craven, years before those two films, that landed him a place in *Nightmare*. "I did the fire burn for Wes on *Swamp Thing*," he says, "and I believe he'd liked that enough that he wanted me on this other one because it, too, had a fire burn."

With that, Cecere had the job. And like many others, he recalls his expectations of first meeting the man behind the film *The Last House on the Left*. "I thought he was gonna be a real weird sort of eerie fellow. What he turned out to be instead was a mild guy who knew what he wanted," offers the stuntman. "Wes was very precise in the things he saw regarding the stunts for this film."

THE (ALMOST) MAN OF THE HOUR

With the film heavy into pre-production and key craftsman in place, the time had come for Craven to focus his sights on casting. It was a task that would begin with the important, possibly make-or-break aspect of filling the role of the film's unique villain.

Though Craven had already put much thought into who the character was on paper, drawing from real-life experiences and fears, finding a flesh and blood person to bring Freddy Krueger to undead life was somewhat more challenging.

"We had a brilliant, young casting woman, Annette Benson, and she found everyone," Risher says.

Starting her career as a casting assistant on films such as *National Lampoon's Class Reunion* (1982), *The Star Chamber* (1983), and *Christine* (1983), Benson eventually moved up to casting director, with her first genre credit being the science-fiction/horror/comedy *Night of the Comet* (1984). After that, she waded into the more serious terrors of *Elm Street*, a move she did not regret in the least.

"I was too naïve to know if moving into horror was a good or bad career move," admits Benson. "I was pretty new at doing my own movies, so it was pretty exciting when I was offered *Elm Street*."

Referred to Shaye and Risher by another casting director to work on Craven's film, Benson did that and more. "After casting *Elm Street* I was offered the position of head of casting for New Line Cinema, which led to nine wonderful years with the company," states Benson.

It also helped that Benson connected with Craven's material. "I loved the script," she says. "It was scary, well written, and I saw the opportunity to find talented actors to bring it to life."

David Warner as Evil in Terry Gilliam's fantasy adventure *Time Bandits*. The face he wouldn't be portraying? Krueger. "I met Robert Englund and mentioned this whole thing to him. I said, 'I was supposedly offered the role, and if you've heard that I've turned it down, it's not true.' He'd never heard that rumor himself," Warner states.

With Benson on board the search began for an actor to play Krueger. The task would quickly reveal Craven's preference that, for his villain, he was looking for someone who could portray more than the decade's prototypical stalk-and-slash malefactor.

"There was the classic argument that Freddy's a real character," Talalay states. "He's not just a man with a hockey mask."

Even Shaye was impressed with Craven's ability to see that the character could, and should, be more. "Most villains cast who don't say very much in these kinds of movies are usually stuntmen," he states. "And Wes' idea was to eventually get a real actor in the role."

The decision came from Craven's early ideas that Krueger would have a true persona, something with which Shaye agreed. "Wes wanted to add some personality and some élan to it," he says. "Which I thought was a very good idea and, clearly, it was."

As the search for the role started, even Risher was on board with what Craven was hoping to find. "He wanted a good actor," she says. "More than anything he didn't want to cast just some creepy guy."

Instead, Craven would look for clever, intelligent performers who could carry off the role.

Some have stated in the past that first in line was a character actor already well known for villainous turns in films such as *Time Bandits* (1981) and *Tron* (1982): David Warner.

It would seem, though, that his potential casting is almost something akin to myth. When asked about the possibility of using Warner, Shaye adds, "I don't know. It's not familiar to me."

It's also not familiar to Warner.

"People have often asked me, 'Well, why didn't you play Freddy Krueger?'" Warner reveals. "I honestly cannot remember being asked to play the character at any stage at all. I was very busy at the time and meeting a lot of people, so unless my agent got it and turned it down without my knowing it, which would be unethical, I really don't remember anything at all in my past regarding *A Nightmare on Elm Street*."

Having done films in multiple genres, Warner admits the kind of horror film *Elm Street* proved to be wasn't something he actively pursued. "They're not the kind of pictures I actually go and see," he laughs. "As an actor you do all sorts of things. I've done a western, I've done a musical, I've done a war movie. I don't know that I would have liked to play the Freddy Krueger kind of character, to be honest with you."

Craven was also not one to confirm the possibility of the actor donning the fedora, sweater, and glove. "I used Dave Warner on *Scream 2* [1997] and I'm an admirer of his," he said, then added, "but for Freddy? I don't think so."

One name that was mentioned belonged to actor Richard Moll who, at the time, was known for his guest-starring roles in many of television's most popular sitcoms and dramas, but who would later gain fame for starring as the seemingly dim-witted, but gentle and kind Nostradamus "Bull" Shannon on NBC's hit *Night Court* (1984-1992).

"Richard was somebody Wes first talked about, as he was a stereotyped 'bad guy,'" recalls Benson. "I'm pretty sure we offered it to him, because Wes liked him and thought he would be right. However, I think he turned us down, which turned out great."

BE NOT AFRAID

Moving forward as he looked for the real Krueger, Craven did recall casting for an older man, as that's how the character of Freddy was written. However, he found himself faced with an issue he hadn't anticipated when searching for someone of age who could bring forth his villain's evil persona: the men he thought could portray the soulless murderer were, simply, too soft. "There was something about having seen so much of life that there was a certain tenderness to them," he remembers. "They couldn't really be evil."

Craven once again tapped into his academic background as he thought about the psychology of the human mind when it comes to portraying malevolence. Realizing nobody believes they have evil within themselves, "If something comes at them that shows evil, whether it's an actor or writer, they'll think, 'Oh, that person is evil. Thank God I'm not,'" he says.

There was, however, an actor who wasn't frightened of such things. Known at the time for his role as the alien Willie from the miniseries *V* (1983), actor Robert Barton Englund had already racked up classical theatre parts and over a dozen film and television roles before meeting with Craven for the role of Freddy Krueger. (He had even auditioned for the role of Han Solo in *Star Wars* [1977]. "They said I was too young," the actor reveals about why he did not get the part.)

The chance to be a part of *Elm Street* started with a traditional interview about which Englund hadn't given much thought. "I was really sort of self-preoccupied with my first bout of success as a result of the miniseries *V* at that time," he says. "It brought

Clockwise from top left: A young Englund meets Saint Nick; Englund, Wendt, and others from the play *Journey's End*; Englund performing in the musical *The Fantasticks*; Englund in the play *Life with Father*; A signed headshot of the actor, dedicated to hair stylist Fleetwood.

about a seminal change in my life and was my first brush with celebrity where people could put a name to my face."

Englund was performing in a play with George Wendt (famous for his role as Norm on the television series *Cheers* [1982–1993]) when the call to meet with Craven came in. "My agent had suggested this film called *A Nightmare on Elm Street*," he says. "Wes Craven was going to direct it."

Englund admits that, at the time, his knowledge of Craven was limited to what he had learned from, of all places, a new wave bar he frequented. "I think I had a minor crush on the braless bartender there," the actor jokes.

Aside from being lovelorn, the actor recalls two old monitors on either end of the bar that simultaneously ran a loop of scenes from David Lynch's *Eraserhead* (1977) on one and clips of Craven's *The Last House on the Left* and *The Hills Have Eyes* on another. "And after a couple of Irish whiskeys, waiting for the band to play and flirting with the bartender, they kind of all got meshed in my mind," states Englund. This strange amalgamation led the actor to consider Craven "very artistic, and very much like a dark prince."

Mentioning the potential meeting with Craven to Wendt, who was familiar with the director's work, he suggested Englund take the interview. It didn't hurt that Englund also knew Benson, whom he had met on a series of callbacks for the film *National Lampoon's*

Class Reunion. "I literally read for just about every male role and I didn't get it. I was sure I was gonna be in the movie, but nada, zip, butkus," he says. "But maybe something that I showed Annette convinced her I was the right guy and she brought me in for Freddy."

Benson is quick to point out bringing Englund in to read for the role was more than just remembering him from a former project. "I brought him in because he's a fabulous actor, a fabulous character actor," she admits. "And I knew him before *Class Reunion* because it was my job to know the good actors in town. I was thrilled to bring him in."

Between his agent, an out-of-the-ordinary indoctrination to Craven's work, advice from George Wendt, befriending Benson and, of course, his talent, it seemed that multiple forces were with Englund by the time he went in to audition. There, he would discover exactly how much Craven lived up to the "dark prince" image in his mind. Unbeknownst to the actor, it would be quite a surprise.

"Wes was a professor. Wes was a teacher. He's a raconteur when he talks. Then when I got the script, it did really wonderful, really magical stuff."

Robert Englund

Going in to meet Craven, Englund was dressed "as punk-rock and psychoed-out as I could be," he says, complete with a four-day beard growth, and ready to meet the man he thought would look like Charlie Manson.

But he was wrong.

Instead, Englund saw his would-be director as "erudite, tall, kind of preppy, Ralph Lauren-attired Wes Craven," he says. Somewhat thrown, the actor recovered and used the unexpected to his advantage. "I tried to shut up as much as possible, but I think I stood myself in good stead with him."

The true test would be what Craven thought and, at first, he seemed to be less than convinced as his search for Krueger continued. "I thought he was totally wrong, even though he had some Shakespearean chops and everything else," Craven recalls. "He looked kind of semi-geeky, and he was younger, much younger than I was looking for."

Benson recollects, "Wes was thinking of a large, oppressive, or threatening actor for the role, but I love casting against type. I always did." She believed that Englund might have been perfect for the role because he did not appear to be a stereotypical bogeyman. "He had a slighter build and he was interesting. As a good actor he could become the part. He felt right to me for the role of Freddy from the beginning," she adds.

Nevertheless, Englund did his best to convince Craven he was the best man for the role. "I think Wes wanted a big guy, you know? And I am not a big guy," admits the actor. So he let Wes do all the talking while he "stared at him with my Lee Harvey Oswald stare."

Craven began to sense there was something fun about the actor and threw caution to the wind. "I thought, 'Okay, fine. Read,'" he recalls.

Englund did, realizing the script "did really wonderful, really magical stuff," he says.

Also appreciated by Englund was Craven describing the film's backstory and how he had hoped to create a strange, almost Grimm-like fairytale wrapped around an incredibly memorable monster. "Freddy is a bogeyman in the truest sense of the word," he offers. "And a bogeyman is a pretty classic ingredient, especially in German literature and Teutonic literature of the horror genre, so I guess you could say he is kind of a classic invention from Wes Craven's mind."

The actor was particularly taken by the dream concept, happily surprised the idea hadn't already been executed in the way Craven had envisioned. "I can't believe someone hadn't thought of it before," Englund contemplates, "to use the nightmare, the bad dream, as a locus for attacking, and punishing, and revenging upon the family and relatives of the people that had wronged Freddy." He also had a more idealistic approach to the idea. "Two wrongs don't make a right, and certainly being burned alive is not, you know, due process."

With both the audition and Englund and Craven's conversations about the character and core of the film over, Englund hoped for the best. "Wes was very kind to me and said that he saw something in me, and perhaps he did," he says. "I hope that's the truth."

It was, as Craven found the quality for which he had been searching. "I realize that there's a certain kind of personality that can dare to put themselves in the position of being evil, and Robert just relished being evil," he recalls. "He wasn't afraid of that. He could be the guy on the sidewalk frightening the kid. And if you don't have somebody who can really personally scare, and is willing to scare, and will go into those places in himself to find that sort of element, you're doomed."

Still, Craven remembered his initial thoughts that Englund might not have been right for the part when he first saw the actor. "I said, 'Okay, fine. This might not work, but we'll try it with this younger guy.'" Then, realizing what Englund could bring to the table in terms of his performance and understanding of the character, the writer and director recognized he might have been remiss in looking solely for an older actor. "The rest was makeup, and once the makeup was on him, you didn't know how old he was anyway," he says. "And it was like, 'Duh, what was I thinking?'"

Coupled with the fact that Craven found Englund to have a "fantastic energy, a willingness to play it, and enthusiasm for it," he says, Englund ultimately won the director over.

Burrows remembers, "Wes came out of the meeting and Robert had left and he told me, 'You know, this man can do this.'"

Not knowing Craven's thoughts after the interview was over, Englund recounts, "I went out drinking because I was right up the street from my favorite hangout at the time. And I got home and it was on the answering machine that I had the role."

Not too bad for a chance meeting that, as Talalay points out, "was really, really smart on Wes' part."

Englund had a theory on what helped him win the role. "The time has long since passed when you could get away with dressing a football player or some other non-acting deformed person as a monster," he says. "The people behind the makeup have to have some acting ability because the monster is the core of these films. If he isn't believable, the rest of the film won't be."

While that was true, the fact that Englund had a following certainly didn't hurt, either.

"Robert was famous, known for *V* at that point, and everyone was just thrilled that he was doing it," Talalay says.

THE ORIGINAL ELM STREET CHILDREN

With a villain set, and behind-the-scenes technical aspects of the film running smoothly, it was time for Craven to find the children his Freddy Krueger would terrorize. Never one to play into stock stereotypes, the director instead opted to craft archetypes in the guise of sympathetic victims and the resourceful heroine who would try to save them all.

Relative newcomer Heather Langenkamp would portray the latter role of Nancy Thompson, described as "a pretty girl in a letter sweater, with an easy, athletic stride and the look of a natural leader." (Incidentally, the character's name was Nancy Wilson in "one of the very first drafts of the script, the one I received at the first production meeting," recalls Cecere.)

Just twenty years old at the time, Langenkamp, a native of Tulsa, Oklahoma, had done little performing. Prior to *Elm Street*, her entrée into acting began when, while working at *The Tulsa Tribune*, she saw an ad looking for extras for Francis Ford Coppola's *The Outsiders* (1983). "They held auditions in an old elementary school, so I went down at lunchtime and met the casting director. They took a Polaroid and said, 'Okay, we'll be calling you. We have some high school scenes in the next couple days,'" she remembers.

And call they did, with the actress being amidst what seemed like hundreds of kids. "We had to be dressed like the fifties. The pay back then was about thirty dollars, so I felt rich," Langenkamp laughs.

That same summer, another Coppola film was being made in the area, *Rumble Fish* (1983), and the actress tagged along with her friend, who had been called to be in a street scene. "Her mother had said she would be more comfortable if I went with her, because it was kind of a sketchy neighborhood and was a night shoot," Langenkamp says. With the casting director notified, and on board, she and her friend arrived, got into wardrobe and prepared to be extras in a wedding scene.

And then Langenkamp was asked to speak.

"The first AD came up to me and said, 'We have a line of dialogue and we'd like to give it to you, Heather,'" recalls Langenkamp. "It was a very simple line, like, 'Hey guys, come on up to the party. No one will care,' or something like that. It seems like we did three or four takes, and we were yelling down to Matt Dillon, and there were all these people dancing in the streets. Francis Ford Coppola always puts together such colorful scenes. It was a really exciting moment for me."

Opposite page: Actress Heather Langenkamp

It was one that also helped Langenkamp get into the Screen Actors Guild. Unfortunately, the scene was cut from the final film, but coming at a moment in her life when she wasn't sure exactly what path she was going to take, "I really felt strongly Hollywood was knocking on my door and I better take advantage of it," the actress states. "I stayed in contact with the casting director, her assistant, and the producer. They all really helped me get a footing in the business when I would be studying at Stanford and then go to Los Angeles on the weekends. That went on for quite a while. It was a whirlwind time and I really owe a lot to the very nice people I met in Tulsa."

Langenkamp's very first Hollywood audition would be for the independent feature *Nickel Mountain* (1984). "I had flown in from Stanford, rented a car, and drove to the casting office. It was really exciting," she says. At least until her vehicle (parked on a busy Cahuenga Boulevard) was hit by a runaway truck while she was reading for the director, Drew Denbaum.

"She embodied what I was looking for, which was a legitimate all-American, girl-next-door. No artificial anything."

Wes Craven on hiring Heather Langenkamp

After the audition, Langenkamp went back into the office and asked if they would help her. "They let me use their phone and it took four or five hours for the tow truck to arrive and clear the car away," she recalls.

The ordeal, however stressful, just might have been a boon for the actress. "That whole time, the director, casting director, and I got to know each other. They ended up liking me and hired me to play the role of Callie for the film," states Langenkamp.

She next played Joanne Woodward and Richard Crenna's daughter in the television film *Passions* (1984). "It was really a time when movies of the week were more like independent films. They had scripts that attracted some star talent," Langenkamp offers. "It was a complex part. Richard plays a philandering husband who has a son with his mistress, so my character was acting like a bridge between these two families."

It was one of the first times anyone would see the actress in a large role, "because certainly nobody saw *Nickel Mountain*," laughs Langenkamp. "I was just doing my best to make myself into a serious actress at that time."

It was then that the chance to appear in a horror film seemed to come from left field, based on her prior work and Langenkamp's admitting she was not, at the time, what one might call a genre aficionado.

"I was absolutely not a horror fan at all. In fact, the only horror movie that I'd really seen was *Burnt Offerings* (1976) and I saw that when I was thirteen," admits Langenkamp. "I did not go out and see horror movies as a general rule. I went to high school, was working really hard, and was trying to get into college."

Even though she admits to not seeing true horror films ("I hadn't seen *Halloween* or *Friday the 13th*," she says), Langenkamp does recall enjoying movies from the master of suspense, Alfred Hitchcock. Having lived in Washington, D.C., she and her friends would find themselves at the Kennedy Center for classic film festivals where they showed many of Hitchcock's pictures.

"That was a period of my life when I was really awakening to the history of film, and I was a total Hitchcock fanatic," says Langenkamp. Unbeknownst to her at the time, it would later prove useful for becoming part of Craven's ensemble as she felt that many of the themes of the director's films hearkened back to the older style of suspense and monsters.

"Nothing much had changed in terms of how you make a scary movie. So I'm glad that I at least had that education," admits Langenkamp, "but I wasn't aware then that Wes was like this horror-meister, as you would call him today."

ALL-AMERICAN GIRL

Langenkamp's meeting with Craven for a role in his film would start like any other, and she wasn't alone. "My agent set me up to audition right in the heart of Hollywood, and there were a lot of girls there on the first day," she recalls. In fact, there weren't even enough chairs to accommodate everyone, necessitating many of them, Langenkamp included, to wait their turn sitting on the floor.

Over the years, it has been stated that some of those chairs may have belonged to actresses whose names are now well-known, including Demi Moore, Courteney Cox, Jennifer Grey, and Tracey Gold. Looking back, Benson says, "Demi Moore, no, as she had two hit movies under her belt already and wouldn't have come in for something like this. As for Courteney, that's also a no. I would have remembered her, but I met her in New York after *Elm Street*. Jennifer, possibly. Tracey Gold, it's also possible." (It should be noted, however, that Gold would have only been fifteen at the time of the film's release, making for an incredibly young Nancy compared to the rest of the cast.)

As for Langenkamp, like Englund before her, Benson had been familiar with the actress, having brought her in to read for the lead in *Night of the Comet*. "For that film, it was between her and Catherine Mary Stuart," she remembers.

Though Stuart ultimately won the role of "Reggie" in that film (one of two "valley girls" who find that most life on Earth has been eradicated after the planet passed through the tail of a comet), Langenkamp thinks back on the process of being put up for a role against others considered her type. "We were all reading for the same things, such as the quarterback's princess, or a teen in a John Hughes movie," she states. She also clearly recalls vying for the female lead in *The Last Starfighter* (1984)—also ultimately going to Stuart. "*Elm Street* was such a low-budget movie Catherine Mary Stewart probably didn't even go up for it. She was the Heather Langenkamp of the 'A movies,'" the actress jokes.

As for her *Elm Street* audition, Langenkamp's reading impressed both Benson and Craven enough to garner a callback. It was then she was asked to perform a scene with eventual fellow cast member Wyss. "We went in together and sat side by side on the couch," the actress recalls.

Clockwise from top left: Langenkamp in high school, playing Nora in *A Doll's House*; The actress in *Passions*; Langenkamp's first SAG card; Langenkamp's 1984 date book showing her *Elm Street* audition and the outcome. Note the date; Behind the scenes of *Nickel Mountain*.

The scene was Nancy recalling a dream for her best friend, Tina. Langenkamp decided to heed the advice of her acting coach to "do something natural," hedging her bet on a simple moment that, in her mind, would be make-or-break. "I looked at Amanda and made this sort of screeching sound with my fingernails going down," she recalls. "And I just thought to myself, 'Oh God, if he doesn't like that, then I'm ruined.'"

But she wasn't. Craven understood, and liked, Langenkamp's ability to internalize the claws of Freddy and bring truthfulness to the character. "Heather was just charming and kind of wonderful, and smart, and just went with it. She was interesting to me because she embodied what I was looking for, which was a legitimate all-American, girl-next-door," he states. "Not anorexia-thin, no artificial anything. Just herself. Very non-Hollywood. There was just something about her that I said, 'That's like kids I grew up with.'"

Craven's feelings carried over to others on the crew as well. "She was such an awesome young lady, she really was," offers Logan. "Very intelligent. Not caught up in that whole Hollywood thing."

Englund also agreed with the assessment of the film's impending leading lady. "She is sort of a subliminal American beauty that, you know, I think works as a heroine," he says. "And I think that the corruption of Heather by the evil of Freddy begets a chemistry that audiences really responded to."

Sparking to that idea, and the thought that Langenkamp was just like the kids he grew up with, Craven knew the importance of casting someone the audience might think would be a pushover for the monster, when in fact she is the only one who can stand up to him. He saw in Langenkamp someone who was charming and smart, sensitive and strong, qualities he imbued into the role after learning a lesson from *Swamp Thing*—and his daughter, Jessica.

"There's a scene where Adrienne Barbeau is running from bad guys and trips and falls down, as practically every young woman in every action film or horror film did at some point," Craven says. "And my daughter said, 'You know, just because I'm a girl doesn't mean I'm clumsy. You don't have to have them falling down.'" And she meant it, when she looked directly at her father and made it clear: don't ever do that again.

Years later, his daughter believes the sentiment to be just as true. "I've never understood why women are portrayed as weak and unintelligent and victims in any number of contexts," says Jessica. "I guess I have never understood why women have to be so hapless. As a child, it didn't make any sense to me that a woman wouldn't be unable to run without tripping the same as any man would be able to."

Raised by a widow, Craven understood that the real world didn't always have the damsel in distress falling, fainting, or being rescued in the arms of a man, so he listened to his daughter. "After that, I wanted very much to have young heroines that didn't trip and fall down," he admits, adding, "who could fight if they had to. And Heather Langenkamp just had the quality in spades."

The actress admits that she had a very different upbringing than the average California teenager, never having gone surfing or hanging out at the beach. "My family's always been a real rugged, kind of farm family and I've always identified with that part," confesses Langenkamp. "My parents never let us whine or make excuses. We were always expected to do our chores and do our homework. So I just think that I was raised in that kind of old-fashioned way. And it made me that kind of a person. So, maybe I was a little bit like the character."

It was then that Craven knew he had found his Nancy. The next step for him was to convince Shaye and Risher. Thankfully, it was an easy task, considering hers was the only audition tape he showed them.

"It was like, 'Yes or no?' And we loved her immediately," Risher says. "She had that innocence, that beauty, and that sweetness, yet she also had the strength that the character needed."

Shaye agreed. "I love Heather," he says. "She is that girl. That feisty, tough-minded, 'I'm not gonna let this guy get me down,' kind of person. She was wonderful."

"Heather was a talented actress who I was thrilled to cast," admits Benson. "It was great to have Heather get the role of Nancy. She deserved it!"

Langenkamp received word directly from Craven that he would like her to play the part, a moment that still resonates with the actress. "I remember it like it was yesterday," she says. "I got the part in late winter, but it didn't start shooting until June. So we all kind of just cooled our heels for a while." During that time, she did not mention that the project she would be starring in was a horror movie. "Because I was not a horror fan, I didn't know what I was getting into," the actress adds.

What she did know was her reaction to the full script and story was real and compelling, allowing her to pull from within to bring her character to life. "Nancy immediately connected with me because she's a 'can-do' kind of girl," says Langenkamp. "She really wants to take charge. And she is not afraid. Sometimes I don't know if I've become Nancy, or if Nancy was like me."

The actress also admits admiring that Nancy was not interchangeable like a lot of other girls who are in more typical horror fare. Of characters like that, Langenkamp states, "They're not given very good material. They can't shine. They can't, as they don't have big personalities. But Nancy really did. And to me, that was remarkable."

Risher agreed, trying to be as influential as she could in making the female lead as strong as possible. "Certainly, Heather's was written as a strong character, and she portrayed the character in a very strong way," she says. "That was something I was really proud of."

Langenkamp adds, "The reason that I think Nancy is so important, and not necessarily me as Nancy, but Nancy herself, is that I really think that she is a totally different kind of heroine. And I do think that there would be no Freddy without Nancy in that first movie."

Feeling such a connection to a role so well-crafted in the things she did and said, Langenkamp recalls making the choice not to take a lot of time to develop a "character" in the way she portrayed Nancy. "I really felt like I was gonna just bring myself to the set, and be as close to me as I could. I didn't prepare in the classic sense," she admits. "I didn't know that was part of the whole thing. I was not a very trained actor at all. I'd taken classes, of course, but I just tried to learn my lines and be on my mark and do those right things."

It was a notion that worked and one that even Englund, playing Langenkamp's nemesis, noticed in her approach. "She's all things to all people," the actor states. "She is a princess, she is a warrior woman, she's a teenage everywoman, she's a survivor girl."

THE BOY NEXT DOOR

The next step in casting would be to locate the young man who would play Glen Lantz, Nancy's ill-fated boyfriend. As the heroine's love interest, Craven wrote he was "a good-natured, bright kid," originally envisioning the part as sort of a romantic lead, and what one might expect in that type of role.

"We were looking at all the standard Hollywood guys," Craven recalls. "I wasn't thinking that it would be that hard, but I didn't see anybody that seemed to be that really, kind of charismatic." But this was Hollywood and, soon enough, an actor with enough charisma, as well as an up-and-coming Tinseltown pedigree, was in the mix.

"At the time, there were so many young kids in Hollywood, you had the whole 'Brat Pack,'" says Langenkamp. "The Sean Penns and the Charlie Sheens, and Rob Lowe, Tom Cruise. All those guys were probably up for this part or at least knew about it."

Once again, there were more than a few actors who have since become recognizable names that were said to have been up for the part. One of those was Jackie Earl Haley, known at the time for his roles in *The Bad News Bears* (1976) and *Breaking Away* (1979). Of him auditioning, Benson says, "I don't remember. It is possible as I do remember bringing him in on various projects." While that may not definitively clarify his potential involvement in Craven's film, the actor's *Elm Street* story would pick up again decades later in the 2010 remake, where he portrayed Freddy Krueger. Other names mentioned over the years have included John Cusack, Brad Pitt, Kiefer Sutherland, Nicolas Cage, and C. Thomas Howell. Thinking on those names, Benson offers, "John Cusack, I don't think so. I met him when he auditioned for *Christine* (1983) and liked him a lot, so I would have remembered. Plus, I believe he lived in Chicago at the time. Brad Pitt, no. I met him in 1987 when casting *Apt Pupil* for director Alan Bridges." (Interestingly, this revelation would also contradict the anecdote that Pitt later auditioned for the sequel to *Elm Street*, which was cast by Benson in 1985.) Benson continues, "Kiefer Sutherland, not that I remember. Nicolas Cage, definitely not. And C. Thomas Howell, possibly."

Sheen, who turned down the role of Glen, subsequently worked (and talked about *Elm Street*) with Depp. "Johnny and I wound up on the battlefields of *Platoon* together just three years later," recalls Sheen.

Casting rumors aside, the actor almost cast as Glen was, in fact, Charlie Sheen. He recalls that his brush with *Elm Street* started, and ended, with reading the script, which didn't quite grab his attention. "I just didn't get it completely, but I still took a meeting with Wes," says the actor. "And when I met him, I said, 'Look, with all due respect, and as a fan of your talents, I just don't see this guy wearing a funny hat with a rotted face and a striped sweater and a bunch of clacky fingers. I just don't see this catching on.'"

The young actor, then coming off of *Red Dawn* (1984) and about to work on *The Boys Next Door* (1985), says, "I wasn't really in a position to turn down any movies, but I also didn't want to start making movies that I wasn't going to be proud of."

Extrapolating on his reaction to the material and the role, Sheen succinctly states, "I didn't want to get eaten by a bed. I want to sleep in a bed. I don't want to get eaten by a bed."

Despite his reaction to the material–and his reluctance to become a meal for blankets and a mattress–there had been talk that Sheen asked for three thousand dollars a week. Not the case, says the actor. "I didn't price myself out of it because I didn't get greedy until years later. That came much later," he laughs. "I just didn't get it, and I've never been more wrong about interpreting a script."

Langenkamp's date book, showing the date and time of her meeting co-star Johnny Depp for the very first time; A Polaroid taken at Depp's *Elm Street* audition; A photo of a young, pre-*Nightmare* Depp

"We offered Charlie the part and he passed on it because his agent wanted double scale," says Benson. "And it wasn't that much, just twice as much as everyone else. But New Line was sticking to their budget and that was the end of Charlie."

No matter who would end up in the role, Shaye was quick to confirm that all they could offer were scale wages which, at the time, was $1,142 per week. "I was so freaked out we weren't going to have anybody," he admits.

As the search continued, what would happen next is the stuff of which many an aspiring actor's dreams are made.

Born in Kentucky and raised in Florida, a young man named Johnny Depp found his way to the auditions for Craven's film in a most serendipitous way. "I moved to Los Angeles in 1983 with a band I was playing with called The Kids," Depp recalls. "And I was selling pens over the phone making about fifty dollars a week." At the time, acting had never entered the aspiring musician's mind, until a mutual friend suggested he try his hand at it.

That friend was actor Nicolas Cage, then known for his roles in films such as *Fast Times at Ridgemont High* (1982) and the cult-classic *Valley Girl* (1983)—which was cast by Benson—not to mention being the nephew of director Francis Ford Coppola. "We had talked, and Nic felt that I should try acting, that I should give it a shot," Depp says.

Cage was gracious enough to introduce Depp to his agent, who saw something in him and quickly sent him off to read for *Elm Street*.

"Johnny's agent called me to say she had just met him through Nic Cage and that she knew I would love him for a role in *Nightmare on Elm Street*," Benson remembers. "Of course I said yes, and set up a meeting for him read for the role."

Luck must have been with Depp that day, as the young man with no acting experience seemed improbably wrong from the moment he walked in, though he admitted the idea of being in a movie was exciting. "The thought was miles away from anything I had ever dreamed of," he says.

Also miles away from Depp was the role Craven had written, which was everything even the actor admits he was not: a big, blonde, surfer-type jock. "I looked completely the opposite," he admits. "I was sort of emaciated, with old hairspray and spiky hair, earrings, a little fucking catacomb dweller."

Craven recalls his apprehension when seeing Depp for the first time. "He had a kind of sallow complexion and chain-smoked, and he had nicotine stains on his fingers. I thought, 'That's not the boy-next-door. Probably no chance for this kid.'"

And then he read, surprising Craven. "He really had sort of a James Dean attraction," he remembers. "That quiet charisma that none of the other actors had."

Benson agrees, saying, "When I met Johnny I knew immediately there was something special about him," says Benson. "It's a gut feeling that is an essential part of the casting process. Trusting your instincts."

Still, Craven had others in mind even as he took a liking to what Depp was bringing to the role.

In what now seems to be part of *Elm Street* folklore, it wasn't just Craven who chose Depp for the part. That honor most certainly also belongs to his daughter, Jessica, and her friend, Melanie, who were together when Jessica had come out to Los Angeles to visit her hardworking father.

"He said, 'We're going to be casting one of the male leads today and if you want, why don't you read the part of the woman in the scene? You guys can take turns and it might be fun,'" recalls Craven's daughter.

That's exactly what they did, reading the scene in Nancy's bedroom when Glen enters through her window at night. "We read the part of Nancy and we took turns doing that, and there were a succession of guys who came in," Jessica remembers.

Although Craven's daughter doesn't recall who those "other guys" were, she can't forget being struck by Depp even before they started the reading.

It began with Jessica showing the actor her "quirky watch with Ritz crackers as the numbers," she recalls. "I somehow managed to break it, and water got into the works so the glass was all befogged. And I was showing it to Johnny in the waiting room and he very kindly said, 'I have a secret trick that will fix that for you.'" At that, Depp took a lighter, held it up to the glass and cleared the vapor.

"I'm not sure if it actually fixed the watch, but I was very struck by this magic trick that he did," Jessica states. "And also he was just tall and incredibly good-looking and charming."

It was then that both she and her friend were "completely smitten by him," says Jessica. "After he left I think we both kind of fell into an enormous squealing fit of, 'Oh my God! He was so cute!'"

Proclaiming that more so for Depp than any other actor, the young girls "were both madly in love in the first second," Jessica admits. "And I think we both probably said that to my dad."

Taking that into consideration, and armed with a few photographs, including Depp's ("I think he had just gone out and had it made and never had one before," Craven says), the writer and director had a decision to make for his leading lady's love interest.

"It was sort of a toss-up between him and a couple of other guys," says Jessica, "and at that point, seeing the way we reacted to him, [Craven] realized that this guy was going to be a star. And it was actually very smart thinking. I think the entire thing was just fortuitous."

Unplanned as it might have been, Craven did have a few reservations when the girls continually gave the edge to Depp. "I said, 'Really? He looks kind of sickly and pale,'" recalls the writer and director.

Not one to let her father's words deter her, Jessica simply replied, "He's beautiful."

Craven knew that was it and looks back on the casting to think, "I could make up all kinds of stories about why I had the perception and prescience to cast Johnny Depp, but I would be a liar," he admitted. "The only smartness I had was that I was smart enough to listen."

"I was very focused on his being cast and that night we all celebrated by going to a club where Johnny's band was playing."

Annette Benson on casting Johnny Depp

Jessica agrees. "I don't think it was a plan of his. I think he just saw a reaction and was like, 'Oh, okay, I guess I should pay attention to that,'" she says. "We were teenage girls and we did what the rest of teenage girls would do when they saw the film."

With that, and only hours after he had met and read for Craven, musician Johnny Depp found himself cast in the film, effectively changing his life forever. "It was wacky," he recalls.

"I was very focused on his being cast," says Benson, adding, "and that night we all celebrated by going to a club where Johnny's band was playing."

Risher certainly approved of the decision to use him. "Johnny hadn't done any acting, I don't think, but he was just adorable and we cast him immediately," she says. "He was just a great kid."

Shaye, too, was pleased with Depp, as much for reasons creative as financial. "I was delighted to see a good-looking guy who was on the ball and would take the money, frankly, and do the job," he admits.

Noticing the "it" factor wasn't reserved for Craven and the producers, as some of the crew could see it, too. "Johnny was so innocent-looking. And so clean cut and he had a really perfect look," Doyle recalls. "First time we saw him on camera, we got it. We understood what Wes saw and what he was doing with the role."

Risher adds, "We just liked the chemistry so much with him and Heather. He was clearly a likable, attractive star in the making."

Langenkamp agrees, understanding the choice of Depp as well. "I think what you could tell about Johnny was that he had a kind of quiet energy that a lot of actors just don't have," she says. "And I think that's why he's become such a superstar."

Prior to becoming a superstar he was simply another character in the film, and Langenkamp found herself lucky enough to take some time to get to know her on-screen boyfriend. "I wanted to have an opportunity to meet Johnny before we started shooting," she recalls.

For that, the actress invited Depp over to her house in Silverlake, California where they would ultimately decide to take a trip to the Griffith Observatory, known famously as a major location in the 1955 film *Rebel Without a Cause*, starring James Dean and Natalie Wood. "We just kind of spent the afternoon together. I don't know why we picked it. We just thought it was cool," recalls Langenkamp.

Getting to know one another and talking about their upcoming roles in the movie was something Langenkamp remembers being a big help come the start of filming. "It really proved to be incredibly valuable because you're relaxed on the first day," she says. It also allowed her to see Depp for who he really was. "Johnny had come from an outside place: he was a musician, he wasn't an actor. He didn't go to high school in Los Angeles. Johnny had this toughness that was just so internal, and he was so available, and open, and he didn't have any affectations."

She would not, however, have the same experience before filming with any of her other teenaged friends in the film. "This was our research in how to be boyfriend and girlfriend. Of course, we didn't do anything except have a conversation," Langenkamp admits. "Just getting to know Johnny really helped me to not be nervous."

Looking back, what does Depp think about his whirlwind introduction to the movie business, meeting castmates, and leaving a potential music career behind, effectively at the hands of Craven's daughter? "She's the reason I started this horseshit," he jokes.

"That's very funny. It's hilarious," admits Jessica, adding that she just happened to be at the right place at the right time "to have the right reaction to launch Johnny Depp on the career that he probably would've been launched on anyway. He's an unbelievably talented guy and I'm sure it would've happened. At times like this you can believe in fate. I happened to have my spring break at the right time, I guess."

As for the man who was not Glen, Sheen not only saw *Elm Street*, but appreciated it, even if a touch of melancholy about his passing it up sunk in. "I was sad not to be in such a big hit because, at the time, that really helped your momentum with what was going on in Hollywood," he says. "But I've always said you can't lose a job that you never had, and if someone with that same role kills it, then you have to root for them."

The actor, who did speak with Depp about his *Nightmare* experience when the two later starred together in Oliver Stone's *Platoon* (1986), also recalls a chance meeting with Craven years later, where the subject came up. "I said, 'It's nice to see you again, Mr. Craven. Sorry about that whole *Elm Street* thing,'" Sheen remembers. "And Wes said, 'Don't worry about it, but Johnny Depp thanks you.'"

THEY WERE THERE FOR TINA

Having found the boyfriend for his heroine, Nancy, Craven set his sights on finding her best friend, Tina Gray. Labeled in the screenplay as "a strong girl of fifteen," she would meet an untimely—and unforgettable—end at the hands of Krueger.

Winning the part would be Manhattan Beach, California native Amanda Wyss, an actress who would come to *Elm Street* with far more on-screen experience than her counterparts.

Known at the time for her work in numerous television movies, guest-starring on several popular series, and appearing in the classic feature *Fast Times at Ridgemont High*, the actress says, "I didn't feel I was, you know, incredibly savvy, or that I had it so going on. I was still very young and, even though I'd worked, I was still trying to figure it all out."

Part of that process would be going to the interview for the role. "I just went in and auditioned for it," Wyss says. "My agent had called and they thought the script was very interesting. The little bit that I knew of it, I just thought it was a fun character."

Benson admits that she very well may have known Wyss from bringing her in on previous projects. "We loved her," she says. "She's adorable and she read well."

The actress also recalls the interesting notion that she, too, was up for the role ultimately played by Langenkamp.

In fact, everybody was.

"Anybody reading for a girl part was reading for Nancy," Wyss states. "Nancy's just such a strong, amazing female character. And especially being that young, it was fun to read for that."

As Craven watched the girls try their hand at portraying the one who would defeat the villain, he narrowed his choices down and threw people together to see how they would click. That meant Langenkamp as Nancy and Wyss as her best friend.

"She had a real intense, but vulnerable quality," Craven says of Wyss. "I thought she actually had the makings of a star. Very sharp, beautiful face. Intelligent and intense."

Benson agrees, stating, "Amanda as Tina was just perfect."

"I loved Amanda. She was so pleasant. Very easy-going," offers Logan.

Even her character's killer, played by Englund, had fantastic things to say of her talents. "She's a really gifted actress."

Those qualities, along with the clear chemistry Wyss had with Langenkamp ("We instantly clicked and became friends, and we're still friends all these years later," admits Wyss), would win her the role. As any actor would be, she was pleased to be working, but also excited to be involved in a genre film that seemed special from her very first reading of the material.

"I was set up as a wholesome yet sexy, slightly-troubled, yet lovable blonde. But there was something intrinsically sad about her because she was sort of a victim of this broken home," offers Wyss. "She's being left to raise herself, and she was manipulated by her boyfriend, which happens to young girls."

Craven felt that Wyss "had a worldliness about her," going on to liken her character to one of the girls in his previous film *The Last House on the Left*. "You have the one kind of innocent and then you have the one that kind of knows the ways of the world. Amanda's character needed to be that," he says. "It just felt like she had been out there and knocked around a little bit by life."

Wyss certainly appreciated not just the characterizations, but the morality tale Craven had written. She understood that Tina would use her body, or any manner of qualities she possessed, to make people love her. It was also clear to the actress there were important distinctions between her character and Langenkamp's. "Nancy was just grounded and real and practical," she says, accepting that those might be abilities that could seem mundane or boring. "But Tina was like, 'Oh, let's all get together and play.' Then you realize the qualities Nancy had are the things that make life work."

Craven found it important for the divergent personalities to be friends. "It just makes an interesting tension to have two characters that are drawn to their antipathies, in a way," he offers.

It was because of these characteristics and nuances Wyss found the script and story to be "unique and very psychological and intellectual, really," she says. She also enjoyed the notion that the characters she and Langenkamp played weren't overtly sexualized. "Even though my character was the 'slutty girl' who has to die, she wasn't sexual in an offensive way. You were able to imprint all your parental love, or your

The many faces of actress Amanda Wyss. "I loved the idea of playing a girl who wasn't just a doting daughter, a school kid, or a complete basket case. Tina was a role that felt like someone dealing with real teenage issues," says Wyss.

sisterly or brotherly love. It was a very visceral, deep, wholesome caring for these children that were dying."

Interesting words from yet another cast member who had also never seen a horror movie. "We rarely had a television, so I wasn't very pop-culture oriented," admits Wyss. "I was much more literary, and I'd never seen a horror film."

Still, she goes on to make a rather humorous clarification. "I knew of them," says Wyss, "but I hadn't really had a visceral experience with them. I wasn't raised in a cave or anything."

UP YOURS...

Next to be found was Tina's bad boy lover Rod Lane, the rebellious "Richard Gere sort in black leather and New Wave studs" as the script stated, which seemed appropriate for the actor who would win the part, Nick Corri. "I thought I was like James Dean," he admits. "I was a bad kid, but I'm not going to judge myself that way."

A New York City native born to Cuban parents who immigrated to the United States in search of a better life, Corri grew up in tough neighborhoods. It was those very places that played a big role in his decision to become an actor, when he found himself faking tears to save himself from being mugged and robbed of his bicycle. The performance worked, Corri was left unharmed with his bike and, he says, "It was then I knew I could act."

Discovering a newfound passion, Corri relocated to Los Angeles at the young age of thirteen, moved into a friend's basement and started a career. His first plan was to study.

"Preparation in those days was watching Marlon Brando movies, and then watching James Dean," Corri says. "James Dean, Marlon Brando, James Dean. Whatever I saw I would sponge in, so there was a sense of Brando in everything."

The next step, this time at the behest of his agent, was a name change. "I'm Cuban, but my agent at the time gave me the name Nick Corri because there were no Latin actors, except for Ricardo Montalban, and he lucked out," he says. "It was taboo. No Latin actor was going to make it, nobody with the name Jesus Garcia, certainly. So I was given the name Nick Corri. I was this Italian, fake guy."

The plan seemed to work, as he got his first break—under yet another stage name, Thom Fox—playing the boyfriend to Coco in an episode of the hit television series *Fame* (1982–1987). In addition to that role, Corri tried his hand at theater, performing in the musical *Grease* and even winning a Drama-Logue award for his performance in the play *Short Eyes*. A Pepsi commercial would be next, which gave the actor admission into the Screen Actors Guild.

Unfortunately, things suddenly came to a stop and Corri didn't work for nearly two years. "I was going to quit, I was on the unemployment line," he says. "I was emotionally destroyed that I was never going to be a James Dean, a Marlon Brando."

It was nearing that rock bottom that may have been the thing that brought him back, using the very sadness and emptiness of his life and career to get the role in *Elm Street*. It also didn't hurt that the actor found the script to be very interesting.

Nick Corri hanging out with his aunt and cousin prior to Elm Street; The actor playing Julio in "Words," an episode of Fame. His character and Coco struggle with whether or not to have sex before he leaves to join the Navy.

"When I read it, I thought, 'Oh, this is cool,'" Corri says. "Wes was brilliant. It was a great psychological premise. The unknown. The dream." As Craven himself might have done, Corri likened the screenplay's premise to something right out of Hamlet's "To be or not to be" soliloquy. "What dreams may come? To me, it's what dreams may come. It's that darkness," he reasons.

Captivated with the material, the actor's next move was to go up for the part and, though he might have felt better about his career, or chances in previous auditions and meetings, his situation at the time might have been exactly what he needed. "When I went in and auditioned for Rod Lane, was I prepared? I was in the perfect condition that Wes had needed me and Rod Lane to be in," states Corri.

It simply may not have hurt that, at the time of the audition, Corri didn't care. "I didn't really have a reference point. It was just an audition for some horror film," he says. But after connecting with the role, and remembering his training, he adds, "I was instilled to work. So I went in, I focused, Wes talked to me, and I was just very real. There was a lot of me in it: cocky, big ego, womanizer. All me, but in a juvenile way."

"Nick was great," says Benson. "I remember him as a passionate actor who fit the bill in the role of Rod Lane."

Craven agreed, seeing a lot of soul and empathy in the interesting young actor. "You felt like he could play a character who wasn't necessarily a bad guy," he says, "but one that hadn't had the breaks that everybody else had."

The real life Corri was living paid off for the reel life he would be playing. When he landed the part, his life experience was something he credits with helping not just him, but the other young actors. "We were all real. Heather was real, and Amanda, and everyone in the movie," he says. "We were all hanging out at Johnny's place, almost like a slumber party, watching Wes' old movies. I do remember it really started off with Wes Craven. We were all kids. Wes was like Dad. For a moment, it was really family, you know? And at that moment, it seemed like everyone was in the zone."

Corri, Wyss, Langenkamp, and Depp, who would portray the original film's *Elm Street* children, bonded off screen as much as they did on. "We were all real. Heather was real, and Amanda, and everyone in the movie," admits Corri. Wyss adds, "I think a lot of it was whether we organically, actually had chemistry together. And we did."

Wyss agrees, saying, "Because we were so young, I think a lot of it was whether we organically, actually had chemistry together. And we did. A lot of it had to do with the casting because we were approachable people, and I think that's easier to identify with."

It was a bond that was shared, in part, because Craven was smart enough to find people who could bring forth and portray a real spirit of themselves and imbue it into the character.

"I think that's why all of us were very successful in portraying that group of teenagers, because the essence of who we are was really played in those characters" Langenkamp says. "You actually wanna see them live. I know you're there to see them die, but you root for them more than you do with other horror movies."

Looking back on his first big film role, Corri adds, "Amanda, me, Heather, and Johnny, we really did the work for the first movie."

It's a point with which Langenkamp concurs, adding, "Just to give you an example of the kind of people that we were back then, we were all pretty new, young, and green. I had a little Alpha Romeo that would hardly ever work and I often gave Nick a ride home, because he lived kind of close to me and he didn't have a car."

In fact, when Langenkamp was not chauffeuring Corri around, he took the bus. "We were all just like kind of beginners, you know, we didn't have a lot of money, that's for sure," she says.

FATHER KNOWS BEST

Though *Elm Street* would feature teenaged victims under attack from the specter of Freddy Krueger, Craven knew having his story work would also hinge on believable performances from two other, key roles in the film: Nancy Thompson's parents. That mandate had the director out to find an actor who could bring authority, gravitas, and an element of mystery to the role of Police Lieutenant Donald Thompson.

"It's interesting, the people you get to work with on low-budget films," Craven says, "because a lot of them have very distinguished careers, and then their careers have maybe gone down a little bit and they don't get that much work."

Luckily for Craven, that wasn't so much the case with the man who would ultimately play the part.

Born Carmine Orrico in Brooklyn, New York in 1936, he had what seemed a typical childhood as the son of a housewife mother and a dockworker father. It wasn't until after graduation that Orrico would take up acting (studying with the famed Stella Adler) and, after appearing on a detective magazine cover, be discovered by talent scout Henry Wilson. Wilson called up the young man's parents, received permission to take the sixteen-year-old to Los Angeles, and promptly renamed him the then much more Hollywood-friendly John Saxon.

It was soon after that the newly christened Saxon found himself under contract with Universal, playing teenager roles in films, including his first sizable part as a delinquent in *The Unguarded Moment* (1956). He moved on to work with many notables, including Bruce Lee in his first film role. Of that experience, Saxon recalls his agent sending the script and telling him, "'Uh, it's got some cockamamie Chinese actor, and they want to shoot it in Hong Kong. Read it and see if you like it.'"

Saxon did like it, ultimately playing opposite the martial artist in *Enter the Dragon* (1973), remembering that his agent had also said, "'You'll put some money in the bank. It's a piece of crap nobody will ever see!'"

History proved his agent wrong. With the film a hit, Saxon racked up numerous television credits, Italian "spaghetti westerns," and police dramas, leading him to his first genre credit, the horror classic *Black Christmas* (1974), directed by Bob Clark (later known for *Porky's* [1982] and *A Christmas Story* [1983]). Other genre fare followed with roles in *Battle Beyond the Stars* (1980), Dario Argento's *Tenebre* (1982), and *Prisoners of the Lost Universe* (1983) before being cast in *Elm Street*.

When Saxon got the call to take part in the film, he admits he wasn't very aware of Craven's work as a director, but that he did have an affinity for the genre outside of his working in it. "I like horror and science fiction because I feel they have a little glimmer of perception about something in the human psyche," he says. "I get a little kick out of scripts that have something like that."

Clearly, Saxon saw much of that in Craven's material, leading him to enjoy the aspect that "dreams had an equal weight, an equal reality, with ordinary reality. I think the idea has a lot of validity," he states.

In addition to finding the screenplay interesting, Saxon appreciated that his character had somewhat hearkened back to his earlier work as the lieutenant he played in *Black Christmas*. "I guess I'd made a bridge between the two in some way," he ponders. "And I admired that film a lot."

Craven was thrilled to get someone with a resume many in the audience would recognize—and for a price on a smaller budget. "It was great to get somebody that's affordable and at the same time has fantastic experience and chops," he says. "He was wonderful. He was like one of the bedrocks of the film."

"I loved that he was in the film," Benson states.

Risher felt similarly, remembering there was enthusiasm over Craven choosing him for the cast. "We were so excited that John Saxon was willing to do it," she says. "He was quite a name at that time."

Corri recalls meeting Saxon for the first time and that, while filming, the older actor didn't hang around the younger kids very much. "I was always judging, 'John's

Clockwise from top left: Saxon with Bruce Lee behind the scenes of *Enter the Dragon*; The young, strapping Saxon in his contract player days; A concerned Saxon as Lieutenant Fuller in Bob Clark' s *Black Christmas*.

relationship, would be Langenkamp as his daughter. Helping the icy connection was the fact that the actress did not meet her movie father until filming. "I didn't have a chance to meet John, which actually worked out great because my parents are divorced in the movie," she says. "My relationship with my father is the most distant and the most difficult for Nancy."

While their first meeting on screen would have a serious undertone to it, Craven recalled a more humorous, early encounter with Saxon at the actor's first makeup session. "He arrived with little boxes, and he opened them up, and they were hairpieces. He says, 'Would you like this one? It's a little bit more full. Or this one, where I'd look a little bit more aged?'"

It's a moment recollected by Logan. "I don't know if he had three or four different toupee boxes, but I do remember he had all these hairpieces that RaMona basically got to choose from," she says. "I believe she tried all of them on, and then we kind of chose one that we all felt most comfortable with. John was great."

"Yes, I did his hairpiece," confirms Fleetwood, adding that it was all part and parcel of creating and building a believable character. "What kind of cop is he? What town is it in? What's his lifestyle? That all will pretty much read into someone's hair and the way they wear it. So we chose the one that was conservative and I thought it was great. He's a brilliant actor."

Preferred hairpieces aside, Craven looked back happily on the casting of Saxon. "He was great. There was nothing like 'I'm a star, treat me special,' or anything. He just always came out and did a really solid job."

A MOTHER'S LOVE

The last major role to be filled would be Marge Thompson (named Marge Simson in early script drafts), the alcoholic mother to Nancy who shared a deadly secret with her ex-husband, Donald. It was these traits that had Craven looking for someone who could bring a solemnity to a character he deemed crucial to the story.

"It was important to me that there was this drift from the woman who was saying, 'You're crazy' to her child," Craven offers. "Because the child is speaking about something that she, the mother, participated in."

It was an act that drove the character of Marge to the bottle to drown out the memories that, in the end, have put the life of her daughter in jeopardy.

The role would eventually go to actress Ronee Blakley, born in 1945 in Nampa, Idaho. Spending many of her early years in the Pacific Northwest, she eventually studied at Mills College, Stanford University, and Juilliard for post-graduate work.

Blakley's first taste of fame came with her work as a singer-songwriter. She released several acclaimed albums in the seventies, though many still associate her with her Academy-Award-nominated performance in the Robert Altman film *Nashville* (1975).

Langenkamp recalls that Blakley "has lived such an incredible life," working with such talents as Bob Dylan, Joni Mitchell, John Ritter, Omar Sharif, and James Coburn. It was a life and career that would continue thriving into the early eighties, with more film roles, television, and work on the Broadway stage.

"Everyone knew that *Nashville* was directed by Robert Altman," admits Corri. "It was a big deal and we all knew who she was. And as you could see in the movie, she was beautiful."

But it was in 1984 that she happened across the role of Marge in Craven's *Elm Street*. And like many before her, Blakley remembers first meeting Craven and being somewhat taken aback.

"I am squeamish, so I can't watch horror movies, but I had heard of Wes because of my very good friend Jeramie Rain, who was an actress in one of Wes' movies [*Last House*]," Blakley recounts. "I would've thought he was the opposite of what he is. I didn't expect him to be so buttoned-down and preppy."

The actress received notice of the casting call for Craven's latest through the director's secretary, who happened to be the secretary of her former husband, film director Wim Wenders. "When I first read the script, I thought it would be a hit," admits Blakley. "I was slightly unsure about doing what some might call a slasher movie and others would call a psychological thriller."

Eventually Blakley went into a general meeting with Craven and, as she recalls, "he liked me and I got it," also remembering Craven wasn't sure she was old enough to play the part. "I pointed out to him that I actually was the correct age to have a child Nancy's age. I was glad to be cast. I wanted the role."

"I also loved that Ronee was in the film," admits Benson, adding that having seasoned, well-known talent like Saxon and Blakley in the film lent the project credibility. "It's not like today where you need Brad Pitt to open a movie, but at that time they were names for us."

Blakley was also ultimately happy to be working with the writer and director on a film and in a part that demanded so much, trying to give a performance that would push boundaries. "It was a difficult role," says Langenkamp, and one that could have been thankless and looked over, but Blakley gamely rose to the challenge. Perhaps, some have said, too much.

"That was just her interpretation of the mother and I tried to rein it in as much as I could, but it did have sort of a blowsy thing," offers Craven. "And I felt like it might just work as a mother who was kind of narcissistic and full of herself and half-stoned all the time on booze."

Talalay, who spent a fair amount of time on set, does recall that the actress was "on a different plane. She viewed the part as the alcoholic mom and, you know, went to town with that. She was a handful."

Offering an explanation of Blakley's portrayal that ties in with the film and its genre is Englund, who cites melodrama should not be cause for concern. "All horror movies have to have a certain amount of melodrama. Melodrama's not a dirty word," he says.

Taking a look at the film through the eyes of those in jeopardy usually requires a viewer to descend into the abyss with them. The same cannot necessarily be said for the villain or, in the case of *Elm Street*, the one who created the evil now with them.

"The Heather character, for instance, has to be real and stoic and reacting to all of this madness around her, but those of us who've played the madness, we're given a little path. We're allowed to go over the top a little bit," admits Englund. "So Freddy can be larger-than-life because he exists in the imagination. And Ronee's character was descending into madness. She was an alcoholic, she's raging with guilt, and I think that what Ronee did was she echoed back to a kind of *What Ever Happened to Baby Jane?* (1962) performance which is, I think, perfect for the bad mom. She is the bad mom."

Blakley viewed the character as a serious-minded woman who tried her best, as a single parent, to help her daughter and keep her safe from "this awful monster who was killing the children of the community. It was obviously an unreal situation in the truest sense," she says. "It was a complete fiction and it was even a dream. But I tried to make it real and I viewed it as realistically as I could."

"Her performance now is looked at as almost sort of campy, because she had to play this alcoholic mother," Langenkamp states. "But in retrospect, I really feel that Ronee's performance actually gives the movie a juiciness that, had she not given it a lot of flavor, would have been lost to history."

"You have to surrender to the exaggeration, and to the surrealism, and to the mythology in horror," insists Englund. "There's always gotta be the wise old priest, or the mad scientist, or the neurotic stool pigeon, whatever character it is. These are certain ingredients."

Heather, too, is an ingredient according to the actor.

"She is the survival girl. But by definition, a survival girl just has to be gritty, and down-to-Earth, and real, and reactive," states Englund. As for Blakley as the mother of such a character, he adds, "I certainly think that she gets a pass just by the nature of what she fulfills in the menu as an ingredient in the film. So I think it's a really appropriate performance and I've never had a problem with it."

Blakley shared most of her screen time with Langenkamp, who goes on to admit that, "The horror genre is filled with, not clichés, but kind of traditions. And there's always one character who is usually kind of the scenery chewer," she offers. "They just get to do that. That's their job."

Scene chewing aside, like she did previously with her on-screen boyfriend, Langenkamp recalls she and Blakley decided early on it might help to form a bond if they were to believably come across as mother and daughter. "I wanted to meet the woman who was gonna play my mother, and she had kind of an illustrious career up to that point," she says. "I was a little nervous."

There was nothing to be nervous about, as Blakley says that Langenkamp "was so mature for her age. We were both Stanford girls, and she was very beautiful and playing a young teenager. She was just so mature beyond her years."

The two took their mutual liking for one another a step further, deciding to do something unorthodox that could break the ice between two women who would have critical screen time together as mother and daughter. They went to the mall.

"We pretended just for that day we were shopping for a prom dress," Langenkamp recalls. "I pretended to be her daughter and she was hilarious. We would get in pretend fights, like, 'Mom, I don't want that!' Of course, I wanted the slutty dress, and she wanted me to have the conservative dress."

Blakley attributes the idea to her penchant for Method acting. "I like to try things out on the street. I feel that if you can make it work there, then it's going to work on the screen," she states.

The domestic one-sheet poster for Robert Altman's *Nashville*. The film received five Academy Award nominations, winning an Oscar for Best Original Song; The cover of Blakley's 1972 folk-rock debut record album; A striking and beautiful Blakley poses for the camera.

Of her and Heather playing their roles in public for an afternoon, Blakley admits, "I think it's charming. We really were trying on dresses and," she adds with a laugh, "if you can't trust your mother, who can you trust?"

YOU REAP WHAT YOU SOW

Now that Craven had found his villain in Englund, a group of young actors to fill the teenaged roles, and two veterans to portray the writer and director's oft-used absent and neglectful parents, the cast had time to delve into, digest, and dissect the material. To all, it would become apparent that Craven was not crafting a typical horror film.

"You never, ever feel like you're in a slasher movie," Langenkamp says. "You feel like you're in an Ingmar Bergman film, talking about the afterlife or what's going to happen to us if we give into our baser passions. I always looked at it as a kind of teenaged struggle, with all of these forces, not only Nancy's parents, but this external bogeyman. It was a parable."

These notions were those with which Wyss agreed, quickly realizing "that it wasn't the norm of a horror film, especially the psychology of it. It was intellectual and thrilling," she says.

It was this pervasive thought among the cast—that they were dealing with more than just mind-numbing gore—that allowed them to understand Craven imbued his material with deeper, more philosophical themes than most.

"Freddy is a warning," says Englund. "It's as if the legend of Freddy promulgated with the children. And it's that old expression, 'You know the chicken's coming home to roost.'"

Craven having written a revenge motif was also saying something more about humanity and its morals. "Freddy had been a child killer, and that's why the parents felt justified in killing him," acknowledges Englund. "It made it a whole moral issue: if he is truly that despicable a human being, do you have the right to take the law into your own hands? That was interesting to me."

The writer and director felt that Freddy was more than just a made-up character, and that he was a collection of propensities of human beings. "Especially males, to be destructive," offers Craven. "And to kind of want to slash and burn, as opposed to nurture and protect."

It was also an opportunity to move forward on something he had explored before, which is the failure of parents and authority figures no matter how hard they try.

"The parents' marriage is falling apart, so right there they're not protecting their daughter," says Langenkamp. "And the cops can't figure out the criminal, and the vigilantes are forced to kill Freddy Krueger in the first place. So there are failures all the time."

Englund furthers the analysis of failure, pointing out his villain does the most damage in the recesses of the mind. "It's just that talking about evil and becoming preoccupied with evil can manifest evil," he says. "Especially because it hinges on recent sins."

Many on the film had felt the intensity of the idea was anything but superficial. "The whole town having their dirty secret that they had committed group murder themselves," says Haitkin, "makes you see the depth of the tale and search your own soul about vigilante justice, and decent people doing bad things in the name of what they consider right."

"Wes calls Freddy 'the bastard father of us all,' and there's a lot of bastard fathers and mothers on Elm Street. Freddy is the monster of the contemporary broken home of America."

Robert Englund

The concept of parental vengeance, which ultimately takes its toll on the very thing they are trying to protect, resonated with Blakley. "These people are desperate parents. Marge was angry and desperate," she says. "And they're dealing with a type of absolutely unreal situation. As an actor, you're trying to make it real, believable, and one would think if that were happening that the parents would be distracted to the point of madness, almost, by the horror and sorrow and helplessness."

The parents' decision, of course, comes with a hefty price, paid not only by them, but their innocent progenies. "With revenge, if you're going to dig a grave for someone, dig one for yourself as well," Wyss states. "Freddy comes back to kill what they love, so there's a karma and a morality that hits us at a gut level, because if you create acts of violence, you'll receive acts of violence."

"Those things were a big element in the structure of the film, the metaphysical structure if you will, of secrets hidden within families," says Craven, "and things the parents had done costing not so much the parents, but their children."

Corri understands the concept and the repercussions of such acts, finding that to be a reason the script resonated with so many. "You take the law into your hands, you kill the dude who was guilty, you killed him wrongly, so the devil in him is going to go after you. That's what makes it interesting. It's a really in-depth story," he says. The actor also found a way to simplify the actions of the angry parental mob: "In the original script, I do remember he may have molested kids and I thought, 'Yeah, burn the fucker.'"

Langenkamp has thought deeply about the powerful concept of an angry mob of parents ending the life of the one who has caused them pain, after he did not receive the punishment all felt was deserved. "I would never want that kind of crime on my hands, but it happens. It happens all the time," she grimly says. "I do think that vigilante justice is an answer to someone like Freddy Krueger."

The actress also feels the elements of the film, its story, and its characters are an exploration in horror and how one handles it. When fear invades, what do you do? What can you do? "That is what these movies are about," Langenkamp asserts. "Especially Nancy, who not only faces her fears, but works to get rid of them and decides to take an active role for what is happening to her."

Englund sums up what the script accomplishes in terms of dealing with those fears and the creation of Krueger. "Two wrongs don't make a right, and Freddy has come back. He's talked about, and he's whispered about, and he's hinted at," he says. The mere thought of the terrible man who had seemingly been vanquished coming back to haunt the dreams of, and destroy, more children "has infiltrated their imaginations," continues the actor, "and by entering their imaginations it's infected their subconscious. He is the sin, and the monster, and the damage that is sort of under the brass of the suburban home."

In Craven's *Nightmare*, those whispered and covered-up wrongs in the past can, indeed, become the bogeyman. "Wes calls Freddy 'the bastard Father of us all,'" Englund adds, "and there's a lot of bastard Fathers and Mothers on Elm Street. Freddy is the monster of the contemporary broken home of America."

READY, SET...NO?

Philosophical examinations of the material aside, the time had come to begin production on Craven's latest, though the writer and director received word from Shaye that would potentially be an end game for the film. With production offices, and a cast and crew ready to begin, Shaye delivered harrowing news just two weeks before principal photography was to start: they lost half the investment to make the movie.

"Bob came into the office and said, 'Wes, I'm sorry to say, but this company in Europe, Smart Egg, which had a significant amount of the money invested, withdrew the money,'" Craven recalls. "It was discovered that they needed the money elsewhere."

The news couldn't have come at a worse time for the film. "In the middle of everything, when the financing had fallen through, the crew was packing up. It was like an unbelievable disaster," says Shaye.

It was also ironic for the producer, at least in terms of timing.

"I'm sitting in New York, waiting to go on stage to give a keynote speech for Price Waterhouse, I think it was, that was having a media seminar and my topic was 'How to Finance an Independent Movie.' It was completely ridiculous," recounts Shaye. "I really agreed to do it because I was hoping I might attract somebody who was interested in it. But it was at that moment that everything was really in terrible shape."

Talalay remembers being privy to a lot of the goings-on at that time, admitting there were, indeed, many problems regarding financing. "I was intimately involved because they had to come to me as accountant and say, 'We can't pay anyone. We've lost this portion of the financing, but we need to keep the film going. We want you to do anything you can to help keep the crew involved and not lose people,'" she says. "It was very, very, very, very tense."

As New Line Cinema had shown in the past, however, adversity can be the mother of invention. This time it would be Risher taking the more hands-on producing role as Shaye stayed back in New York to search for the needed funds. This left Risher with the unenviable task of informing cast and crew of their dire financial position. It seemed, though, that some people had begun to catch on prior to the announcement.

"After I had been signed to do the movie," Saxon says, "I was told that, 'Oh, we'll call you in a short while for wardrobe changes and some things like that, okay?'" Saxon waited. And waited, until finally he made a call to the production inquiring when they would have him in. "And there was the biggest silence," he recalls. "And I got the picture of what was happening pretty quickly."

Also figuring out the situation, and articulating it quite clearly, was Corri. "They were broke. There was zero money," he says. "But you're young. You don't care about the waiting, but there was waiting."

Having to deal with a situation that was escalating from supposition to certainty among those she was trying to put at ease, Risher remembers, "I was six months pregnant at the time and I had to announce that we wouldn't be able to pay the crew, the cast, or anyone that week."

Confident the money would ultimately be secured, Risher and Shaye weren't sure what the reaction at that moment would be from the talent they were, in essence, asking to work for free, at least for a short time. Risher credits her pregnancy as a possible factor in the outcome. "I think that because I was pregnant, we didn't lose any crew members or anything," she states.

It also didn't hurt that Risher was well liked. "She was very friendly and easy to talk to," says Cook.

"To keep a crew together for the period we did and keep it going was remarkable," says Talalay.

Perhaps it was a sympathy factor, combined with everyone's passion for Craven's project that kept them going, though Langenkamp admits she understood how the movie's precarious finances could affect more than a few cast and crew. To many, this was more than just another "gig." It was a way to stay in Hollywood, find their way, and make it.

"You're not thinking about the big picture," Langenkamp offers. "You're thinking about your rent that's due on the first of the month. And it sounds so unglamorous, but I think that a lot of people on the movie were thinking the same thing."

The actress was right, though there was a small financial buffer from an unlikely source when, in addition to Shaye funding it out of his own pocket (the amount being a few thousand dollars), Burrows ponied up some of his own cash. It helped out the others who, perhaps, could not last another week or two without pay.

"That's correct," Shaye confirms. "I didn't actually know that for a fact until afterwards, but John Burrows agreed not to take a salary himself, and I think he may have paid a couple of people."

Artistic renderings of Craven's dream killer, Freddy Krueger, showcasing his evil persona.

Despite the financial burden placed on the production, Talalay is seen enjoying a serene moment on the studio lot. "That is one of the most resonant memories of my New Line time: the vulnerability of being that far along and then somebody pulling a trick to get the money," she states. (Note the car on which she is sitting.)

Having just come off of a film, and having some extra money, Burrows believed that *Elm Street* shutting down would have been a mistake. "I thought maybe we could keep two or three people on; the people looking for props and certain other people that were involved in the making of the home location on the stage," he states. "So I used ten thousand dollars and paid the people that were working. They never knew. People used to tell me, 'This is your picture, John.' Of course, as soon as the company had the money allocated, I was paid back."

"He ultimately went two weeks without a paycheck, so he was amazing," Risher recalls.

Even with what Burrows was so generously able to do, when the time came to move forward and sit down for the script read-through, there was one person who did not show up: the writer and director. It was not necessarily Craven's choice, however, as his agent advised him it was against Director's Guild of America rules to show up when the company didn't have the money to pay everybody.

"And so he didn't come. We had our first reading without the director," Risher admits.

Craven dealt with the situation as best he could, pouring himself into a new activity that would keep his mind off the financial turmoil his would-be film was going through. "I went home, bought a bicycle, and just pedaled from Santa Monica down to Long Beach, which is a long way, but just sort of in despair that, 'Damn, another thing's fallen through,'" he says. "It just felt like I'm never going to get out from under this horrible, bleak period of three years where I lost all my savings, and anything I had made from *Swamp Thing* and *Deadly Blessing* had long ago been spent on keeping an assistant and a publicist and everything."

Craven, though, was able to look back and inject some humor into the situation as he remembered something that was said to him when he was working on those previous two films back-to-back. "Be nice to people on your way up, Wes, because you'll be passing them on your way down," he says with a laugh. "Sure enough, there were three years of absolutely no income and it was pretty awful. So that was a very bad time when New Line lost the money."

Fortunately, he didn't have to pedal in despair for long trying to keep his mind off whether he would ever begin filming. The same couldn't be said for Shaye, who worked long and hard to wrangle a deal that would keep the show on track.

"Bob eventually found the money we needed with Media Home Entertainment as our partner, and a couple of other people who came in as partners," Risher says.

Not without some sacrifice, as Shaye points out. "With great pain and suffering, I will tell you that," he reveals. "As much pain and suffering you go through making a film is nowhere near the pain and suffering you go through financing it. In this case, I had to raise all the money outside."

After one final meeting with Media Home Entertainment's owner, Joseph Wolf, Shaye finally made a deal. "The tipping point was the devil's agreement. I made an agreement with Joe, and he agreed to buy the video rights for a certain amount of money. But he made us guarantee that if we didn't do certain things like buy additional prints and open in a certain number of theaters, that he had the right to take the film away from us and give us nothing for it," recalls Shaye. "And that was the only deal I could make. And that finished the financing for us."

"Bob didn't like it, but he had to take it. He was stuck," Burrows remembers. "Bob will always remember that he was really giving his blood, you know? He said, 'John, I hate it, I hate it, I hate it.'"

Haitkin, while not directly involved with any of the financial dealings, does recall an interesting meeting in his apartment. In attendance with him were Craven and Shaye, who let it be known just how important *Elm Street* was to New Line Cinema. "Bob said to both of us that the future of the company was riding on this movie," he recalls. "To think that it was such a big financial issue that a company's life depended on less than two million dollars was pretty amazing."

"That is one of the most resonant memories of my New Line time: the vulnerability of being that far along and then somebody pulling a trick to get the money," Talalay states.

"Through coercion, diligence, begging, anything we could, we finally got agreements from people to either finance the film or lend money to it and we got it going," Shaye admits.

Even Craven recalled the tension Shaye must have been under while trying to rectify the financial situation. "I think he gave up a lot of his points because the other financial entity just kind of crucified him," he says. "They took a lot of what he had in that movie away from him during the course of that negotiation."

As much as Craven understood the stress and tenuous financial waters Shaye must have been treading, he admitted it was not something about which he ultimately had to worry. "I just was waiting for that phone call to say, 'We're on again.'"

Soon enough, they were. With full financing behind them, and a cast and crew eager to begin, Craven and New Line Cinema would soon start physical production on what the writer and director stated could be his "watershed movie."

THE FACE OF EVIL

At the top of the list of things to do was the creation of what the film's villain, Freddy Krueger, would look like, something on which the makeup artist in charge worked diligently to please Craven.

That responsibility went to David B. Miller (later to work on such films as *Tremors* [1990], *The Addams Family* [1991], and *Batman & Robin* [1997]), who already had a working relationship with Craven from an earlier foray into the swamps.

"My involvement came about because I worked on *Swamp Thing*, and there was this guy on that film who was the production manager on the first *Elm Street*," Miller recalls. Consequently, he received a call that Wes was about to embark on a new project—a monster film with a very low budget—that they thought would be perfect for him. "So I went in for an interview with Wes, and met with Jim Doyle, and basically got the job right there," he says. "They looked through my portfolio and liked everything they saw and that's when I got the job."

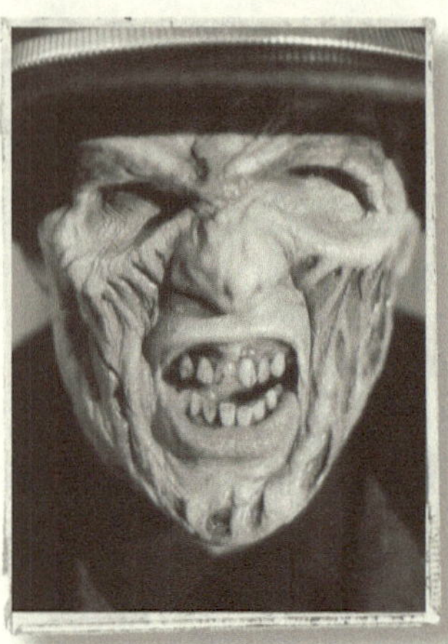

"I did a zombie cop makeup in *Night of the Comet* (1984). Wes saw that picture and said, 'This is very close to what I want Freddy to look like.' I thought, 'Okay, well that's easy. I've already done it,'" laughs Miller. "But after that it was a trial and error process to get the right look."

What the job would entail, though, was still somewhat vague. "All Wes told me was that he wanted something really, really hideous; an older-looking guy with pus and slime dripping from his face. Something monstrous," Miller states.

Another aspect Miller recalls after having conversations with Craven, who asked for a makeup that went deeper, was a design in which Krueger's teeth would show through a rotted jaw. That was jettisoned after explanations from Miller on why it simply wouldn't work. "There's no way you can do that with a real actor," he states. "You can paste teeth on the outside of the appliance, but it just doesn't look right. So that whole idea was gone."

Deciding what would and would not be feasible, Miller continued to come up with a look for Krueger, making sure to base as much as possible on fact. "I am a real stickler about research into a character," he admits. "So when Wes said it was a burned character I went to the UCLA medical center bookstore and found all these burn unit books." In his search, Miller saw how real burn victims looked and started basing his idea on that.

Now that he had an idea of where his makeup would go, the effects artist worked hard on a meager budget of approximately twenty thousand dollars, ultimately presenting his director with five different sculptures. "One of them was very skull-like, not much skin on it, just more bone. Another one was more translucent skin, very thin," Miller recalls. "There was also one with burned skin that was pulled tight across the skull. Those are the ones I can remember."

Instead of selecting one design, however, Craven's reaction surprised Miller. "Wes chose different things from each sculpture. He said, 'I'd like to see that, and that, and that combined onto one head,'" remembers Miller. He took the elements that Craven asked for and set about designing a new look for Freddy which, though loosely based on the images of real life burn victims, would have its final inspiration from the most unlikely of places. "The final design for Freddy, and this is a true story, is pepperoni pizza," he admits.

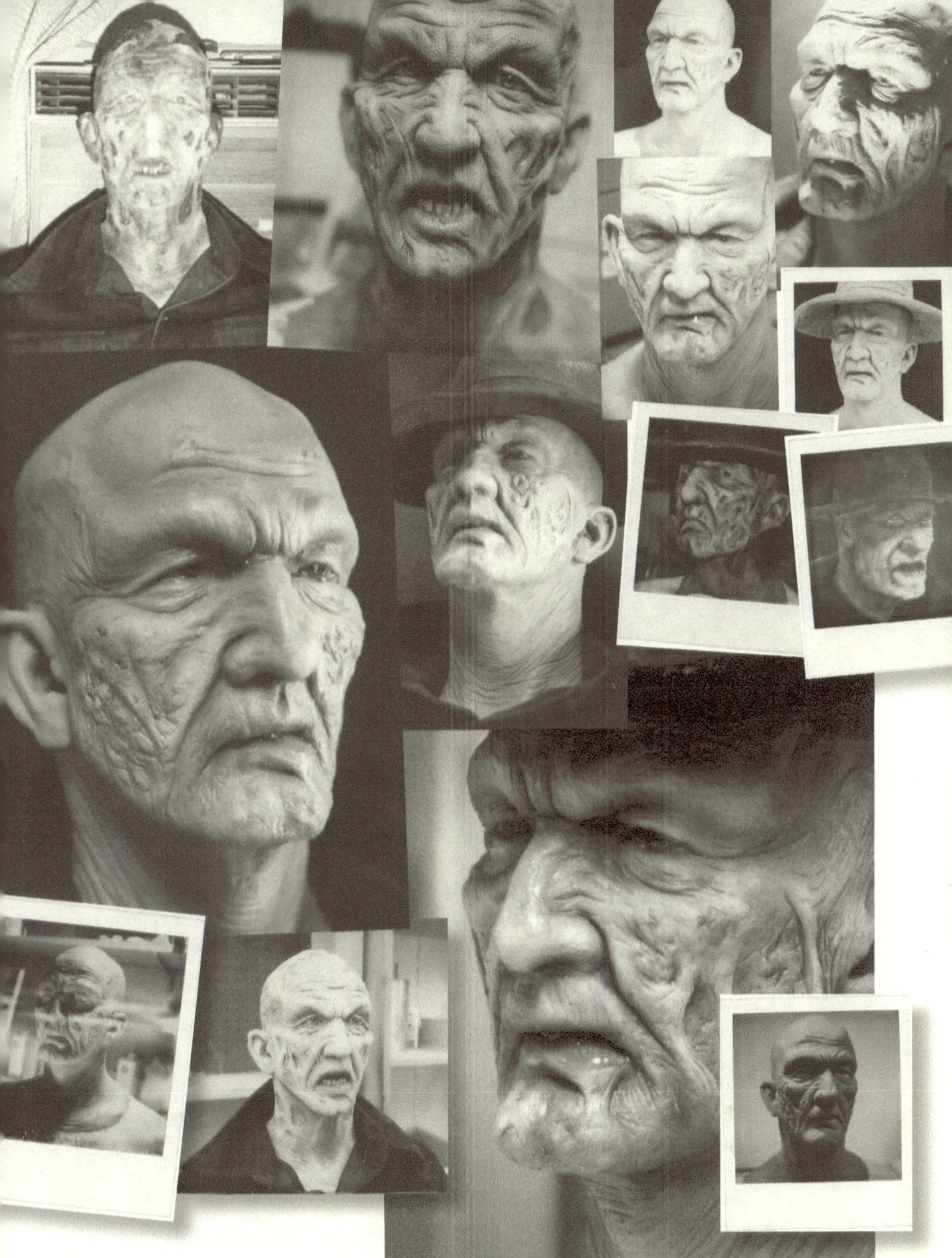

With an edict from his director, and armed with real-life burn research, Miller toiled on the numerous looks of Freddy Krueger. Ultimately, it was a pizza dinner that provided the final inspiration for a look Craven approved.

Miller found himself at a restaurant one evening, deep in thought, when he started playing around with the cheese and pepperoni on his pizza, realizing that he had, in essence, created Freddy Krueger's face. "I thought, 'That's a cool look. It looks like melted skin around muscle,'" he says.

An inspired design at the ready, Miller went to his home workshop, started sculpting and found himself with yet another idea, which was to create layered appliances for the inner and outer skin of Freddy. "I did separate prosthetics on the face that represented muscle," he recalls, "and then over that was the outer skin layer that looked all cheesy and stretchy."

To heighten the effect of masses of destroyed flesh, Miller only glued the edges of the outer layer. "What would happen was when Robert moved the skin would move separately around the muscle, and that's what ended up being Freddy. It was a very interesting look," he says.

"My whole thing with the face was it needed to have enough to sort of show the violence of what the parents had done, and it needed to be sort of mask-like, because I was convinced that at that time all the slasher films had masks," Craven states. He also wanted to be sure that the mask had a personality to it, as he did not want to hide the human being underneath, much like other horror films had done. "So," he adds, "what we came up with was very, very good."

CLOTHES MAKE THE MONSTER

Also a part of Krueger's look was the very clothing he would wear, which was an extension of Craven's desire that his villain have a twisted sense of humor—in this case, the trademark striped sweater for which Freddy would become known.

Craven has said his creation of Freddy was very deliberate, and the iconic clothing was not concocted arbitrarily. In fact, as he had many times before, Craven found assistance from a scholarly source. Dipping into the annals of mythology, he decided he would have loved for Krueger to be able to shapeshift into different forms, an important aspect of mythological creatures. "I thought at times he should be able to get out of the symbology of his own body and do something greater," he says.

Budgetary and effects limitations prevented that notion from coming to full fruition, though Craven found another way to play with the concept. "I wanted him to have something instantly recognizable."

That item became the now familiar striped sweater, which was not originally the color scheme viewers have come to associate with Krueger. In early versions of the script, the colors Freddy wore were red and yellow. Craven, though, did not want to leave the design to chance, and a change was soon made.

"The red and the green together actually were from an issue of *Scientific American*," Craven recalls. He admitted to never having gone back to find it, but the article "detailed the complexities of how the human retina discerns colors, particularly when they are close together."

Certain colors, Craven learned, are not easy on the eye and difficult to process visually. That being the case, the writer and director turned a seemingly innocuous bit of clothing into a twisted piece of Krueger's arsenal. "I literally made him into a painful sort of optical effect on the human eye just in the sweater," he stated.

That optical effect almost had less material to work with, if not for opposition by the director's makeup man. "There was a sleeveless sweater version of Freddy that was dismissed by David Miller," says Craven, "because in addition to the face that had a gazillion different parts, he would also have to make up the arms. So we decided, 'Okay, fine. Long sleeves.'"

But there was another, similar argument made by Englund that Miller lost, and it was in regard to whether or not there needed to be much makeup on Krueger's scalp, something normally hidden underneath the character's fedora. The infamous accessory was almost jettisoned by Craven as the actor tried many variations, "all these different hats, and they were all ludicrous," Englund says. "I'm getting the Freddy makeup tweaked as they're hanging flanges of translucent flesh behind my ear, Dave Miller's got a brush up my nose and hair dryer up my butt, and I'm sitting there and they're trying these different hats on me."

Fighting for what Craven originally wrote in the script, and described to him upon their first meeting, Englund was able to keep Krueger's fedora. "I remember they put a paperboy hat on me and I said, 'You guys, Wes, it's in the script, it's in your mind's eye. The fedora. It means something,'" the actor argued.

That was when Englund decided to stop talking and start demonstrating, placing the fedora back on his head and making sure his shadow was on the wall of the small storage room they were in, showcasing the silhouette of Freddy and his clawed hand. "And then I did my little Bob Fosse tip of the hat and I turned to Jacques and I said, 'Look, you can hide Freddy in the shadows of the brim,'" the actor remembers.

Craven and the others were sold.

"If I did anything for Freddy at that moment, I saved the fedora. I fought for the hat," Englund happily recalls.

It wasn't just a good look that made the fedora work for some, such as Miller. The makeup man was momentarily pleased, as it could have meant less makeup for him to design, though he quickly discovered Englund, even with the hat, had other ideas.

"I think David sort of figured that because the hat was in the screenplay that he wouldn't have to work so hard on all of the suppurating wounds on my scalp," Englund says. "But I said to him, 'David, you've gotta keep them. I want those looking nasty because I wanna show those. I think it's one of the genius things of the design.'"

THE APPLICATION OF TERROR

Makeup design complete, another one of the film's demanding items was about to surface: the daily task of turning Englund into the monstrous Freddy Krueger. And while it would (and did, to many) seem an unenviable chore to sit through the arduous process, the one person with the most potential to complain did exactly the opposite.

Englund, who would endure hour after hour in a makeup chair, and day after day under hot lights, clearly recalls how the idea of being covered in prosthetics took him back to his love of horror movies like *Frankenstein* (1931), *The Mummy* (1932), and famous made-up actors like Lon Chaney.

"I had this revelation as I remembered the fourteen-year-old boy in me who'd gone to the Saturday matinee and couldn't figure out who the creature was in *Forbidden Planet* (1956)," Englund states. "I remembered reading a *Life Magazine Goes to the Movies* coffee table book when I was nine years old and I loved the classic horror section from the thirties with a two-page fold out."

It left Englund wondering if somehow, even subliminally, he had longed to take part in that ritual. "I'd always had a hard-on to really try the makeup. I think when I did *Nightmare*, I was exorcising that fascination I had as a little boy," he says. "And as a young theater actor, the old men would come in with their hotel towels and spread them out with their good luck coffee mugs, and their pencils, and their scissors, and tubes of makeup, and these guys would do these fantastic makeups. I was kind of fascinated with that. I must say, it was something I always thought was cool when I was young. And things that are cool when you're young, they never leave you."

It also didn't hurt that Miller was coming to *Elm Street* fresh off one of the most popular videos of all time, courtesy of Michael Jackson and a famed genre director. "We forget how big *Thriller* (1983) was then, and David created that makeup with John Landis," Englund says. "And so I knew I was in good hands." Looking back on the combination of factors, he realizes, "I think that had something to do with me saying yes and me really wanting to play Freddy. I really wanted that experience."

That experience would be taken care of by the expert hands of Miller and his makeup team, though Miller recalls the first time he saw Englund as the one to play Krueger, he thought, "This is gonna be a challenge." He knew of the actor from his work on a film called *Stay Hungry* (1976) and, somewhat unsure of the choice, thought, "They want him to play Freddy?" He believed the actor, who was not talkative at first, might not like him, but once he got his face cast for the makeup sculpting ("It was all new to me. It was an adventure," Englund says) he opened up and, as Miller recalls, "got so excited about being in the makeup."

What that makeup would be was a mystery to Englund until the moment Miller pulled him aside to discuss the realistic burns he had researched and said, "This is what we're gonna do on you, and Robert said, 'You're kidding,'" Miller remembers.

The moment still plays vividly in the actor's mind. "David just whipped open this medical textbook for me the first day I sat down," Englund says. "I was kind of trapped in this antique barber chair in his garage in Pacoima or somewhere." Seeing the pages and pages of real, disfigured burn victims had an effect on him. "I'd never seen anything like that before," he says. "That was like, at that time, the scariest thing I'd ever seen."

Exactly the effect Craven wanted Miller to create.

"Because David had worked so hard and created something everyone thought was special," Langenkamp says, "the makeup artists involved were so devoted to their work."

One of those technicians was Mark Shostrom, a friend of Miller's who would later go on to create effects for other *Elm Street* ventures, in addition to popular genre fare such

Clockwise from top left: Miller focuses intently on sculpting; A technician diligently works in Miller's shop; An early test photo features Englund as Krueger, sporting a paperboy hat; A sticker that was placed on official reference photos of Englund in full makeup; A behind-the-scenes Polaroid captures Englund.

as *Evil Dead 2* (1987) and *Phantasm II* (1988). His job on the first film, however, would start without ever seeing a word Craven wrote, or even reporting to the set.

"To be honest, I never read the script," Shostrom says. "I got called to do the film by Dave Miller, who hired me for a week to work in his garage on many things. And one thing I had to do was run the foam for all the Freddy pieces every day while Dave was stuck on set."

Working strictly out of Miller's garage shop, Shostrom's job of running the foam saw him, several times a day, processing the actual appliances Englund would wear. Using a machine very much like a Mixmaster, the components were combined until they were like whipped cream. Then, Shostrom would pour it into the sculpted molds Miller had created for the prosthetics to be glued onto Englund's face. The low budget of the film, however, would rear its head even off set where Shostrom worked day after day.

"We had run those molds so many times that they were falling apart," Shostrom remembers. "They were about an inch thick and I had to superglue the things together like pieces of a jigsaw puzzle." Thus, it became a daily grind simply to keep the molds useable since new ones could not be created.

To keep the process as simple as possible, while still getting the best looking result, Miller's design was overlapping pieces which would fit together very much like a puzzle.

"What Dave had done was very clever," Shostrom says. "He designed it in layers so you had one kind of burn layer that went on Robert first, and then a second series of appliances that went over that." He recalls the effect being very much like Swiss cheese, with pieces you could almost see through and "very smart, though for me it was a lot of pieces to run."

Those pieces included one for Englund's forehead, back of the head, nose, upper lip, and parts for each cheek. "They came all the way down to my chest and maybe an eighth of the way down my back at that time," says the actor. "They were up to the edge of my shoulders. It was a lot of makeup."

Now that the makeup had been crafted to give the horrifying impression for which Craven and Miller were hoping, the time had come to actually attach the appliances to Englund, transforming him into Freddy Krueger.

Langenkamp, who would not have to endure any major makeup applications on the film, saw firsthand how the effects artists needed to have a very tender kind of caretaker relationship with their actor. "They're so close all the time, always touching, always prodding at the face," she says. "I don't know how Robert did it sometimes."

One of the people in such close proximity to Englund was Louis Lazzara, who was hired directly by Miller. "My job, originally, was to basically just take Robert's makeup off. But after a few days, I ended up applying it as well," he says. "So I ended up just staying with Robert, because Dave had to go to the set every day."

The task of applying the Krueger makeup "at first took about three-and-a-half hours," says Miller. But the most difficult thing during those marathon makeup sessions? "Trying to keep Robert still in the chair and not talking," Lazzara says. "He's a fantastic actor, but he can't sit still. And I love him for every ant in his pants."

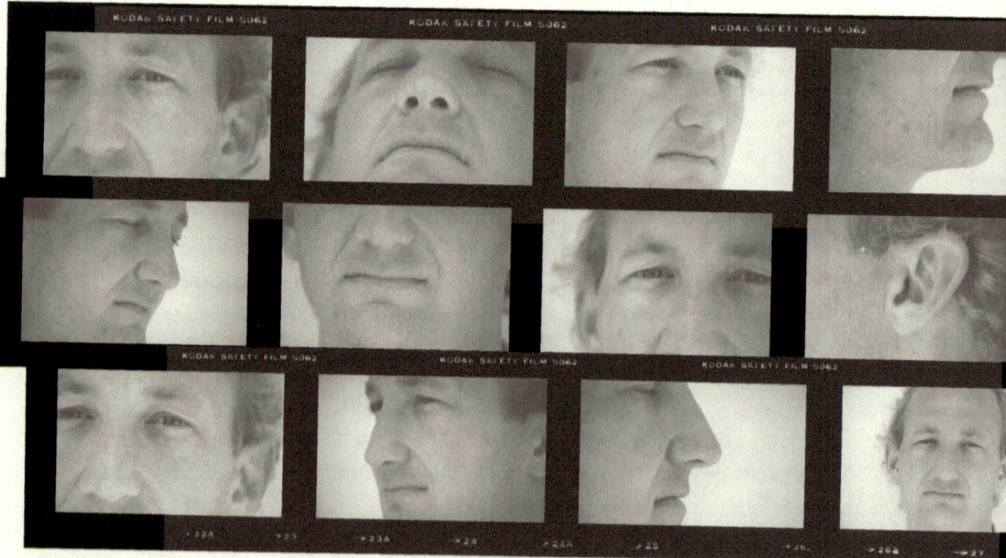

Blakley, who only had to watch Englund endure the process, was sympathetic. "To see what he had to go through with his makeup was extraordinary. He really had to suffer with his skin, which was extremely sensitive to all the latex and materials he had to endure for hours a day," she says.

Miller has similar words for the man he transformed. "He went through the mill," he says. "He'd go through a makeup session for hours, and sometimes have to stand by for six hours in makeup, just in case he was needed. He was just great."

How did Englund feel about finally having his face poked, prodded, and glued? Just fine, apparently. "The makeup appliances were so light that you hardly knew they were on," he states.

Miller, however, recalls the first time Englund was in full makeup the actor "was afraid to move, worried the appliances might actually fall off."

That didn't happen, but Englund's virgin experience with facial prosthetics did give him pause. "I was aware of how intensive the project was, how many pieces were involved and, after sitting through that process for so many hours, I was intimidated. I could feel them binding on my own musculature and my own face," says the actor. "I was just afraid that maybe they would tear on the jaw line or, if I turned my head from side to side, I'd tear the neck. I could feel the tightness of the medical adhesive, and I wanted to know what the limitations were."

Eventually learning that the materials were strong enough and had the elasticity to allow his performance to shine through, Englund says, "I did discover I had to animate more underneath to make it come alive."

Opposite page: Reference photos of Englund's face Miller used while creating the Krueger makeup.
This page: Englund waits to be transformed into the film's villain; A bust of the Krueger makeup.

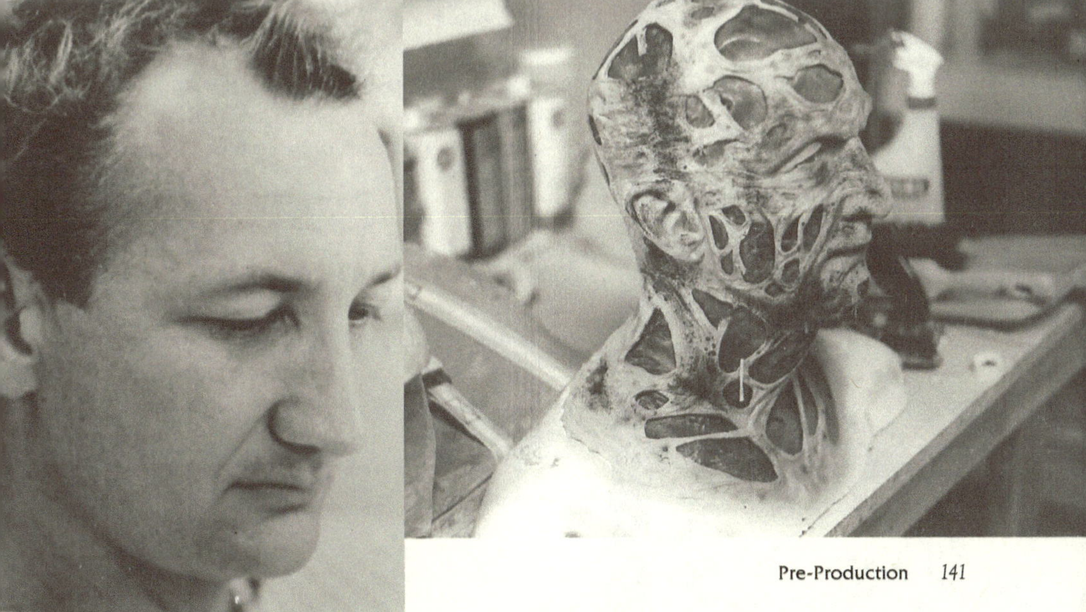

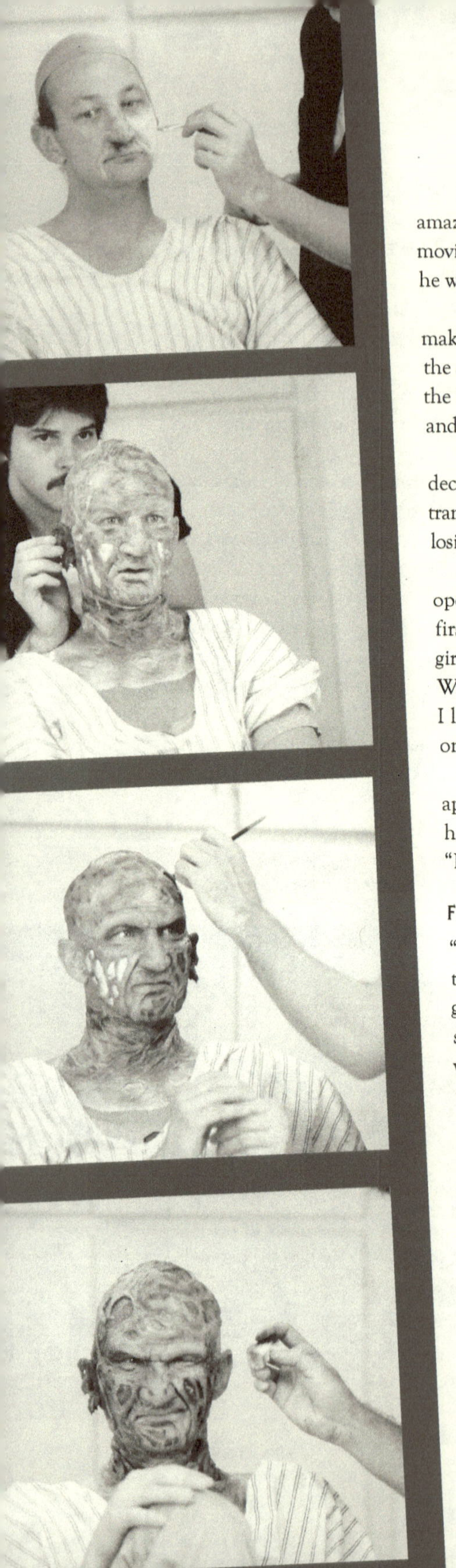

Miller recalls the actor's reaction. "He said, 'This is amazing. It all holds together and it moves.' And he started moving his mouth around and moving his eyebrows and he was just all excited after that."

"It didn't look artificial," Englund says of the makeup. "I see a lot of makeup effects that don't go with the scale of the actor wearing it, and I always thought that the Freddy makeup was done in the right scale to my body and my silhouette and my physiognomy."

At one point there was talk of having flanges of burnt, decayed skin hanging off Englund's ears, in addition to translucent wattles under his neck, as if he were always losing flesh. Those ideas, however, were quickly abandoned.

"The continuity can of worms that would have opened was just something we decided not to do after the first day or so, because it would've driven the continuity girl, me, and David Miller crazy," admits Englund. "And Wes, I think, realized it would've driven him crazy, too. I loved that idea, but it would've just been a nightmare on a low-budget movie."

Eventually streamlining the final makeup application process to about ninety minutes, Englund has nothing but kind words for his alter ego's creator. "David Miller is a genius. He treated me like gold."

FINDING FREDDY KRUEGER

"I don't know what wells Robert went to, to bring out the elements of Freddy," confesses Craven. Englund getting used to the makeup process that would visually showcase Krueger was one, though an added bonus was simply the experience of being transformed into the character.

"A lot of what I discovered to play Freddy was during those first makeup applications," states Englund. Whether riffing with Miller about movies they loved and hated, complaining about the lights, being itchy, hot, or directly yelling at Miller to get a makeup brush out of his eye, the actor used it all to formulate the persona audiences would be seeing on screen and, hopefully, of which they would be terrified.

There was, however, more than simply using the sometime aggravation of the makeup, or what

Opposite page: Englund endures the long, multi-step process of becoming Krueger.

This page: Miller enjoys applying Freddy's skull while Englund talks away his time in the makeup chair.

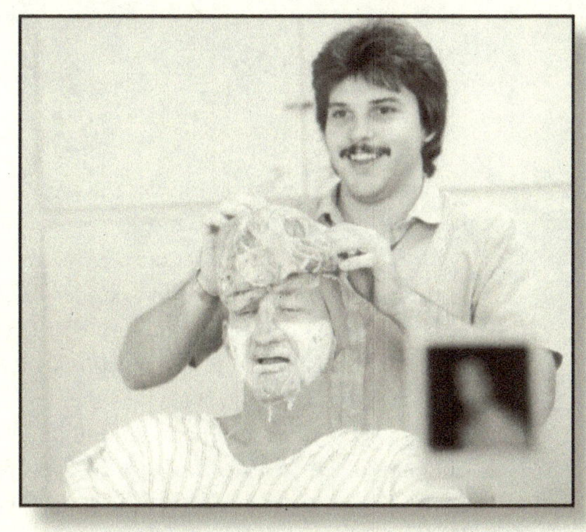

it would allow him to do, to truly generate the character. The makeup itself was a liberating factor for Englund that allowed him to stray from what he termed indulgent behavioral work. "I thought, 'The makeup is so extensive that I need some humanity in my eyes. My darting, little, beady eyes will be the humanity,'" he says.

"He would always be doing these looks, practicing what he was going to do in the scene," says Langenkamp, offering that as one reason Englund became so good at portraying Krueger. "For all those hours he spent in the makeup chair, he's really focusing a lot on when and how the makeup looks best. He really learned to work that makeup."

Englund was also aware that he could, while under all that makeup, physically move differently than he normally would. "I was able to make myself look bigger than I am. I was able to make myself look tougher than I am. I was able to play myself older than I was when I began Freddy, certainly," he states. "I even changed my voice for the role."

A variety of elements helped Englund create a sort of cruel, Vaudevillian clown of a man, replete with a sadistic undercurrent that, says the actor, "was really fun to do." To compliment that, he went further than just letting the makeup do the work of distancing Englund the person from Krueger the character. "I'd recently seen the Klaus Kinski film *Nosferatu the Vampyre* (1979) and was very influenced by his look," he says. "I realized I could borrow a little bit of Klaus' thrust neck, and I really wanted to preserve that."

Kinski wasn't the only classic inspiration for Englund. "I also used a little bit of Jimmy Cagney in there," he admits. "You know, 'You dirty rat,' that little kind of spread-legged, strong, gangster stance that Cagney used was something I kind of had going on in the back of my head, too."

Externally, Englund found he received good direction from Craven as to whom the character should—and should not—be, in addition to being granted ample freedom to explore. "I gave him guidelines of what I saw when I was writing it," Craven says.

The writer and director, though, was very much interested in what Englund was bringing to the role. "I would say, 'Try this, but what do you think?'" remembers Craven. "It's better in some ways not to stipulate too much when you're directing."

Eventually, Craven realized that Englund was bringing far more physicality to the role than what he might have imagined, and that it was a good thing. "He was ready and enthusiastic about exploring that persona in a way that came from his own imagination, as well as mine," he recalls. "The physicality of the character, for instance, was not necessarily on the page. Much of it was Robert experimenting and improvising based on a theme."

"Wes wanted me to get outrageous at times and he would have me do scenes two or three takes because I tended to underplay it," Englund says. "I originally thought the elaborate makeup would do most of that for me."

Freddy's ability to terrorize was not limited to his physical abilities, or the burned and scarred look of the character—there had to be a psychological motivation as well. One aspect came from Englund's childhood, as he recalled in third-grade a seemingly out-of-place girl on Valentine's Day get very few missives. "But," he says, "there was also a boy that didn't get any. All my life I remembered that. And I think that boy was Freddy Krueger. It's hard to act that, but if you've seen it, then you can believe that could be enough for somebody to be that."

The actor, as an adult, also found inspiration in spades with the very people his Krueger would soon be after. "I remember once looking at Johnny and Heather as they were being made up," Englund says, sarcastically adding, "as if these two young, beautiful kids needed it."

Using that as a basis for Krueger's pain and hatred, Englund watched them frolic in the light as he was "basted like a turkey with KY jelly," he jokes.

It's something Langenkamp remembers with a laugh. "You know, there are always the makeup effects guys around with KY jelly," she says. "That gets a lot of laughs all the time: 'More KY!'"

It was less amusing for the man under the effects, so it didn't take long for Englund to see that he could channel the envy of their youth and beauty and make it a part of his character. "A light bulb went off where I realized I can use this as Freddy," he admits.

On Englund's finding the character, and the fact that so much of the film would rest on his portrayal of Krueger, Langenkamp says, "Robert was a very seasoned actor, had been in lots of movies, and had worked with incredibly famous people. So we were all like bowing at his feet. Robert had the whole package. I mean, he knew how to move, he knew how to use his props, he knew how to have perfect diction, he knew all the tricks of the microphone. He had so much to offer. We were all really looking to him as the person who was carrying this movie. It was gonna live or die based on his performance, really. I think we all knew that."

SCREEEECH...

More than just makeup, a hat, and sweater, many (even non-horror aficionados) know Freddy Krueger is synonymous with his trademark, razor-fingered glove.

"It's gotta be the scariest looking thing. It just looked so homemade. It looked like something that some psychopath would've made," concedes Langenkamp.

Opposite page: The life and times of Freddy Krueger. Often, Englund would endure a complete makeup session only to wait for hours to be called to set. It was just one thing that assisted in the formation of the evil the actor would portray behind Krueger's eyes.

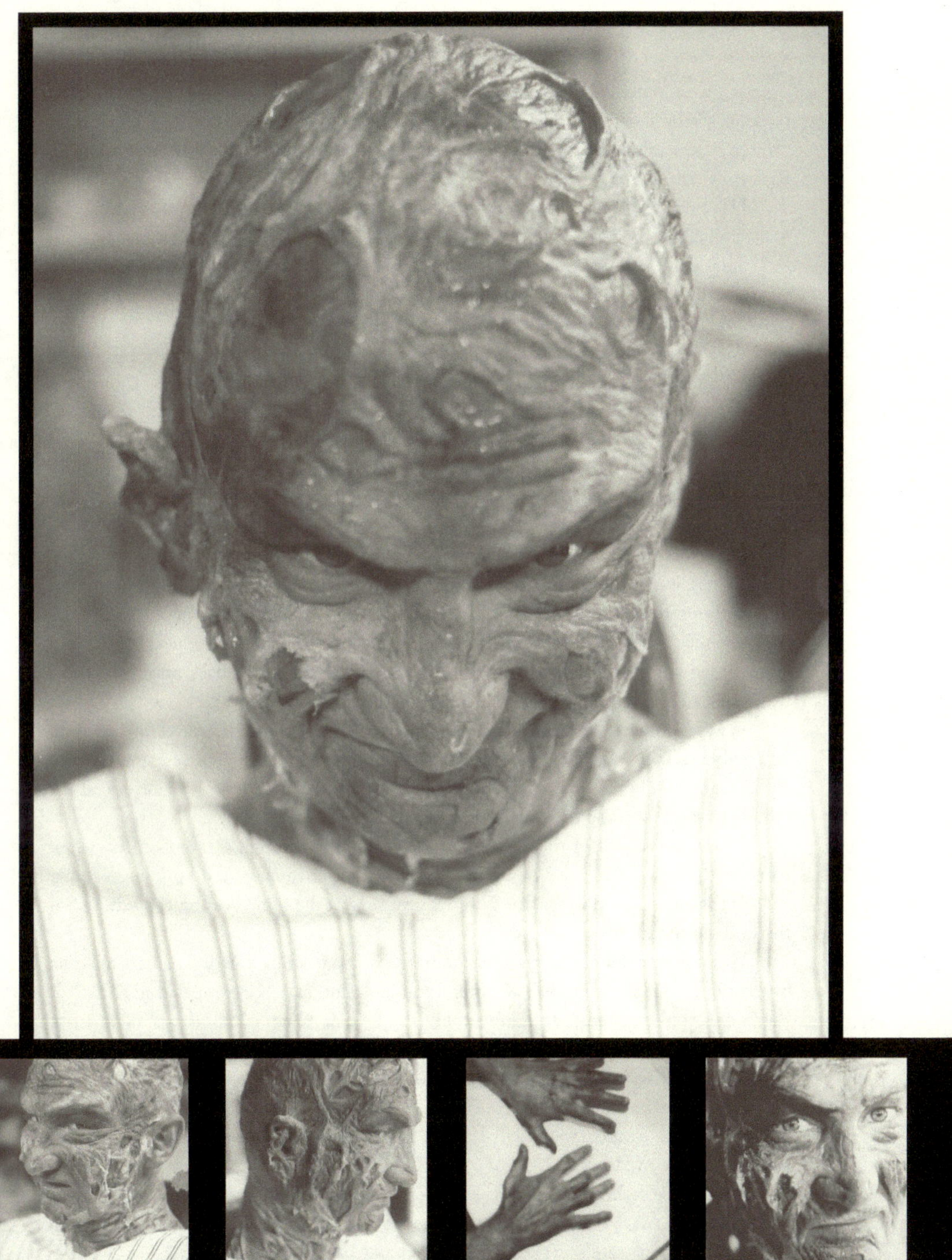

It was a prop that took much forethought, planning, and execution before it became, all by itself, an icon. Starting once again with Craven's words, Doyle gave the script to Carlucci and had him assist in figuring out how to create the weapon on Krueger's right hand.

"He said, 'Read the script, and by the way, there's a glove in there, and you have to make some knives on it,'" Carlucci remembers.

That glove's description in the script stated, "Then the man's hand slips into this glove-like apparatus, filling it out and transforming it into an awesome, deadly, claw-hand with four razor/talons gleaming at its blackened fingertips."

After reading, Carlucci devoured the task, realizing he had never seen anything quite like the weapon he was to design. Excited about the possibilities, the effects assistant was energized as he dreamt up ideas for Freddy's claw. "To me, it was the hero," he says. "This is the true villain of this film, this glove."

The process started with Carlucci trying to understand the conceptually primordial, yet technologically modern, weapon that was an extension of Freddy. "I was making this beast that was described as slashing this person, and sparking off of that, and cutting this," he remembers.

"There were about four or five of us that stood around with the prop master and he was trying to sort of figure it out," recalls Huntley. "Should there be a bend to the claws? He had work gloves, he had all these things, and we all sort of stood there and commented, and I think that Greg Fonseca was also there. I look back on it now and I think that such an important, iconic image of Freddy was that glove."

It was an instrument that had to be powerful, but crude, indicative of a layman being able to construct it in a basement, much like Freddy did. "It was something he could make in a boiler room," Doyle recalls. "The blades had to be horrific and shiny and dirty at the same time."

Doyle realized all of these thoughts were running through Craven's mind when he came up with the idea, so he went off, created some sketches, and built a test finger of how the glove would function. When Craven saw it, he signed off on everything but the knife in the finger.

"I don't remember exactly the description in the script, but it was basically just 'work gloves and steak knives,' or something like that," says Craven. "I don't know if they were even designated steak knives, but that's what he ended up using." (The script actually states, "Close on same hands dumping four fishing knives out of a filthy bag.")

The next day, Fonseca came in with two sets of knives, and the team chose the one that looked the best. Once tested, it was deemed perfect. In actuality, the blades selected to construct the weapon were neither steak nor fishing—they were tomato knives, a no-longer-available model XXP210 from W.R. Case and Sons Cutlery.

"It was the right shape, it was stainless steel, we could do everything we wanted with it," Doyle says. "They very well could have been tomato knives. We just called them steak knives. They were everything we wanted and Wes bought off on it."

Craven certainly did. "I thought it was terrific."

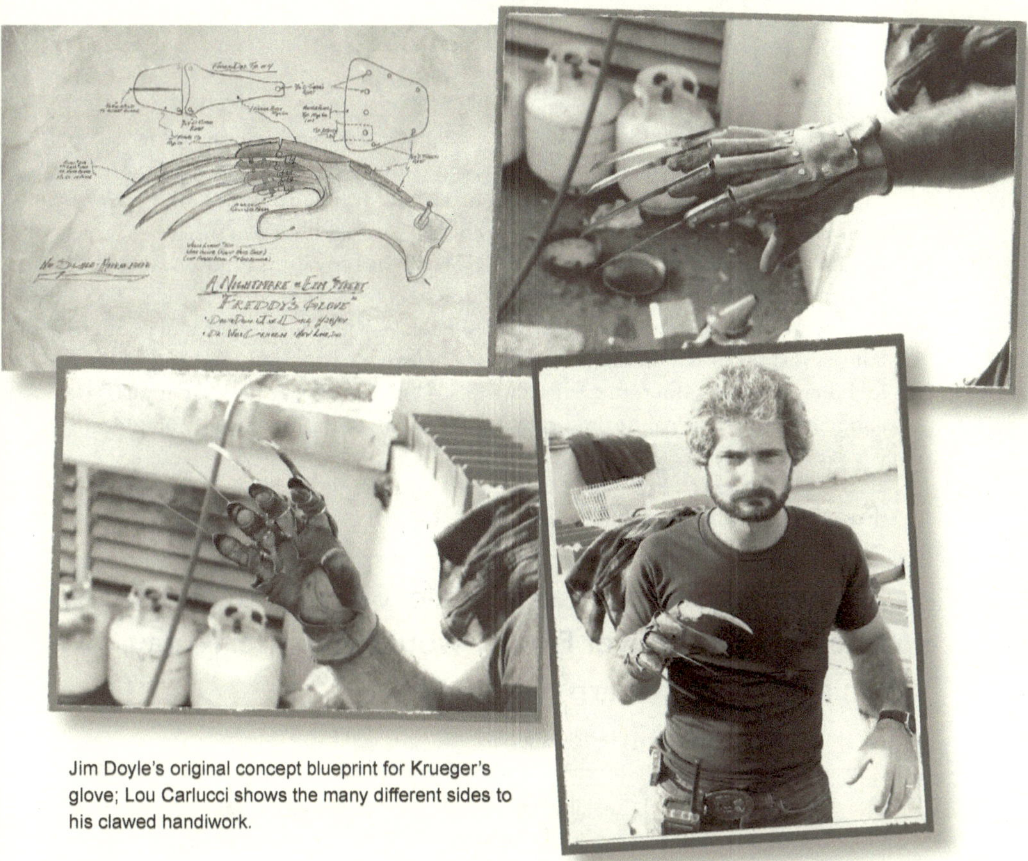

Jim Doyle's original concept blueprint for Krueger's glove; Lou Carlucci shows the many different sides to his clawed handiwork.

The man who would be wearing it was sold as well. "It's a vicious thing, but there's something very wonderfully homemade and rustic about it, too," says Englund.

With a greenlight on the concept, Doyle set Carlucci off to begin construction based on his drawings and, though the script was particularly descriptive when it came to the glove, Carlucci found his relative inexperience a blessing in disguise. "I wasn't an experienced prop maker, by any means," he admits, "so it worked out well. Looking back, if I was more experienced I might have made it look too pretty, or too perfect."

With the approved parameters in mind, Carlucci worked to take the one finger and one claw that Doyle had shown him and duplicate them, because all the fingers were identical. Made out of copper pipe, which was split-shuddered and hammered in ways that a tinsmith in a boiler room could actually do, Doyle remembers, "The real glove with the real sharp knives was rarely used. It was really dangerous to play with that thing."

Langenkamp recalls making sure the right gloves were used at the right time, though that wasn't always the case. "They had sharp ones, plastic ones, and non-sharp ones, and whenever Freddy would grab me, I'd say, 'This is the non-sharp one, right?' And often they would have forgotten to switch them out. Someone would say, 'Oh no, this is the sharp one!'"

Luckily, the actress wasn't hurt by the mix-up of real or fake Freddy knives, but short on time and funds, Carlucci recalls, "By the time I finished making the first glove, extra parts, and a couple of stunt gloves made out of plastic so no one would be hurt, it took me about a week." It was clear that there was neither the time nor money to spend on making duplicates. "We thought that if anything would break, I had extra parts to put on the gloves," he says, noting he constructed one glove that worked out well. "It was very durable."

Between keeping the talons sharp for some shots ("I had one guy that did nothing but sharpen the blades on that knife for the whole film," Doyle says) and dulling them for others, Carlucci admits that "the glove took a lot of abuse, but worked out well." He also remembers showing the finished glove to Craven for the first time. "Hands down, it was perfect, just great for what he wanted to do."

Englund agrees. "I just loved it so much," he says. "It's a fabulous prop and one that extends Freddy. It extends his anger, his revenge. I like that."

"They had sharp ones, plastic ones, and non-sharp ones, and whenever Freddy would grab me, I'd say, 'This is the non-sharp one, right?'"

Heather Langenkamp on Freddy's glove

As Langenkamp had, Englund would make sure the proper glove was used at the proper time, though Doyle recalls the moment the actor tried the glove on for the very first time. "First thing he did was cut himself, like everybody did, because we didn't realize that if you folded your fingers all the way, the knives went into your wrist," he says.

It didn't take long for Englund to feel the power of what Craven had envisioned, give his director a look and, as Doyle recalls, "He got that smile on his face. He was walking around for a day, just trying different things he could do that were going to be interesting and scary, but graceful. He was great with that thing."

Once again, Englund took the concept of the glove's construction and turned it into a means for character motivation. "I love the idea that behind one of those garage doors in a white trash neighborhood, Fred Krueger was there with his vice and his files, making that thing, and dreaming and fantasizing about what he was gonna do," he says. "And when he put it on it emboldened him to terrible and terrifying acts of violence. I think all those elements have combined to make it this incredibly symbolic thing. A symbolic hand of evil."

That malevolence would not only be seen, but also heard, with the sounds of Krueger's blade becoming an indelible part of the film's iconography. "The sound people in New York experimented endlessly trying to find the right sound for the scraping claws, and what they finally used was a steak knife on the underside of a metal folding chair," reveals Craven. "They wanted to find a sound that would set everybody's teeth on edge, and they finally found it that way."

With the design, construction, and sound of the film's iconic weapon approved, the mechanical effects team, responsible for the many complicated, on-set effects pieces in the film, prepared to move on to other aspects requiring their detailed attention. "It was just a culmination of putting our heads together and saying, 'Okay, this has never been done. How can we create this look of what they're trying to achieve here?'" Carlucci remembers.

They discovered there was one, and possibly the only, way to pull things off: cheaply.

"There was a lot of pressure on the original film because there was no money. And it was cheap, cheap, cheap," Lazzara states. "Yeah, if I remember correctly, they had no money."

Even though that might have been the case, the cast and crew worked hard to make up for the lack of funds with an abundance of ingenuity.

"To be honest with you, we ran out of money making the first one," says Englund, though he is still proud of what they were able to accomplish in such a short time and on such a low budget.

Meyer-Craven, too, recalls the stretching of the budget, likening it to old monster movies like *Voyage to the Bottom of the Sea* (1961). "In those films special effects were like, 'Push in the sea monster!' and you could see the broomstick," she offers. "Well, *Elm Street* was just this side of that, only all the broomsticks were hidden, so the stunts and effects worked really well. It's just a very special movie. It was different and it changed the face of things in horror. You look at movies now, with all the green screen, and then you look back at *Elm Street* and you think, 'I'm sorry, but that works. It just works.'"

"It was, in fact, all rubber bands and paper clips," agrees Langenkamp. "And not only did it work, it was also a lot of fun. It was much more of a unit on the film."

WHO'S THE BOSS?

As production moved to a start, that unit was ready to set sail with Craven commanding the ship. Luckily, he was a director who knew the rounds of working to get the most out of everyone behind, and in front of, the camera. It made for a place that felt safe, flexible and, for the most part, relaxed. In the shadow of what they were all about to undertake, it came as a welcome relief to many.

Miller was one person who had the experience of working with Craven a second time, though in a markedly different capacity. "Working with Wes on *Swamp Thing* wasn't as intimate as working on *Elm Street*, because [*Swamp Thing*] was a much larger film," he says. His second go with the director was the one that made Miller understand more fully who Craven was as a person as well as a filmmaker. "He was more like your older brother. Everyone called him the 'college professor.' He didn't seem like a director, as he was very calm about everything," he recalls.

Besides Craven's palliative influence, he had endeared himself to many on the production for another reason: his competence. "Wes knows what he wants, and I respected that so much," Risher says. "He's a very efficient shooter. He gets his scenes and moves on."

That aspect of his abilities was something cinematographer Haitkin would appreciate, more so because although Craven knew what he was after, he didn't have a rigidity about it that handcuffed the creative process.

"He was flexible, and that's what made Wes a really good director, is that he could draw from people's ideas," says Haitkin. "That's why he selected people that were into understanding what he was doing."

Because of that, many crew members were self-starters who were quickly able to deliver Craven their best work. "He basically left all of us alone to our own devices," says Logan. "He may have given us a little bit of direction, but I don't think there was a lot of telling us exactly what to do. I think he let our creativity shine, which is always nice."

Remembering Craven being excited and happy about the effects when they were presented to him, Lazzara says, "It was a good working spirit. He let us use a lot of the creativity within ourselves, which was a really wonderful thing, especially back then."

Burrows remembers, "Wes accepted people. He wasn't, 'I have to do it my way and that's it.' He was the kind that would take notice of other people that had ideas. He told the crew, 'I'll take ideas.' He'd talk about things and he was good at that. He really had a great mind."

Even though some on the crew, such as Diers, had less interaction with Craven, they do believe their presence was felt. "I think he knew who Debbie the Cat was, and I think he liked my Xerox art, vaguely. But that's my memory. Everybody liked Debbie," he laughs.

"Wes is really, really a gentlemen," Jensen says. "He really makes everyone feel like they're part of the process of making this fun thing work. It's fun. It wasn't just blood and gore and guts. It was magic, and he loved being the head magician."

It also made the time on set for the actors a more pleasant experience. "He was so amazing with all of us, because we were all really just kids," Wyss says. "He was just such a calm, reassuring presence, and he knew how to talk to each of us."

That talk would often be to make sure the performers knew what he was after and how to get it from them as quickly as possible, often needing only one take.

"I think that one of the most brilliant aspects of Wes Craven's directing is that he is confident," Langenkamp says. "He just knew what he wanted and it was, 'I got it. I don't have to do another take.'" Even when insecurities arose and an actor might want confirmation, Craven knew when he had what he needed to move on.

"I seem to recall that from most of the things that I did with him," says Saxon. "I had in mind what I wanted to do, and I showed him, and he just accepted it."

Blakley also found her time under Craven's guidance to be fulfilling. "Wes is a great director. He was easy to work with, fun to work with," she admits. "He's an elegant man, with fine manners and a soft voice. He was thoughtful and considerate of the actors, and helpful."

More accolades for the director would come from Corri. "He'll always be an important person in my life because he started my career and he gave me a break when nobody would," the actor says. "He's Wes, he's 'Daddy Wes.'"

"He was just one of the kindest men," offers Benson. "A sweet soul. Intelligent and professional. He was amazing."

Clockwise from top left: Craven making his way, and enjoying himself, amongst his crew; Cast and crew hang out behind the scenes, enjoying some down time; Fleetwood shares her shear talent with Shaye.

Perhaps it is Englund who best boils down what it was like to be under Craven's employ. Simply put, Englund explains, "Wes was a dream to work for. He has kind of a fourteen-year-old, wisecracking, punning schoolboy inside of him."

With such an easy director at the helm, coupled with that sense of playfulness, one would be right to imagine that the set had its times of levity, even in the face of such dark and brooding material. "It was a very good vibe on the set," Miller says. "Everyone seemed to have a lot of fun."

That fun happened more than once when cast and crew decided to riff on their director. "He's a very professorial, clearly literary gentleman," says Talalay. "And that's the Wes that comes out when you meet him and work with him."

Craven's demeanor extended to his choice of clothing, which tended to the more serious sweater, or shirt and tie look. "I had heard Truffaut had said in an interview that he was a quiet man and he was always concerned about the crew really respecting him, so he found three things that always made a crew really respect you," he says. "One was to wear a hearing aid, two was to wear glasses, and three was to wear a tie. So I went with one of those."

That directorial look was a perfect point of attack for a cast and crew ready to have a good-natured laugh at Craven's expense. "I remember one day we all dressed to match Wes, and walked around and matched his mannerisms and everything," Miller says.

Langenkamp recalls the day, organized by the grip department. "We had plaid shirt and tie day. People liked to pull his leg and he had such a good sense of humor about it," she says.

That sense of humor is remembered by Cook, who recalls that members of the grip department "were all wearing khaki pants and plaid shirts just like Wes did," she says. "And they had their hands on their chins and they're looking very thoughtful and all pointing in different directions. He got a big kick out of it."

But the fun didn't stop with Craven being the punchline as he, too, found a way to get in on the act. Haitkin, in order to avoid any distractions while looking through his camera viewfinder with one eye, would wear a patch over the other eye. The notion, Craven explained, was ripe for riffing. "One day he saw we all had eye patches on, which he might not have taken as lightly as the crew dressing up like me, but it was in good fun."

Haitkin's decision to cover one eye was not something germane to just this film, as Cook found out when calling around to other filmmakers in the course of her duties. "I called this one guy that I'd worked with and I said, 'We're doing this and that with Wes,' and he said, 'Great. Who's the DP?' and I said, 'Jacques Haitkin,'" she remembers. "And then there was a pause, and then he said, 'Is that the guy with the eye patch?'"

Intrigued by the notion, Langenkamp went to its source. "I did ask him if it was part of his technique," she says. "Because when you're looking through the camera with one eye, you develop this ability to see just through that eye. Whatever you're seeing through the other eye kind of dims and becomes less important. But when you put the eye patch on, suddenly all you're seeing is what's through the eyepiece. And I think it allows your eyes to relax. But it did make him look kind of, I think, very menacing and more intimidating than he probably had to."

With both director and cinematographer on the receiving end, many thought the cast needed their moment in the mocking sunshine, too. "I know we had a 'Nancy Day' when everybody wore bedclothes," Craven remembers. "Even one of the gaffers had slippers with bunnies on them. It was a really great crew and we had a lot of fun."

"Yeah, every week we had a certain dress up day, and there were probably five or six weeks. Nancy Day was easy," says Langenkamp. "Everybody has pajamas and slippers."

"I do remember Pajama Day was funny," says Englund. "You need that, especially on a horror movie, because it does get kind of silly and ridiculous. But that's one of the first times I remember that. I'm sure whoever thought of it had done it on another movie. It's sort of the movie equivalent of Casual Friday."

Langenkamp also remembers moments with Craven that were more down-to-earth, as well as cerebrally amusing. "The one thing with Wes that I always tried to do was stump him with a vocabulary word, which is simply impossible," she says. "He would say something like, 'Oh, time for a little postprandial nap.' And I would say, 'You know, I'm worried about my sartorial image.'"

As the days where actress and director tried to impress one another went on, many around them received a nice education on terminology. "He just had such a fantastic range of words at his disposal. 'Postprandial' is one of the best words," says Langenkamp. "It was just silly, silly, silly."

GRAB KNIFE, CUT TENSION

That sense of humor and easiness on set did not always translate to every situation, or every person. In fact, it was known that there were slight tensions between Wes and members of the production team, whether real or simply perceived, that did not go unnoticed by some.

One of those people was Talalay. "There was just a lot of tension between Bob and Wes," she says. "They just didn't get along particularly well."

What's more, Talalay herself felt some undue pressures simply because she, as a production person with New Line Cinema, was on the side of Shaye. "Wes always considered me Bob's person and the corporate spy, especially being the accountant," she says, going on to emphatically confirm, "I had no say in anything! But he definitely was suspicious of me all the time."

Craven's comment on the matter of whether Talalay was, indeed, a company mole? "I think she probably was."

"He didn't want me hanging out," admits Talalay. "He wanted me signing checks."

The bigger tensions on set, though, did at times seem to be reserved for Craven and Shaye, something Cecere recalls well. "There was some friction in there and, at one particular time, we wouldn't film any time Bob was on the set," he laughs.

While Cecere admits he can't be sure what Craven's thought process was of deciding not to shoot when Shaye was near, he does say, "Bob always wanted to do things his way and not necessarily Wes' way."

One reason for that, at least in Craven's mind, may have had to do with Shaye's former career trajectory. "It's very difficult if you're dealing with somebody else that also is a director or wants to be a director," he offers. "Or thinks they could step in and do it better. So there was a certain amount of tension about that."

Shaye does admit that there were times he and Craven "had a little bit of a disagreement about who was doing what, and he wanted me to stick in my role as a producer," he says.

"They're just such very different kinds of men," adds Langenkamp. "I don't think under the best circumstances that they would've been chummy, good friends. They're also just such different personalities. And I do think that Bob is a very creative soul. He has a lot to add to a creative endeavor and I think that's one of the reasons why he's been so successful."

Risher confesses to understanding both sides, but does say, "Bob was so passionate about *Nightmare*. He wanted it to look good."

"I mean, look, Bob is the guy who got the money to make that film. If he had failed, there wasn't anybody else that was gonna make that happen, because I'd explored

Craven and Haitkin prepare for a take.

all other avenues," Craven admits. "Bob had been a director once before that time and there's always that struggle between the producer or the studio, whichever it is—in this case it was the creative producer—as to who's going to put the imprint on it and who's going to have the final say on the way it goes. So there was always that sort of tension. But in the long run, it worked out pretty damn well."

While many could feel the tension between director and producer ("It was obvious to everybody," says Doyle), the true, underlying cause was not entirely known: to keep the film on track, "Bob had mortgaged his company and his life and his house and everything to create this film," Doyle adds.

At the same time, Craven had signed away all of his rights to the film and characters, essentially leaving both men to stake their careers on this project. Strain could have been expected.

"Obviously there is going to be some tension," offers Doyle. "Bob was, of course, looking at the money flowing out the door every morning on production reports. Wes was looking at the film they weren't getting every morning with the dailies. So there was some tension."

Haitkin was also aware of the struggles between his director and producer. "Yeah, there was conflict between them, but for a cinematographer, I'm harvesting setups," he says. "I work for both of them, they both are my boss, so I let them sort it out. Ultimately, Wes tells me what to do. So if Wes said, 'Don't shoot that,' I wouldn't shoot it. If Bob said, 'Shoot it,' and Wes said, 'No,' I wouldn't shoot it, because I work for the director ultimately, but I also work for the producer. My goal is to get the best result overall."

And while it was clear that Craven and Shaye were two strong personalities who both shared a vision to get to the end of the project, it was equally apparent that they might not have agreed on how to arrive there. Looking back on the issues, Craven says, "Ultimately, Bob and I both respected each other all the way through. We both knew we had everything to win or lose with the film. And he never forced me to do anything."

"Bob was, at times, a very difficult and demanding personality," says Cook, "but that's what producers are. He could be bossy and kind of short with you, but he wasn't impossible. Basically, if he was happy with the dailies, and stuff was going well, great." If things weren't, she says, "Then Bob would yell about it. But it certainly wasn't the most difficult and unbearable show I ever worked on. Far from it."

Cecere believes that any troubles between director and producer never seemed to be truly detrimental problems and, he adds, "Sometimes seemed more like a joking problem."

Doyle agrees and says, "There was some yelling behind doors. But I didn't think there would be a breakup of the family. The good news is in front of the crew the guys would come out and they were still working together. And that was to their credit."

IS IT OR ISN'T IT?

As the film moved forward and differences were being ironed out, there was at least one other matter that needed attention. Because the film dealt so heavily with blending together reality and the dream world, one thing Craven wanted was to keep the exact line between dreams and waking life less than obvious. It was a choice that seemed antithetical to Haitkin's understanding.

"I wanted to put a very strong effect so that you'd know you're in a nightmare, so that it would really be scary," Haitkin says of his lighting choices. It was something that, as he would learn, was paradoxical to Craven's vision. "Wes said, 'No, no, no, no, no, I don't want to let people know we're in a nightmare. It's just the opposite.'"

A tricky tactic to employ, it was one of the most effective concepts Craven had in mind. "You could be in a nightmare and it might look real, or in the real world and it might look nightmarish," Haitkin says. "We wanted the audience to not know to keep them off-balance. What's scary is when stuff is a little real. I wanted to get enough naturalism in there so that it felt like it could really be happening."

It was a concept that was an important part of the film for Langenkamp. "You don't know, and it leaves the audience wondering, for at least a few seconds at the top of a dream, whether they're asleep or not," she says. "If it's suddenly gone black-and-white, or if it suddenly had gone psychedelic, or mist or something, it would've given the audience too big of a help to kind of figure it out. And that's the fun part of the movie to me."

Wyss concurs that it's also one of the reasons people were fascinated and attracted to the material. "Is it a dream? Is it real? You're never really certain."

Audiences would eventually find out.

4

Production

Three, Four, Better Lock Your Door...

As the film moved forward, and creative issues and personal differences were being ironed out, production on *A Nightmare on Elm Street*'s tight thirty-one-day shooting schedule was finally ready to start on June 11th, 1984.

THE HAND OF REVENGE

Though it wasn't the first to be filmed ("We shot this very close to the end," recalls Craven), the opening scene would set the tone of the movie, teasing audiences of horrors yet to come by giving them a glimpse of what is now one of the genre's most iconic images.

Opening in a boiler room, viewers are assaulted with steam, damp grime, and the shadow of fire and dark energy. "We looked at a lot of boiler rooms and most of them were very clean and kind of contemporary, and I wanted something very dungeon-like," says Craven. "And the one we used just fit the bill. All of these pipes had been wrapped in this insulation, and it was all broken open and this stuff was falling out."

Close and teasing shots revealed an unknown man's ragged feet, then dirty, nail-bitten fingers as they pick up pieces of metal to hammer, weld, and shape a taloned apparatus. It was the tool

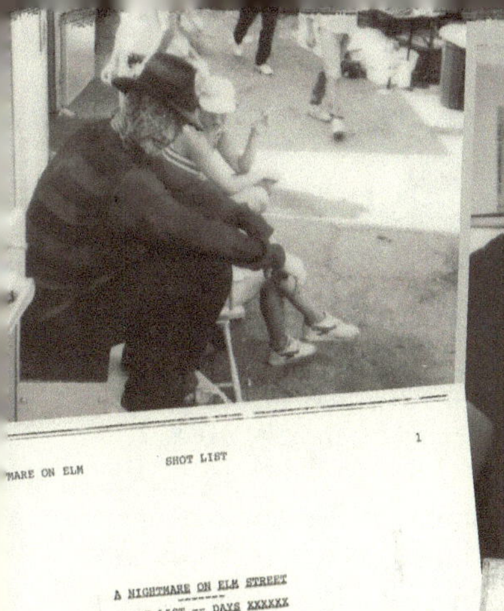

MARE ON ELM SHOT LIST 1

A NIGHTMARE ON ELM STREET

SHOT LIST -- DAYS XXXXXX

SCENE: 1A (MONTAGE)
ACTION: FRED BUILDS KNIFE-GLOVE
LOCATION: BOILER ROOM

CUT IS FROM: This opens picture
CUT IS TO: TINA in tunnel

1. LOW ANGLE DOLLY SHOT ON FRED'S FEET, TRACKING before them, then letting them pass, SEEING him as a dark silhouette, and SEEING around him the FIRE of the boilers, the STEAMING PIPES, etc.
2. ENDING SHOT to display the claw and take us to the corridor. Either cutting of the canvas, or of something else. ABOVE IS TO BE SHOT ON LOCATION. THE REMAINDER OF MONTAGE IS TO BE SHOT ON STAGE AS INSERTS.

SCENE: 2
ACTION: TINA RUNS
LOCATION: CONCRETE TUNNEL

CUT IS FROM: CLAW SLASHING CANVAS
CUT IS TO: TINA IN BOILER ROOM

1. CLOSE ON TINA reacting to OVERLAPPED SOUND OF CLAW. She listens, hears nothing more, starts forward.

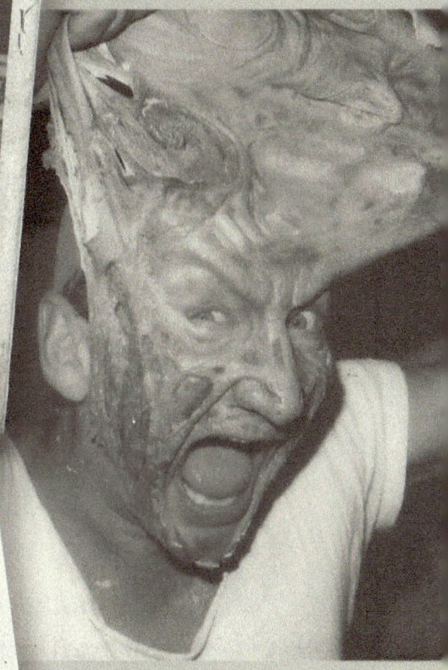

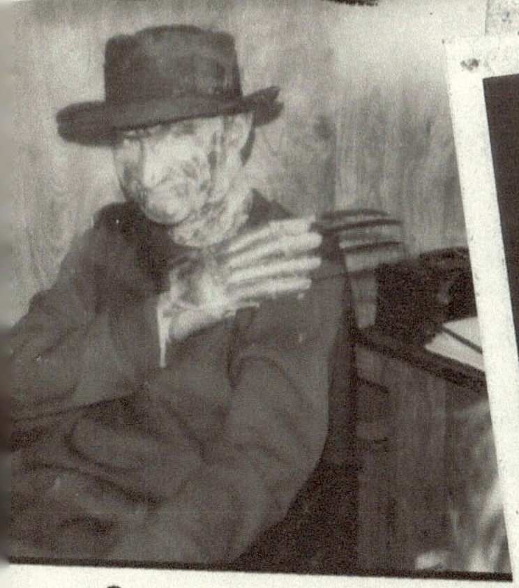

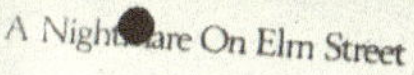

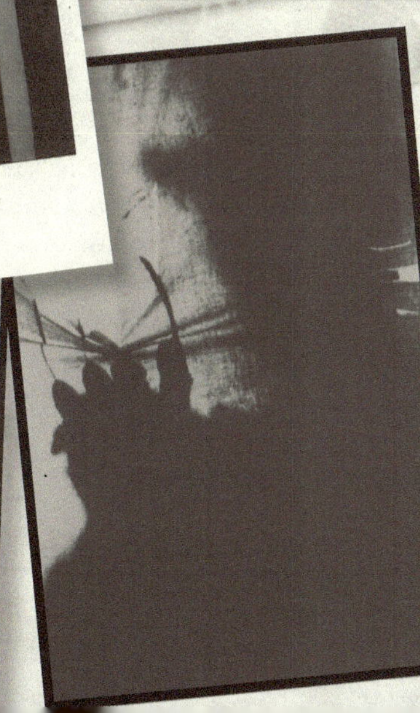

A Nightmare On Elm Street

ACTORS DA

ARTISTS NAME	WORK STATUS	START TIME	1st MEAL FROM	1st MEAL TO	2nd MEAL FROM			
HEATHER LANGENKAMP	W	8 50 A	12 45 p	1 45 p	7 45 p	8 15 p	9 30 p	Heather Langenkamp
JOHNNY DEPP	WF	12 Noon	12 45 p	1 45 p	7 45 p	8 15 p	10p	
RONEE BLAKLEY	H							
ROBERT ENGLUND	W	9A	12 45 p	1 45 p	7 45 p	8 15 p	9P	
TONY CECERE	SWF	7A	12 45 p	1 45 p	7 45 p	8 15 p	9 45 p	Taylor
TANYA RUSSELL	SWF	7A	12 45 p	1 45 p	7 45 p	8 15 p	9 45 p	Tanya Russell
PAUL SHAVER	SWF	7A	12 45 p	1 45 p			3p	

Freddy Krueger would use to destroy innocent lives. Tighter, claustrophobic moments added to the feeling of menace and terror, but they were also practical. "It was all shot on a table. A little tabletop," admits Craven.

While Doyle and his team already had plans for how to create the infamous weapon, the filming of its construction would be another matter entirely, an event that had two people portraying the wicked Krueger.

"The hands building Freddy's glove in the beginning of the film were mostly Charlie Belardinelli, my third on the film. It was his first effects film," Doyle says. Because Belardinelli worked a lot on the glove, in addition to his hands being the right size and shape, Craven "cast" him as Krueger's on-screen hand model. As a craftsman who understood the natural movements involved, he was happy to oblige.

"I put the sweater on, cut the fingers off gloves, did a little bit of filing, a little bit of using the torch, and worked the prop a little bit," remembers Belardinelli. "It was a lot of fun and a spur-of-the-moment thing."

But the effects artist also knew he had to do more than make the glove: he had to do justice as a stand-in for Englund, so he asked the actor what the best approach would be. Belardinelli recalls, "Bob Englund came over to me and said, 'Charlie, you gotta think sick. Think real sickness,' and I said, 'Okay.'"

In addition to Belardinelli, Doyle says, "There are a couple of scenes, a couple of quick shots, where part of the arm is Carlucci, who was my second on the film."

Thinking back on the mere concept of the glove and its powerful introduction at the beginning of the film, Englund says, "There's something there. There's something of armor to it."

Carlucci agrees, but feels that as interesting a prop it is in and of itself, "The glove is nothing without Robert, and that's the extension of him," he says.

LAMB TO THE SLAUGHTER

That chilling weapon, and the ambiguity of dream versus reality, would be seen when audiences first meet Tina. Dressed only in a nightgown, the young girl walks through a dark, concrete corridor.

The moment was something Doyle remembers as sounding easy to capture on film, though was actually anything but. "The first time you see Tina in the boiler room hallway in the nightgown, that took them weeks to figure out what was the right nightgown," he says, "and how transparent it would be, how we would light it, and how Jacques was gonna put the background up."

Haitkin also points out that the steam emanating from the pipes was, in fact, real steam and not just stage smoke. "The credit is to Wes that we used real steam. It was a big deal to him and you had to use real boilers," he says. "There's nothing like it for quality."

Filmed at the now-closed Lincoln Heights Jail in La Habra, California, Wyss has not-so-pleasant memories of the location. "It's a very creepy, scary, bad-energy place. I was terrified," she says. In fact, she admits to never going anywhere in the building

1 Rev. 4/30/84

1A. INT. (MONTAGE). 1A

NIGHTMARE MUSIC THEME begins as we FADE UP on a SERIES OF SHOTS, all CLOSE and teasing.

-- A man's FEET, in shabby work shoes, stalking through a junk bin in a dark, fire-lit, ash-dusted place. A huge BOILER ROOM is what it is, although we only glimpse it piecemeal. Then we SEE a MAN'S HAND, dirty and nail-bitten, reach INTO FRAME and pick up a piece of METAL.

-- ANOTHER ANGLE as the HAND grabs a grimey WORKGLOVE and slashes at it with a straight razor, until its fingertips are off.

-- CLOSE ON SAME HANDS dumping four fishing knives out of a filthy bag. Their blades are thin, curved, gleaming sharp.

-- MORE ANGLES, EVEN CLOSER. We can HEAR the MAN's wheezing BREATHING, but we still haven't seen his face. We never will. We just SEE more metal being assembled with crude tools, into some sort of linkage -- a splayed, spidery sort of apparatus, against a background light of FIRE, and a deep rushing of STEAM and HEAVY, DARK ENERGY.

-- And then we see this linkage attached to the glove.

-- Then the BLADES attached to all of it.

-- Then the MAN'S HAND slips into this glove-like apparatus, filling it out and transforming it into an awesome, deadly claw-hand with four razor/talons gleaming at its blackened fingertips. Suddenly the HAND arches and STRIKES FORWARD, SLASHING THROUGH a DARK CANVAS, tearing it to shreds.

1 EXT. LOS ANGELES. NIGHT. (2nd Unit) 1

A PULSATION OF LIGHT AND SHADOW. MUSIC DROPS AWAY to a hushed RUSHING OF WIND and DISTANT SIRENS. CAMERA RACKS INTO FOCUS on a HIGH PANORAMA of the San Fernando Valley, its night sky lit from within by a strange GREENISH LIGHT. TITLES BEGIN.

CAMERA TILTS DOWN and ZOOMS SWIFTLY into the valley's web of light.

CUT TO:

Belardinelli, channeling his inner Krueger, prepares to fill Englund's shoes for the terrifying opening sequence; The opening moments of the film as seen in the screenplay. (Note the numbers and marked passages, showcasing effects work.)

alone, not even from her dressing room to the set. "It was clearly a place filled with so much anguished emotion," she adds. "God only knows what happened in there, and I wouldn't stand anywhere on the set by myself. If the whole group moved, I moved."

She wasn't alone in her assessment. "It felt absolutely haunted, horribly depressing, and grim," states Cook. "It definitely put the crew in a mood. Even in broad daylight you think of how depressing it must have been when it was actually in operation."

Perceived fears aside, some look back at the more real worries of having filmed at the location. What Craven and his crew would find out much later was that the building had actually been closed down because it was full of hazardous material. "We realized we were all in there, sucking up asbestos for a week," the writer and director revealed.

Haitkin confirms, "It's now condemned, and we spent weeks down there breathing."

Craven jokingly adds, "I always thought we'd all end up dying at the same time, twenty years after that."

That type of setting was perfect for the beginning of Tina's nightmare, where she and viewers received their first taste of Krueger in pursuit, though he would still remain barely visible. Instead, the young girl first shares her nightmare with a lamb, something many have questioned.

"I think it is such great imagery combining terror and sweetness. It was such an anachronistic thing happening while this person is scared," Wyss offers. "There's something about it. Some commentary on innocence."

"I get more questions about that lamb than almost any other aspect of the film," laughs Langenkamp.

Craven explains, "This was my tribute to Buñuel, the lamb."

Luis Buñuel Portolés was a Spanish filmmaker often associated with the surrealistic movement. Upon his death at the age of eighty-three in 1983, his obituary in *The New York Times* called him "an iconoclast, moralist, and revolutionary who was a leader of avant-garde surrealism in his youth and a dominant international movie director half a century later." That said, while the lamb's appearance might have been lost on some viewers, it might have also been lost on the animal.

"Everybody was helping because the lamb was really scared," remembers Jensen. "The hallway looks so empty, but there was so much camera equipment, and lights, and cables, and it was echoey and loud. It had to come out through a doorway and, by the time we were ready to shoot, that lamb was beside itself. We were all tucked back in corners and, at a certain point, the lamb would just go where it wanted to go."

"It was supposed to streak across the hall and it wouldn't move," Craven says, "so they finally ended up kicking it."

Even after the animal needed some prodding to do its part, Wyss recalls that the scene went smoothly and that working with the four-legged creature was anything but difficult. "The only danger is being totally upstaged by something so adorable!" the actress states..

With her non-human co-star having done its job, Wyss may have been frightened of the locale, but she does remember seeing a lighter side to the entire scene, at least while filming it. "There were some funny things, because I had to run like I was in molasses," she says. "It was kind of hard to create that effect, and I felt kind of silly at first, but then I got into it." Helping her to achieve the movement when her legs were off screen was the fact that she was running on a treadmill attached to the dolly.

Wyss also found some comfort with the man trying to end her character's life, as even when Englund was in full makeup and character, "He would be saying these incredibly funny, intelligent things, and then he would just turn into Freddy and they'd call 'Action!'" she says. "But I was like, 'No, I'm still laughing. Wait!'"

A creepy setting and funny offscreen moments aside, the scene would play out relatively smoothly, with only one potential issue rearing its head to effects man Doyle: the need for yellow dust to come out of Tina's mouth during a silent scream when Freddy appears behind her.

"When I first saw what they were going to use for Tina screaming and having the dust come out, I thought, 'There is no way that will work,'" Doyle says. The chosen formula that so worried him? Crumbled up Cap'n Crunch cereal, another indicator of the film's budget and ingenuity. Thankfully, Doyle's fear that it would just mix with the actress's saliva and come out as mush did not come to pass. "They ground it into a really fine powder and it worked," he adds. "Since it's edible, you can put it in your mouth and she just spit it out. It actually worked."

JUST A DREAM, MA

Just as Tina is about to fall victim to Krueger, who shocks the girl by suddenly appearing behind her, she wakes up in her room. Drenched with sweat, the young girl is looked in on by her mother. The actress playing the part was Donna Woodrum, whose previous brush with the genre came when she was in a crowd scene in the horror comedy *Attack of the Killer Tomatoes* (1978). Although the actress did little performing afterward, Craven liked what she brought to his film. "I always thought she was very good. It really set the tone for Tina," he stated.

"The audition for this film was the very first audition I had with the agent that I had at the time. So it was a whole new experience for me," says Woodrum. "I got the sides, I read the part they wanted me to read for, and I went in. That afternoon, I guess maybe an hour or so later, my agent called and said, 'Well, I don't know what you did, but they really like you.' It was that quick."

As for Tina's mother's boyfriend, who seems far more interested in having her back in bed than whether Tina is all right, actor Paul Grenier made his debut, something that Craven recalls. "It was like a huge thrill for him, because he got into SAG, I think, on that, because he

Wyss shared her first scene with an adorable but frightened, not always-cooperative lamb; Tina (and audiences) get a fleeting, shadowy glimpse of the man who is on the attack, Freddy Krueger.

got a line." It was also Grenier's sole genre credit before moving into sound and casting work.

"He was a friend of mine and I met him in an acting class in Hollywood," reveals Woodrum. "I was startled that I knew this person that I was supposed to be running away with. I don't remember him doing anything else, but he did a lot of theater."

Tina's mother was someone who quickly ignored her daughter's problem, with Woodrum offering that denial was a big factor in portraying the character. "So what do you do when you're in denial? You ignore the obvious, so that's what I was trying to do," she says. "I was sort of being taken in by it, but knowing if I said anything about it, there goes the trip to Vegas, and this doesn't look like anything I know how to deal with. So the best way to handle it is try to be a good, stern parent and say, 'You gotta stop that kind of dreaming,' and then I get out of the picture, literally. Exit stage left. And that's what I did."

Both mother and boyfriend may have had a small amount of screen time, but the scene did its job quickly, setting the tone for at least one theme of the film, which was the abandoned teenager.

"Let this be a warning to you parents out there: these kids need supervision because there are evil forces out there out to get them," says Woodrum. "And I liked the way they did my character, showing her as this self-seeking, searching, lost woman, who was trying to find love in all the wrong places when her real interest should have been at home."

Like mother like daughter in many ways, but not off screen. "Amanda was nothing like the character she played. In the film it was all teen angst and all that stuff going on. But in actuality, she was a hoot-and-a-half. She was a jokester. She was laughing and smiling all the time," recalls Woodrum.

The actress reveals that there was a moment she worried she might not even be sharing screen time with Wyss, as both time and money were running out. "I was in one of the first scenes in the film, which was the last to be shot. They weren't even sure they were gonna film that because it was close to midnight, and it would've been going into the next day. The Union would've been involved, which means more pay, more money," Woodrum discloses. "I mentioned one time, 'Wes, I really want to do this scene,' and he said, 'Donna, I'm doing everything I can to see that we do.'"

Getting to the set at seven in the morning, Woodrum waited and waited, hoping the moment would come, even if her surroundings seemingly proved otherwise. "I waited all day and all night to do that scene. You can't tell, but, behind that little room set, everything was torn apart. They were already striking everything out of the warehouse," she says. "They were closing down the whole thing. And all I wanted was to do the scene. I didn't want them to cancel it."

Luckily it wasn't, but that didn't mean Woodrum was able to bring everything she might have planned. Years later, she's interested in a second take. "I have to tell you, I've really not been very happy with the scene I delivered. It was not the one I had in my mind and I've redone that scene over and over again," the actress admits. "I could have played up the differences in the two characters even more. Here was this girl, terrified, and here is this mother, frozen, trying not to be terrified, and just passing it off as, 'Oh well, not that important. Just do this and don't do that and you'll be fine. Bye.' But there was absolutely no time to do that."

She does not, in any way, hold Craven responsible. "I don't blame him whatsoever. Listen, he was not only a great director, he was a great technician," Woodrum praises. "He really knew as an artist what he was after."

JUST LIKE YOU AND ME

The next big scene in the film was significant, as it introduced the core cast as a unit, including the film's ultimate heroine, Nancy. But first, audiences would get a glimpse of characters that have become synonymous with *Elm Street*: the ethereal, jump-roping children.

The moment would lead to an iconic part of the film, and its mythos, with the introduction of the now-infamous "One, two, Freddy's coming for you" nursery rhyme. Sung by the aforementioned girls jumping rope (who are not credited in the final film), the four youngsters have seemingly long been a mystery.

"Two of them were my daughters. Coye is the one holding the ball, and the one jumping at the other end of the rope was Adri-Anne," explains Cecere.

"I was eight years old when we filmed the scene and, actually, RaMona was very instrumental in my sister and I working on the film," says Adri-Anne Cecere, the dark-haired girl near the bottom of the hill. "She knew that my dad had two little girls, so she asked Wes."

Fine with the idea, Craven then had the hair stylist ask Cecere. "I think at first he pretty much said, 'no' because of the type of film it was," Adri-Anne recalls. "And then he thought about it and he said, 'Sure, why not?'"

Originally excited to be part of the movie, ultimately, "They didn't wanna be there, especially the youngest one," Cecere says with a laugh. "She was really in a bad mood. Believe me."

"Correct, I was not in the best mood," laughs Coye Cecere, remembering the reason for her disposition. "At first, Wes gave me a teddy bear to hold and I was excited about that, but it turned out that the teddy bear ended up looking too big, because I was so little."

In its place, the four-year-old at the top of the hill was given a ball, something that did not sit well with her. "I was unhappy that they took a toy away from me," explains Coye, "but also that I was wearing a dress, and I was a very Tomboy-ish girl, so putting me in a dress and tights didn't make me want to work."

Her father jokingly offers another aspect that might have played a small part in both daughters' lackluster enthusiasm, though it would seem to be par for the course on the film. "They didn't wanna pay them much," Cecere says in jest.

It's something that did not faze his young girls; in fact, they were happy to be paid anything at all. "They basically just presented this opportunity to us, and my sister and I wanted extra money to be able to buy a fish tank and Disney socks," Adri-Anne says with a laugh.

One young girl, who completed the quartet of jump-ropers, recalls that her involvement was apparently a case of knowing the right people at the right time. "I

Adri-Anne & Coye Cecere (left) and Annie Rusoff, three of the little girls seen in real life at the time of *Elm Street*; In reel life, they were a triumvirate of ethereal jump rope girls who introduce audiences to the creepy and memorable "One, two, Freddy's coming for you" nursery rhyme.

"They just presented this opportunity to us, and my sister and I just wanted extra money to be able to buy a fish tank and Disney socks."

Adri-Anne Cecere on being a jump rope girl

---

don't actually, totally remember how I got the part, but I assume it was through Rachel Talalay," says Annie Rusoff. "She is a dear old, old family friend. So I believe that probably she just said, 'Do you wanna do this?'"

If getting the part seemed easy enough, so too was the playing of it. "There was no direction. It was just, 'Jump rope,' because I think we were all too young to really understand anything about it," Rusoff recalls. "When we first met Wes, I think it was just time to do the actual shot. And so we'd already done a bunch of other stuff to prepare for it. I think that I just met him for a second right before and I just thought it was cool."

Adri-Anne also remembers little interaction with Craven regarding the scene. "He just came up and said to us, 'Don't pay any attention to the cameras. Just do what we've asked you and just turn the rope,'" she says. "I think he told the other girl, 'Go ahead and jump the rope and have a good time with it.'"

"I also don't think he wanted to scare us," says Rusoff. "Plus, there were a lot of other people around the scene to make it work."

One of them was Haitkin, who would end up marrying multiple, new techniques to achieve the feeling Craven wanted—methods that today would be done with the magic of computers. "Not back then," says Haitkin. "There's a moment when you see these kids on a lawn, and it's all diffused and everything, and they're in slow motion. And the camera, without a cut, transitions from them, zooms back, goes out of slow motion, the filtration goes off the camera, and then we're suddenly in a walk-and-talk dialogue scene."

In order to achieve the effect, six people were needed to work the camera, and Haitkin created a prototype mechanism using pieces of glass with diffusion material sprayed on in a graduated way. It was once again proof that even on this low-budget film, the creativity of the crew would invent a way to give Craven the look he was after. "The speed aperture computer, when we used it, was just a steel box with alligator clips. It was a very primitive tool," Haitkin says, "but it's now a standard item built into cameras."

Rusoff remembers less of the movie magic and more of the practical side of how she and the other girls disappeared. "When they pan over away from us and then again back toward us, the girls are gone," she says, "but it was simply that they had some person who moved us out of the shot really fast. We were still standing on that lawn, but we were on the side, just wrangled off so we 'vanished.'"

The disappearing act is confirmed by Adri-Anne. "I remember as soon as it was done, they pretty much shooed us out of the way because they needed us clear for the rest of the scene," she recalls.

Combining innovation and simplicity, Haitkin felt they achieved what they needed to. "It was a metaphor for what Wes wanted to do in the film, that you never knew whether or not you were in a dream," he says. "First you're in a tight shot on the girls jumping rope, and then you're suddenly at the school where the teens are walking and talking. It's two different worlds."

It was, after all, part of Craven's mandate. "That interpretation coming fairly early in the film, right after the main, opening action sequence was important in the storytelling," adds Haitkin.

Also central was seeing the teenaged characters interact for the first time. "Just watching the kids when they get out of the convertible when it drives up, and they walk by, I remember that being a pretty poignant moment," offers Adri-Anne.

Staged in a way that allowed the audience to believe in them and, more importantly, care for them, it was a notion that many of the cast carried over from script to real life when they began filming in front of John Marshall High School in Silverlake, California. "It's a beautiful high school and was totally anomalous to the rest of the neighborhood," says Craven, which assisted in his achieving a Midwestern United States look.

"We shot right outside the school," says Langenkamp (who, at the time, lived just a block away), "where it's the car driving up, and we get out and have the conversation about, 'Oh, I had a dream last night.'"

Corri recalls, "That was my old school. I loved it there."

One of the many facets of the film that Langenkamp responded to was, in fact, the interaction among the characters, specifically centered around Nancy.

"She had her relationship with her boyfriend, her relationship with her best friend, her relationship with her best friend's

The film showcases the core teenage cast in a way that allows audiences to understand, empathize with, and like them.

boyfriend, and then her mother and her father," Langenkamp points out. "So there's five people that, I knew when I got the part, I was gonna have to have these really important scenes with each of them. And I think it's kind of rare in horror movies that the heroine has so many different relationships going through the plotlines."

"Right when we all met, we clicked. So I knew as an actor, 'This is gonna be fun,'" says Wyss. "Because even in the car driving up into the shot, everybody's character sort of came alive just in the way we were interacting with each other. So in a way we already were these defined people coming together in this group, and I felt like we'd all been friends."

It was a good thing, considering Langenkamp was the only person to have met a cast member—Depp—prior to filming. "You just don't have a lot of pre-production time, and so any of these kinds of moments you can have with the person, and get to know them, it really proved to be incredibly valuable," she says.

Wyss recalls that due to her schedule on a film prior to *Elm Street*, "I didn't have a whole lot of time to make overtures to anybody else in the cast to get together, so my first time meeting everyone was when we shot that scene," she recalls.

"I think you can tell we're all a little nervous," Langenkamp concedes, but Wyss adds, "It ended up working out and we definitely worked really well as a group."

Regarding Depp, who unbeknownst to all at the time would go on to be one of the world's biggest stars, the cast and crew has nothing but good things to say, particularly since it was the musician-turned-actor's first film venture. Being on a movie set for the first time also had Depp take notice of some things, one of them being the crew's reaction to his look. "I remember everybody on [the set] was so freaked out, going, 'Jesus, the kid's got tattoos!'" says the actor.

Corri, whose character seemed to fit more who Depp appeared to be in real life, recalls, "He looked like a rock star wanting to be an actor, and then he really immersed himself in it," he says. "I remember one time walking with Johnny, and I'll never forget the difference between us, when a corvette pulls over and picks him up, while I walked!"

Of note to Corri was the man behind the wheel. "It was Nicolas Cage. That was the defining moment, like, I'm not quite sure that he knew he was going to become big, but he was destined to it," he says.

True or not, at the time, Depp was, like many on the film, still finding his place. "If I remember correctly, he was married, I think, and he was living in his car," Lazzara says. "And there was no money. I remember he hadn't gotten a check for a long time. For weeks and weeks and weeks. And they kept telling him, 'You know, your check goes to your agent.' And he said, 'I don't have an agent.'"

It was that innocence of the situation that many believed helped him. "He was so honest, and he comes from a place of honesty. And that's where every actor wants to come from, you know?" says Corri.

"He was exactly who you think he is," adds Wyss. "He was sweet, and cool, and handsome ,and laid back, artistic and genuine. Working with him was fun. The four of us really did have a great time."

Though his castmates saw one side of him, Craven saw a decidedly different aspect of Depp on set. "Johnny was so terrified when he was first performing. He'd always be on the set in a cold, clammy sweat. His hands would be trembling," he said.

Even with that, the writer and director gave the new actor accolades. "He was really pushing himself into an area that was totally different, and I don't think something he felt prepared for at all, except he was driven by this impulse," Craven offers. "He had this incredible talent."

Depp's attitude to seeing himself in the role of Glen might more closely resemble the actor Craven first met on set. "I went to see dailies. I was twenty-one, and didn't know what was going on," Depp says. "It was like looking in a huge mirror. It wasn't how I looked that bothered me, though I did look like a geek in that movie. It was seeing myself up there pretending. I didn't actually vomit, but I felt like vomiting."

Craven recalls that Depp "always thought he was doing terrible work, but he ended up doing a really interesting character."

"I don't wanna say Johnny Depp was insecure, because he wasn't really insecure, he was just a little unsure of himself and his abilities," says Logan. "And he and I had a conversation at one point and I said, 'Hang on to your seat, kiddo, because you're going to go far in this business.' And he said, 'No, do you really think so?' He was being very truthful and honest. I said, 'Yes, you're going to be a huge star.' And guess what? He is."

Depp's potential sickness—or stardom—at the time aside, the cast did, indeed, work well together as they began their journey into the world of *Elm Street* and Freddy Krueger.

"Wes, in his genius, picked all the right people to play the right parts. He clearly saw the chemistry," Wyss says.

It was chemistry that has stayed with many of them.

"It sounds so silly, but Heather and I would sit down on the steps of our dressing rooms and do the crossword puzzle together," Wyss reveals. "And we've been the closest of friends ever since. So Wes just knew. It was like Match.com."

THAT'S WHAT FRIENDS ARE FOR

After a brief discussion of their nightmares, Nancy and Glen spend an evening at Tina's house to comfort her and make her feel safe. Wyss points out that filming the scene wasn't always easy. "It was a lot of dialogue, a lot of action, and sound effects. The sound effects were actually on the tape Johnny was playing," she says.

Langenkamp recalls that Depp had some troubles. "Johnny had a hard time queuing up the spot," she laughs.

One of the first scenes that Depp would film, Jensen recalls the actor was uneasy. "I remember his hands were literally shaking. He was very, very nervous," she says. "But he accepts people calming him and I think hair and makeup and I did, too. You touch somebody and let them know it's okay, they look good, they're fine. And he accepted it. It was really that the door was opened not just in his career, but also his heart and his being."

Offscreen anxiety gave way to a moment of levity on screen as Glen tries to use an airport sound effects tape to fool his mother into thinking that he's staying at a cousin's house, as opposed to shacking up with the girls. Amusing, but somewhat tough to catch on celluloid the first few times out.

"Oh my God, we did it so many times!" laughs Wyss. "Now they would do the sound in post-production, but back then the timing had to be perfect and it was so, so difficult to get the tape to stop, play, rewind, and do all the different things we needed it to do."

In spite of the time it took to film, Wyss does remember, "That was one of the most fun scenes to shoot, really, because of all the camaraderie and being together."

The actress also has fond memories of the location where they shot her character's home. "It was on the canals of Venice and was a real funky, probably 1920s beach house. It was a real eye-opener to go to Venice," Wyss states, referring to the eclectic mix of bodybuilders, vendors and vagabonds.

Also interesting about the location was its being randomly connected to fellow cast member and jump rope girl, Rusoff. "A lot of Tina's house was actually shot in my house," she says, admitting it was more of a fluke than a plan to do so. "It was kind of a coincidence where they said, 'Oh, hey, it's the same contact people.' So I think it was me being cast first and then the idea to use the house."

Rusoff recalls the scenes in the living room because "a lot of the furniture that was in the house was ours. So it's really funny to look back and watch it because I'll say, 'I remember that couch, I remember that lamp,'" she states.

Ultimately, she and her family were relocated for a week while Craven and crew took over. "They had to totally rearrange the whole living room," remembers Rusoff. She also recalls one detail that might have been overlooked by the crew, the audience or, perhaps, both.

"Every time I think back on it, the very first thing that jumps out in my brain is when they are all in the backyard at Tina's house. In one shot you can see a plastic Bob's Big Boy character statue hanging by its neck in the window," Rusoff states. "And that was actually

The alley location of Tina's house in Venice, California as it appears today; Back in 1984, Jensen hangs outside of the house, waiting for filming to begin.

always there. My mom had it, and I thought it was funny that they left it in the movie. It's like he's being hung. I always wondered if they purposely left it there or if they didn't notice."

Huntley admits, "I don't remember it. I think if I had seen it I probably would have taken it down as it would not have been correct for Tina's house as far as a character goes. It's pretty funny though. A funny little anecdote."

The group of kids did, indeed, leave the relative safety of the living room to do what has become a horror movie trope—check on a scary noise coming from outside in the dark. Accomplishing the shot without a cut had Haitkin placing the camera on a large dolly track. "It went all the way across the yard," recalls Langenkamp.

Craven adds, "It was all very practical," with the yard being behind the house and the alley being behind the yard. At least in theory.

It wasn't easy, recalls Talalay, to find such a specific locale. "There were always complicated things, especially with Tina's house in Venice," she admits. "It couldn't just be a house. You had to be able to get to the back alley, but the back alley wasn't directly behind the house. There was a back house between it, so we had to figure out how to handle that. And yet, it is a great location."

Haitkin recalls that because they were filming in what was deemed by some to be a bad neighborhood, he encouraged crew members to take a buddy with them to the work trucks.

Craven was more specific in his fears. "I remember the guy who was in the big condor, the big light tower. I was worried he was going to get shot at," he joked.

Thankfully nothing untoward happened, and the on-screen rumblings turn out to be Rod, going for the scare. "We had a great time when we were all working together, especially in the back yard of the house when I am making the creepy sounds with the little garden tool," recalls Corri. "No one wants to confess what's going down, that we each have had some weird experience with this crazy man in our dreams. And I'm going over to the house to get Tina, but not really confessing that I am scared."

It's at that moment that audiences are teased with the notion that all four of the kids are having the nightmare. "In my mind, that is the scene where everything changes. Where you start to realize the real horror is about to begin," says Wyss. "The audience was afraid, then they can laugh with the characters, but then we start to die."

Corri states that his character would not have admitted to dreaming of Krueger, instead choosing to be jocular about the situation. "I'm too macho to confess that. I just want to be tough and get laid," he says of Rod, adding very honestly, "When I look at the acting, I just can't judge it because I don't want to look back on it. I was just very cocky."

At the time, Corri thought he knew it all, and that he was "a badass or like James Dean," before finally revealing that he ultimately "played an amalgamation of something that wasn't really me." He does divulge one aspect of the character that was not so difficult to judge or play. "Being in bed with Tina, played by Amanda, was great!" he exclaims.

Soon after, Rod and Tina leave, claiming they would take her parent's bed for what, at first, would be anything but sleeping. Nancy and Glen would find they, too, had a moment to themselves. It was in this instant that Langenkamp and Depp would share an on-screen kiss—the first for him.

"People always ask me what it was like to kiss Johnny Depp. I wish I could remember and say that it was the most romantic thing ever, but back then he wasn't the Johnny that the world knows now," says Langenkamp. "When we were filming, Wes pulled back on the scope of the moment because he didn't think, with everything going on and me being there for my best friend, that Nancy would just fall into the arms of passion."

Undercutting the romanticism still left room for sexual overtones. Glen's line, "Morality sucks," as he listens, alone, to Tina and Rod's lovemaking, is quite memorable. It was also a moment based on a real incident from Craven's life, the first time the young director was away from home.

Spending the night in a Chicago artist's loft, he heard the host couple making love in the next room. "I was a complete virgin, and it was the most miserable night of my life," laughs Craven.

The moment of on-screen sex between Rod and Tina was also not the most pleasant experience for Wyss. "I found that mortifying," confesses the actress. "Not because I didn't think Nick was adorable, but because we were simulating sex. I was just horribly uncomfortable."

Citing the scene as one of the hardest to film for her, Wyss admits, "I find being semi-naked and rolling around with somebody that you're not actually intimate with uncomfortable. But as an actor, I am ready to do the scene and find the truth in it. But it can be awkward."

SECOND TIME AROUND

Sexual proclivities complete, Rod and Tina soon find themselves ready for sleep, while viewers are treated to a bit of foreshadowing of the terrors to come. In the May 8, 1984 screenplay draft, Rod "rolls over, practically snoring, and pulls another cover over his head. A dirty red and yellow cover." Adroit viewers will notice the action is retained, but the colors were transposed to the now-iconic red and green. Tina also pulls a cover—pale blue in color—over her head, unaware she would soon be entering the nightmare once again.

It happens when the young girl quickly wakes in the middle of the night to a rattling sound, and a voice which cruelly whispers her name. It was another of Craven's clever ways of playing with audience expectations for what was the waking world and what was the nightmare.

"It was brilliant the way Wes had written the story," says Doyle. "He starts giving you indications of what's real and what is not, and then twists those around on you and makes you very uncertain." This time, though, Tina was, indeed, dreaming.

Tragically, for the last time.

It would begin with a small moment that illustrated what the darker-than-black, evil Freddy Krueger could throw down. "As Tina wakes up," Wyss says, "I hear what I think are pebbles hitting my bedroom window, and it turns out to be a tooth, which is really just gross." Craven credited it as his "Roman Polanski moment," referring to a point in *The Tenant* (1976) when a character pulls a tooth out of the wall.

Unpleasant as the movie moment may have been, filming it was another story, with the actress finding she had to really focus so as not to give the scare away. "I'm standing at the window, and the cameraman and Wes are right there, and I know they're about to flick these pebbles at the glass," Wyss says. "And I kept flinching before anything happened. And Wes is just like, 'Yeah, you know, you can't do that. We're looking at the window, too.'"

The actress finally managed to recoil at the correct time, though it took Craven's reassuring hand on her shoulder the moment before they got the take they needed, telling her, "Just relax until it happens."

NOW I LAY ME DOWN TO SLEEP

Though Freddy was busy tormenting Tina in the dreamscape, his evil plan did not stop there. At the same time best friend Nancy was drifting off to sleep in another room, though she would not be alone. It was a moment that would visually display not just Krueger's transformational power in a memorable way, but also the ingenuity of the special effects craftsmen.

"The scene where I'm in bed at Tina's house, and the ceiling magically starts pushing out towards me in the shape of Freddy Krueger's face, I don't remember what the description read in the script," says Langenkamp, "but that was an example of Jim Doyle coming up with an incredibly original idea in the spur of the moment."

Such ideas were often necessary because the majority of the film's effects were done on set, in camera, and not in a computer. "One of the things was that we didn't have any digital technology. Everything we did was real," says Talalay. "Even if it was like Freddy putting his face through the wall, which was hard to figure out how to make it scary."

But they did, and the solution, when Burrows quickly inquired how they could possibly pull off the effect, was as simple back then as it was new. At least to some on *Elm Street.*

Spandex, a flexible synthetic fiber, was created in 1959 in DuPont's Washington laboratory, but gained popularity in the seventies and eighties. "It was kind of all the rage. Jane Fonda and everybody were all in love with spandex," Langenkamp says. "So Jim went to the fabric store, bought a bolt, and stretched it across the wall."

Painted gray to match the rest of the set and lit just right, it was Doyle who put Krueger's glove on, leaning on apple boxes to slowly push through as Freddy to terrify a sleeping Nancy. When the girl stirs awake, "We did the 'Cut!' and they put the real wall back in so I could knock on it," says Langenkamp.

Craven admitted that they weren't sure what it was going to ultimately look like, but as Doyle pressed against the fabric "we all went, 'Woah, that's really terrific!'"

Looking back, Englund appreciates the low-budget nature of the film and what they had to work with. "The face pushing through the wall beside the crucifix over Heather, I think that was about a dollar ninety-five effect," he says. Still, he was more than aware cast and crew wished there were additional funds, and, looking back, even a shot of CGI or two here and there throughout the film.

"It sounds so low-rent, but it was so effective," says Langenkamp. "And you could still do that effect today. Jim just pushed forward with his own face into the spandex and made that image. And it works."

The specter of Freddy Krueger pulsates along the wall above a sleeping Nancy. The effect, one of the film's most creative, was also one of its cheapest, utilizing spandex, apple crates, and effects man Doyle. "It sounds so low-rent, but it was so effective. And you could still do that effect today. Jim just pushed forward with his own face into the spandex and made that image. And it works," says Langenkamp.

Talalay sums up the budget-friendly, creative idea. "I think it is really the simplicity of that which makes it super effective," she says.

Langenkamp adds, "It was just Jim's imagination coming up with that idea."

"These were effects where you really had to start getting creative," Carlucci says, relating they were asking themselves, "How am I gonna do this practically? It's never been done before." Back in 1984, without the benefit of digital technology, he continues, "Nobody on the team was thinking, 'Maybe we can have the computer help us a little.'"

The notion of Krueger invading what would seem to be reality was something Craven thought a lot about, explaining that dreams are elastic, allowing one to float, fly, or fall. Taking the concept further, he says that what is happening to the character on the screen depends on their level of consciousness.

"So if you are awake Freddy can't get you, because Freddy represents the thing that can only get you when you're asleep. However, if you're fighting sleep and are half-asleep and half-awake, then he can impinge on your world," Craven says, offering that Freddy pushing through the wall in an effort to get Nancy "makes perfect sense because she was half-asleep and half-awake."

In the screenplay dated April 30, 1984, Freddy's presence was ultimately more corporeal, with Craven having Nancy "touching her hair and feeling the plaster dust." Nancy and the audience would also have noticed that the wall did not (as in the finished film) go back to its original shape, unaffected by Krueger's invasion. Instead, she would see that "there are three parallel cuts in the plaster there. About eight inches long. As if cut by sharp knives. Nothing else."

In the final cut, Nancy simply knocks on the solid wall to reassure herself it was, after all, just another dream.

THE LONG ARM(S) OF FREDDY'S LAW

With Nancy more fully awake for the moment, Krueger kept his attention on a frightened, dreaming Tina, who finds herself wandering through a darkened alley. "We shot that in the middle of the night in Venice," Wyss says. "It was freezing, but I just remember thinking, 'This is so cool. This is my chance to fight Freddy,' which I eventually do," she says.

The confrontation would begin when Tina faces her tormentor in the alley. If the effects team had one of their first successes with spandex and ingenuity, they were about to come across an idea in the script that wouldn't run quite so smoothly. Although a plan was in place for how the film's next gag could be done, not everyone was sure it would play.

"The extending arms didn't work at all," reveals Talalay.

Referring to the moment when Freddy demonstrates to Tina his inhuman reach, cinematographer Haitkin recalls his trepidation. "Slinky arms, I call them. I'll never forget that night because when I first saw how the effect looked, I was a little concerned that it was gonna look too fakey, too cheesy, not scary enough, and not be usable."

Once again, Doyle figured a way to make the effect of Freddy's impossibly long arms happen. "That was all simple marionetting. There were two guys on garage roofs who have long versions of fishing poles, and each fishing pole has two wires to each arm, and as you work the fishing pole you can get the arm to extend out," he states. "So they not only unfold, the forearms stretched."

At least one person was vocal about how he thought the effect was going, even with a plan of action at the ready.

"It looked ridiculous," admits Haitkin.

Doyle points out that he probably had good reason to feel that way. "Not only did he have two wires in frame in a backlit scene—so everything is glowing and we're trying to knock the brightness off the wires—he's also got two fishing poles overhead that are making walking shadows," he recalls.

Whether it was the zeitgeist of low-budget moviemaking, or just the general pallor among the crew that what could be a truly frightening image just isn't coming together, Talalay says, "The thing I remember most was how depressed Wes was and how angry Jacques was. It was just one of those moments where everything is shit and there's just no way this is going to work."

The man in the shot, Englund, also remembers the moment and its difficulties, in addition to his director's choice in vehicles. "I had to get ready for the scene, and it took them so long to rig that moment. I think Wes had an old XK-E Jaguar and I kept looking at Wes' really cool car."

While the actor spent time waxing over the automobile, the crew involved was working to prepare the shot. In addition to the aforementioned issues with fishing poles and monofilament, Englund recalls another complication, which turned into a slight frustration. "It was really difficult for the guys on the roof because they had to kind of walk with me and keep the arms at the same height," he says. "That was the big trick, to get the speed of my walk together with them walking alongside."

They also had the tough task of coordinating the height of the arms, ensuring that they wouldn't sag too low. "I remember I couldn't walk the way I liked Freddy to move," says Englund. "I think that Wes had me run on one of them, or do a little kind of jogging step. It wasn't really the way I felt Freddy would move. I remember never being quite happy with that."

There was, however, one aspect of the low-budget moment that Englund recalls fondly. "I think for some insert shots they actually used caps from old cowboy cap guns to get the sparks when the claws drag along the wall," he says. "I remember that because it seemed kind of surreal to me, using the technology from toy cowboy guns. That was a sort of a Marcel Proust flash for my childhood, and here I am in Venice, California at two in the morning, in all this makeup, trying to hold these extend-arms out as much as I can to support them."

Craven also revealed another way the crew created the sparking effect. "It was just a car battery hooked up to the glove, and there was some sort of plate on the wall that just made sparks."

Haitkin still remembers the scene in general as a particular challenge. "It's all done in camera. It's one take. You either get it or you don't," he says. And everybody turns to me and says, 'Did we get it? Does it look good?'"

Eventually, they completed the shot.

"It was a very complicated gag to achieve, and took quite a while to make it work, but it is a really memorable effect," states Carlucci.

It was concluded that the best option, and what made the final film, was to show Freddy and his arms in silhouette. It was more a cost-measuring decision than anything technical, as painting out the wires frame-by-frame if they were visible in direct light would be too expensive.

"The fun of this movie was that Wes had written this wacky stuff, and it was our job to figure out how to illustrate it, and turn it into pictures," Haitkin says.

Crediting a great team, Talalay also gives accolades to the director for turning a difficult effect into a winner. "The extending arms didn't work at all. And yet Wes managed it. You can imagine what the image was in the script, and what we got," she says, "was fishing poles

A look at one of the many times the effect for Freddy's extending arms did not go as planned (left); The full effect of Freddy's limitless reach, a moment many worried might not work, but what ultimately became one of the film's most memorable images.

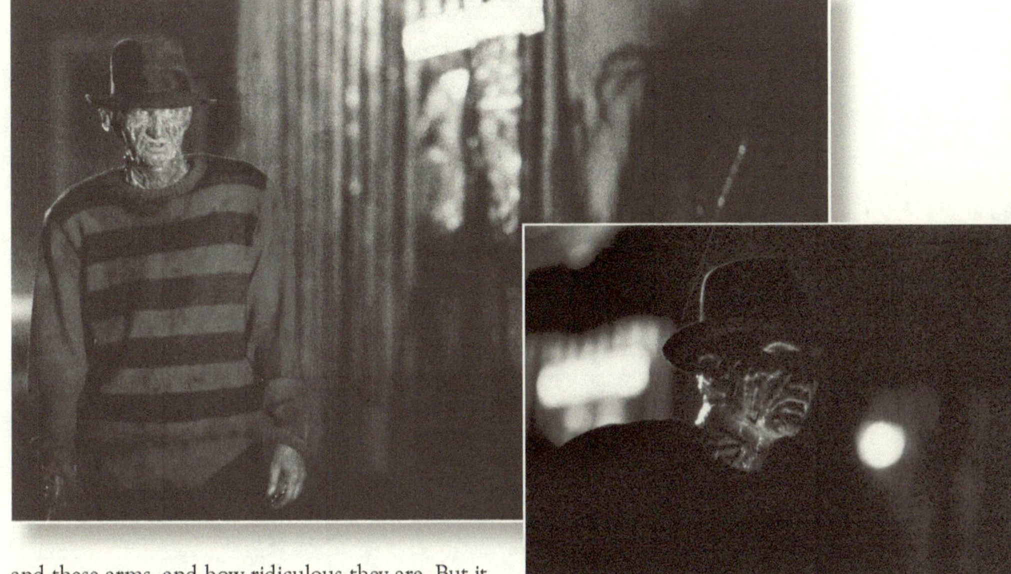

Englund, in full character, waits for "Action!" so he can begin terrorizing Tina in her nightmare. The man behind Freddy still believes that Tina's demise is "pretty brutal stuff."

and these arms, and how ridiculous they are. But it actually works brilliantly. That's a credit to Wes for making it work on set on the day."

With the general consensus being that a difficult effect ultimately worked, looking back, Doyle still isn't entirely convinced. "I don't like that shot. I wish we could have spent more time with it and got it smoother," he says. He does add, however, "But it's many people's favorite and it works for them. It scares everybody, I think."

Indeed, with Craven having remarked, "So many people tell me it's one of the scariest moments."

A GLIMPSE OF EVIL

As Freddy's arms stretched and his gloved hand scraped and sparked, Tina would stare in disbelief at her dream world attacker. It would be the first time moviegoers would get a somewhat prolonged, close-up view of Krueger, leading to discussions about just how much Freddy should come out of the shadows.

It was a conversation that started earlier in pre-production due to Miller's excellent makeup work on Englund. Craven was so impressed he had originally intended to shoot Freddy in brighter light to highlight the look of the character. However, Miller felt otherwise, suggesting to Craven, who agreed, that he keep Freddy further in the shadows.

"Because the appliances on the makeup were so thick, it just made some really interesting shadows," Miller remembers. "It was just more mysterious looking and, if it's in the dark, it leaves more up to the imagination."

That was an aspect Fleetwood understood and appreciated about Craven's style. "I love the way Wes shoots, because he doesn't put it all out there," she says. "He leaves some imagination space for you when he films. It was like he didn't have to show the monster a hundred times for you to be afraid."

DOYLE ENTERPRISES, INC. - THEATRICAL ENGINES
SPECIAL EFFECTS BREAKDOWN — BY FX#, SC#, ST#,

PROD NIGHTMARE ON ELM STREET FOR KATJA M.P.C. / W. Craven as of 5/5/84

DOC# #84-009 PREP DATE 5/15/84 SCRIPT DATE 4/30/84 PAGE 1 OF 3

FX#	PG#	SC#	ST#	DAY#	GAG	LOC/ST.	SETTING D/N	INT/EXT	Ø	NOTES	
1	1	1A			Boiler room-----Talon montage (pipe tunnel in B.R.)	L	Boiler room	I		Establish & maintain atmosphere Shoot assembly o. Talons	XXX
2	1	1a			Hand slashes dark canvas	L	" "	I	Ø	Optical element + FX #3	XXX
3	1	1			Wide over S.F. Valley--Greenish light	L	2nd unit	E	Ø	Op. El. + cloud element(see end notes, last page)	XXX
4	2	2			Lamb	L	Boiler room	I		Live Lamb (temporarily, at least)	
5	1a	3			Saliva-Tina	L	" "	I		Methyl Cellulose-3mm pipette	
6	1a	3			Blades rip thick fabric	L	" "	I		Assist props as nesc.	
7	1a	3			Dry yellow dust - Tina	L	" "	I		(in camera optical)	XXX
8	3	6			(kids jumprope)	L	High School	E		(assist as nesc.)	
9	5	8			"Sky strangely clouded"	L	Tina House	E	Ø	Op. El. + cloud element	XXX
10	7	9			Gas fireplace	L	" "	I		(type T.B.D.)	
11	13	14			Tina & Rod -"blanket creeps"	S	Tina's mom's room	I		ROTATING ROOM mono rig	
12	13	15			Nancy-Wall bulges, plaster, etc.	S	Tina's room	I		Spandex wall, plaster insert (UV for "glow")	XXX
13	14	17-22			Pebbles on window	S & L	Tina's Mom's room	I & E		Series of views-pebbles hit win.	
14	15	23			(pebble breaks window) Pebble imbeds in window, actually cow tooth	S	"	I		Lock-off-Tina's P.O.V...Replace glass	XXX
15	16	26			Talons on wall - sparks	L	Alley-Tina	E	Ø ?	Minor pyro, (St. Elmo's fire?)	XXX
16	16	26			Arms elongate	L	" "	E		Pneumatic & Elect.--Fishpole art.	XXX
17	16	28			Krueger fr. behind tree	L	Tina's frnt. Yard	E		In camera optical- black drapes	XXX
18	17	30			Rod first sees struggle-under covers	S	Tina's mom's bedroom	I		Rig bed w. space at foot	XXX
18a	17	30a			" sees struggle-his P.O.V. looking under	(S)	(" ")	I		Insert corner	XXX
19	17	30a			Tina - "awful jolt"	S	" "	I		Assist as nesc.	XXX
20	18	30a			Tina lifted & thrown at Rod, smashing into lamp	S	" "	I		B/W lamp-Rod & Tina stunt-Sparks R. Room 90° out-fly rig	XXX
21	18	31			"Blue Flashes"- electrical gag	S	" "	I		T. Coil--100KV power supply-- 110VDC, 400A arc supply (TBD)	XXX
22	"	31			Tina dragged up wall	S	" "	I		Rot. Room moving--Rod secure	XXX
23	"	31			Tina P.O.V. - Forced perspective wall	(S)	(" ")	I		Insert Corner (DOLLY OR STEDI C)	(XXX)
22a	"	31			Inverted swag (chain) lamp	S	" "	I		Rig lamp on spring wire-sparks R. ROOM 180° out	XXX
"b	"	31			Furrows from fingernails	S	" "	I		Pre-set ceiling	XXXX
"c	"	31			Tina-dies, flops loose	S	" "	I		Rig actress on ceiling for death	XXX
"d	"	31			" falls into bed, blood splats	S	" "	I		Stunt rig to ceiling, drop on cue, rig bed w. blood	XXX
24	18a	33			Glen breaks in door	S	Tina's M's B.R.-Hall	I		Door rig, slick floor	
////	19	35			Broken window, Rod gone	S	Tina's Mom's B. Room	I		Provide "broken" window	
////	23	39a			(Video sync) Newscast	S	Nancy's Kit.	I		Assist as nesc.	
25	27	45			Body Bag-from classroom	L	High school	I		Assist--Classroom atmos.	
26	27a	50			" " -Hand, slides out of scene	L	" "	I		Rig occupant-pull off camera	
27	28	53			" " -fall down stairs	L	" "	I		Stunt	
28	29	55			Boiler room----See FX #1	L	Boilerroom	I		Atmosphere	
29	29	58			(Pipe tunnel) Boilerroom	L	" "	I		"Hot pipe"	
30	29	58			" " " Nancy burn's arm	L	" "	I		"Burn Nancy's arm"	
31	35	68			Nancy in bathtub	S	Bathroom	I		Warm water, "soapy water"	
					END / MORE					END / MORE	

A page from the special effects breakdown created by Jim Doyle. The document illustrates moments in the film requiring effects: the script page, scene number, description, and what Doyle and his team needed to do in order for the nightmares to come to life.

Haitkin, always keeping an eye on making the film look simultaneously good and creepy, did not disagree. "The cinematographer always wants it darker, and the producers always want it brighter so everyone can see," he says. The decision to keep things dark was utilized because "they knew the value of the film was to scare people."

SHE DREAMT THIS WOULD HAPPEN

Those scares would continue as Freddy raises his gleaming, taloned glove, announcing to a terrified Tina, "This is God!" before chasing after her. It was actually a moment that left many a viewer remarking that Freddy appeared rather diminutive in his pursuit. The sentiment is not lost on Craven, admitting that Englund's stand-in for that shot "looked about four feet tall. It was the only guy we could get!" he stated.

Craven also revealed that the original chase was much more extensive, "going all the way around the block and then would come back through another house and everything else," but admitted they were never able to shoot it that way. The script dated April 30, 1984 reveals Tina does make her way to another home, pounding on the windows only to see "ashen faces appear, recoil, pull curtains closed and disappear in fright." Going further, the only response to Tina's pleas is for all the front porch lights to be turned out.

A continuity photo for a scene which never made the final film: when Tina, still in her nightmare, races to other houses for help and is only given strange looks by people with ashen faces.

"I remember thinking when I read the script that that was amazing," Wyss says. And even with the finished version, the first real glimpse of Freddy Krueger imparted terror. "I did a lot of running and screaming that night in the alley."

Her character would find no help in the nightmare despite how much she screamed, but in the real world that wasn't exactly the case. "The neighbors in the nearby area had been told that we were filming there, but people a block away didn't know and they called the police," Wyss states.

Rusoff remembers the offscreen dramatics as well. "It was going late at night and there was some complaining," she states.

Burrows also recalls, "The neighborhood was very upset at us. There weren't too many films going around on the streets in those days. Then they became interested in the picture when they saw shooting at night, and when Freddy was out walking around. 'Oh, look at him! There he is, there he is!'"

Interest in moviemaking or Freddy notwithstanding, some none-too-happy people in the area did have a slight impact on filming. "Some residents might have had something to do with the shooting schedule changing slightly, where they were only allowed to shoot for a few hours once it got dark," Rusoff recalls. "And then I think they had to put a notice up in the surrounding area. Something about that they're filming a horror movie and there would be screaming."

Wyss clearly recalls the irony that, although she was screaming for help, people "only complained about the noise, not that someone might be in trouble. I mean, it was the eighties, so who knows," she muses.

PEEK-A-BOO!

A helpless victim is exactly what Freddy relished, and in this major sequence Krueger continued to play with Tina, making sure she was terrified even as he toyed with her. It gave Freddy a chance to demonstrate the seemingly limitless possibilities in which he could frighten those he was after, but also a chance for Craven and his craftsmen to display their inventiveness in bringing nightmares to life.

"We didn't have money for opticals on the film, but we wanted to have one little gag where Freddy could jump out from behind a tree that's too small for a guy to hide behind," recalls Doyle. "So instead of going the optical direction, we went to the old beam splitter direction."

That necessitated working with a company in Burbank, California that made specialized mirrors big enough that would exactly match the shape of the tree. "The tree is there, but he's really at right angles to the camera," reveals Craven.

Doyle also remembers that the effect was simple enough to complete while other scenes were being shot inside the house. "We brought Freddy out, got him lit and all he had to do was this one move and you had it. It was a ten-minute shot, a simple trick with mirrors: Freddy is on one side, the beam splitter another, and the real tree yet another. And everything in Freddy's frame is just blacked out, except that line of the tree," he says. "It really was just a mirror gag. It was really easy to do."

Also relatively easy and effective were the two moments that followed, both impressive displays of the games in Krueger's twisted mind. Jumping from behind the impossibly slim tree, the monster calls to Tina and beckons her to "Watch this." When she does, she is treated to Freddy performing an act of self-mutilation as he slices off two of his own fingers, which spit out an unnatural fluid.

"It was just a fake hand and arm up to the elbow of Robert," reveals Miller. "It had tubes running up inside the fingers and it was all pre-cut, and we just barely packed the fingers back on."

As for the "blood," "Wes wanted the stuff coming out of his fingers to be glowing. So I thought, 'Okay, what can I use?' and I thought of glow sticks, the kind that you break and you shake them up," Miller says. "So we did a bunch of those and put them into a syringe, and as soon as he cut his fingers off, or pretended to cut his fingers off, we pumped the glow stuff out. That was the early pre-CG version of glowing blood."

It's a moment that showcased Freddy as diabolical, proving that if he could do that to himself, just what terrible things would he do to Tina? "We had to do that a

The skull cast and sculpt that would be the basis of Krueger's face tearing off; Miller and his team prepare the fake torso for filming; A final touch up to the bloody skull underneath the removable face; Preparing to rip away the horror; The final look of a faceless Freddy. The sequence was another terrifying and effective nightmare moment, courtesy of the makeup effects team (and plenty of KY Jelly).

lot of times," says Englund. "It's a practical effect and it seems very rudimentary and primitive now. They had a hydraulic for the fingers running down my arm, underneath the sweater, and wrapped around my groin and down my leg. So just outside of the frame of that shot there's a couple of effects guys pumping that green shit."

"The moment is effective," says Doyle. "It's another one that really got to people."

Horrified, Tina tries to race away, but cannot get inside her house, instead winding up with Krueger on top of her. Putting her hand up to his face to block out the horror, she quickly finds herself tearing the monster's visage right off.

"That was pretty interesting. We had to keep reapplying that face, and Wes wanted it a certain way and he got it," remembers Lazzara.

"That was a puppet head of Robert," says Miller. "We basically took one of his lifecasts, cast it in clay, and sculpted down from that and put a skull face on there. It was a bit of a process, and we made a little thin membrane with Freddy's face to go over that. And instead of gluing it down as she's ripping it off, we just packed it on with a lot of KY Jelly because it had to smear off really easy."

Slicing off Freddy's finger and tearing off his face were both moments thought up by Craven to demonstrate the dark, evil humor that Krueger could exhibit, and which Englund was able to bring forth so effectively.

"I had written some of the scares and lines in a way that was deeply ironic and almost comic," admits Craven. "And Robert was able to do it just right, in almost a funny way."

"At least half the people who watch the film are frightened of Freddy, and at least another half cheer him on in a sort of nihilistic way. It's a personality," Englund offers.

TINA, WE HARDLY KNEW YOU

"The neat thing about my character, I thought, was that she appeared to be a little bit of a red herring," states Wyss. "You almost think Tina's going to be the heroine at the beginning, in a way. It's a little bit of a nod to Hitchcock, I think. And I found that interesting and fun."

It was her character's death scene that inspired the talk of homage to the master of suspense. Like Marion Crane's demise in *Psycho*, Tina's violent murder was a catalyst that propelled the other characters into action. Wyss sees some similarities between her portrayal and that of the Janet Leigh character, but there is one area in which she knows Leigh ruled.

"Sometimes when I see our movie I'm like, 'What was I thinking with my hair?' It looks a little more Geraldine Ferraro than Janet Leigh, but what can you do?" Wyss jokingly asks.

It was not something she'd have to worry about for long, as Tina would see her young life come to an end a mere eighteen minutes into the film. "That's the real nod to Hitchcock. My death so early on, and I believe audiences were shocked not only that, 'Oh, I thought she was gonna be in the whole film,' but that Tina was taken out with such extreme force," Wyss says.

The actress was also aware of the genre undertones (some might say clichés) that permeate many viewers' minds when watching the film. "There's the simple, direct way where people would say, 'Tina was having sex, so she had to die,' because that's part of a morality tale," Wyss states.

Thinking more deeply about the character, Wyss decided early on that sex doesn't have to equal death, or be the reason she succumbed to Freddy's blades. "I think Tina was living in a home where her mom was drinking and there was just not that much value on life. She simply looked for ways to escape the life that she had," says the actress. "Whereas I think people pictured Nancy as the girl that got straight A's in school, and she did what was in front of her, and she did it well. But I don't think Tina was as much of a survivor. I just don't think she had the tools to fight the force of Freddy."

Langenkamp takes the notion a step further with her own character, and the realization of what Nancy can, and cannot, do. "I could not solve Tina's problems.

And I do think that as hard as Nancy tries, the only one she can save is herself," the actress states. "And I think that's actually kind of a very tragic part of Nancy's character is that she tries, but she just isn't that successful."

TURN, TURN, TURN

"Okay, so everybody wants to know about the death scene," says Wyss, forming a sly smile that proves she knows it was one of the most interesting and iconic events in the film—if not in recent genre history.

"It was filmed at the studio and they had built a revolving room, like basically a box on a spit or a rotisserie, based on an old Fred Astaire movie," Wyss reveals.

The death of Tina in the now-famous revolving room would begin with the script of course, but also with conversations between Doyle and Craven. "Jacques had already been hired, and Greg Fonseca had been hired, and we had begun to work with Wes on the specific dream sequences," Doyle says.

"I remember at the reading, everybody was describing how they were gonna do things. And people were dumbfounded about how they could possibly do what they say they're gonna do," remembers Risher. "Like the way to have the person walk on the ceiling was to turn the whole room around. Of course, we had no idea how to do that, but Bob had a determination to make things work. Even if we didn't have the money to do it right, he would make sure they could find a way to do it anyway."

The suggestion for turning the room around, as well as the way to implement it, came from Doyle. "Wes being a classical writing professor, and with my background in theater, we talked about the structure of the script," he says, revealing that Craven clued him in to the idea that you must hook the audience by the first reel, or you might lose them. "And this first killing happened at the end of the first reel. Wes told me, 'This has got to be the one. This thing has got to be so big and so broad, and so out there, and so strange that the viewer is really going to be taken in, and that we're going to be able to keep them.'"

The writer and director revealed that the sequence of events was crafted as a slow build that ultimately "goes from bad to worse. It just gives the audience absolutely no relief," says Craven. "You wake up, think you're safe, and then it still gets worse."

Since Craven wanted something big and fantastic for Tina's death, Doyle ultimately suggested they do the rotating room where, he said, "We could disconnect the reality by doing that, and so we did."

As Craven points out, "What are the bulwarks of consciousness, the rocks of Gibraltar we depend on? If you punch a wall, it will hurt. Gravity is pinning your feet at the ground. Night is night and day is day. I realized in dreams none of that is true. When Freddy strikes, gravity would be abrogated."

And the notion of dragging a semi-conscious, bloody teenage girl up a wall and over the ceiling? "People found that very upsetting," Craven says, "because it violated the basic rule that you can't go up the wall and over the ceiling without something holding you or being on a ladder."

To complete what would be a fairly large undertaking on a small budget, Doyle called in more than a few favors to complete the project, but a major component of its creation was Belardinelli.

"Jim Doyle had explained it, and he had a model showing us what exactly we were building. So the concept was there and then he explained to us what scenes it would work for, with the girl walking up the walls, walking across the ceiling," explains Belardinelli. "We started building that room at the USC theater shop, where Jim Doyle had gone to school and knew some people. So we did some preliminary cutting and welding with the steel. I pretty much did every nut and bolt in that room. And that was a lot of work."

Carlucci remembers the difficulties in creating the set piece, but also its rewards. "The rotating room was probably the coolest thing we've done, I feel. Jim was an excellent mechanical engineer and designed it in a way to be perfectly balanced before anything was put in it."

It was an important point as once the set was dressed with the required elements, the effects team would go in and counterbalance the room so each wall would be equal in weight.

"The room would be sitting on these massive bearings, but since everything was balanced, it would take a couple of people to just turn that room and actually make it move without using any mechanical means, heavy duty hydraulics or some other ways of turning it," Carlucci reveals.

Haitkin recalls the genius of the design as well. "Because the thing was perfectly weighted, even though it had so much mass, it could be turned by hand," he says. "And it was safe that way. You didn't have to worry about a machine. If somebody went 'Hold it! Hold it!' we could just stop it."

Belardinelli certainly recalls the moment the fruits of his and the others' labor would be tested. "I had worked days and weeks on that rotating room," he says, "and the very first time we finished it and had it all erected, Jim Doyle, with just one hand, took that thing and spun it. And it just spun around freely by itself. I looked at it and said, 'Wow, we did it.'"

It was a design that was great for an independent film trying to break new ground. "It was brilliant," says Risher. "He then used it for many commercials and things afterwards. I hope it made his money back, because we paid him very little."

Doyle admits that he absorbed much of the cost of what was a thirty-thousand-dollar effect on an effects budget of about fifty thousand. "In return, I rented it out four or five times after that."

In fact, in addition to commercials, the room would reap rewards in at least one other feature.

"We did use it again in a film called *Breakin' 2: Electric Boogaloo* (1984), and it worked out very well," Carlucci says. "We were very excited about that room."

The mechanics of the room were certainly exciting to some, but the idea of its use proved to be somewhat problematic for the team whose job it was to get the illusion on film. The logistical ease was enjoyed by the effects team, but Haitkin acknowledges, "The most difficult scene for me was the rotating room," he says. "First off, because a lot of the lighting in that scene is coming from outside, the lighting had to be suspended on armatures outside and on the room itself."

Craven also had the worry of what could have gone wrong with that setup. "All the lights that were attached had to perfectly rotate with the room and, more importantly, not fall apart when it was upside down," he says. That didn't happen, thankfully, but Craven pointed out another obvious issue. "It had to rotate in a way that, obviously, you couldn't see any curtains or anything move. Nothing could move."

"Everything in that room was a total challenge in making it not move while that room is turning," Carlucci says. "We were always getting creative with, 'Okay, now what can we do?'"

The idea was to add items that would throw audiences off so they just couldn't tell the room was moving. "The entire rig was just monumental. It was an incredible amount of work," recalls Rideout, who found herself in the position of figuring out the best way to make sure nothing in that room would budge. "I don't even know how many hours I spent in that room gluing down every single tchotchke, and lid, and hairbrush, and stiffening the fabrics."

Huntley remembers that all of her set dressings were, indeed, starched, stapled, or glued to the walls. "Nothing moved and it all appeared to be the correct way," she says. "That was a lot of

A glimpse of the crew rigging lights on the full-size rotating room. "Jim Doyle had explained it and he had a model showing us what exactly we were building. So the concept was there and then he explained to us what would it work for," explains Belardinelli; A view of the rotating room's outer shell construction.

work because all the curtains have to look like they're hanging naturally and all that kind of stuff."

The latter was another bit of inspiration and learning for the crew, when Doyle inquired what would be best to keep all the fabric in the room stationary when the room was turned.

Rideout had the answer. "I said, 'Well, spray starch would be the obvious answer, but Aqua Net is the better one,'" she states.

Super Hold Aqua Net, to be exact.

According to Rideout, "I remember going through cases of Aqua Net, and I had hot glue and hot glue burns all over my hands and forearms for, I don't know, a week, probably."

"All the set dressing crew were stapling and hot gluing every object in the room," recalls Diers. "And at that time I did think, 'This is a pretty spectacular kind of gag for a film like this.'"

Corri, whose character also failed to save Tina, adds, "To me, it was an amazing piece of art that they had everything locked down."

Just when Rideout thought she was in the clear, another matter was raised, one in which she would, quite literally, take center stage. "We had to then actually turn the room with someone in it, and it was a huge deal. I remember it well because I was the one who tested it!" she says.

Rideout was the first "live body" in the room, tasked with making sure that an actor would survive its turning. It was a memory that stays with her.

"The camera rigs were all locked into place and everything. They were watching me on the monitors, hoping that I wouldn't break any bones," she recalls. After the successful experiment (one that she called "a trip"), Rideout also tested all of the flying rigs, which were built on her body since she, like Wyss, was a smaller woman. "They were actually built on my body and I was able to coach Amanda on what she needed to do in order to get through her stunt."

YOU COULD JUST SEE THE CUTS HAPPENING

Before any on-camera stunts and falls were needed, there was the tearing apart of Tina by an unseen, clawed hand. It was an effect that sticks in the minds of many viewers, as four, deep gashes simultaneously appear and slice Tina's chest open.

"When I saw that Tina would be dragged up onto the ceiling and slashed with the finger knives, I just didn't have an image in my head," Langenkamp recalls. "But I was really interested in how it was done."

Because there would be no visible knives or blades, the effect proved an interesting challenge for makeup man Miller. "I had to make a torso of her using a urethane material, which looks like skin, and I sculpted four slits in it. Already pre-made, pre-slashed," he says.

The next step was to create the effect of the slashing-in-progress, achieved through monofilament covered in latex and embedded in the slits, which were then shielded with morticians wax. After filling it in, Miller put final makeup on the appliances so they looked like they weren't there at all.

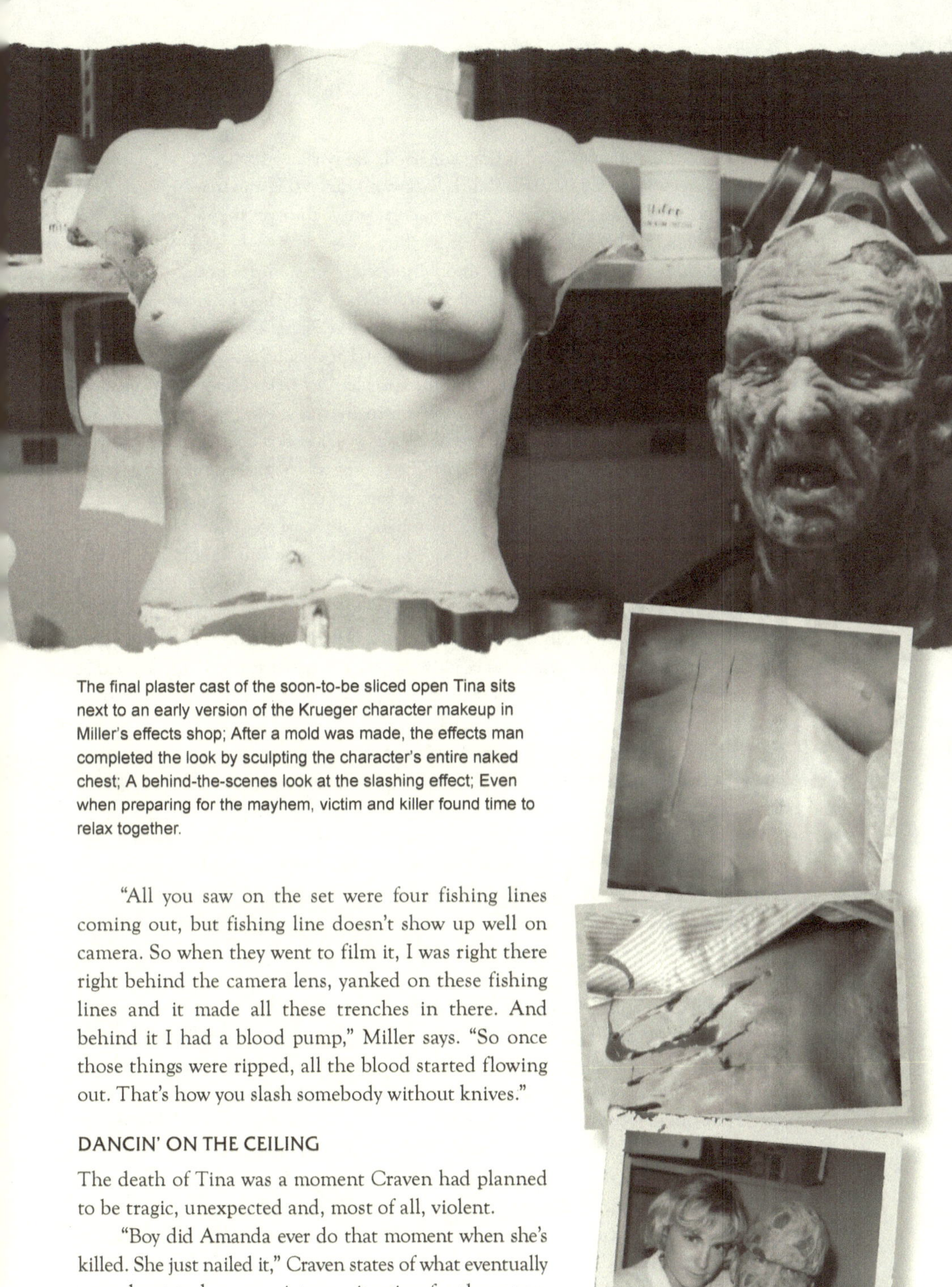

The final plaster cast of the soon-to-be sliced open Tina sits next to an early version of the Krueger character makeup in Miller's effects shop; After a mold was made, the effects man completed the look by sculpting the character's entire naked chest; A behind-the-scenes look at the slashing effect; Even when preparing for the mayhem, victim and killer found time to relax together.

"All you saw on the set were four fishing lines coming out, but fishing line doesn't show up well on camera. So when they went to film it, I was right there right behind the camera lens, yanked on these fishing lines and it made all these trenches in there. And behind it I had a blood pump," Miller says. "So once those things were ripped, all the blood started flowing out. That's how you slash somebody without knives."

DANCIN' ON THE CEILING

The death of Tina was a moment Craven had planned to be tragic, unexpected and, most of all, violent.

"Boy did Amanda ever do that moment when she's killed. She just nailed it," Craven states of what eventually turned out to be a very intense situation for the actress and, subsequently, himself. "When she's dragged up the wall, there were no wires or anything dragging her. It was when we finally rotated the entire set with her in it. So she was actually sliding backwards down this wall that appeared to be going up and across the ceiling piece. And it was extremely disorienting."

So much so that Wyss found herself battling a case of vertigo, standing up at the end of take after take barely able to move. "I just completely flipped out," she admits, "and was like, 'Stop! I have to get out! I have to get out!' And then here comes Wes, all calm, sticking his head up through the window, he's like, 'Check this out. I'm standing on the ground. You're laying right here. We're looking at each other, you're not falling.'"

It wasn't just Craven who remembered the episode. "Amanda was totally freaked out about doing that scene because it was so visually convincing that she was really on the ceiling, even though she was on all fours," Cook states. "She was terrified of raising her hand up because she was afraid that she would fall, even though she was on the level ground."

Craven did his best to reassure Wyss, but the actress concedes that she simply could not wrap her mind around the concept. "Through that whole scene I was like, 'Oh my God!' Every time we'd start again I was like, 'I'm falling! Everything's gonna fall on me. The camera's going to kill me!'" she says. "I don't know, but I was always on the floor. As the room rotated I was either crawling or being dragged, but I completely flipped out."

Getting out of the room was no small challenge for her, either, recalls Cecere. "Amanda was completely baffled and couldn't figure out how to get out of the set. She couldn't realize, all of a sudden, the whole room was upside down," he says. "So we actually had to step in on the set and help her out."

The offscreen dramatics were remembered well by Craven. "I literally had to come into the set and stand next to her and say, 'Okay, this is up. Just go through the door and you'll be okay.'"

But even the writer and director fell victim to a job well done by his effects team. "As soon as she was out of the set, she was okay. But as I looked around, thinking I was going to reassure her, I started to feel nauseous," he disclosed. "It was a very, very strange set."

Englund, who was not a party to the mechanics of the room while attacking Wyss' character in the final edit of the film, does recall the dynamics and power of the scene. "It's pretty brutal stuff and it really holds up," he says. "The blood and her being dragged up the walls and down the walls, it's like that Fred Astaire number only taken to a hellacious place."

The actor also understands the subtle sexuality of the scene, something Craven did not hammer home like other teenaged-themed horror films of the eighties, instead deciding to keep it as dark subtext. "You don't have to draw that much attention to [the sexuality] because Freddy's in those teenage girls' bedrooms. He's in their bed with them. He's in their dreams with them, in their nighties, under the sheets, in that drawer with their private diary," expresses Englund. "And so I think that in and of itself is one of the great hooks, that Freddy is violating that private place. Even more private than genitalia, you know?"

Englund feels the death of Tina is special for more than any unspoken meaning or its raw brutality and power, but for its technical merits as well. He notes that the scene was "really wonderful and kind of expressionistically lit. Jacques and Wes did such a great thing on that."

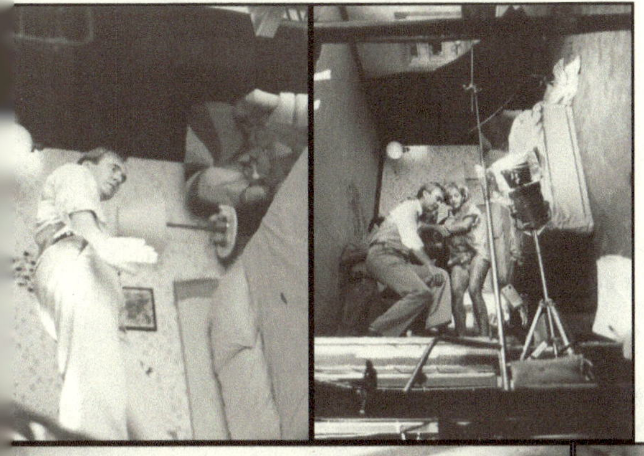

Clockwise from top left: The writer and director patiently surveys the surroundings of the rotating room; Craven works to reassure Wyss in the turned-on-its-side set, even though he, too, succumbed to the effect; Tina reaches out for help as she is dragged across the ceiling. The moment was difficult for Wyss, as she was afraid raising her arm up would cause her to fall; Technicians prepare the rigging that will allow the illusion of Tina (a stuntwoman in this case) to fall from the ceiling onto the bed.

While Haitkin would appreciate the compliment on the work, he remembers the work itself as less than easy to accomplish. "As you get turned upside down, you're still operating the camera, but your brain is upside down and you're not used to it. So everything is opposite. And it's spinning around. It's crazy," he says. "Dealing with all the lighting, the camera operating, the problems of it, I would say that was one of the most difficult effects for me."

Difficult, yes, but ultimately satisfying for both the crew and the audience.

Langenkamp has memories of watching the moment unfold, this time from behind the scenes. "We were all watching it go around and around. It was like watching a ride at Disneyland, because everyone was strapped in, and it took a couple of hours to get it all lit and safely secured," she says. "Just observing that process was really interesting."

Corri's memory of shooting the scene includes the shot where his character watches as a screaming Tina is dragged up the wall and across the ceiling, her bloodied arms

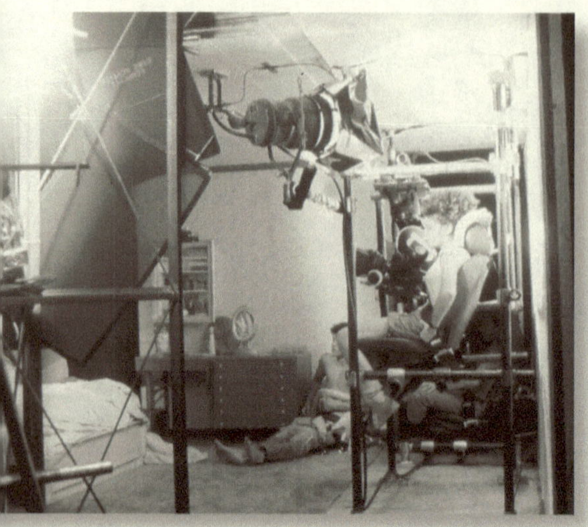

Behind the scenes in the rotating room used for Tina's death. Corri is strapped to the floor for his moment, and the rigging and jump seats used to keep the cameras and their operators stable can be seen.

reaching out for his. "Basically, I'm in the shot where I was upside down reaching for her and she's actually walking on the floor, which is the ceiling," he states.

It was not only powerful visually, but technically as well. Unlike how the effect was used in the musicals of Gene Kelly or Fred Astaire, or even the chilling scene in *Poltergeist* (1982) in which JoBeth Williams is pulled up her bedroom wall by an unseen force, Craven took his nightmare a step further by being the first to place two people in a rotating room, each on different surfaces.

"It's very disorienting because you start with that great shot of the boy seeing his lover up there, and she's wearing barely anything," says Englund. "And it's not sexual because she's so vulnerable up there on the ceiling being thrashed around by Freddy in her little nightgown. It's very disorienting."

Even down to the smallest details relating to Corri's character, Doyle elaborates on how they accomplished the effect. "We just tied him to the floor and turned the room and glued his hair down," he recalls. "The gold chain he had around his neck we glued to his chest so it wouldn't fly. Since he was nude from the waist up, we just put him in a waist harness."

Corri recalls, "I was like, 'Holy shit.' I was a kid, I was like, 'Let's do this.'" And they did, with the actor being "upside down with the camera over my shoulder. It was an amazing effect," he adds.

The excitement Corri remembers might not have come into play for the actor, had it not been for a conversation, and a few minutes of calming, with his hair stylist.

"Before we did the gimbal room where Tina goes up on the ceiling and stuff, Nick was really freaked out. I mean really freaked out," divulges Fleetwood. "As a hairdresser you become these people's private friend, and it was to the point where he wasn't going to do the shot. And I always thought that as a professional, you keep all the crap away from your director, if at all possible."

In order to help assuage the actor's anxiety, Fleetwood took Corri outside, where the two walked around the studio for several minutes. "It calmed him down so he would go in and do the shot," she says.

The shooting of the scene does hold some grim memories for the actor, even as he was backstage while other aspects were being filmed. "What I remember the most was that I was outside the room and there were these guys playing cards below while they were shooting," says Corri, "and the door was open to the rotating room, and when Amanda falls on the bed there are gallons of blood. I remember the stunt woman slammed onto the bed, blood slapped me on the face and it was eerie. It was creepy and I was ill."

A stuntwoman was used in place of Wyss for the moment when Tina falls from the ceiling onto the bed, and, Doyle says, "It was a dangerous stunt. It was still early in the schedule and we couldn't afford to lose [Amanda] at that point."

To keep the illusion as long as possible that it was, indeed, Wyss, the actress was used as the room spun around while she essentially crawled and dragged herself against and up the wall, eventually "landing" on the ceiling. Cecere remembers the switch from actress to stuntwoman. "When it was time for Tina to fall, we took the stunt girl and placed her up on the ceiling and had her cabled up against it," he says.

Langenkamp recalls watching those moments and the trepidation she had felt. "It was horrifying. It was the only scene I think I've ever been part of that was more frightening in real life. What if it falls off its hinges? What if somebody falls and lands on the ground? It seemed like so much could go wrong," she says.

Luckily for everyone involved, nothing did. With safety protocols in place, Cecere and his team would "at a given command, release the cable. The stunt lady then fell down, hit the bed and then bounced off," says the stuntman.

"It all worked perfectly," Langenkamp states.

And though she didn't take the fall, the final, bloody moment for Tina still sticks in Wyss' mind as a testament to the abilities of Craven and his crew. "In that scene, you can feel all the tension and the fear because I really was terrified," she says. "I just felt that the mechanics of that room, Wes' direction, and him being such a calming presence all worked together so brilliantly. It was such a shoestring budget and people's genius put that together."

WHAT WAS SHE DOING THERE?

The story now fully set into motion, the film next introduces Saxon's character, Lieutenant Thompson, working to get to the bottom of what had just happened, particularly because his daughter was at the scene of the crime.

Giving him the rundown of events is Sergeant Parker, played by Joseph Whipp. The actor, who would go on to play roles in several of Craven's later works (perhaps most notably as the Sheriff to David Arquette's Deputy Dewey in *Scream*), got the part after his first meeting with Craven.

"I knew just a little bit about him and this was the first time I'd ever met him. I went in, and it was somewhat informal, and we hit it off very well," Whipp says.

Receiving word he got the part came quickly. "There were no callbacks involved in this," states Whipp. "Evidently, they liked my audition enough to just give me the role. They just called me afterwards to confirm it."

"Joseph is someone who I met when he was cast in the Richard Brooks film *Wrong Is Right* (1982) when I was working as Karen Rea's casting assistant," says Benson. "He's a fabulous character actor and I was thrilled when he was hired to play Sergeant Parker."

Having a rapport with Benson, and the swiftness with which Whipp earned the role, was mirrored by actor Joe Unger (later to play in more than one genre film, including New Line Cinema's own *Leatherface: Texas Chainsaw Massacre III* [1990]), who would play the role of Sergeant Garcia. "I had worked with Annette Benson before and we had become friends, so she called me about it," says the actor.

"Joe was an actor who I always felt honored to cast," Benson states. "Throughout the years I was casting, if I had a role that he was right for, I would bring him in to read or, if I could, just offer him the part. He is interesting and a talented actor."

With the formality of meeting the casting director already taken care of, Unger found himself meeting Craven at the house location in West Hollywood. "I actually met him on the set, we chatted for a few minutes and he said, 'Good to go,'" Unger recalls. "Wes was such a down-to-earth guy. We just chatted and he asked me to do the role."

In the scene, Parker brings Thompson to the station, where we first see Garcia. "He was doing the same job he does every night with the same people he works with every night, so it was a matter of trying to create that world," Unger says. "I had gone and visited a desk sergeant at the LAPD in Hollywood, just to talk with him for a few moments and watch."

Saxon as Lieutenant Donald Thompson, distant father to Nancy, trying to figure out the murders surrounding his daughter.

Unger's character quickly ushers Parker and Thompson into the latter's office to see his distraught daughter, who sits stoically with her mother, Marge, also introduced to the audience for the first time. It was another moment for Craven to remind viewers that there was more to *Elm Street* than blood and guts: he had striven to develop real characters with real problems, on top of the horrific events they were already facing.

It was also one of the early days of filming for Whipp, who remembers meeting much of the cast that night. "It was the first day I was working. It was a long night, but it was a lot of fun," he says.

Part of that fun was his character getting a glimpse into the murky waters Craven was crafting for the Thompson family dynamic. Of Nancy's character, Langenkamp ponders, "Her parents have split up, and the only time I get the feeling that she sees her father is like maybe once a month if he has some free time. So when I get hauled into the police station, and see my dad under terrible circumstances, I think the fact that I didn't know John Saxon at all made that relationship a little bit colder, a little bit uncomfortable for Nancy."

The rapport between Saxon and Langenkamp was also interesting—at least from his point of view. "She was young, smart, and beautiful, which was hard to ignore. Because of that, I'll admit, it wasn't always easy to see her as my 'daughter,'" he gamely states.

On screen, Nancy's parents might have been the first divorced couple Craven had in one of his films. "It was kind of interesting because, by that time, I had gone through a divorce and my parents had divorced just before my father died," he says. "It was really a part of my life and person that I felt comfortable looking at." Divorce had also become so common at the time the film was made, "I felt that it was appropriate," he added.

Craven also observed it marked a division between the two adults where, if they had truly done what is eventually revealed they did do, that "a divorce is quite likely because of the stresses and strains."

Blakley, too, thought about the relationship between Marge and her ex-husband. "They were a divorced couple who obviously had some issues. Perhaps control issues? Perhaps dominance issues?" she asks understandingly. "I don't think Marge liked anyone to tell her what to do, and John's character was a very sensitive cop, and a very attractive cop, and also a classic male role model type."

I'M NOT GONNA HURT YOU!

"I think that there were some scary moments that were supposed to make you feel uneasy, especially about whether or not Nancy was safe," Langenkamp states, referring to the time her character walks to school and is being followed by someone unknown. "That guy was just meant to be seen in the background, and then you realize that she's been set up for a sting with Rod, to capture him. They figure that Rod will try to contact Nancy, which he does, and they catch him. That was Lieutenant Thompson's big, great idea."

Craven made sure to give just a taste of Nancy's possible paranoia with small, strange things and red herrings such as the man being there one moment, then gone the next. While there is just a vestige of the unease, his presence was deemed necessary by the actress. "Otherwise," offers Langenkamp, "they wouldn't have been able to really effectively capture Rod, which is really what they needed to do in the script, I think."

She continues to say that, before the capture, "When Rod grabs me as I'm walking to school the day after Tina's death, it's a funny scene. By that, I mean I didn't buy that Nancy scene at all," Langenkamp admits, more secure in revealing her feelings decades later, but remembering that she wasn't as seasoned or confident to talk to Craven about it then. "I wasn't brave enough to bring that up with Wes at the time, but if I had to do it again, I would have said, 'She knows that it's not him. She's not gonna ask him.'"

It was an important distinction Langenkamp wished she brought to the character. "She wants to help him, she doesn't wanna give him the third degree. So I didn't like those scenes very much," she confesses.

Corri agrees with the actress. "Oh, Nancy knew. And I think she had a hard time standing up to her dad," says the actor. "Her dad wants to get the criminal and she's saying, 'No, he didn't do it.'"

As for the logistics of shooting the scene (filmed on the street in Venice, California where Craven had lived at the time), while Langenkamp remembers the difficulty in standing up for what she thought might have played better for her character, Corri recalls the trouble he had in simply standing.

Or in this case, running.

"I was barefoot and everything hurt. I remember running back-and-forth," Corri says, admitting his decision to be more Method. "But it was really hard asphalt! And just going back-and-forth: running, running, running. I was just skinny as a rail. I was just trying to be an actor and this was my first big movie. And all this stuff I had learned from acting class, I was just going for it. And that's it."

Craven admitted that the actor was "shredding his bare feet," and afterward "we had to hospitalize him, practically," the director joked.

Langenkamp looks back at the scene and feels that her on-screen father might have been right when he asks what she was thinking by going to school the day after her best friend had been murdered. "He had a really good point," laughs the actress.

Ultimately, the sequence is telling as it furthers the story set into motion with Tina's death that someone, or something, is out to get them.

A SONNET TO DIE FOR

Nancy may have had an uncomfortable interrogation with her parents at the police station, and an unlikely encounter with Rod in the bushes, but she would soon come upon something much more terrifying. And it would happen in one of the most inauspicious places.

"We also shot the classroom scene at Marshall High, and it's a really beautiful, old school," Langenkamp says. "It's just an iconic high school. Three stories, all brick, and a beautiful building."

The scene in question would mark the appearance of Lin Shaye, an actress who was not a newcomer to being on camera. With several small film and television roles prior to *Elm Street*, the actress isn't shy about admitting she might have had an ace in the hole on getting the role of Nancy's English teacher.

"Well, Robert Shaye, my big brother I'm proud to say, he was looking out for his sister and I think it really came directly from Bob," the actress admits. "You know, they were looking for a little role, and I met Wes, and we just hit it off completely. It almost was like, 'Forget about Bob, forget about everybody else.'"

With that meeting, Lin was cast. "When I first read the script I thought it sounded really scary, and I was just rooting for it, basically, having met Wes and, of course, it being in my family as well," she says.

Now that her familial connection and subsequent hit-it-off meeting with Craven landed her the part, Lin was surprised at the amount of recognition the character has received. "I gotta say I was somewhat shocked how much impact the English teacher had on people," she says. "That they remembered her and say, 'I have a teacher just like that.' The character was mean, but then she was funny, and it's exciting as an actress to feel that you've made an impact, even with a small character like that."

While likability was certainly one reason for the character being memorable, it was also the small touches the actress brought to the role; things, she believes, made a difference.

The exterior high school location as it is seen today. John Marshall High School, still in operation, first opened its doors on January 26, 1931.

"I remember there was the thing with the pencil. This kid is sleeping and I bop him on the head with the eraser," Lin states. "And that was my idea. Even in a small scene, the idea that you bring something personal and something creative to that moment is very fulfilling for an actor. Those were my favorite parts, the little grace notes that I was able to add."

It also helped that the scene was full of young students all eager to please, as Langenkamp remembers. "When you have a lot of extras in your scenes, it adds a certain amount of energy anyway, because they're all so jazzed, and they all get to be in this movie, and everybody's really excited."

The scene was definitively more than just an English teacher lecturing, as it also marked the true beginning of the audience witnessing Nancy's nightmarish relationship with Freddy Krueger. It signaled another moment where viewers are left to wonder if it is, or isn't, a nightmare, and would begin with a reading from Shakespeare.

"Don Hannah, who is actress Daryl Hannah's (*Splash* [1984]) brother, read the *Hamlet* piece. And he did a wonderful job with that," Langenkamp says.

Before getting that role however, Hannah was up for another part in the film: Glen. He and Depp auditioned until the word came in. "I just got called and they said that I didn't get the part that I was up for and that Johnny did, but that I did get a speaking role," Hannah recalls. "I think that we both got our SAG cards based on that, so I was stoked, you know."

Though the role wasn't going to have much screen time, Hannah took it seriously. "I rehearsed a lot on that part. Not only did I learn how to surf, because I was a surfer, but I just worked really hard on that," he says of his first speaking part. And while Hannah did exactly what Craven had asked of him, it was Langenkamp who was, once again, having a bit of trouble accepting the scene and her character's part in it.

"In the high school class where I'm sitting there, we had Don Hannah reading the piece from Shakespeare, which is so Wes Craven to include a classical reference in his modern horror movie. And Don did such a great job, but when he started going into that ghostly, weird voice, I really didn't buy it at first," admits Langenkamp.

"When I got up to do my bit, I read it straight and then Wes came up and asked me if I'd repeat it again in a stage whisper," Hannah says. "I did, and everybody sort of laid their heads on the desk and when 'Cut!' was called, people started kind of laughing. They enjoyed it, so that was pretty cool."

For her part, Langenkamp recalls not being as enthused about the goings on. "I didn't think it was gonna look good in this movie. It was early into the film and I wasn't really aware of how Wes was gonna incorporate all this kind of dream fantasy into real life," she says. "And it was one of the times where I saw, 'Oh, Wes is going to be doing all these kinds of trippy, imaginary things!' And we're supposed to be living our normal, everyday life."

To make sure she understood, the actress decided this time she would speak up. "I just kept thinking, 'God, this is so weird. Will people buy it?' And after talking to Wes about it, he and I always had a joke where I'd say, 'Can you try to explain this to me, Wes?' And Wes' reply would be, 'I can't explain it. It's just a dream.' And I'm like, 'Ok, thank you,'" Langenkamp laughs.

That pithy explanation may have emerged because the film was the first of Craven's to tackle the dream state with any real depth and power. "Some of it was based on knowledge—the dreams I've had—and some of it was based on intuition," stated the writer and director. "So most of that is too lengthy to explain to an actor or actress on the set. I tried to tell the actors everything they need to know about what's going on in their teenage lives at that moment. It was its own reality."

Craven, though, had a more grounded rationale for including the bit. "I went to Hollywood High to research what school kids looked like in 1983," he says, revealing that the instructor was teaching the very same Shakespearean passage. "And I just wrote it down and thought, 'My God, this is it, this is kismet.'"

Behind-the-scenes moments with Hannah wearing a Krueger stunt mask and with a member of the crew. "These Polaroid's were taken just before the classroom scene was shot," states Hannah. "The Freddy latex mask was on a mannequin head in the hair & makeup trailer and I just couldn't resist. The other picture was taken with electrician Toni Semple in the hallway of the high school location."

As Langenkamp tried to get clarity from Craven on what was, in fact, happening, Hannah recalls a much greater moment that ultimately never came to fruition.

"The original script that I received for my character was going to be a big effects scene, where hair was supposed to come flowing out of my face, and I think I was supposed to die in this very gruesome way," remembers Hannah. While early script drafts do not include a death scene, they do reveal that the character has "his face wreathed by white hair."

Though the follicular aspect didn't occur, Hannah tried to make the most out of what he was given, simply thrilled he had done what he set out to do. "It obviously worked because of the reaction I got, so I was thrilled with it, and I liked the simplicity of it. I came in, I did my thing, and I was gone."

FRIENDS ARE FOREVER

Hannah's time on set may have been short-lived, but another cast member was about to make the second of three appearances, this time much worse for wear and out to terrify a best friend. The question in audience's minds of whether Nancy was, indeed, on the other side of the waking world was about to be answered affirmatively in a horrific way.

"With Mandy in the body bag in the hallway," says Langenkamp, "I believe we shot that at a different high school and on a different day."

Wyss definitely has more specific memories of the filming. "Oh, yeah, the body bag scene. First of all, your psyche does not wanna be in a body bag when you're alive. Your body and your brain say, 'Don't let them zip this up!'" she says.

Having realized there was no zipper on the inside, the actress found herself at the mercy of crew members who she didn't always know very well. "You really are having to trust the people taking care of you," admits Wyss, "so I was literally like, 'Hey, don't zip me up all the way.'"

It was something Talalay could understand. "The body bag terrified me in the script and it scared me in the film, too," she says.

Nancy soon sees her bloodied friend dragged away in the body bag which, interestingly, was written to sport the original Krueger colors of red and yellow, but was replaced by a translucent plastic for the film. Pulled by an unseen force a trail of black fluid is left in the dead girl's wake, inspired, Craven says, "by the slime trails left by snails," and achieved when the crew ran down the hallway with a big bag of ooze. It's then the audience knows that, once again, something terrible is on the horizon.

"It's the first time that Heather is really confronted with the dream," says Lin, "so it was important to see her react to that in the most profound way."

As Nancy follows her friend being hauled off, Craven once again gave praise to Wyss. "Amanda did a great job of being dead," he says. "It sounds like a joke, but just the way her hand flapped over and landed so lifelessly. It was absolutely chilling."

Enough so that a concerned and confused Nancy races to her friend, only to end up coming face-to-face with another character that has a moment—and a line of dialogue—almost as iconic as Freddy's glove.

SCREW YOUR PASS!

"I am a stuntwoman, and in this industry it is a lot easier to hire a stuntwoman to do the stunt and also say the lines," says Leslie Hoffman, who would run into Langenkamp's character and eventually don the now-familiar red and green sweater, as well as Freddy's claw. "I'm just as much an actress as I am a stunt woman, so it was just easier to have the stunt coordinator hire the hall monitor for the stunt. Tony knew I could act, and that's how I got the part," she says.

"Oh yeah, I actually was the one who suggested they use Leslie," says Cecere. "Leslie came in and all she'd ever done was stunt work prior to that. I'd rehearsed it with her so she would actually take most of the fall and not actually have Heather bang into her."

Behind the scenes, Hoffman shows off her look as Krueger.

That didn't mean she knew exactly what she'd be doing while acting and doing a stunt. "Actors are usually given the script and they go over it and they develop their character. In my case, I arrived on the set and had no idea what I was doing, was put in this sweater and my hair put up in ponytails," Hoffman says. "Wes came over to me and said, 'I want you and Nancy to run into each other, and you are going to fall to the ground. You're going to look at her and say, "Where's your pass?!"'"

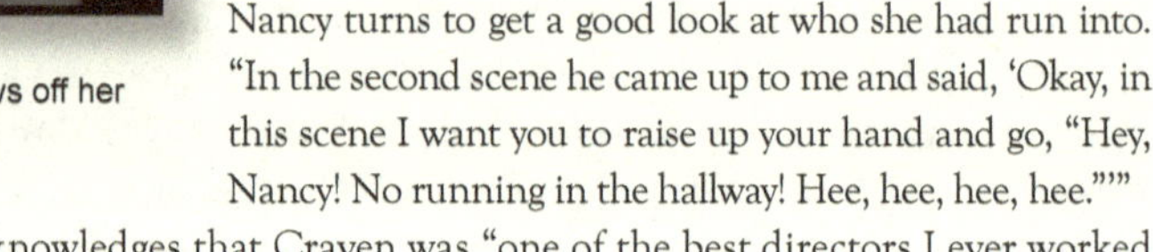

Craven took the direction further the moment Nancy turns to get a good look at who she had run into. "In the second scene he came up to me and said, 'Okay, in this scene I want you to raise up your hand and go, "Hey, Nancy! No running in the hallway! Hee, hee, hee, hee."'"

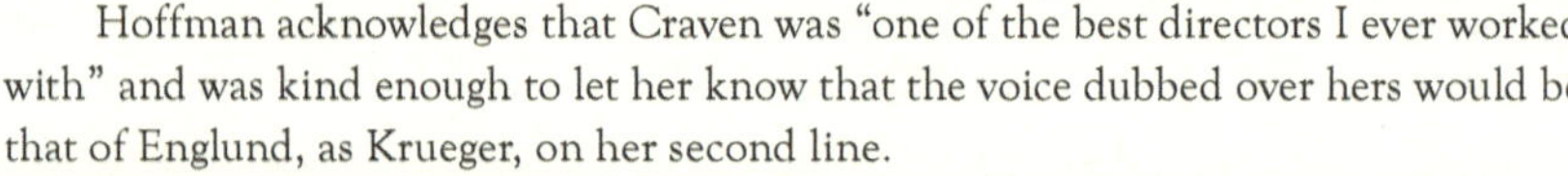

Hoffman acknowledges that Craven was "one of the best directors I ever worked with" and was kind enough to let her know that the voice dubbed over hers would be that of Englund, as Krueger, on her second line.

"That's very gracious for the director to let you know that," admits Hoffman, adding, "And when the film was done, it was very rare that stunt people would get credit. In this case Wes gave me credit not only as the hall guard, but under stunts."

The stuntwoman also provides information about Freddy's sweater that many, except Krueger die-hards, might not have noticed—at least until it's pointed out. "The interesting thing is that in the original film, the sleeves are a solid red. There are no stripes on the sleeves," Hoffman reveals. "But every single sequel afterwards, maybe because they couldn't find the same sweater, they found a sweater that had green and red stripes on the sleeves."

Hoffman admits she came to California to be remembered, but had no idea it would be for a role in a low-budget horror movie. "When people ask me what movies I've been in, I start naming movies, and they say, 'No, I didn't see that.' I ask if they saw the original *Nightmare on Elm Street*. 'Yes!' 'Well, remember the hall monitor?' And they say, 'That was you? That movie scared me! I still have nightmares about it. When Robert

Englund's voice comes out of your mouth, it still upsets me,'" she recounts. "So aside from having the glove and sweater, I guess that's what makes that scene so iconic."

The moment is also one which showcases a shift in the blurred lines between the dream state and waking life. Referencing the fact that the hallways have become a bit darker and filled with wind and dead leaves, Craven says, "There's a lot of moments in this movie where people look at me like I'm crazy when I say, 'Let's have some leaves blowing around.'"

It was, admitted Craven, a turning point for the audience as, once again, "You never know when you're in a dream and when you're in reality. It's very, very frightening."

Haitkin, whose job it was to assist in creating that blurred line, agrees, stating, "That's the essence of this piece."

WHO ARE YOU?

The scene quickly shifts from the high school hallway to Krueger's boiler room, as did the filming locations.

"We went from the actual high school to filming at the Lincoln Heights jail. And how do you make it seem like the same place?" Craven jokingly asks. "You put the 'No Students Allowed' sign," he answers, referring to the simple insignia placed on the wall behind Langenkamp—the same one seen as she descends the stairs—as she creeps in to where she doesn't belong.

Craven enjoys watching Langenkamp prepare for her first encounter with Krueger in the boiler room nightmare.

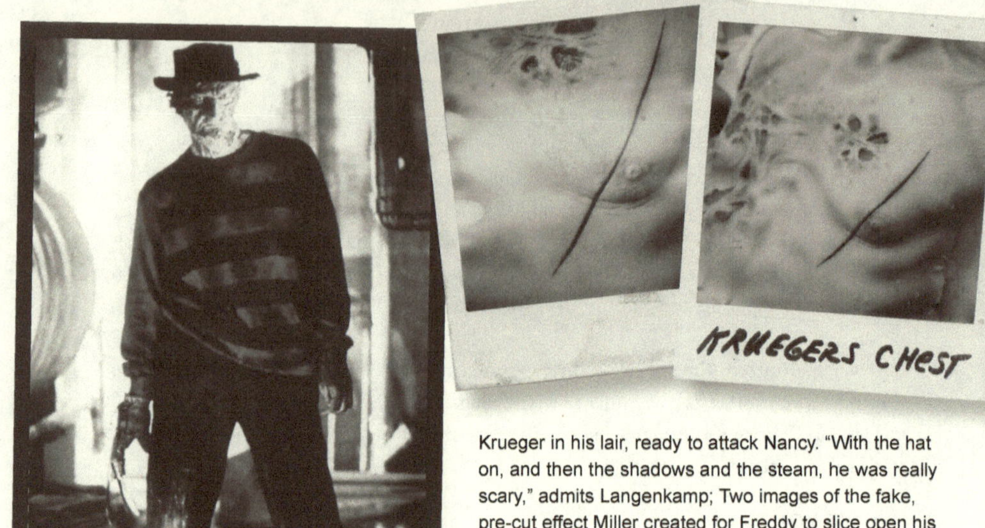

Krueger in his lair, ready to attack Nancy. "With the hat on, and then the shadows and the steam, he was really scary," admits Langenkamp; Two images of the fake, pre-cut effect Miller created for Freddy to slice open his own chest.

"It could've been something I did," admits Diers, "because that would've been the kind of thing that an art department production assistant would be asked to do. It also could be something that the scenic artist would have done, or one of the scenic painters, because they often do signage, but in those days you did everything because it was non-union."

"I think the first scene we shot was in one of the boiler rooms. It's in my dream when I'm in the high school," recalls Langenkamp. It was important for her character as much as it was the audience, because it's the first time Nancy is seen in the dream with Freddy. "With the hat on, and then the shadows and the steam, he was really scary," she adds.

"I loved the lighting combined with the catwalks that we were working on. The light really came through that kind of waffled, cross-hatched metal," says Englund. "It just did some really great dappling effects bottom-lighting Heather and myself. And I had to trust that the light would catch my eyes, or the parts of my makeup that we had accented with Vaseline or KY Jelly. And I know that Heather was perspiring a little bit because it was hot in there and she had one of her little eighties sweaters. There was something kind of strange about Nancy's little girl look combined with Heather's beauty combined with her perspiration. It was sort of a sexy, strange fairy tale."

The juxtaposition of industrial filth with Langenkamp's softness was something that helped the tension between the two characters. "The lighting and the contrast of Heather's little wardrobe against all of that roughness had something that I liked. It really helped me create a moment, and it made me kind of dance with Heather a little bit there," Englund says. "I also began on that day to discover a little more of Freddy's body language with the scenery, knowing that this world was a little bit kicked up, and a little bit exaggerated, and a little bit larger than life. We weren't in a real world, it was a dream world."

His prey at the moment agreed, seeing Krueger for what he truly was. "I think in those boiler room scenes, he's the scariest because he was always scratching those nails against the pipes. It was incredibly scary, and I realized, 'This is gonna work,'" Langenkamp says.

Englund was known to really use the claw scraping to agitate people on set, leaving many to fear, if not the actor under makeup, the horrendous sound he would make with his character's signature prop. "Everybody would just hear it and be like, 'Ahhhh!' It was really annoying to have that kind of a weapon that close to you all the time," says Langenkamp.

"There's an old expression that actors use called 'wearing the scenery,' and it's when you get on a set you haven't been on, whether it's in the theater, or it's on location, or on a sound stage, that has to be lived in," explains Englund, who wasn't afraid to touch and use his physical surroundings to the benefit of his character and performance. "Instead of standing in the middle of it all, at some point I decided I'd like to scratch the railing with the glove. I'm not sure if I scratched it for a sound, whether that was in the script, or if I did a little tap. But it was a combination of something that was in Wes' script and something I found with the real set."

Langenkamp remembers the instant she felt that Freddy Krueger was truly going to instill fear in audiences, partially because she, herself, was afraid: when Freddy comes out from behind the boiler in her nightmare, one shoulder stooped lower than the other. It was also a moment that Englund realized the importance of the glove, not just to the film, but his portrayal of the character.

"The glove affected me because it's heavy, and when I put it on, one shoulder dropped a bit," Englund states. "It affected my movement and it affected my posture, and I immediately thought it's like having a holster. It's like a gunslinger's thing. It's like reaching for the gun."

More than creepy posture, Krueger answers Nancy's "Who are you?" by demonstrating his complete willingness to terrify with another act of self-mutilation as he slices open his own chest, revealing innards of a most grotesque nature.

Also present, but much less afraid, was David Miller, who was tasked with creating the injury. "For the scene where Freddy slashes himself, he lifts his sweater up and slashes down. They lifted the sweater on him and we cut to a fake torso I made of Freddy's chest," he reveals.

It was the only chest cast they had of Englund and, though it looks like Krueger's blade slices open the wound, it was, in fact, precut. "It just looked like he cut into it and we had little cables in there that would widen it," Miller reveals.

Englund remembers the experience well. "I'm rigged with little hydraulics and little tubes and things, and it's like being on *The Muppet Show* (1976–1981)," he says. "It always seems like there are five guys wearing black cloth over them, and hoodies, and they're all squeezing things up inside me to make an effect work."

Making those effects work can, frequently, get a little silly. "There's literally a guy with his hand wrapped around your testicles. I'm not exaggerating. It's been that way on several of the movies. And it's like, 'We must stop meeting like this,'" laughs Englund. "You get to the point where you have to crack jokes with the guys who haven't slept in twenty-four hours, who are doing their best to make the effect work."

Wisecracks aside, Miller says it did. "It really looked good as his finger was going down the split we made. It would widen, and inside was a pump that was like blood and methylcellulose, which is slime."

There was also one other item Miller made sure was forced out of the oozing wound. "Oh, and maggots," he laughs.

Real maggots, which is what Craven had requested. It was something that didn't quite sit well with Jensen. "The maggots started to get to me and I started to faint. Wes was right behind me and caught me. He was pushing me up by my shoulders and then I went outside, put my head between my legs, and then I came back," she laughs. "They were some kind of South American maggots, and when they shone light on them they got hyperactive and they wiggled. They were in yellow, slightly fluorescent goo, and I just remember losing it."

It was a feeling Langenkamp could appreciate. "It's Freddy at his best and most frightening," she feels. "You have the silhouette, then he cuts himself and all that terrible stuff comes out, and there's also his dripping face right before he comes after me. It was, and he was, scary."

"The glove affected me because it's heavy, and when I put it on, one shoulder dropped a bit."

Robert Englund

The truth is the actual fear may have helped, as Langenkamp had reservations about her performance in some of those intense moments, having never done anything like it before. "I was really scared about how I was coming across and wanted to do a good job," she says.

Helping her was Englund's performance, as he conveyed Krueger's sense of nastiness and gallows humor. "Part of it was the cat-and-mouse chase between Heather and I," offers Englund. "That kind of colors him a little differently, whether it's crueler, funnier, sexier, whatever. And that's a rich thing to explore as an actor."

Langenkamp and Jensen might have been frightened and repulsed, respectively, of Freddy in that moment, but it was Englund who was having a hard time with one aspect of his character. Or more pointedly, his character's attire.

"I can remember Wes was really married to the idea of these really oily, shiny pants that had boiler room grease all over them. And I remember when I first put them on they looked great, but that's not how I was lit," offers Englund. "I could've worn black Levis in the whole fucking movie because I was lit so dark. I remember about a week in saying, 'Wes, I love you, man, but it takes an hour a day for the girls to oil these. It takes two hours a day for me to clean myself after I take them off. This shit goes up my butt and everywhere else and into my pores. And I'm miserable the whole time I'm here and it doesn't show.'"

Keeping Englund's wardrobe in such a state was the responsibility of Jensen. "His costumes were heavy and greasy. And I do remember him not wanting it. It was like, 'Oh God, again?'" she laughs.

Thinking about it practically, which happened to play into his less-than-enthused attitude about having to wear the clothing in such a way, Englund says, "Unless you're doing inserts of my greasy, oily, slick, awful, old-man slacks, they're just pants on film."

Lubricious or not, as Krueger found new and innovative ways to torture the dreams of the Elm Street children, this particular nightmare saw Nancy flee from Freddy for the first time, literally with nowhere to run. "That scene where my back's pressed up against the wall is a very heavy scene, because Nancy's in this dream and she's not sure of what it all means yet," says Langenkamp. "But it's also the point where she has the moment of realization, 'If I burn myself on the pipe, maybe I'll wake up.' And I love that scene! We do have those powers in our dreams. We really all do. It's just like we only know about the ten percent of the brain we're actually using. I mean, Wes really put something in that scene."

Indeed he did, as Craven was well aware. In what is termed "lucid dreaming," the dreamer is able to exert some degree of control over their involvement within the dream, much like Nancy does.

"It's such a magical concept," Langenkamp says. "You see the beginning of Nancy's ingenuity in that moment. It's kind of her defining, brave action."

After Nancy survives her classroom nightmare and the encounter with Krueger, Langenkamp became convinced that Craven confusing the line between dreams and reality was something worth watching. "There were the times where I was nervous about how a scene was going. And then, when you see the final cut, of course Wes knows what he was doing. But there's times when you do participate in a scene, and you're not one hundred percent with the program," she says. "I love when I wake in horror, and I'm screaming, and I look around and there's all these kids. I like that scene."

Lin agrees. "I finished my day in school, and it was a wonderfully written role because it did have a little bit of angst to it from the teacher that had sort of a frustration with her students. And a little bit of comedy at the end," she says. "The 'You'll need a hall pass' line has, of course, become a favorite of people's. So I pretty much satisfied myself with having done my job."

It was also important to Craven that, along with Tina's dream at the beginning with her slashed nightgown, this scene is another primer of "things that happen to you in the dream come with you," he says. "If you're hurt in the dream, you'll be hurt when you wake up, which is the spookiest part of the whole concept."

The layering of that intellection was crucial because, as Haitkin points out, "Amidst all this insanity, there's a logic."

Langenkamp used the unfolding events, and Craven's smarts in keeping things as real as possible, to her advantage. "That's the key to acting in a horror film as well, is you have to always realize that, for that character, what's going on is totally logical," she says.

Craven gives the actress high marks for her portrayal of what he had crafted, finding a way to sell the audience on the fact that Nancy was a strong, young woman truly going through a horrific experience. "[She] somehow has the strength to figure it out and believe in herself."

Craven demonstrates what it's like to lie behind bars; An incarcerated Rod tries to convince Nancy of his innocence and about the man with knives for fingers, who has also appeared in his dreams.

HE HAD KNIVES FOR FINGERS

Her terrifying encounter over, and carrying a burn from her dream to remember it, Nancy realizes now more than ever she must talk to Rod to better understand what happened to Tina. "She now knows what [Rod] is experiencing, too, and has to confirm with him, and make him admit that he's had the similar kind of dreams," Craven explains.

Langenkamp, however, judged it might have been unnecessary. Or worse, unbelievable. "I have to say that doing the scene with Nick in the jail, I remember not really being comfortable with my lines," she says. In addition, the actress admits to simply not being satisfied with the on-screen moments between her and Corri's character. "I just didn't really like a lot of my scenes with him. You know, I'm not really good friends with him as a character, and yet I'm truly trying to find out all this information, and I really need to know the truth from him."

The actress felt it was a hard sell in the expositional moments they shared, something she carried over from the first scene in the bushes when she tried to make asking if Rod was guilty, work. "I never really felt like those were my best scenes. And in a way, I think Nancy would have known he didn't do it. And she kept saying, 'Did you do it? Did you do it?'" states Langenkamp. Believing that Nancy knew the answer, she adds, "Of course he didn't do it. She already knew there was a Freddy out there getting the kids in their dreams, especially after the nightmare she had just had in the school, so I think the dialogue gave me a lot of problems in the jail."

Her co-star also remembers the difficulty of the scene. For him, however, it had nothing to do with dialogue or character. Instead, it was the real world that was infiltrating the moment. "Well, the jail scene, I was really depressed," admits Corri, who goes on to a much more startling acknowledgement. "I am not going to say the drug I was doing, but I was ripped in the jail scene. I passed out and Wes was like, 'Are you ready for the shoot?'"

Corri goes on to say how deeply being under the influence affected his work. "This drug was allowing me to get into this crazed position. In that scene, when Nancy's in front of me and I'm crying, I'm really fucked up," the actor reveals. "So I'm crying not because of the scene, I'm crying because my life is shitty at the time. It was the first and last time I ever did drugs on the set. I'd never violated the art form again. I felt really bad."

It didn't affect Langenkamp's opinion of his abilities, stating that the actor was very good in the scene. "I remember being kind of mesmerized by his intensity," she says.

Decades later, Corri reflects back on that situation. "It was a matter of using a lot of pain from my own life. I was a Method actor back then," he says. "On the set, I lived in that jail cell until they were ready to shoot. So I just created this pain and delivered Wes Craven's words. That's probably the last time I'll be a Method actor. It's too painful."

In the end, even he states more could have been done in the scene and with his character. "I probably would have been a little bit more real," considers Corri. "More in the scene, which is 'What do I want from Nancy?' instead of looking at it as just me. A lot of actors back then were self-absorbed."

WARM MILK? GROSS.

While Corri might look back at problems that affected his performance, and Langenkamp harbored issues with her dialogue, it was her character that was about to endure a much more immediate, deadly, and wet problem. In what is arguably one of the most memorable scenes in the film, Nancy relaxes in a hot bath, essentially hoping to forget her troubles. What happens, instead, is an invitation for an even greater threat.

"It might be my favorite scene on film," Langenkamp states.

"The bathtub scene," says Doyle, "was another favorite of mine, actually. And that was just a regular bathtub, which Greg Fonseca built on the second floor. We had a two story set and we just built a box, and set the bathtub on a box, and the water was all in the box."

Langenkamp recalls how the sequence was created. "They built a bathtub that had no bottom. Instead, it had a tank underneath and I was just sitting on a very narrow board," she says.

Under that board, at least in the film, was the stuff of nightmares. In this case, one in which Nancy drifts off to sleep, giving Freddy yet another opportunity to attack.

"There were just all kinds of people immediately out of range," states Rideout. "I was directly behind Heather's head with all this smoke pouring out, which was supposed to be steam from the bath. There were a lot of people all around doing all sorts of things. It was very intimate, because we were all crowded into the tiniest little space you can imagine." Even with the set's moveable walls, the space didn't end up being much bigger than the bathroom Nancy was supposed to be in. "It was a really small space for everyone," she adds.

Issues of space aside, the moment in question was the haunting instant Freddy's claw comes sneaking out of the sudsy water, hoping to tear into Nancy. A plan was set in motion to start filming, but an issue, Doyle remembers, quickly reared its head. "The day of the shot, one of my guys was sitting in the bathtub and he could just bring his hand up and do that gag," he says. "We were ready to do it, but it turned out the guy going underwater couldn't hold his breath very long. He just didn't feel comfortable."

Once Doyle was told the crewmember wasn't sure he could stay under the water for nearly a minute, it wasn't only Doyle's ideas that came to the rescue, it was Doyle.

"We had to get going, so I just jumped in there and did it," he says. It gave the effects man the distinct pleasure of Langenkamp sitting on his knees, with her feet resting on his shoulders for an entire day, while Wes yelled so Doyle could hear the cues.

"Jim Doyle was wearing a full scuba diving rig and was just underneath me. And I'm just balancing on a board. And it's his hand with the Freddy glove on it and then, on Wes' cue, he pulls me down," says Langenkamp.

As interesting as it sounds, the actress did admit to one thing while filming what was undeniably a technical scene to pull off. "They did a lot of camera angles in that so I did, frankly, get really jaded by the end of the day. When you do something that many times over and over again, it's hard to keep it fresh," reveals Langenkamp. "It was a very challenging day trying to create drama and trying to create excitement when the real lines on the page are quite small and quite still."

That said, Langenkamp was ultimately pleased with what was captured. "I think we did a good job. I think we made it a good scene," she adds.

Good enough that even as audiences would be wondering what could possibly happen next while Nancy was in Freddy's clutches under the water, amusingly, so did Langenkamp. "All of the scenes that are under the water they did after we wrapped," she says, admitting she wasn't even aware there would be underwater photography. "I didn't really know that they were gonna have all that thrashing. I thought that it was just gonna be a shot from on top of the bathtub. But Wes obviously liked the idea of showing her in this unlimited water space."

Once Langenkamp's character was in that space, the question on many fans' minds was whether or not they caught a glimpse of a naked Heather Langenkamp. The answer, much to the chagrin of many an admirer, is no. "Sorry, they did that with a stunt lady," she says.

Or as Rideout remembers, a woman who ended up being the stunt lady. "I essentially ended up body-doubling Heather because we were the same size and shape, and that, of course, is how I ended up under the water when Freddy grabs her in the bathtub," she says.

Filming the scene wasn't just a few scattered thoughts tucked away in memory for Rideout. On the contrary, as she vividly recalls one very physical aspect. "It was very cold. Lou Carlucci's pool, which is where we filmed that, was, and I cannot stress this enough, not heated!" she says.

The scene was filmed after they finished wrapping principal photography. "It was the day after the wrap party and we were all horribly hung over," remembers Craven, who was suited up for the underwater work.

"Wes was down there at the bottom of the pool and they put visqueen over the top of the pool, so it was like swimming in a big trash bag," Rideout says.

The look it gave, Burrows recalls, was that "you couldn't tell how deep the pool was and it looked like it went forever down there."

What made the entire ordeal more terrifying for someone without much, if any, actual stunt experience was the simple fact that Rideout also had zero scuba experience. For a scene where she would be pulled, and kept, under the water in order for the character to potentially

Clockwise from top left: A sticker playfully describes Doyle as the "Amphibious Krueger"; The effects man rehearses the moment before submerging himself under the water; Nancy struggles to not fall victim to Freddy; Langenkamp patiently waits for the next take.

meet her doom, Rideout was glad she had at least one person on her side. "Doyle, as I recall, was underwater with me. He had the regulator and stuff for me. The big thing, of course, was to not panic, because there was only a tiny little square cut out of the plastic over the top of the pool that was, in theory, the light from the bathtub in the bathroom shining down through," she says. "It was a little scary doing that shot, because I knew if I panicked, if I tried to break the surface of the water of the pool, I wasn't going to get any air, because I was essentially swimming inside a plastic bag. So that was a little unnerving."

Luckily, the shot didn't take long, worked just as it should have, and Rideout came through it unscathed, albeit a little chilly. She also got something else out of it. "It's how I got my SAG card. It's my war story of how I got in the Union, as I was Taft-Hartley'd in as being Heather's body double for that stunt," she says.

With Rideout recounting her experience, Talalay sums up the scene and her feelings about it. "To me the bathtub scene is a favorite. The situation is normal. The victim is vulnerable. The tension is built and dissipated with mastery. It's a masterpiece," she states.

CHECKING ON THE JAILBIRD

Now armed with the knowledge that Krueger had the terrifying ability to get to her no matter where she was, for all he needed was her drifting off to sleep, Nancy decides it's time to take matters into her own hands. In her room, trying hard to stay awake, she watches television. The program she views is Sam Raimi's *Evil Dead*, an in-joke for which the director was given a "special thanks" credit.

"He had put something of one of my films in the basement of one of his films," Craven says.

Raimi elaborates on the back-and-forth. "There's a torn-up poster of *Jaws* (1975) in *The Hills Have Eyes*, so I thought it would be funny to tear a *Hills Have Eyes* poster into pieces in *The Evil Dead*, to tell Wes, 'No, this is the real horror, pal,'" says Raimi. "So then, in *A Nightmare on Elm Street*, Wes put *The Evil Dead* on a television set, saying basically, 'No, Sam, *The Evil Dead* is just pop entertainment. This is real horror.'"

Raimi would later respond in *Evil Dead II* (1987) by putting one of Freddy's gloves above the door in the tool shed where Ash (played by Bruce Campbell) chainsaws his girlfriend. Though Craven and Raimi hadn't known each other at the time, they did meet at the Cannes Film Festival years after both movies had come out. "He'd been very kind to me ever since," states Raimi.

In her room, Nancy desperately tries to stay awake. "I thought the design of Nancy's room was such an important aspect to the character. There were a lot of little touches that made it feel very real and very grounded," Langenkamp states.

If staying awake in front of the television proved difficult, Nancy soon found herself with an ally, Glen, aiding her in what could seem like a futile task. "It was so romantic that he climbed up the rose trellis," Langenkamp offers. "There was so much sweetness, so much of what teenagers do, and the way that they deal with each other is so sweet. It's a nice counterpoint to the terror."

Talking to Glen, Langenkamp's character recites a line that is "the biggest laugh of the film, usually!" she exclaims. "The line where I am so serious when I say I look twenty years old is really funny, because I was playing a sixteen-year-old girl, and for her to say that was obviously an exaggeration. Now that I'm well over that age I find it really humorous."

In truth, Langenkamp was just shy of twenty during filming, and the line was not concocted as an inside joke, or simply for exaggeration. It actually had its origins much closer to home. "Wes' daughter actually told me she was the person who originally said that line, and she really did say it," Langenkamp states. "It was a bad memory for her, actually. And her dad kind of took it and put it in the script."

That memory had to do with the very real ramifications of her parents' divorce. "It was hard. The effects of the divorce were not easy on my family. And my brother and I fought a lot," Jessica recalls. "The pain of the divorce manifested in a lot of strife between us, and I believe that when we went to visit my dad, it generally got worse."

Such was the case when, on one of their visits, the two siblings had a terrible fight in which Craven had gotten involved. "I have very sort of shapeless memories of it, but

I do know that I'd been crying hysterically for a very, very long time when I looked in the mirror and said, 'My God, I look twenty,'" Jessica recalls.

Feeling very old before her time, Jessica also admits to remembering "very little of [her] childhood," claiming that particular time was not a light time in her life. "But I do remember that moment very clearly for its sort of pain. I felt poorly treated, and unseen and unheard, and so that statement sort of came out of a moment of feeling very despondent. And that's fine. I think every teenager, or pre-teen, or child, does. I might've felt it a little bit more than some, but that's okay," she laughs. "It's character building and all that."

All past pain and wit aside, Langenkamp remembers the bedroom scene with Depp as being another of her favorites. "I really did like the moment with Johnny on the bed where I'm telling him, 'We've gotta stay awake and go in the dream,' and I have all this really crazy stuff to explain," says the actress. "I just think that's a very sweet scene and I trust him so much. It's just the kind of relationship between boyfriend and girlfriend you don't get to see on film that much where they're just really good friends, and she's trusting him to do something for her. It's so cute and sweet."

"She was able to talk to him, and he came over when he was concerned about her," Craven offers. "He was her last chance to have an ally in this fight against Freddy and that was an important character for her. An important thing that, of course, had to be stripped away at the last minute for Nancy to face Freddy alone. But it was very much a romantic relationship between them."

It was exactly what Craven had wanted. "You care about the people," he added.

Though Glen doesn't seem to take the surreal notions Nancy claims are true completely seriously, she does entrust him with her life as she makes the choice to fall asleep, enter the dream, and do some investigating of her own. Part of that would entail Glen keeping an eye on Nancy.

It was something Huntley hoped the sets would reflect.

"In Heather's bedroom, I had put a lot of sort of faces," Huntley says. "There's a pillow with a face, there's some dolls that are facing the camera. There was sort of this quality that Heather was being watched. One of my intentions was sort of to capture that subliminally that there were faces always watching her."

Such thoughts put into the dressing of the set were understood, and appreciated, by Langenkamp. "Eyes never were closed, in a way," she says, adding that she believes Nancy's bedroom set to be one of the finest of a horror movie in quite some time. From the naturalistic room, to utilizing themes that play into the conceit of the film, the actress valued what the art department was able to do to convey a girl on the verge of womanhood.

"That room is very memorable to me. It's so perfect for her," Langenkamp says. "The rose trellis as the gateway to her boyfriend through the window. And just the junk, the little pictures and things. It was so helpful to me, as an actor, to really ground myself in that part. I walked into the room and I immediately was like, 'Oh, I'm in my room.' It really felt like a sixteen-year-old girl's bedroom."

One aspect the actress says hit home was that the room was full of everyday, real things, a lesson to be learned in modern movies. "It's very hard to find that in movies these days. Everyone looks like they're in a hotel. Everyone looks like they have a Pottery Barn interior designer coming in to neaten everything up as they walk through their lives. And we all know that girls are not like that," Langenkamp laughs. "We are not like that at all."

The filming of Nancy leaving the house, under the watchful eye of Glen, and walking down the street was complicated, specifically because it was one, long Steadicam shot. "At the time it was very, very new, the use of that kind of equipment," says Craven. It was also rare on a lower-budgeted production. "It was remarkable what got pulled off with the budget that we had, or didn't have."

All around, it was a hard show for many. "We were trying to make a big-budget feature on a small budget," considers Huntley. "It seemed like there were eighteen-hour days every day. Like shooting Heather's house exteriors, we did shots with all the rose vines up, then we'd have to take them down and shoot something else and we'd put them back up. It just went on and on and it felt like twenty-four hours. Up, down, up, down, up, down."

As Nancy meanders through her dream, checking to see if Glen is still observing, she ends up in an alley that "was filmed in several different locations," recalls Langenkamp, including areas in Venice and on Melrose Avenue near Downtown Los Angeles. The nightmare for Haitkin and his crew was that they were fighting with the inevitable sunrise as they shot the scene just before dawn.

"You can see in at least one shot of Glen standing by the tree that it's just contaminated with light," Haitkin says.

"It's always the worst time," states Langenkamp, jokingly adding, "You don't even want to get near Jacques, or Wes!"

Unfortunately for Nancy, she quickly realizes that when you're on Freddy's turf nothing is what it seems, and that her visit to see Rod also meant seeing Krueger. It was a brief moment in the film, but one that had a lasting impression, coupled with a revelation.

"Freddy goes through the bars. Does he go through the bars? Oh my God, he went like *Terminator 2* (1991). *Terminator 2* stole it!" Corri jokes.

"I find it very interesting, and I'd like to think there was a tip of the hat to it in *Terminator 2*," admits Craven.

An unsubstantiated, clearly comical claim of cinematic idea-borrowing aside, the shot of Krueger passing through the closed and locked jail cell was one of the scant opticals in the film. Achieved by filming the prison bars by themselves, then removing them and filming Freddy walking through the same area, "they rotoscoped the shots together as one so it looked like Freddy walked right through them," Doyle recalls.

But because it's a dream, anything can happen, and what started with Nancy visiting Rod quickly turned into something more upsetting. "That was such a hard day. A very hard day," Langenkamp remembers of filming the scene where Nancy checking on Rod from afar goes awry. "Just ask Amanda," the actress implores.

"Yeah, it was terribly gross," Wyss admits.

The moment has Nancy checking in on her locked-up friend, only to be confronted again with the corpse of Tina, this time in a further state of decomposition and, literally, full of terrible things.

"Wes wanted creepy-crawly things coming out of it, he didn't just want a body bag," recalls Burrows. "He said, 'John, you gotta find some huge spiders, tarantulas, huge worms, I want stuff coming out of the bag!'"

Eventually they found someone with the requisite slimy creatures who "brought these things out of a big suitcase and put them on my desk, and Wes said, 'No, no, that's it, you got the job,'" Burrows recalls.

"There were real centipedes. And there were snakes and goo around her feet. It was a day of a lot of creature feature stuff," says Jensen.

Those creatures would ultimately provide the requisite on-screen shocks, but also bring slight offscreen discomfort to Wyss. "Everyone was very caring, but it was still disturbing," she admits.

"We were trying to make a big-budget feature on a small budget. It seemed like there were eighteen-hour days every day."

Anne Huntley on the rigors of filming

"Nobody wants to get in a body bag full of centipedes, and snakes, and slithering, grody things," agrees Langenkamp. "So my heart was going out to Amanda because she had to do the grossest things, and she's always such a trooper. They always kind of pushed the envelope to see how much she would do."

But according to Langenkamp, there was a limit. "Finally, she would say, 'Okay! Three centipedes, that's enough.' But it was gross. It was really gross," remembers the actress.

It was easy to see why, as everything Wyss had to do in the film seemed to deal with blood, slime, snakes, and insects. "She had the worst part, really, if you were even remotely afraid of any of those things," insists Langenkamp.

There was small consolation that Wyss didn't have to endure every insect indignity herself.

"When the centipede came out of my mouth, they actually did a cast of my head. So when we filmed, obviously I used a rubber centipede that came out," Wyss says. "But then they were able to cut with the fake head of me with a real centipede."

"We did a cast of Amanda and a whole sculpture thing," says Miller. "Wes still wanted her eyes closed and wanted her mouth open slightly." As for how they got the live centipede to do what was required, "We actually used a paper towel tube and put it behind the mouth. And then they put the centipede inside the little paper towel tube from the back and blew air in there and forced it to come out of the mouth," he reveals.

"So it was all very interesting. It was brilliant editing that made it very seamless, I think," Wyss states.

Craven recounted more than just Wyss' abilities to accept being surrounded by vermin, mainly when the centipede got loose on the set. "Everyone refused to go back

in because they couldn't find it," he says. Eventually, the bug, a poisonous centipede usually native to the Amazon, was located.

Back on set, Wyss had to survive other, real critters. "There was, like, hundreds of eels at her feet!" Craven laughs.

It was something Langenkamp watched, quickly concluding, "Amanda was always brave. I don't think I could have been so brave."

Viewing at a safe distance behind camera, Jensen also gives the actress high marks. "She really worked up to being incredibly brave," she says. "You could tell the terror on her face wasn't just acting. She had to do it and she did it."

Courage aside, even the movie magic of it all eventually found a way to get under Wyss' skin. "It was a very Outward Bound experience. It was like being sent into the woods on my own with a piece of string and a fork. And listen, I know it was fake, but the rubber centipede was still terribly gross."

"I'm not sure if I was halfway in the makeup or halfway out of the makeup, or if I came in on a break for a donut and a cup of coffee," says Englund, admitting he was there to see Wyss go through the ordeal, and that it reminds him of the film's iconography and reach beyond the United States.

"For years, I would go over to The Brussels Film Festival in Belgium and I remember one year, going up this great, grand staircase, I saw a huge vertical poster, probably at least twenty feet high, of Amanda in the body bag with the bugs coming out of her mouth," Englund says. "To this day, that's how I remember that sequence. That was sort of the first time I realized what an iconic image that particular moment was from the film. That was the day my bell rang and I became cognizant of just how dense and iconic and international *Nightmare on Elm Street* had become."

NOT UP HEATHER'S ALLEY

Realizing Glen has left her for sleep, Nancy tears away from the specter of a dead Tina and the threat of Freddy at every turn. On the way to her house, she finds herself in an alley where the uneven feeling of a nightmare actually came to pass during filming.

"There was a day when we had two or three units. I know Sean Cunningham came in and shot some things of Nancy running that were part of her nightmare outside, running down the alley," Craven recalls.

"In the middle of all of this," Cunningham says, "I was talking to Wes and asking him how it was going, and he was telling me about the shortage of time, and money, and so on, and I volunteered to come in and try to shoot second unit to pick up shots."

Opposite page (top to bottom): Englund waits for "Action!" as Craven prepares the scene where Freddy leaps out from the bushes; Miller's clay sculpture of Tina's head that allowed the character to regurgitate a live centipede; Before a fake head and real centipede were used, Wyss forced a rubber version from her own mouth. The size was much larger than the actual creature, and something not fully seen in the final cut of the film; The actual critter, which was temporarily lost on set, but eventually found; Englund (background) gets into character before chasing Nancy.

The *Friday the 13th* creator was aware that there was enormous pressure on Craven "because he had believed in it for so long and now it was sort of like 'put up or shut up,' and he was working with an insufficient budget, and a very short shooting schedule, trying to figure out how to do it," Cunningham says.

One answer was Cunningham not only helping film scenes of Nancy running, but helping to complete shots of an Elm Street sign, something never used in the final cut of the film and only surfacing in deleted scenes.

"They needed to extend Heather's jeopardy, so there were these really great girl-in-jeopardy shots of Heather in her little pajamas," recalls Englund. "I liked Sean a lot, and I think he's a very influential director in late twentieth century horror and responsible for some great stuff, but I remember everybody feeling rushed that day. It was very, very rushed. And the crew probably hadn't slept that day, and we were down to the splinter art department crew. We didn't have the 'A' team."

The situation for Langenkamp became more than rushed when an accident happened. "It's really hard to forget," says the actress. "We were doing a running scene, I cut my foot and had to go get stitches and that was on Sean's watch. And I really do feel like he was rushing us. He was not letting the people do their jobs properly, and I didn't have any footwear, so I ended up going to the hospital. I wasn't very happy that day."

"There was kind of a sense of 'What can we throw in front of the camera next? What might help us edit this whole thing together? Is this scary? Is this not scary?'"

Heather Langenkamp on the tight production schedule

Neither was her hair stylist, who recalls being upset enough that she wanted to take a swing at anybody who wasn't ready to defend the actress. "I remember the costume supervisor, Lisa, grabbing my hand and saying, 'It's not worth it,'" Fleetwood states. "When Heather Langenkamp was pumping blood out of an arterial cut on the bottom of her foot, as I'm carrying her to get her into a car to get her to a hospital, that's when I just said, 'Really?!' She had all these stitches put in her foot. I was really disappointed."

It was a time that Englund, who had experience on both smaller and larger-budgeted films, felt he needed to make a statement. "I remember using my grown-up voice and saying, 'Whoa, whoa, whoa.' I didn't really get into it with Sean or anything, but I just sort of said, 'Let's sweep this fucking floor. Actors are working here.' I wanted to protect the space," he says. "And I wasn't being hero for Heather as much as it was just I could feel us rushing too much."

The actress, expressing an understanding, is also somewhat passive about the ordeal. "It's especially hard when they've obviously hired a second unit director, and things aren't going very well, and we don't have a lot of time," Langenkamp says. "I just found that after working with Wes, who by then we'd established a pretty great shorthand for what he wanted, I didn't feel like it was easy to have to readjust and start speaking to a new director."

Labeling Cunningham—at least in those instances—as the opposite of Craven, Langenkamp adds, "Right at the moment when everyone's at high anxiety because they're not even sure if they're going to get this movie done, and you bring in someone with that kind of personality, I probably was really stressed out."

Further revealing that the actress was not very sure of what Cunningham wanted, Craven admits that, "Heather actually came to me and said, 'I just want you to be the director here,' and Sean went home the next day. But he did come and pitch in. And I think, to my memory, that's the only thing that Sean did."

"I'm sure that Sean provided a great favor to him, and did that work probably for nothing or close to it, so I could totally understand the necessity," Langenkamp says. "But I also felt that it's just really hard to have someone new come in and order people around, literally telling them what to do, and then be in charge when no relationships have really been made at that point. I don't think we knew each other from Adam at the beginning of the day, or by the end of the day, either. And that's too bad. I wish we'd had more time."

In what was clearly an already tight production, even Doyle remembers the rush to make their days, especially since a lot of footage was to be filmed at night. "Shooting a nighttime movie in June wasn't the best thing to do since you have only seven hours of dark," states the effects man. "Wes was running first unit, we're shooting four effects units, Bob Shaye was running one of the insert units, Tony Cecere was running the stunt insert unit, and others were shooting on locations we missed, just because of time limitations. A couple of Wes' friends came in to direct some of these things. It was really the only way to get it all done."

Langenkamp was not only aware of the busy atmosphere, she was in the middle of it. "There was kind of a sense of 'What can we throw in front of the camera next? What might help us edit this whole thing together? Is this scary? Is this not scary?'" she says. "They were doing inserts of my hand, and grabbing my jewelry off at one moment, and me putting it back on the next. I just remember people constantly taking off parts of my wardrobe and putting it on someone else so they could do a little scene that they needed. I don't remember it being frantic, but we were definitely focused on getting as much into camera as we could."

"I knew everybody in the office at that point and I kind of had the skinny on what we were having to shoot by the end of the show," says Diers, who was privy to the needed cutaway or reaction shots. "It was definitely a beat-the-clock kind of time."

THERE'S NO PLACE LIKE HOME

As time ticked away, getting it done also meant Nancy getting away from Freddy and into the supposed safety of her home, 1428 Elm Street, a house like many others. But as time would tell, it would become a star in its own right replete with Hollywood tours driving by. It also became synonymous with terror, even though nobody knew it was to become an icon in the series.

Because the shooting schedule saw the film working around the Fourth of July holiday, cast and crew held a barbecue to celebrate. Clockwise from bottom left: Jensen, Fleetwood, and Logan showcase the talents of costume, hair, and makeup; The festivities saw a statuesque Blakley mimic Lady Liberty; The costume, makeup, and hair ladies don their best red, white, and blue; Depp, years before he would actually move to France, sports a beret, a wine glass, and loaf of the country's bread.

"We were shooting in Los Angeles, but everything had to look like Ohio. So finding a sort of house where you would believe that, and that was on a street that didn't have palm trees, was the first objective," Talalay says.

And of the now well-remembered address?

"The actual house number was 1428," Langenkamp recalls. "I mean, we didn't have the money to change the numbers on a house!"

As difficult as it might have been to find a home on a street in southern California that didn't look it, that's exactly what Craven ordered. "I think there seems to be one, maybe two, streets in Los Angeles where you don't see palm trees," says Cook. "I know that was a big thing for Wes is that he really wanted it to look generic Midwest, if nothing else." Because of the mandate, there weren't a lot of options. "I can't swear to this, but I think because of that reason the street was always being shot on, which might have made it more expensive," she offers.

Film finances weren't only affecting what went up on screen, as the production found out while prepping the practical house location. The day before they were set to shoot, the IRS had posted a lien on the property, causing the set decorators to tell the government agent they were going to be shooting in fourteen hours.

Burrows recalls, "The IRS man said, 'I don't care what you say, I've heard every excuse!'" The official then informed them that they were not to take the sign down, and that it had to be there twenty-four hours a day. "So we got there the next morning and we took it down. We didn't hear from anybody, so it was down for a week," adds Burrows.

"I don't remember that," admits Craven. "But it wouldn't surprise me if it did happen. Sometimes those things happen and the director doesn't even know about it."

"It's funny, because those kinds of things happen all the time on these low-budget films," admits Diers. "That is absolutely no surprise to me. I don't want to say anything hurtful to the people who owned the house, but maybe that was the reason that they were having filming at the house. Maybe they needed the money."

If that wasn't issue enough, the next interruption would be made by the film production's neighbors. It was much more of a noisy affair, occurring at the studio the film was using.

"Since I was brought on so early with Gerry, I had to look around for the right studio facility. We went to Desilu," recalls Cook.

"Desilu Studios had been established on Gower Street in Hollywood," says Langenkamp. "So after Desilu, after Lucille Ball and that whole era had passed, it was in quite a bit of disrepair, and I think that's how the production got it so cheap."

With multiple stages to work with, including one with a pit that was required for the production, "It was great to have two stages so we could be building on one and shooting on the other. And it was a great location," Cook says.

"I remember Kathy and Ronee and I, on the Fourth of July we were filming, and I remember we had a big blowout. A big Fourth of July dress-up thing," says Fleetwood. "We had fun."

Cook agrees, stating, "We had a barbecue. It was really our home during the whole time of making that movie, and it had a lot to do with sort of the family atmosphere. It really was just a homey, sort of private, protected lot that not many people knew about, really. I have fond memories of that."

Englund recalls, "We were in this perfect, miniature lot in the heart of Hollywood. Everybody had easy access parking, our dressing rooms were little offices that maybe had been Desi Arnaz or Lucille Ball's offices," he says. "There was still scenery there from *The Brady Bunch* (1969–1974) or *The Partridge Family* (1970–1974) or one of those shows that shot there."

Past television behind, it was now the year of the very successful Los Angeles Olympics Arts Festival. "I know rehearsing in the adjacent soundstage was Le Théâtre du Soleil, which is arguably the best theater in Europe," says Englund.

As the theater company worked to put on their big, staged productions, they eventually had hundreds of people attending nightly, in addition to a band. "All their excitement, and clapping, you could hear it on our stage and the sound man, he was going nuts," says Burrows. "So I complained and Bob Shaye called them and said that he was gonna sue if they didn't do something about the sound. So they actually cut the band out and told the audience 'Don't clap!' for the next twelve days. And that settled it."

"It sounds a little bit out of my style, but it's possible," Shaye says of the tale.

Finally able to continue on, though they "did shoot quite a bit at the house, especially outside," Langenkamp recalls, "a lot of the work was at the stage. We shot most of the interiors there."

It was there, Burrows says, "We actually built the whole house on the stage, first and second floor."

Haitkin elaborates on the independent film mimicking a bigger Hollywood movie. "It was done, in a way, like a studio," he says. "The film was shot on a lot. Even though it did have a lot of location filming, it was based in an independent stage in Hollywood where sets were being built, pretty elaborate sets."

But the house, whether real or on the soundstage, was seen by Craven as more than just a place for Nancy to live, something Langenkamp appreciated. "Wes has a lot of ideas, philosophical ideas, and he has a lot of ideas about what the words actually mean. In a 'way out of this world level,' that sometimes can be extremely deep," she says. "For example, Wes was reading a philosopher, and I wish I could remember the name, when he wrote *Nightmare*, and the house is actually a representation of the psyche itself. You know, you have so many levels of the house because there are so many levels of our psyche. And he actually is thinking of those things when he's directing the movie. And he's letting you know that he's thinking of those things when he's directing the movie, which is fantastic."

STUCK!

Craven shot some, but not all, of the scenes at the actual house location. It was now the sanctuary to which Nancy desperately tried to get after her encounter with Tina's corpse and Freddy outside the jail. But in true *Elm Street* fashion, Krueger wasn't going to let that happen so easily, putting Nancy in a sticky situation. The notion came to life differently than what was in Craven's screenplay, while also bringing out the creative talents of producer Shaye.

In an early version of the script, Nancy runs down the street away from Krueger, but the nightmare doesn't make it easy for her. Running at top speed, she crashes through a sawhorse and "into a new sidewalk, sinking into the wet cement over her ankles. The stuff sticks to her legs in long gluey gobs and she can barely pull her feet loose." Krueger gives chase, almost slashing her, but Nancy does get away into her house, where another change was made.

That same draft has Nancy watching as Krueger claws at a window in the kitchen, trying to get in. He is "prying at the glass with his big knife-fingers, the sharp blades sizzling against the edges of the glass as they crack it away from the frame." It is at that moment the young girl turns and runs upstairs, prompting what is seen in the final version of the film.

"The Bob Shaye imprint in large measure came from some of my own nightmares. That's why I was just offering them up to Wes," Shaye states. "The one that I specifically recall was the sticky stairs episode."

Risher remembers the idea originating with him as well. "When Nancy puts her feet in the stairs, yes," she says, "that was Bob's idea. We called them the 'oatmeal stairs.'"

Shaye's notion was also confirmed by Talalay. "Bob had an image of, really, that idea of running and not being able to move. Trying to get away and not being able to get anywhere."

"I think it's just a really common dream, from what I've understood: people getting stuck as they're walking. It was kind of the idea behind it," offers Langenkamp.

Nancy rushes up the staircase, only to find that her feet have literally sunk into each step. Recalls Langenkamp, "They decided to just cut the carpet, and then they poured in a bunch of oatmeal mixed with mushroom soup or something like that to make it that sticky, sticky consistency."

The stories of soup and oatmeal offer one explanation, but the movie magic material that was really used? Rideout, who offered up the solution, explains. "Doyle said, 'What's the stickiest, stringiest, nastiest thing you can think of that the stairs can turn into?'" she remembers. "I looked at him and I said, 'Bisquick.'"

Doyle was surprised at Rideout's fast answer, as well as the idea she could be right. As he found out, she was. "If you mix Bisquick up too thick, and let it sit for an hour, it becomes the most sticky, gooey, tenacious stuff on the planet," Doyle says.

On a note that fit in well with the production, it was also very cheap.

But make-it-at-home batter wasn't all the effect had going for it. "There were just boxes built into the stairs and we mixed the Bisquick up, and laid it in there, and got it all flattened out. And then we took sliced-up carpet and layed it over," Doyle says. "Obviously, it was a cheap effect. When you see it and you watch it closely you can see the spots where she's gonna step where it's not quite level."

Talalay isn't shy about what she thought of the final product. "Listen, they put the sticky stuff over the stairs and, well, it kind of looks like it!" she says. "It was never planned properly and that was a cheesy effect."

Nancy was, at least for a few moments, effectively stopped in her tracks, with a "stunt foot" performance by Rideout. "It's actually my feet in the stairs, too. I did a number of inserts. And let me tell you, that Bisquick will follow you anywhere!" she jokes.

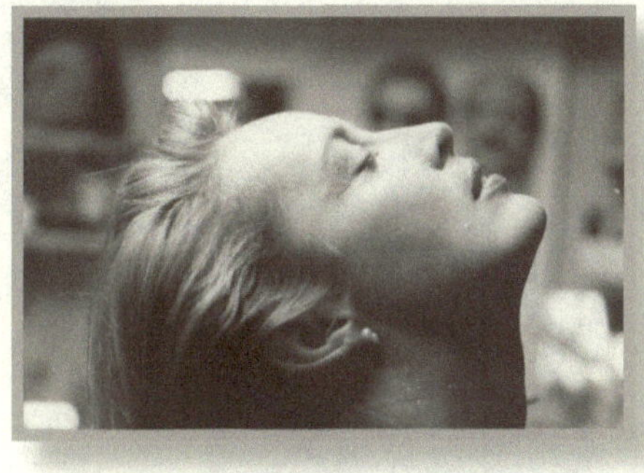

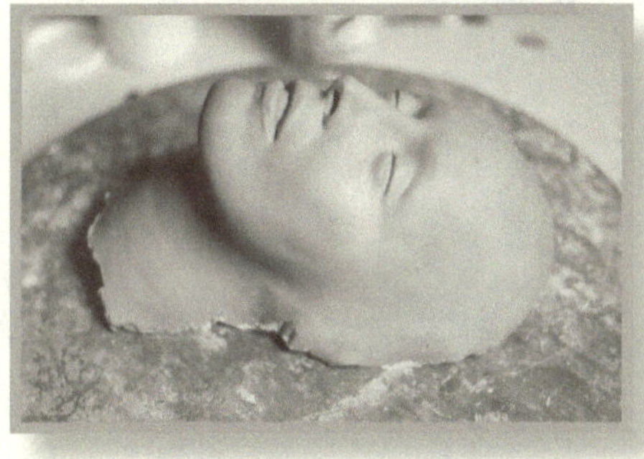

Special effects reference photo (top) used to create the lifecast of Blakley for the moment where Freddy torments Nancy by wearing the face of her mother. The plaster cast (bottom) also provided Miller the ability to create a second mask for use on another effect at the end of the film.

Englund looks back at why he feels those simple nightmare sequences are so effective. "For me, one of the things that always works in a movie is when somebody's barefoot and they have to run. Anybody running around in their backyard, or being chased by somebody, barefoot, or in their nightgown or something. You're doubly, cathartically involved," he says, "because you can imagine, 'Oh my God! It'd be hard enough if there was a fire in my house to get out, to get my wife and my dog, but I'm

Top to bottom: Englund is all smiles as Miller (who feigns a fright) touches up his makeup; Wanting to get in on the act, Depp (in his character's letterman jacket) tries on one of the Freddy stunt masks; Depp takes a moment to have some fun with hair, makeup, and effects; A fully made up and ready-to-film Englund waits patiently for his cue.

Johnny Boy

gonna be barefoot, I gotta crawl over my roof, I gotta jump in the cactus.' And the idea of being stuck when you know you absolutely must get away. Ewww! We all have that common experience."

As Nancy fights to free her feet, Krueger is not far behind. Smashing the front door window, he tries to frighten the girl with a decidedly more psychological approach; one that may surprise longtime fans of the film. "When I am on the stairs trying to get away, and Freddy smashes through the window, he's wearing a mask of Ronee, of my mother," reveals Langenkamp.

For some time, it's been seemingly decided that Krueger was actually taunting Nancy with the face and voice of her murdered friend, Tina.

Not the case, says Langenkamp. "Tina is already dead, and I've seen her that way twice. At that point in the film, the only female in my life is my mom. That's who Freddy was imitating."

That idea is also reinforced by the man responsible for creating the false countenance. "It was a mask of

Ronee Blakley's face. We didn't do a mask of Tina's face for that moment," admits Miller. "It was definitely the mother because we had a mold of her face to make the skeletal remains of her when she is in the bed at the end. The mask at the door and the mask on the Marge dummy are the same. In the script it read kind of like, 'Oh, she recognizes it's not Freddy. It's her mother.'"

Further confirming the notion is the actress whose voice it has been said haunted Nancy. "I never did that ADR. It was Ronee," offers Wyss.

What did Craven have to say when pressed for clarification? "I have no idea."

"We just did one take of the sticky stairs scene," says Langenkamp. "It didn't take any time at all, but it was kind of toward the end, and we were doing things really fast, as I remember, 'Ok, let's do this, let's do that, let's do this.'"

Haitkin remembers the pressure on set to get things done, on time and on budget. "Pressure? Definitely," he says, "because we didn't have a lot of money and it was an extremely ambitious project. The film had a ton of custom work."

He further reveals that at least two-thirds of the film was figured out as they went along, mainly because there was nothing truly standard about it at the time. "Every shot has to have a certain look to it, every shot has to be part of that whole," Haitkin says. "So you have to groom it and get everything ready. There was no money, there was no time, and that was sort of the challenge."

Without the funds for an additional day of shooting, and needing to get everything completed, Craven recalled the multiple units all working on the same stage, as he went from one to the other "setting up shots and shooting, and then going to the next set up," he says of the frenetic goings-on around him. "I know Freddy building his glove, and Nancy sinking down into the steps, the mother being sucked through the front door, and I think Rod's sheet coming around him in the prison cell, were all being shot simultaneously along with the main speaking scene."

By the end of the film, with so many units working, people had to be careful not to enter, and potentially ruin, another shot in what could seem like a circus of setups. "There were sets cobbled together like a Rubik's Cube," laughs Diers. "A piece of that set, and an insert of that set, and something from this set, and somebody's lighting was with people shooting third unit over here. We were trying to finish on time and send the equipment back and get the crew off the payroll. And I just remember the comedy of literally, 'Which unit are you on? Which shot are you guys working on?'"

It was the "we have to get it done" attitude that seemingly caused another, even if shallow at the time, rift between Shaye and Craven. "One of the big fights I remember between Bob and Wes was over the sticky stairs," Talalay says, "and my recollection, which could be incorrect because it really was a long time ago, was that Bob was obsessed with this image of the sticky stairs. And Wes wasn't particularly interested in it, and there wasn't any extra time to shoot an extra day, so it ended up sort of being Bob forcing us to shoot this," she says.

"Wes and I did have a little bit of a disagreement about who was doing what," Shaye admits. "He wanted me to stick in my role as a producer."

Shaye did, until there came a moment when time and money were running short. "The very last night, the camera crew was threatening to walk off the set and we were shooting all the stairwell stuff," Shaye recalls.

"Bob normally was in New York, but would come to visit occasionally," said Craven, "And we were shooting the stairwell scene, and we had the oatmeal in there already, to my recollection. And I said, 'Bob, why don't you direct this one?' And he essentially said, 'Action' and 'Cut,' but I was there on the set and we had been filming all day."

Also present was Risher, recalling that Shaye "came at the end when we were shooting the oatmeal stairs because Wes wanted him to direct it. So Bob directed [that]."

"Bob was managing that one. He was helping because it was his dream idea," Langenkamp says.

Whether due to a forcing of hands or something simply necessitated by circumstances, Shaye says, "There wasn't much directing to go on, but Wes finally deigned to let me say 'Action,' at least."

"That was kind of a goodwill gesture," admits Craven.

REFLECTIONS OF EVIL

With Craven, the crew, and the cast surviving the peril of the sticky stairs, the scene on which Shaye was temporarily back in the director's chair ended as Langenkamp's character races into her bedroom.

"The classic Wes Craven scare moment is when Nancy is standing in front of a mirror, and says, 'This is just a dream, he isn't real!'" says editor Shaine. "And with perfect timing, Freddy launches out of the mirror." It's a moment he admits to revisiting more than once because "it's just a perfectly timed scare. And nobody but Wes does it better."

It can also be said that it might not have been done at all, as the moment was not in earlier drafts of the script. Instead, Nancy makes it to her room, seemingly safe, until Freddy strikes, as stated in the April 30, 1984 script, where "the killer dives through her window and seizes her in a shower of shattered glass!"

The moment changed to Krueger crashing through a mirror on Nancy's door. "I think it's kind of an example of probably Jacques and Wes deciding that they had this opportunity to do some *Alice in Wonderland*-like, *Through the Looking-Glass* ideas that just breaking through the window wouldn't have been as interesting," Langenkamp says, adding, "I'm also sure Jim Doyle had a lot to do with it."

"The mirror that breaks when Freddy comes through the door, into Heather's reflection, allowed Wes to say some interesting things," Doyle says. "The fact that Freddy was coming through her reflection, through her visage, was important to him from a structural standpoint."

Examining the notion of whether Nancy is, or isn't, in a dream, and whether the character knows the difference, is intriguing to Langenkamp. "On top of the *Alice in Wonderland* reference, or when people go through mirrors, the other thing is, the whole dream metaphor is that a dream is a reflection of our life," she states. "When Nancy's in the dream, she doesn't know whether she's in her real life or in her dream sometimes. She says,

'This is only a dream, this is only a dream,' and then Freddy comes crashing through the mirror. It's just an example of how Nancy's always checking, 'Am I awake or am I asleep?'"

Worries of whether she was conscious or slumbering would quickly be set aside, as Nancy was jolted when Krueger bursts through her own likeness. "That was me," reveals Cecere. "I was the one that came crashing through the mirror and then fought on the bed with Heather."

The stuntman goes on to explain his part in the thrilling scene, admitting that a double was used for Langenkamp as she stands in front of the mirror with her hands at her face. "I didn't want to take a chance on some of the glass getting in her eyes," says Cecere, "but then throughout the scene it was a stunt girl some of the time, and some of the time it was Heather."

Although Langenkamp didn't take issue with a stuntwoman doubling her for the effect and some moments in the scene, Englund did, according to Cecere. "Robert didn't particularly care for me doubling him because I wasn't his size," he says, though the stuntman freely admits that isn't on the whole unusual. "A lot of actors don't particularly enjoy it. They find every flaw that a stunt person has. It's just like, if you ever see me side by side, or even some of the shots, sure, I'm not built like Robert, and I do understand the importance of that."

Also imperative was the simple fact of making the mirror effect work, one that proved to be somewhat groundbreaking. "As far as I knew at the time, nobody had tried to do a breakaway mirror that size before," Doyle states. But that wasn't his only issue with the effect, as he found out "when you take breakaway glass and put the mirror on it through vacuumed metalizing, you have to do it quickly, within a few hours, because the vacuumed metalizing shrinks slightly. As it cures, it breaks the glass."

Being ready meant, for people like Haitkin and his camera crew, coordinating with the effects and other departments ahead of time to make sure complicated shots like the breaking mirror go off without a hitch.

"There's no improvising on set for certain action sequences, visual effects, mechanical effects. Those things all have to be planned," says Haitkin. "And when you have departments that are working independent of each other preparing all these sequences, it's necessary to work off pictures because people interpret words in different ways. And the only way to keep everybody of one mind is to storyboard, so when Freddy was breaking through the mirror door, that was something that was preset and all worked out."

Indeed, as Doyle remembers. "We stuck the mirror on and we said, 'Now,' and they were ready to go. They did a good job."

It was also a job that, if done incorrectly, could beg the question: what would happen if they didn't get the shot?

"We had that thought about a hundred times a day on that film!" admits Craven. "Certainly with a stunt or anything like that. And I was worried about the glass flying into somebody's eyes or all sorts of things. But it was one of those cases where it worked the first time and you say, 'Thank you, we're moving on now.'"

Behind the scenes, Langenkamp and Englund rehearse the battle; Nancy fights with Freddy, using her strength to keep his talons from tearing in to her.

Krueger crashing through the mirror and leaping upon Nancy would be the first time Langenkamp was able to physically demonstrate that her character was, indeed, a fighter. It's something the actress appreciated. "It's rare in modern films, and certainly in the films that I've seen in my life, where the protagonist and the antagonist are so clearly defined. Where they actually represent good and evil with no equivocation at all," the actress says. "Robert Englund and I talked a lot about the underlying symbolism of our battle."

The man behind Krueger also found their on-screen relationship interesting and complicated. "There is some kind of Cocteau *Beauty and the Beast* (1946) thing between Heather and I, and I don't know what it is, but there is a dance between us that has sort of become archetypical," Englund says. "The audiences respond to that on a subliminal level."

Elaborating on what Englund sees in their on-screen rapport, Langenkamp says, "Robert is a very intelligent person and a very highly-trained actor, so in a lot of ways he encouraged me to think of the battle on a much higher level, as if we're talking about a Greek tragedy."

Englund, on the other hand, states it in more simplified, perhaps salacious, terms. "Audiences don't want to see us get it on, but they'd like to see us butt heads. I think they'd like to see Freddy force a kiss on her."

The actress ruminates on the recipe for success between the two characters, accepting the sexual element, even if it is one-sided. "I've always thought that one of the keys to their relationship is that there is ambiguity. I don't think Nancy loves Freddy, but

I do think that Freddy loves Nancy," contemplates Langenkamp. "She's not only fighting him off to save her life, she's also fighting off this untoward approach by a man."

Whether that man is getting too close, putting his face into their space, or leaning his body on theirs, Langenkamp feels it's something that almost every girl and woman has felt. "From a boy in school to a creepy uncle, to a co-worker around the water cooler. If you're a woman, you've experienced that," she says.

It's also one of the characteristics that make Nancy a symbol of femininity for the actress, even when others might see the character differently. "When everyone's like, 'Oh, she has this very masculine quality,' I don't really get that," considers Langenkamp. "I really feel like she's so innocent and she's fending off Freddy in all these different aspects."

Filmed at the end of an eighteen-hour day, Nancy and Krueger's platonic, and almost deadly, roll in the sheets saw "all those feathers everywhere," recalls Langenkamp, as Freddy tears into the pillow Nancy holds in front of her.

Craven recalled Risher being on set, nearly eight months pregnant, sitting in a corner. "She had a big air mask over her face so she wouldn't breathe feathers, because somebody told us that you could inhale feathers and die."

Risher confirms the moment, "Yes, I had heard that inhaling feathers was harmful, so I had covered my mouth," she laughs.

Thanks to an alarm clock, Nancy wakes up seemingly less afraid of her encounter with Krueger and his deadly advances and more frustrated with the one who should be kissing her: the supposed-to-be-watching Glen. In charge of waking her up if it looked like she was having a nightmare, it was one of the first big scenes for newcomer Depp and, much like his character, the actor confessed that back then he was "scared and lost. Fortunately, Wes was very patient and gentle," Depp says. "He didn't mind when I asked him stupid questions like, 'What's action?'"

Craven remembered Johnny "being pretty green. But he did pick it up pretty fast and was eager to participate in the process. He seemed to automatically understand what acting was and what creating a character was."

If Depp was working hard to acclimate to life on a movie set and to find his character, Blakley admits she was also working hard on hers, going so far as to use not just her talents, but her person, to bring Marge to life. "As an actor, I used my hair as a character prop, and started her out with a very tidy hairdo and then brought her hair down, messier and messier as the movie went along, to signify her unraveling," Blakley says.

"She wanted her hair to look a certain way," Woodrum confirms. "So it was a lot of work to make her hair look good, but that's what Ronee loved. And when her hair looked good, she was a very confident and great person, although her character wasn't. But that just tells you how good she was."

While Craven might have appreciated the actress's delving deep into her character, in addition to Blakley's hair experimentation, he does politely add that "she was never quite satisfied with her makeup, so she would usually go and fiddle with it after the makeup and hair [departments] were done with her, so we never knew quite what she would look like when she got to the set."

It's something that is remembered well by the women in charge of such tasks.

"I did her makeup and she was not terribly pleased with it, although I have to say everybody thought she looked fabulous, including myself," says Logan. "She went to her room and put on a bunch of orange makeup. Orange eye shadow, orange blusher, orange lipstick, orange everything. And she proceeded to walk out to the set, unbeknownst to me."

Logan was made aware when a second assistant director summoned her to the set to confer with Craven. The makeup artist saw Blakley and, without saying a word, made it clear to the writer and director that the cosmetic application she witnessed on the actress was not her original doing.

"Wes later said to me the expression on my face when I saw her for the first time led him to believe that I had no idea that she had done that, and it certainly wasn't my work," recalls Logan. "So I had my kit there and I redid her makeup. Wes was standing there, I looked at him for approval, he gave me the basic thumbs up and said it was great."

"I think what was happening to her was so torturous, such a torment, that she sought solace where she could find it, which was in the bottle."

Ronee Blakley on her character's drinking

It wasn't, Logan points out, a onetime occurrence. "Every single day, that's what happened. I had to figure out how to not let that happen," she says.

Which is exactly what she did.

"First thing in the morning, when Ronee would come in, I would go through her purse in front of her, take all of her makeup out, give her back her purse, and lock her makeup in a drawer in the makeup room, which was locked after I left," Logan states.

Fleetwood was not immune to the situation, either. "She was constantly changing her hair, and you did not ever know what she was going to do," she states. "It was a continuity challenge, but I was constantly on it. The hair moves, and when you have someone moving the hair for you, it's going to do even more so. It was one of the biggest challenges for me on the show."

The situation did, however, seem to work out. At least for Logan. "She gave me a fabulous gift at the end of the show," she laughs.

Langenkamp does seem to have an understanding for the situation, revealing that she and her other, younger castmates wore very little makeup. "Ronee was probably the one who sat in the chair longer than most of us. We kind of went on our merry way after about five minutes," she says. "And now that I'm the age that Ronee was when she played the role, if you're surrounded by gorgeous teenagers, if you're surrounded by Johnny Depp, I can only empathize with Ronee wanting to look her very best."

Whatever Blakley was doing, particularly with her hair, did seem to work, adding yet another layer to the character of Nancy's mother. Nowhere was the start of Marge's unraveling more apparent than when she bursts into Nancy's room (forcing Glen back down the rose trellis from which he came), clearly drunk, and showcasing the actress's unkempt hair notions.

"I think Marge's drinking was a problem for her," admits Blakley. "I think that it wasn't helpful for her daughter that she drank too much. And I think what was happening to her was so torturous, such a torment, that she sought solace where she could find it, which was in the bottle."

HANG TIGHT

Just as Depp heeded the advice of those around him, his character would also listen to Nancy, who forces him to go with her to check on Rod. From her previous nightmare, she realizes their friend might actually get a visit from Krueger, which could only spell trouble. As Nancy and Glen make their way into the police station, they are stopped short by a less-than-willing-to-help Garcia.

"It was overnight in a suburban police station. I've worked the graveyard shift in jobs before and there's fatigue involved and you just wanna get through it, basically," Unger concedes. "And to have hysterical kids running in, especially when one of them is your boss' daughter, you don't know how to deal with it, you know?"

Trying to convince him that they must see Rod, Nancy and Glen next face her father. It was a moment where Saxon recalled his on-screen brushes with Depp.

"Johnny kept referring to me as 'Mr. Saxon,' and I thought, 'Well, come on, hey, ya know, just call me John,'" he says. "I mean, who knew that one day he was going to be 'Mr. Depp?'"

Though Saxon didn't have many scenes with "Mr. Depp," even he realized the future star's ability to understand and absorb what was going on around him. "Although I didn't have much to do personally with him in the film, it was clear he was always paying attention. It was just some things that I saw him do," the veteran actor says.

Langenkamp, too, was impressed with Depp's ability to be aware of what he needed to do, and what he didn't actually understand. "I remember [Johnny] being very serious about not pretending he knew what he was doing when he didn't, and about listening, not just to Wes, but to everyone on the set," she says. "He was so real, and as a result, I think he was so refreshing. He was shy and unassuming. He didn't hog the camera. He didn't demand any special treatment. It was just really nice to have someone like that as a co-star."

"He was in awe of everything that was going on around him," Logan says. "And always wanted to learn and better himself."

Craven also gave the first-time actor praise for his work and work ethic. "He had very, very high standards."

As Nancy begs her father to check on Rod, Craven was happy with the performance that Saxon was giving his character, the long-suffering parent. "I think [John] did a wonderful job as sort of a guy who really cared for his daughter, but he thought maybe she was going crazy, or she was just being totally weird or whatever," he says.

"You need a character that's sort of with it, and also finds it incredible," Saxon adds.

Craven felt there was a lot of nuance in Saxon's portrayal. "He's not just a stupid cop, which is so common in these films," he offered.

Taking his daughter seriously or, at the very least, humoring her, Thompson summons the keys to Rod's cell from Garcia. When he can't find them, the moment offers tension as the audience is aware of something the adults are not: for Rod, every second matters.

"We played the thing like 'Where are the keys?' and Wes directed to that point while I'm dicking around looking," Unger says. "I don't know that the guy's being hung, you know? It did add to the suspense of that moment."

As the scene progressed and moved toward trying to save Rod in his jail cell, Corri recalls that, in his mind, Rod's death left much to be desired. "My death, I think, was stupid. I get hanged, you know? Tina goes through hell in her bed. And then this dude's choking me out in my cell and I'm screaming like a little girl. I was just like this tough guy yelling, 'No!' but Tina fought it out with him. I don't know," he says, joking, "I'd love to get some reshoots on that."

Englund has a different take on why, even when Freddy isn't visible at the scene of the crime, he still permeates the narrative. "There's something kind of wonderful in that it's like that old game of telephone that you play at camp with the Dixie cups," he says, "and you hear the whisper in everybody's ear all the way around and see how the story changes. So Freddy can kind of be a little different in everybody's dream. Sometimes you see him, sometimes you don't. But he's always there."

The actor is also quick to clarify that Krueger does, indeed, murder Rod. "Freddy strangles him with his own bed sheets. And I just love that because it was an excuse for another kind of kill, a more creative kill that shows how Freddy can manifest," Englund says. "And I always loved that. I think that's really effective even if I am not in it because it's just so apt as to be something from Freddy's imagination, or a tool that he would use, or a kind of mean kill. It's a mean taunting that he would use. And I think that actually really holds up, that kill. I think it holds up today."

Differing viewpoints on the matter aside, Corri does give high marks to some of the team that brought about his Freddy-less end, but first takes umbrage with at least one person involved: the makeup girl. "She put too much white powder on me, as if I lost blood after I'm dead. So that was kind of weird," he admits, but goes on to say, "The effects guys were amazing. Everything was done like the old days, real stuff. Where today it's green screen, CGI. When they were hanging me, the thing going around my neck, they shot it backwards. They did the knot and then they unraveled it."

Detailing the secrets of Rod's death at the hands of an unseen Krueger, Doyle says, "It was technically complicated because there were a lot of little scenes that had to be cut together and, when the sheet snakes around his neck, if you really look at it, you can tell it's being pulled backwards."

Doyle admits that to avoid this potential flaw he and his team tried to pull the sheet forward, but the fishing line pulling at the fabric was too obvious. "So we would pull slowly backwards, and in printing the film they may have sped up and slowed some things down. It was very carefully laid out with Wes and Jacques," he says.

Haitkin admits, "There were a lot of different things going on with that."

What wasn't perfectly laid out was the first attempt at hanging Corri's character. Wearing a harness vest with the wire to lift him wrapped in towels, and a hook behind his neck, the actor recalls, "They're pulling me up and I don't have anything under my feet, and the harness is around your scrotum and it's like wearing a really tight bathing suit."

The issue began when the effects team started to lift him up on the line to hang him. "The thing

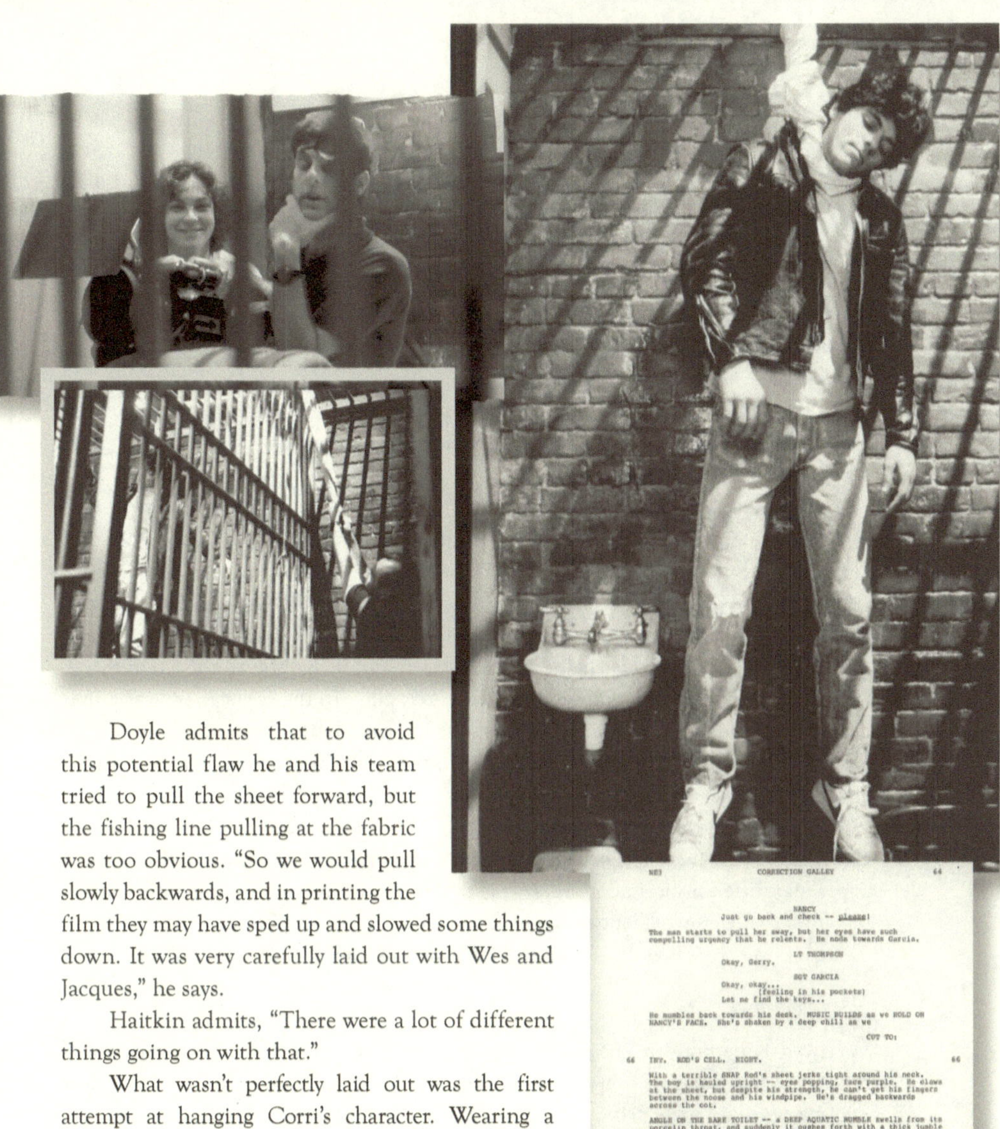

NE3 CORRECTION GALLEY 64

NANCY
Just go back and check -- please!

The man starts to pull her away, but her eyes have such compelling urgency that he relents. He nods towards Garcia.

LT THOMPSON
Okay, Gerry.

SGT GARCIA
Okay, okay...
(feeling in his pockets)
Let me find the keys...

He mumbles back towards his desk. MUSIC BUILDS as we HOLD ON NANCY'S FACE. She's shaken by a deep chill as we

CUT TO:

66 INT. ROD'S CELL. NIGHT. 66

With a terrible SNAP Rod's sheet jerks tight around his neck. The boy is hauled upright -- eyes popping, face purple. He claws at the sheet, but despite his strength, he can't get his fingers between the noose and his windpipe. He's dragged backwards across the cot.

ANGLE ON THE BARE TOILET -- a DEEP AQUATIC RUMBLE swells from its porcelin throat, and suddenly it gushes forth with a thick jumble of water and sewage.

Thrashing in pure panic now, Rod is hauled backwards across the splashing floor, gasping and struggling in vain against the powerful pull, untill he sees the filthy fountain he's being dragged towards. Then he really goes berserk -- fighting it with every ounce of strength in his body -- water is everywhere, a giant stream shooting up and smashing off the ceiling, cascading down the walls and rushing out through the bars into the cellblock. And Rod is dragged forward despite all his struggle not to be.

ANGLE ON THE TOILET -- the front of the sheet dives into its column of water like a water snake, quick and strong, dragging the helpless boy at its far end headfirst into the water. Rod's arms brace on the edge of the bowl -- his muscles and veins pop out in supreme struggle -- but the power of whoever it is pulling on the far end is far superior -- his arms break their lock -- his head and shoulders are pulled under water and held solid as a rock.

His feet kick and spin and thrash, but it only earns him an even harder jerk, that seems to crush his shoulders right down into

CORRECTION GALLEY

Clockwise from top left: Haitkin and first assistant camera operator Anne Coffey set up a shot in the jail; Rod meets his end by hanging, a moment Corri felt could have been a bit more exciting; A script page describing Rod's original "death by toilet"; A peek behind the scenes of the "mechanics" of Rod's death.

snapped. The wire wasn't strong enough. So the first time I crashed and burned. I fell three feet," Corri remembers. "They then did it with a harness where they lift you up and secure you. But it was the old days."

Also thinking back on the effect, Carlucci echoes Corri's sentiment about the way it was done. "Again, these were the old methods of achieving these type of effects that nowadays it might be more convenient to do it computer generated and to have a different look," he says.

Old school techniques or not, Corri is firm on one aspect of the effect. "I wanted to die after Johnny Depp so I could be in the movie longer. I just loved acting and I didn't want to get killed off," he declares.

Corri's character being disposed of on screen did have an impact on Langenkamp's real life. "The strange thing about being in these movies is that you see things that actors do that sometimes you never see in real life," she says. "You're sitting there looking at a hanging man and you say, 'Is that what a hanging man really looks like?' You, yourself, don't really know, so now my image of a hanging man is [Nick] hanging from a sheet."

Unger, whose character helps cut Rod down and bring him to the floor, recalls a moment of his that was changed and ultimately cut. "In the script there was a line, when we find the body, that my character says in Spanish," he says.

That dialogue, in early drafts of the screenplay, was, "Goddam loco kid—he didn't have t'do that—Madre dios!"

"I'm not Hispanic, and I didn't grow up in that milieu, but I didn't see any reason to change the name, because in America, people have all kinds of different last names and different heritages," says Unger. "I've known a lot of people with Spanish surnames that weren't fluent in Spanish. And I tried it, and to me it wasn't working. I talked it over with Wes and he said, 'Don't worry about it,' so we just changed it."

LANE TO REST

With Rod Lane now another victim of Krueger, Nancy attends his funeral, quietly trying to make sense of everything. Playing the Minister presiding over the service was Jack Shea, an actor who, at the time, was looking for a talent manager and not necessarily his break on *Elm Street*.

"I was living in Los Angeles, pursuing my acting career, and went to a person who was recommended," Shea remembers. "He was interested and, at the time, I was appearing in a play in Los Angeles called *Bleacher Bums*. He sent his assistant to see me perform." That assistant happened to be Craven's wife, Mimi, who brought Craven along. "Afterwards, I met them both. They were very gracious, very kind, and I wound up being called in by Wes to read. That's how I got the part."

Filming the scene, recalls Langenkamp, began with a discussion "on whether or not Nancy would have owned a black dress," she says, hence her wearing bright blue to the service, something that clearly makes the young woman stand out.

"When you're innocent and young, the idea of going to a funeral is the last thing on your mind. In fact, personally, I don't think I ever owned any black clothing until I moved to California, because it was hip," laughs Langenkamp. "But it's something that a young person wouldn't have, a mourning costume. And that funeral was the next day or two days later. So maybe you don't have the opportunity to go buy new clothes."

Remembering the color choice, Shea adds, "[Heather] was the protagonist in the film, and I believe they were using costuming and color as a way to pull her out. Other people in that kind of monochromatic black and white would kind of recede into the background, while that blue would pull her out. That's one of the ways that costume designers do it, through color and ornamentation."

Langenkamp also offers that with Marge in a seemingly general state of denial, coupled with bouts of drunkenness, Nancy's mother may not have particularly cared whether or not her daughter was dressed appropriately. "So all these little justifications for wearing the blue dress do make sense and, in the end, it does make Nancy stand out," the actress states.

The burial scene (left), filmed at the Boyle Heights Evergreen Cemetery, is the only moment audiences get a brief glimpse of Rod's parents. It also showcases Nancy in what many would not deem typical funeral attire, something that was by design; The original Pietà (right) that is shown at the very start of Rod's funeral. "After the show wrapped, I begged set decorator Anne Huntley for the plaster statue," admits Diers, with whom the piece now resides.

And it wasn't just the funeral wear doing that. "Nancy stood out a lot with her clothing in general. She wasn't trendy, and she didn't care, and time and time again you just realize, obviously, *Teen Vogue* just wasn't knocking on her door," jokes Langenkamp.

Jensen offers her opinion on the subject, something that, even though she did not design the clothing, she understands and felt worked for the film rather than against it. "I think that they were just real people. They were all kids that would hang together, and be neighbors, and it didn't seem fashion-y at all. It didn't seem fake," she says. "It seemed like they really were a team of kids that just lived and studied together, were in the same school and in the same neighborhood and, ultimately, were in the same nightmare."

Nancy looks on at her parents as she begins to describe her tormenter. The notion forces Marge to take action to help Nancy end the nightmare.

That viewpoint is echoed by Langenkamp. "One of the most successful aspects of it is that it's a kind of timeless wardrobe for these kids. Nobody's really wearing trendy outfits," she says. "I think a lot of modern horror has the girls look so great, and they're wearing very stylish clothes and jewelry, and it dates the project a lot, I think. I remember talking to the wardrobe people, saying, 'We just don't wanna do that.'"

While Langenkamp and Jensen recall the clothing choices, the actress also remembers the bucolic location where they were shooting. "It took place at a cemetery in Boyle Heights, California. It was a really old, beautiful, and classic Los Angeles cemetery," she says.

"We did it in just a very few takes," recalls Shea, "and I believe I was there on the very first day of principal photography. The filming itself went very smoothly and Wes was very nice towards us."

Shaye vividly recalls the scene, which was one of the very first to be shot, for other, very important reasons: it being a lesson on interacting with talent. "We were shooting the cemetery scene and I had just met John Saxon for the first time, and he comes up to me and says, 'Who is this guy, Shaye? What kind of movie is this? I know what it is, but who are the people that are putting all this together?'" the producer recalls. "So I pretended I wasn't me and I said, 'Oh, they're really good guys.' I figured we'd sort it all out later."

He also thinks back to another instance, this time with Craven. "The first or second shot of the film was people standing in a graveyard. The second shot was a car pulling away, and it was either supposed to be a reflection in the rear window, or something," Shaye recalls. "So Wes does one take, two takes, three takes, and I walked up to Wes and said, 'I think we got enough, don't you?' And he turned around and said, 'If you think you're gonna start telling me how to make this movie, you'd better think again, because I'm gonna do it the way you're supposed to do it. And you're the producer, just go stand over there.'"

The moment might have been the one to set the stage for any tensions that were simmering between producer and director, so Shaye took notice and, looking back with a laugh, remembers responding to Craven with, "Okay, I get it."

As the scene unfolded, it quickly becomes clear to Nancy's parents that she is on to something regarding the killer; something about which Donald and Marge aren't enthused.

"What I like so much about the story, and John Saxon and Ronee Blakley's portrayal," Langenkamp says, "is that you don't really understand in the beginning why these two adults have this conspiratorial relationship. You get the feeling that they're both upset about Nancy, but the minute she mentions Freddy Krueger, it clicks for them that the sins of the past might be coming around again."

Of course, both Donald and Marge are carrying with them the unspoken, awful truth of what they have done. "It's where he knows it's connected to Freddy," says Saxon.

"She killed Freddy. She's a murderer," Blakley says ruefully of her character.

Saxon felt it, too. "I do remember a little bit more about the relationship. It was the first scene I did with Ronee and Heather, which was the funeral," he says, admitting that the "relationship between husband and wife was not good. And at the same time, I think Heather was saying things about 'Freddy, Freddy,' and I wanted to stop that kind of stuff, to let her know that was nonsense."

The reaction from Nancy's parents wasn't necessarily something Langenkamp felt her character noticed. "I think it's a good example of Wes subtly moving the story along through a look. Marge just does this breath in, and Lieutenant Thompson scowls. Basically, it's not a big give away," she offers. "That's the way Wes kind of brings that story along. And at that point Nancy's very innocent, and she doesn't think that her parents would possibly have any idea of what she was talking about. It makes her betrayal later that much more devastating."

Before Nancy would find out the truth behind her parents' lying eyes, she would recognize that, unlike what her father had hoped to convey, Freddy Krueger was anything but nonsense.

"The dad was just not willing to go there and admit that Nancy's having these real dreams, but he knows he's somehow involved, and it's the same with Ronee Blakley's character," Langenkamp says. "Ronee becomes such an important yin to my yang. I mean, I just want somebody to believe me, and understand that I'm in this dire circumstance with a guy in my dreams who's trying to kill me. And then my mother is just pulling equally hard in this direction of protection and escape."

Blakley understood her character's motivation, saying, "We had to play it that way, of course. We deny it, but we know it may be true."

As Nancy is taken away by her mother, she can only stare at her wordless father. "I actually enjoyed playing with—having come from a divorced family myself—sort of the feelings of a kid that needs the parents to be together," Craven says. "And instead they're fighting with each other."

IF YOU DON'T DREAM, YOU GO

Shortly after the funeral for Rod, it was Blakley's character who decides that her daughter needs some protection.

And sleep.

To see that happen, she takes Nancy to a clinic named the "UCLA School of Medicine, Institute for the Study of Sleep Disorders" in the May 5, 1984 draft of the script, but which was changed to the "Katja Institute" for the film. (It was named after one of Shaye's daughters.) It's inside that Marge is hoping someone can answer the questions about what her daughter has been dreaming.

It was an important moment for Blakley's character because in her mind, she believed Marge would feel the need to "do anything to help my child. Anything to get her well. Anything to make this horror stop," she says. "It can't be real. But what if it is?"

The scene also had a fan from the crew. "I like the dream sequence where Nancy goes to the sleep clinic, just because that starts out as such a normal, scientific, reassuring scene, and then starts to get out of control," says editor Shaine, "and you're kind of with the dream technician, who is freaking out as the scene progresses."

That dream technician, Dr. King, was played by Charles Fleischer, an actor who had steady work in television before his role on *Elm Street*, in series such as *Welcome Back, Kotter* (1975–1979) and *Laverne & Shirley* (1976–1983), among many others. After his role in the Craven film, he would best become known just a few years later for his work as the titular voice in *Who Framed Roger Rabbit?* (1988). He recalls that he got the *Nightmare* job like many others had before him.

"I was called in to read for it. I read for Wes, got the part, went in there, and worked with Ronee and Heather, and it was great," Fleischer says.

Blakley also remembers her work with the actor to be a good time. "It was enjoyable. A good working relationship."

Craven and crew recalled his doing a myriad of voices to keep them entertained, amongst other things. "He's remarkable at doing voices. He's remarkable in many ways," says Craven.

Meyer-Craven, who played Dr. King's nurse, agrees with the testaments to Fleischer's talents—both on camera and in between takes. "That guy is hilarious. I call him 'Dr. Charles,'" she states. "When you're shooting, he was like a regular doctor in the clinic, and seemed like a very professional guy, but the minute they cut, and he looked around and had forty-five people staring, it was off to the races. He would have characters, and voices, and they're peeling him off the ceiling. But when they yelled, 'Rolling! Action!' he would come back."

The actress admits that the behind-the-scenes fun Fleischer was having did take a small toll on her ability to deliver for her character. "I'm trying to be, you know, the best professional I could be at the moment. But, in between takes, Dr. Charles was just evil," she says playfully. "If you watch it you can see me trying to keep it together."

Holding back laughter would be essential, for the scene was crucial as the audience—along with Nancy—discovers more about just how tangible her nightmares are. "Wes gave me a lot of direction in the scene, I remember," says Langenkamp. "How my eyes should move back and forth to look like REM sleep and the certain jerking around." Keeping it real was important, down to the machines "busily beeping and blipping, of course, and then suddenly they just go wild!" she adds.

It's at that moment the actress wondered just how she might perform what was needed of her.

"That's another example, kind of like the bathtub scene, where you absolutely have no idea how you're going to do it," Langenkamp says. "Nancy has to wear all these little monitors, she has a blanket on, and it was very technical. I just keep thinking over and over again how we didn't ever rehearse things. We never had the day before to run lines, so we'd just show up in our costumes and everyone would go through the scene. And Wes, sometimes he didn't think about some of the details, and other times he came out with really strong ideas of what the action would be."

Fleischer as Dr. King and Meyer-Craven as his nurse prepare Nancy for the tests they will run while she is inside the nightmare.

In this instance it would be Nancy fighting wildly, while an unseen and in-her-dream Krueger was on the attack. "The thrashing part is all me," Langenkamp states. "Wes wanted it to be violent at the time when the meter is just going off the charts. And I have to say, the physicality of Nancy is one of the things that makes her so unique. Every opportunity that Wes gave Nancy to have a physical action, from banging on the side of the bathtub and reaching for the sky, to being in the bed struggling and having this really scary spasming, I just trusted him so much."

Langenkamp knew that with Craven she could "always go for the biggest thing first, and if he thought it was too big, we'd always tame it down. But what I learned in that movie is that in horror you have to go big. You cannot be subtle," she states. "If you study Lawrence Olivier or whoever, they're subtle. They're doing things with their eyebrows. But you just can't be that subtle with your body when you're in a horror movie, because you're fighting Freddy."

Fleischer felt that the big action in the small scene would be crucial. "I had a suspicion that it was gonna be important, but I don't think anyone could know the depths that it would reach," he states.

That extent would include the shocking and clever twist of Nancy actually bringing something from her nightmare into the waking, physical world. "I don't know how Wes wove all that in and out, the supposedly real parts with the supposedly dream parts. It all became amorphous, in a way," says Blakley. "That was a key moment and it really spooked audiences. Everybody instantly knew that, somehow, it was real."

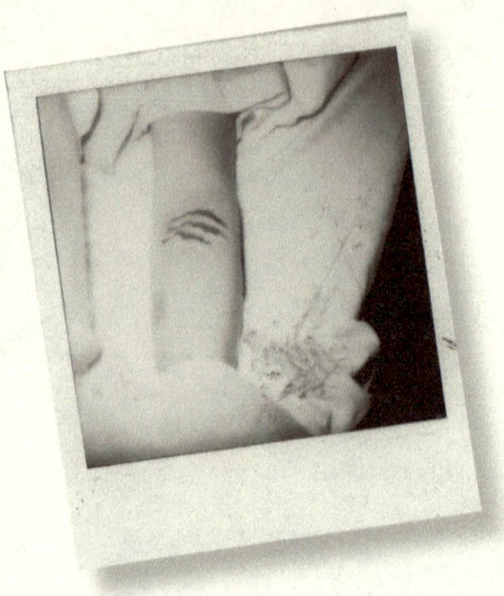

This page: Continuity photograph of the slashes Nancy endures from her dream clinic nightmare.

Opposite page: Behind the scenes, Langenkamp poses for hair and makeup continuity; Two markedly different photos showcase the gray hair Nancy might have sported in the film—a look Langenkamp did not miss. "With my blue eyes and all that white hair, it was just a bad combination," the actress explains.

That sense of fluidity, brought to life by such a simple gesture, was something that struck the film's editor as well. "It was kind of a wonderful touch to bring the hat from under the covers," says Shaine. "A simple prop, and yet, in the course of the movie, it had so much power to it."

Englund agrees, adding that since Freddy is "manifested in dreams and in nightmares, that is where he can do his damage," it would make sense that for Nancy to find a way to stop him, she must bring him to her world.

"This part to Heather was very important and she had to do her work and say, 'Okay, I have to make this believable,'" says Meyer-Craven. "It's the one moment in the film where Nancy proves Freddy's existence. She proves that he's able to affect the living. That one moment in time in the movie, if it didn't work, you know, the movie didn't really work. Heather is pulling a hat off the dead guy and pulling it into the living, so she could say, 'Wait a minute, I'm not crazy, here it is.' I was very impressed by Heather's dedication."

"I remember very vividly trying to figure out how to say the line, 'I grabbed it off his head,'" says Langenkamp. "Once in a while as an actor you really feel like you nail the delivery of a line. You give it exactly the feeling that you want to, and it's hard to do sometimes."

Admitting that it can be either thinking there are many different ways to say a line, or the director could be offering multiple ideas, the actress says on that line, she was pleased with her performance. "I just really remember leaving that scene and going, 'That's exactly the way that I wanted to say that,'" Langenkamp admits. "It was this sense of wonder, shock, understanding, but not believing. It just had all of these little aspects to that line reading. And also to impress upon her mother that this is real. All those emotions I remember coming together in that line reading and feeling very happy with it."

"That's when I really started poking around with lucid dreaming, and that concept that you can go into a dream and be awake," Craven states. "And I just invented this little conceit that if you were holding something when you woke up, it would come back with you into your reality."

The writer in Craven admitted he needed a way to figure out just how his heroine could vanquish a villain powerful enough to kill her in a dream when she would have to, eventually, fall asleep. "It finally occurred to me that she could bring him out," he says.

"First, Nancy burning herself in the boiler room and waking herself up, but finally in the sleep clinic struggle, coming out with Freddy's hat and realizing that she can bring Freddy out. That was the turning point," Craven offers. "That was where you can say, 'Okay, now you can take what is evil in the dream, and overwhelming, and bring it out into your world and have a fighting chance, because Freddy is not that familiar with the waking world.' That was the turning point for making the story work for the third act, and the third act is always the killer. It's always the thing that, 'How do you make that work?' And that was what made that work."

Even Fleischer understood the inherent concept at work when it came to Craven's villain. "I think that Freddy Krueger represents this anthropomorphic vision of evil that somehow relates to everyone. It's an archetype that Wes just tapped into," he says. "Even the clothes that he wears. The stripes and the claws. He just hit all the right notes. It's kind of magical to go into the subconscious and extrapolate data that is applicable to everyone."

The question posed by Marge of, "What the hell are dreams, anyway?" received a slight answer from Fleischer's character, and when asked if there is an explanation, the actor states, "I don't think so. I think dreams will always be a mystery as will life, but I think there's something that speaks to Wes' genius, which is that Freddy Krueger transcends the fantastic atmosphere of certain monsters. Frankenstein's not gonna really happen. And Dracula? Yeah, right. But this Freddy Krueger character, there's something about him that could be that it was real. Sure, it's fantastic in the dreams. But it touched an archetypical nerve that transcends some guy with bolts in his neck and some guy sucking blood. So it's like, it's all just a dream and it goes on forever."

GRAY MATTER

Nancy's ability to slowly understand her adversary was not just psychological, as it came with physical costs. In addition to her arm being sliced by Krueger's blades, she found out it was possible for hair to turn white from fright.

At least a part of it.

"Because Heather was so young, and she was so fresh and beautiful, it was very important that because of all the scares and the things she went through that her hair turned gray," Risher states.

Even in very early drafts of the script, Craven described "her hair is electrified, standing on end and graying before their very eyes!"

"In the script, that idea read brilliantly and we thought it was great," states Risher. In theory, at least. "So Wes has her try on a wig and she looked ridiculous with gray hair. It was just stupid."

Langenkamp remembers it well and doesn't disagree. "They sent me to a wig maker where they fit my head to make this very long, white wig," the actress says. "So, as much hair as I have, imagine it all white. And it was a fortune for him to make that wig, but we put it on and it just didn't go with me at all. It made me look like a total freak. There's no way it could have ever been in the movie, because I did look absolutely, one hundred percent crazy, and otherworldly, alien, weird-looking."

Blakley did not differ in her assessment, saying, "Something like that, you really have to work because you don't want it to come off funny, you want it to come off horrifying."

Someone with first-hand knowledge, who makes it clear she disavowed the wig the moment she saw it, was Fleetwood. "I had nothing to do with that wig, ever," she emphatically states. "Apparently, before I was hired, a gray wig showed up out of the blue. They handed it to me in prep a few days before we started shooting, had me put it on Heather and it was horrible. The colors were all wrong; it made her skin look green. It just wasn't a good wig."

It was an issue that Craven could also see, as Risher recalls, "So we met with him and he said, 'Look, I gotta change this. I think I'll just give her a gray streak and it'll look sort of pretty.' So we all agreed."

The conversation was one in which Fleetwood seemed to not only take part, but take charge. "I said, 'Well, you're only trying to sell the story of the fact that the lack of sleep is throwing some shock into the hair. Why can't we just cut some of the pieces of the wig out, I will put them in clips and it will be great for continuity because I can just put them in and out?'" she recalls. "So that was my idea and that's what we did."

It seemed to be yet another moment of time-sensitive, independent filmmaking ingenuity. "I cut up a couple of gray streaks and we made clip-ons. It was a complete clip-on and it was another one of those three-minute deals," adds Fleetwood.

In a revision of the script dated May 8, 1984, Dr. King does say to Nancy as they prep her for sleep, "Don't worry, you're not gonna change into the Bride of Frankenstein or anything," which, though cut, eventually sees Nancy's character somewhat echoing the classic Universal monster's iconic white-streaked hair.

"Ultimately, we went with just the streak and tips when I come out from the dream," says Langenkamp. "And I think it actually looked really good."

Langenkamp's date book marks when she once again spoke to Depp outside of filming and also shows the date and time of her white wig fitting.

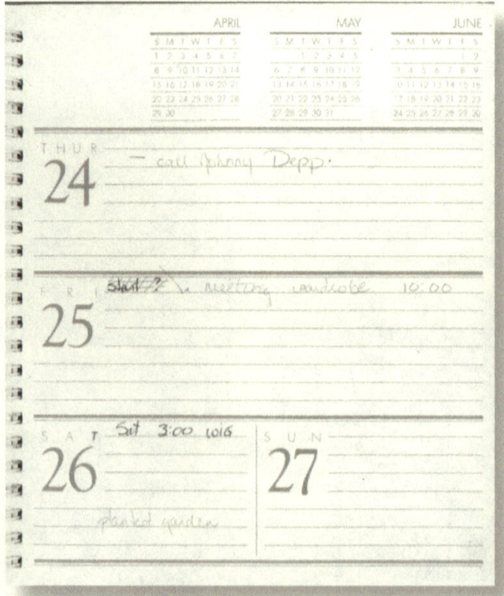

The actress does think back how it might have been a small creative misstep, but one that was much bigger financially for the film. "I think they were disappointed, because whenever you spend thousands of dollars on something, and it's not gonna get used, it's kind of a crushing blow on a low budget," Langenkamp adds. "But what we ended up doing really got the idea across."

That it did, particularly for Krueger's past killer, Marge. "There's the horrid realization that it's real and he's back," admits Blakley.

PARENTAL GUIDANCE SUGGESTED

The new streak of gray would remind Nancy of the nightmare she seemingly could not escape, but it was the tattered, brown fedora, inexplicably pulled from Krueger's head and into the real world, that led the young girl closer to the truth—and pushed her mother further into a corner.

A short, but important, scene between the two characters over how Nancy found the hat, and from whom she retrieved it, would escalate into the bigger truth having to be revealed.

"I loved the scene in the kitchen where I confront my mother," Langenkamp says of Blakley's character trying to fend off the accusation that she knows something about Krueger. "I am showing her proof that I'm not crazy and she's treating me like I'm crazy. She knows it's Freddy, but instead of admitting it, she slaps me." The actress continues, remembering the intensity of the moment. "Ronee really slapped me. We were both very buried in that scene."

Aside from the nuts and bolts of actually choreographing and filming the moment ("Wes, Ronee, and I had to really work out the movements," Langenkamp says), Blakley recalls the emotional aspects. "Although I know in the movie they are at each other's throats a few times, I think Marge adored her daughter, but with these horrendous things happening, it put such a strain on their relationship that it's no wonder that they had a hard time," she says, remarking that the specifics of the scene were not always easy to play. "You're supposed to behave as if you were just in your kitchen with your daughter in such a situation, hiding a bottle and slapping and beating your daughter, which is tremendously awful."

The actress adds that while she and Langenkamp had no problems acting together, the moment did feel awful. "To put yourself in that place as a mother is a terrible place to be. You have to feel sorry for Marge because of all those things, but she's not admirable in that scene. Sympathetic, perhaps," offers Blakley, "but she's the villain. Hopefully I was able to give her some sympathetic understanding, so that she could be rounded as a character and not be seen as a one hundred percent villain."

But Nancy can take no more. Marge feels her daughter only needs some sleep, causing the young girl to smash her mother's vodka bottle to the floor and scream, "Screw sleep!" With that, Nancy "is finally getting strong enough to confront her mother," Langenkamp says, "and that's a big, important moment."

It was something Craven planned. "It's actually a reversal of roles, where Nancy goes from being the child to being the adult, and the mother goes from being the mother to being the child," he stated.

"I think so many kids really find themselves in that position, and the outcomes are often way more tragic than that scene, but, you know, parents just lose it sometimes," offers Langenkamp. "I thought the scene was one of the most realistic parent-child scenes in the whole movie."

WHAT'RE YOU READING THAT FOR?

After Nancy storms out of the house she meets up with Glen, who notices his tired girlfriend reading *Booby Traps and Improvised Anti-Personel Devices*, a book on survival.

"One of my favorite lines is in the scene where I say, 'I found it at this great survivalist bookstore,'" laughs the actress. While the line does appear in an early draft of the script, it was subsequently edited out.

The scene, which saw Depp and Langenkamp in a master shot on a small bridge in Venice, California, actually had the close-ups of the actors filmed elsewhere. "It was on top of the roof at the studio," Langenkamp states, "because they didn't have time to get the shots on the actual bridge."

Another interesting notion of the scene is the palm trees seen swaying in the background. Though they worked well to visually connect the dual-location shots, they did not necessarily coincide with the notion of the Midwestern look and feel Craven was after.

In the scene, we learn that whenever Glen gets nervous, he eats or sleeps, which was planted by Craven to be more than innocuous. "I once studied with an Eastern teacher who said everybody goes out various doors to get away from being conscious, because it's very painful. So some people go out sex, some people go out drugs, or food and sleep and booze," he stated, referring to the characters played by Depp and Blakley, both of whom failed to protect Nancy.

Looking at the concept as a mirror to real life, Langenkamp states, "We live in a world where everyone's looking at a video screen all day long. I mean, people are losing their ability to look at their fears and face their fears. It's like a muscle that's not being exercised. And we are so good at avoiding the realities in our life, because we can have all these diversions. Nobody knows how to face their fears very well these days."

It's something Nancy knows she must do and, furthering that line of thought, Glen speaks of the Balinese way of dreaming, telling Nancy that in order to defeat a monster, they "turn their back on it, take away its energy, and it disappears."

Good advice, but when Nancy returns home, she finds she must first deal with what seems like horror in real life—

her mother has barred every possible window on the house.

When asked exactly how the art department gave the house realistic iron bars, Diers comments, "I don't remember, but I have since done that same gag, and we just made them out of wood. You don't want them to be too heavy, and the landlord doesn't want you to nail into their house."

That may have been the case on other projects, but Diers admits, "Back in the eighties, people were a little more naive. You walked in the door and you were 'Hollywood,' and people respected you. They believed it was going to all go well. Little do they know it's sort of,

FM 5–31
DEPARTMENT OF THE ARMY FIELD MANUAL

BOOBYTRAPS

HEADQUARTERS, DEPARTMENT OF THE ARMY
SEPTEMBER 1965

The survival manual (left) Glen sees Nancy reading, prompting her to reveal that she is "into survival." Little does she know how important the information in its pages will become; Many of the traps seen in the film were pulled from a real Department of the Army Field Manual (above): FM 5-31, "Boobytraps."

'We're working on a movie and the movie comes first. Your house is kind of secondary.'"

Whatever the process used, it turned 1428 Elm Street into a makeshift prison, strikingly reinforcing the idea that Marge will stop at nothing to keep terrifying and fascinating secrets from escaping.

"She also cuts down the rose trellis to prevent access to the boyfriend," Craven says, with Langenkamp pointedly adding, "It's like cutting down her youth."

To some the entire concept might seem crazy, but not to Blakley or her character. "I don't think it was. She was doing whatever she could to protect her daughter, and probably losing a bit of her sanity in the process," believes the actress.

Langenkamp feels it was an important moment that signified the beginning of the end. "The scene with the bars, you know, I believe it's one of the first parts of the final act," she says. "My character comes in and she realizes that her battle's about to be enjoined with Freddy, and it's going to take place in the house. And what her mom's done by putting up bars has ensured that there will be no escape. There will be no getting out of that house."

Blakley also feels it was a moment where, as the parent, Marge has ostensibly tried everything, to no avail. This was a slightly illogical next step, though she was filled with concern for her daughter. "Desperate worry. And desperation," she says. "These parents are dealing with murders. The children are being killed horrifically."

It was a moment that Nancy had to move past quickly. "She kind of has to take it with a grain of salt, and go about her business in getting ready to defeat Freddy,"

NE3 CORRECTION GALLEY 98

oaked clothes, naked and drunk and asleep,
with his weird glove of steel blades right
by his side...

She winks at the daughter, as if Nancy knows that thing all too well.

NANCY
(dreading it)
Go on...

Marge reaches over and taps a dusky two-gallon jug of gasoline near the lawn mower.

MARGE
Couple of the men screwed his door shut from
outside. Screws don't make a bit of noise,
y'know, screwed it shut like a coffin lid.
Then we poured gasoline around it and...

She mimes striking a match --

MARGE (CONTD)
WHOOSH!!!

Arms up, eyes are wide with the light of that fire, there's awe in her voice.

MARGE (CONTD)
But just as the fire was everywhere -- just
when it seemed not even the devil could live
in there any more -- he crashed out through
the window like a banshee -- screaming and
all on fire -- swinging that big knife every
which direction --
(hushed, remembering)
screaming at the top of his lungs he... he
was going to kill <u>all</u> our kids, now...

She stops with a sudden quake. A clear string of mucous flags from her nose. She swipes it away with the back of her hand, and drinks for a long moment. But the intake of the liquor doesn't hide the image.

Her face bathed in tears, she looks at her daughter and shakes her head.

MARGE (CONTD)
There were all those men, but none of them
could do what had to be done -- his rolling
and screaming in the grass so the whole state
could hear -- no one could take those knifes
from him and cut his throat good and proper
except <u>me</u>.

CORRECTION GALLEY

Langenkamp says. "I think that Nancy is so embattled at that moment, at the idea of these bars, that she just flicks it off and keeps on going."

Like audiences, Nancy was not fully prepared for where the story would be taking her. Or the fact that it was a journey that could only be led by her mother.

THE TRUTH SHALL SET YOU FREE

"Marge, when she's in the furnace, in the basement scene, she goes into it," Blakley states, further revealing that Craven not only knew what he wanted, but helped the actress achieve it.

"Wes was very determined that day in his directorial advice. He made sure the set was absolutely quiet and you could almost hear a pin drop," says Blakley. "He really tried to help me with it. As an actor, your job is to make it believable. And that's what I tried to do."

Haitkin also believed that, in the midst of such horror and fantasy, Langenkamp's commitment to the scene "really helps pull it all together."

"It's a very subtle twist to the story when Nancy's mother takes her down into the basement and shows her the glove that she's been hiding in the furnace all these years," says Langenkamp. "When Nancy sees the glove, it just gives her the heebie-jeebies. And the audience, too."

Declaring it another of her favorite scenes, the actress enjoyed the notion of the mother handing down terrible, hidden-for-years secrets to her daughter. "It shows Nancy's mother at her ultimate weakness as she is confiding this information," offers Langenkamp.

For Craven, the moment helps to illustrate the fears that the film (and many of his works) addressed. "Living in a world that has adults in it who are either misinformed, have your worst, rather than your best, interests at heart, or are too frightened to speak the truth about the way things really are," he explained, which is certainly the case until Nancy's mother feels she must acknowledge the sins of her past.

"Of course, Marge is carrying that awful secret of being a murderer," says a thoughtful Blakley.

That murder was the killing of Krueger, the man haunting the dreams of Nancy and her friends, which is revealed to audiences in a potent monologue by Blakley that all but cemented her character's status as memorable, at least to Langenkamp.

"Playing the mom can be such a cliché part in horror movies," Langenkamp says. "The parent is always this throwaway part that just has to be there to kind of take up space, just to make it seem like the kid has somebody they're living with. But Ronee's performance is so unforgettable, and almost extreme in a way, especially in that basement scene. I just don't think the movie would have been what it was without her being a little bit more intense, I think, than the average parent character is these days."

Opposite page: Nancy listens to her mother confess how the parents of Elm Street took justice into their own hands and murdered Fred Krueger a decade earlier. Cut from the final film were moments that revealed Nancy had a sibling who was killed by Freddy; A script page detailing moments of Marge's dialogue that were cut from the final film. The words impart the notion that Nancy's mother had a much greater part in Krueger's demise; An artist's rendering of an ethereal, in-custody Krueger.

Langenkamp elaborates on why the expository scene was not just compelling for the audience, but for the film's characters as well. "Marge actually has the weight of the world on her shoulders, because she has the crime in creating Freddy Krueger those many years ago," she states. "It's like the Achilles heel of the character, but she must face it in order to save her daughter, or at least try to. It's a very tender scene, and Ronee played it beautifully."

Helping the tender relationship may have been the bonding on-screen mother and daughter did when they were cast. "I felt very close and friendly with Heather and admired her a great deal," says Blakley.

Of the moment Marge reveals everything, "She was so caring, and she just had a great maternal 'I wanna take care of you' feeling, which didn't show up in a lot of other scenes," admits Langenkamp.

With the knowledge that her parents had, in vigilante style, burned Krueger alive, Nancy could finally piece together the reason for her nightmares: revenge. Remarkably, not in the film is an exchange from the May 8, 1984 script draft that further supports why Krueger chose his victims. When Nancy asks her mother if Tina and Rod's parents were also involved, Marge tells her daughter, "Sure, and Glen's. All of us."

"Sleep, by design, is supposed to refresh and renew us. It gives us a break from reality. And in the world that Wes created, it was a doorway to hell."

Joe Unger on Craven's concept

It's a moment cut from the film, but not from the adult characters' minds, with the subtext seemingly creeping into the portrayal of a group of people simultaneously hiding the truth while also having to face it.

"I think there's a lot to that, and it's one of the things that makes this film so compelling. These are terrorized people, and none of them are in their right mind because of such a horrible event," says Woodrum. "And what do people do that are in situations that are so extreme that no one will believe them? They try to repress it. They try to get on with life."

As Marge has shown, they also try to make things normal, which may never again be possible.

"They try to recapture what it was like before the event, even though their own families have been destroyed, their own psyche has been destroyed, and now come to find out everything they did to try and get rid of this monster has not worked. And now he's after the rest of their children," Woodrum states.

Englund elaborates on the power of Nancy's mother coming clean, and how it distresses not just the characters in the film, but the audience as well. "It affects our subconscious. It's the great story around the campfire. 'There's this street called Elm Street, and there were some children killed there. The parents did an unspeakable thing,'" he offers.

The shocking events which unfolded under the watchful eye of Marge and the other parents, only to come back to haunt them, is something Unger appreciated about Craven's film. "It came back with a fury and with a vengeance. And then to put that in a context of not being able to sleep, that's pretty horrific," he says. "You don't need three-headed monsters or space aliens to go with that concept. Sleep, by design, is supposed to refresh and renew us. It gives us a break from reality. And in the world that Wes created, it was a doorway to hell. And I just think that was an incredibly ingenious idea, and he executed it wonderfully."

The parental revenge motif is portrayed in fictitious fashion for the film, but Langenkamp does admit to understanding the place from where her character's parents were coming when they acted as they did. "If there was a person hurting my child in the neighborhood, and other people's children, and nobody could get him behind bars, and the justice system was failing us, and he was still out, yes, of course, I think people would take it into their own hands," she states.

Elaborating on a reasonable motive, Langenkamp adds, "I think that if they didn't, they would be irresponsible."

It is something Craven addresses when he reveals, "Given the right circumstances I think that any of us could astonish ourselves with what we might do. And I think we need to go through life prepared for that."

"It really is a commentary on the culture of the time, and what everybody goes through trying to deal with monstrous situations in our life that really are unbearable," states Woodrum. "We just do the best we can. We're all flawed. And sometimes we do okay, but most of the time we don't."

That being the case, Craven reasoned why Marge must come clean to her daughter. "At a certain point, it's so overwhelming what's happening that she tells the child. She has to."

BASEBALL BATS AND BOGEYMEN

As Nancy was busy digesting the tale of vengeance her mother was serving in the basement of 1428 Elm Street, she phones Glen, who lives across the way.

"We actually shot from two practical houses," Craven remembers.

Haitkin adds "shooting tie-ins at actual locations" was not the norm.

Locating and securing the Thompson residence ended up being the easier of two housing location-related issues.

"What ended up being more difficult than finding Nancy's house, actually, was we had to find a house that was directly across the street within window distance," Talalay says, "so they [Nancy and Glen] could talk to each other through the windows and actually do that."

"I remember being in the upstairs bedroom of the house on Genesee [the street where the house is located] and looking out at Johnny across the street," says Langenkamp. "Those houses really have that relationship on the street." She also reveals that she and Depp "actually were talking to each other on the telephone."

On the phone in real life, yes, but directly across the street from each other, not quite. It's something Talalay found near impossible. "You had to look from one house across the street to the other and go window to window in both directions. That's a huge assignment for nice houses in LA. It was really, really difficult and there weren't a huge number of choices," she says. "We weren't able to get the house directly across the street, and it took Wes some time to come to accept the fact that the house was kitty corner rather than directly across. I was really feeling frustrated that I had to say, 'I don't think I'm going to do any better than this street. So can we make this work?'"

Craven did, thinking back on the area, saying, "It's a historic street now, not for *Nightmare*, but for the origins of it," he says. "It's a remarkable Midwestern-looking street in Los Angeles. The trees are all gigantic Elms and Oaks."

Langenkamp offers a more direct thought to the usage of both homes, as well as the street, for filmic purposes. "This is the world's most amenable neighborhood!" she laughs.

As Nancy begins to explain things to her still-disbelieving boyfriend, Langenkamp thinks back and comments on the choice of costuming for Depp. "I think that cropped football jersey was an A-plus idea!" she exclaims.

"It does look like a little sex-kitten when it's on him," admits Jensen. "What he was wearing, if he really was to play a jock, that's a practice football jersey. You wear it over your pads, and it's cut short so when you're just practicing you breathe, you sweat. It's a real thing."

No matter his wardrobe, Glen would soon be ignoring Nancy's now-legendary warning, "Whatever you do, don't fall asleep!" ("The defining line of the script," Craven states.)

Perhaps apropos to Craven's scholarly background, Nancy had previously mentioned to Glen that she had been awake for nearly seven days, but not to worry because "the record's eleven."

She was, at the time, correct. In 1965 a San Diego high school senior named Randy Gardner set the record for the longest period a human being had intentionally gone without sleep: eleven days. While others have claimed to subsequently break the record, Gardner's experiment was the most scientifically documented.

Sadly, for Depp's character, such facts could not prevent him from slumber, allowing Freddy to mess up the sheets. Craven remarked that when Nancy tries calling to keep Glen awake—an event stopped by his disapproving parents—"It's almost *Romeo and Juliet*-ish in that sense of the star-crossed lovers, at the last moment if she could just have wakened him up, you know, they would have been all right," he says. "But the parents come between."

One of those parents was actress Sandy Lipton, who played Glen's mother. The actress had a handful of popular television credits to her name, such as *CHiPs* (1977–1983) and *Knots Landing* (1979–1993) and, like Unger before her, got the role after meeting and talking with Craven.

"I didn't do a reading. I think what got me the meeting was that I looked 'housewife-y.' I wasn't glamorous when I went in," Lipton says. "We sat and talked for about twenty minutes, maybe about my family. I didn't have a callback. He just said, 'That's it' and I guess I got a call from my agent and I was told I had the part."

While the meeting went well, and Lipton snagged the role, she wasn't exactly sure the type of movie for which she had just met. That detail could have made all the difference. "If I had known it was a horror movie, I think I would've turned it down. I'm afraid of horror films," laughs the actress.

Like many others, Lipton enjoyed the freedom Craven gave her. "I didn't feel like I was being overly directed or questioned. I was comfortable with him," she says. "I think we just did the discussion on the porch, and the discussion in the hallway, before I went upstairs to check on my son in the bedroom, in very few takes."

With regard to her being a party to stopping Nancy and Glen meeting, the actress recalls that her husband in the scene (played by the late Ed Call) probably had a very logical reason. "There was never any explanation given to me about why he slammed the phone down," she says, offering, "I always just figured he did it because it was late that night and what mother wants her kid to get phone calls that late at night? That was my take."

ONE LAST KISS

With Glen one step closer to falling victim to Krueger, the dream killer made sure that Nancy would know her boyfriend was not long for this world, and in a way she would never forget. "I always liked the tongue coming out of the phone because it was one of the most startling parts of the first film," states Craven.

The surreal moment occurs when Nancy's ripped-from-the-wall (and decidedly not working) telephone rings continuously, forcing her to answer. "I told Heather, 'Now hold up the cord so they can see you pulled it out of the wall,'" Craven remembers, also telling her, "Okay, now wrap it up around the phone."

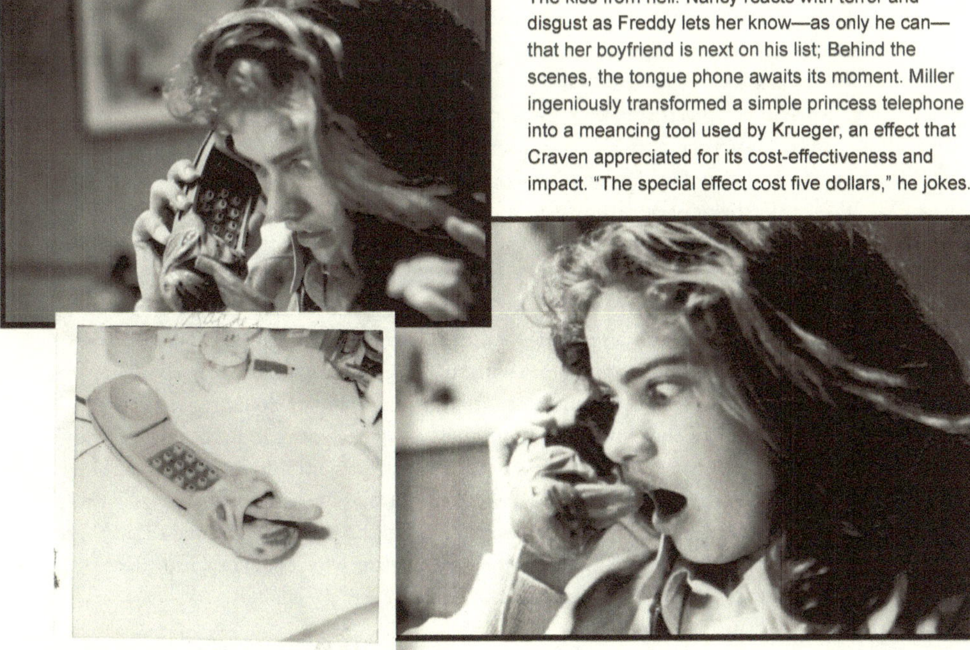

The kiss from hell. Nancy reacts with terror and disgust as Freddy lets her know—as only he can—that her boyfriend is next on his list; Behind the scenes, the tongue phone awaits its moment. Miller ingeniously transformed a simple princess telephone into a meancing tool used by Krueger, an effect that Craven appreciated for its cost-effectiveness and impact. "The special effect cost five dollars," he jokes.

On the other end of the seemingly supernatural line? Freddy Krueger, with the memorable line, "I'm your boyfriend now, Nancy!"

"Wes described it just as, 'I want Freddy's mouth to appear on the end of the phone, and a tongue to come out and go into Heather's mouth,'" makeup man Miller recalls, whose job it was to create the effect.

Like so many other aspects of the film, it was cheap. "The special effect cost five dollars," reveals Craven. "It was just a princess telephone, and a tongue that we had on a little lever and you would squeeze it and it would come out of the phone. That shocked people so much."

"I'm so glad that cell phones weren't invented in that age because I can't imagine the tongue coming out of a cell phone. There's something so great that it was a phone on a desk," says Langenkamp. "The period of time since then, when people use cell phones for so many plot points, and so many different aspects of their horror movies, there's just something so refreshing that that's not in *Nightmare on Elm Street*."

When the idea was run by Miller, "I thought, 'Okay,'" he remembers, laughing. "Wes came up with the idea in the middle of filming and he said he wanted to do it towards the end. So I had to come up with the whole prosthetic for the phone that looked like Freddy's mouth, with a little mechanical opening and another cable that pushed the tongue out. And the cable could bend so I could actually have the tongue come out and go into her mouth for real. So it was a very strange thing to see, but it was very effective."

Effective, yes, but Langenkamp recalls the difficulties she had in giving Craven what he wanted in the moment. "It took a long time to get that eye movement that I do," she says of the moment her terrified gaze moves down as she cradles the phone. "First of all, I have to work with this thing, so how am I gonna make this look believable? How am I gonna make this a prop that actually says something? And it was very technical. I had to have my face completely still, and my eyeballs going left and right, and Wes had all these really technical, precise movements that I had to make with this phone."

That wasn't the actress' only concern, going on to say in general, "The gag with the tongue and the phone is just not my favorite gag in the whole thing," admits Langenkamp. "It's actually the most disturbing part of having acted in *A Nightmare on Elm Street*. That's the one nightmare that I do have, is that feeling of violation of the Freddy tongue. It's a really great symbol of violation and I've always thought of it that way."

The desecration of Nancy as a concept was not one that passed Englund by, either. "There's something to the idea of the tongue," says Englund. "There's all sorts of things that come into connotation with that, such as oral sex and French kissing. It's just such a great way to bring all those latent images into an adolescent mind."

It's a moment that underlines, without having to work too hard for it, Freddy's sexuality. The choice to have Krueger French kiss his victim is not only a harbinger of murder to come, but a way for the evil to play itself out in a subtextual, vulgar way.

"We're beyond *Beauty and the Beast* now. The Beast wants to taint Beauty. The Beast wants to lick Beauty," Englund says, punctuating what could be the ultimate idea behind the moment. "The Beast wants to fuck Beauty," he adds.

With such a powerful concept at play, the memories of Langenkamp regarding the device Freddy used to assault Nancy are somewhat at odds with the recollections by Miller. "During the filming of the tongue phone sequence, Heather wanted to eventually take that thing home. And we thought it was a little strange!" he says. "I don't know what she was going to do with it, and am not sure what she means by saying she didn't want to do that scene, because she wanted to take the prop home. She really did."

"Maybe I told them I wanted it as a souvenir, but it was gross. It was really, really gross," offers Langenkamp. "The thing that I've realized is that when those kinds of props came to the set, I'd say anything that involved a tongue, or something that was very sexual, the guys are always way more excited about it than me. And they're so proud of themselves for coming up with such a hideous thing."

"I wasn't there when we did that scene, as my line reading to Heather was done in post, but I did see some kidding around on set with the prop," recalls Englund. "It was so bizarre. People were putting it up their butt, putting it in the front, putting it in their ears. We all joked around with that prop."

Potential prurient excitement from surrounding crew aside, Langenkamp is steadfast in her belief the item was not high on her list of keepsakes from the film. "I don't think I loved the phone, and I don't think I wanted to adamantly take it home because I loved it," she states. "I probably just wanted it as a souvenir of what I thought were tough days."

Tough or not, Englund purports that it is something with which one has to "just roll with in a rock and roll kind of way. Heather's got all of these images where she's sort of being violated on all these different levels by Freddy," he says. "He's in the tub with her, he's tonguing her with an eighties phone, and all these things."

It's also something the actor feels she must live with, and carry, for good reason. "It's her onus as a survivor girl," Englund declares.

With the truth of her desire to take the prop home something that may never be crystal clear, Langenkamp does admit, Krueger's tongue notwithstanding, she did appreciate one moment in the scene. "It's when I realize that Freddy is going to kill Glen."

Whether or not Marge could ever be considered an unwitting accomplice to Glen's murder, by way of the fact that it was her choice to bar and lock the house, Blakley thinks for a moment and states, "I think she couldn't take care of everything. She couldn't know what was happening for sure, and she was probably drunk as well."

"It would explain the kookiness of the parents and their sort of detachedness in how to deal with this situation," offers Woodrum.

The scene did allow Blakley to showcase her character's ability to be both in control and, paradoxically, out of touch with reality. "There's a line that Ronee has in the film where Nancy comes home and there's bars on all the windows. And she goes to her mother for the keys and the mother says, 'Locked, locked, locked,'" Craven says, admiring the actress' ability to imbue the seriousness of the line with a wonderful flamboyance. "It's my favorite Ronee Blakley line. It's unusual. It's kind of almost funny, but it's also kind of scary that the parent is so incompetent and kind of loony."

Langenkamp appreciated the scene for Marge's aloofness, which underscored the suffering Nancy was experiencing in that same moment. "She knew that Krueger killed her boyfriend, and there was nothing she could do," says the actress. "I look up, grab my hair, and I just go, 'Noooo!' I just love that."

ONE-TAKE WONDER

"I like Johnny's death scene, and not because he's a star right now," says Corri, even though he wasn't present for the filming. "He's got his headphones on and all of a sudden, 'slurp,' he gets sucked in. That's kinda cool."

Lipton recalls her interactions with Depp as his character states he is watching "Miss Nude America."

"He says, 'Who cares what she has to say?' And if I remember right, his eyebrows kind of raised. A little smug flirtiness. I remember being so thrown over by him. His attitude was so cute and so, the only word I can think of is, flirty," Lipton says. "Not with me, but kind of with his character's mom and making fun of something. He was just adorable. Adorable."

After the exchange with his mother, and just before the actual moment of his untimely death, astute listeners will hear the television station he was watching sign off: KRGR, an homage, of course, to the dream killer. Like Corri, Depp also thought his character's death was cool. "I love this stuff," the actor says. "The kid falls asleep and it's all over. He's sucked right into the bed and spat out as blood."

In fact, his apparent enjoyment went so far as to question the production's notion of using a double, when Depp was more than game to handle the effect himself. "I heard some talk about having a dummy, but I said, 'Hey, I want to do this. It'll be fun,'" the actor says.

Craven remembered it, too. "He kept telling me how wild the whole thing sounded. He was really disappointed when I told him that we would bring a stunt double in to actually do the gag," he says. "He begged me to allow him to do it himself, and finally I relented and let him go for it."

To accomplish the action of Freddy's arms reaching from under the bed and pulling Glen down into the mattress, Doyle employed one of his crewmen who had "really, really long arms. [He's] laying right underneath Johnny, the bed is pre-cut, and all he had to do was punch his arms up through there, grab him around the waist, and haul him down," he says. After that moment, they would both be standing on a platform. "That was pretty much all there was to it, except for the television hitting my guy in the head," Doyle adds, laughing. "He hadn't counted on that!"

Craven hadn't either, but he, Doyle, and Haitkin remark it was interesting to see the television stay lit while it went down the hole, followed by the stereo.

As for the room itself after Glen is pulled away, "It was the same room that they used for Tina's death scene. The same exact room. They just redressed it and went through the same process where they locked everything down so it wouldn't move," Langenkamp recalls.

Keeping a close eye on many things, including numbers, was Talalay, who also appreciated the room's reuse, even if she did have some concerns. "What I remember about the sequence was that this revolving room, given the budget on the film, was more of the budget than anything else we did," she says.

The rotating room was reused for Glen's death, to shocking effect. Here, its outer shell can be seen as the crew prepares for a take.

"Oh, yes, the rotating room and Johnny Depp's death, when the blood goes up the wall and falls down," Craven remembers, not immune to the complexities he and his crew would be facing when it came time for Krueger to dispose of Glen. "It was Jacques Haitkin and myself. And I, as the director, saying, 'It's not dangerous. I'll be next to you.' So we had these two jump seats that were nailed to the wall, literally, and we were in three-point harnesses," he recalled.

Haitkin elaborates on how the effect was achieved. "When you see Johnny in the bed, he's watching TV, the room is right-side up and there's a hole in the bed. We pulled Johnny down through the hole and got him out of the way."

A good thing for the first-time actor because the moment he is swept away from set, the room is turned one hundred eighty degrees so that the bed hole is now in the ceiling—all in real time. "And like before, you can't see the room turning because everything is fixed. All the lighting is fixed, the camera is fixed, so you don't see the room turning at all," says Haitkin.

Behind the scenes, once again, were "all the men, who are each on these handles, pushing the room, making it go around again," says Langenkamp.

"The rotating room was designed so that you actually build the room in it, and then you would balance it," Doyle states. "So, literally, you could turn the thing with one finger. The furniture loaded in the room is on the floor, so when the room is actually sitting level it's higher than you think it would be, and the axel is lower than you think it would be. So when you rotate it, it stays balanced because all the furniture is on the bottom."

The goal? "When the hole in the bed gets to twelve o'clock, there's a guy waiting to dump blood," Haitkin says, "so it comes through the hole, but it looks like it's coming up out of the bed."

"And it was just buckets of blood that are poured down the chute," Langenkamp recalls. "I don't know how many gallons they used, probably hundreds it seems like."

"There was a real fear that there would only be one take on this because of the number of buckets of blood that were going to be used, and where the blood was going to go," says Talalay. "The kind of issue you're dealing with on a really low-budget film."

It was a notion Langenkamp says was prevalent on the set. "This was a 'one-take-Sally,'" she reveals. "There's just no re-dressing this room after all the blood's been pumped in."

There was, indeed, huge pressure to make it work while everyone was trying to anticipate what was going to happen—or what might go wrong. "We were now up top with these drums to dump this blood into the bottom of the bed," Carlucci says, straightforwardly explaining what was supposed to happen, "and blood would come down and hit the floor. The camera was turned upside down, so everything would look normal once you flipped that film."

Doyle adds, "We balanced the whole thing, and we figured this much blood is going to weigh this much, and Charlie Belardinelli would pull the plug and all the blood would come down. And once all the blood was down, Wes was strapped to one of the camera chairs and he would say, 'Go,' and you would see the blood go up the wall and onto the ceiling."

A fantastic plan, worked on with meticulous preparation, but one that had few anticipating what ultimately would go wrong.

A SHOCKING EFFECT

"That was quite a nightmare with all the electrical cables and everything," remembers Huntley. "That really was a tricky set. I have done that other times on other shows, but with a gimbaled room there are always a lot of details."

"We had gallons and gallons and gallons of blood that had to come out of the center of that thing," remarks Belardinelli on the beginning of what might be called the most electrifying moment the film faced. "I remember I was holding, on my shoulder, this big tube where the dump tank of blood was. As the blood was pouring out, it hit some electrical somewhere on the stage, or in that rotating room, and I was getting electrocuted."

It was mild enough that the show could go on, with Belardinelli gritting his teeth during the electric shock that lasted the ten or fifteen seconds the shot required. "It was wild," he says. "I wasn't laughing at the time, but I laughed when it was over. My whole body was just shaking, and I was saying, 'Oh, man, this hurts.' But I stayed with it."

"There was a real fear that there would only be one take on this because of the number of buckets of blood that were going to be used, and where the blood was going to go." Rachel Talalay on Glen's death

---

Craven's earlier, and subsequently wrong, notion that everything would be fine was not lost on him, either. "The water went into all the lights and there were these huge flashes and then dark, and we were spinning in the dark with sparks going off," he remembered.

If slight electrocution and being trapped in the dark room weren't enough, the effect also went awry in another way. The second mishap, however, would ultimately work to the film's advantage.

Again going back to the blood, Craven explains, "We put a lot of blood in there. I don't know, like two hundred gallons or something like that, which threw the weight off entirely and the whole thing suddenly just shifted and spun."

Talalay elaborates how things continued to spin out of control. "And when it came time to make that moment work, they revolved the room in the wrong way to start with. They turned it clockwise instead of the other way around," she says.

Doyle elaborates that "a little failure in calculation meant the blood ran to the other side of the room and out-of-balanced it while we were unlocking it."

The immediate consequence was the stage blood literally pouring everywhere. "They realized they've kind of screwed up and all the blood, instead of dripping down the wall, as it was supposed to, came flooding back on us who were watching," remembers Langenkamp.

So does Carlucci. "We were up there, jumping out of the way of cables and ropes that were ripping out because the room was now turning on its own, and there was no way we were stopping it. And all that blood just started pouring out of the stage window," he says.

Back in the room, "It rolled all the way over and poured blood onto everybody that was working in the room, and Jacques made a noise that no man should ever make while they are still alive," Doyle says. "But we didn't hear a peep out of Wes. And he was strapped in the other camera chair. There was only one operating camera, and Wes was just going along for the ride. He got kind of the ride of his life. He enjoyed it. I don't think Jacques did as much."

Multiple reference photos of Depp were taken for a fake head of the actor that was created and originally going to be used in Glen's death scene; The actor sits in the makeup chair after having a lifecast made.

Craven agreed, recalling that the room stopped moving in a less-than-desirable position as he and his crew were left "hanging upside down for at least twenty minutes" before other crew could get lights in the room and get them out.

"I remember that Wes and Jacques were strapped into these chairs with the camera, flipped upside down, and were hanging there," says Cook. "And of course, you can't leave them hanging there for too long because all the blood goes up into their head. So there was all this anxiety."

After the alarm the events had caused subsided, it was clear that what they ended up shooting might have been well worth it. "It all changed the way the effect worked and everyone was like, 'Oh my God, it's ruined! It's ruined!' But of course, it just came out so totally cool. So part of the reason the effect looks like that is because of this gratuitous mistake," adds Talalay.

In Doyle's mind, too, it turned out for the better. "The blood sort of just runs off the ceiling and disappears out of frame, and you don't know where it went. But if you watch just at the very end of that scene, just as the blood is coming up hitting the ceiling, you'll start to see the liquid moving away from the ceiling, going off the ceiling, off to the side, out of frame," he says. "And that's actually the room spinning, and the blood going out the window while we were all jumping frantically out of the way."

Some crew prepared by wearing raincoats and plastic bags with holes cut in them "because that blood was going to go everywhere, and it was very sticky because it was Karo syrup, which is the base of most of that movie blood," Cook remarks. "And I just remember that was a really exciting and astounding thing to watch that get done and then to see it in dailies."

A continuity photo of the coroner, a character that was cut from the final film and only mentioned in dialogue.

"It was," Craven says, "the Ferris wheel from hell."

GLEN, GOING, GONE

Now that the effect of Glen's death was complete (with Burrows' son tasked, for the princely sum of about ten dollars, to clean up the blood still left at the stage), the time had come to incorporate what the filmmakers had wanted with what they ultimately achieved. That meant a slight alteration of the dramatics of the scene and, more specifically, what reaction would be achieved when the remains (or lack thereof) of Glen's character would be discovered.

"The intention was we were gonna have Glen's mother walk in the room and see her son spread across the floor, as whatever it was that came out of the bed," Doyle remembers. "But as it worked out, it was a better shot to have her walk in and her eyes drift up and you see the drips falling in front of her. That worked out really, really great. I think it worked out better."

8.15.84 NYC

Dear Sandy:

Just a late note of thanks to you for your portrayal of Glen's mom in 'Elm Street.' You did a really fine job throughout, and your screaming scene was so memorable it's still ringing in my ears!

Regards,

Wes

Between takes, Lipton watches as Saxon pays close attention to direction; A letter sent from Craven to Lipton, in which the writer and director praises the actress' performance (and her scream).

Lipton's aversion to genre films also helped make the scene play out realistically. "I think that's what made it possible for me to be so real in the scream scene, because there was nothing really shown to me of what I was screaming about. That was all added afterwards," she reveals. "If I had known what I was seeing when I was screaming, I don't know that I'd have been able to go through with it."

Instead, the actress found herself opening the door to a room that wasn't there, staring into the camera with Craven directing her. "There was no room, no evidence of a room, no evidence of anything there. I just opened the door and there was the camera and I just started screaming. I think he just said, 'You've opened the door and you found your son in the bedroom dead,'" remembers Lipton. "When I saw the clip, and I saw what was done after shooting was done, I couldn't believe it. It just was unreal to me that the scream came out exactly the way it should have for what was being shown on screen."

What did not work out, however, was an ultimately unused idea to see Glen come back out of the bed. It's a moment that has been hinted at in photos and behind-the-scenes video, but never has the actual scene itself been played out in full form. In fact, it's become something of *Elm Street* lore as to why it was shot and, perhaps, who shot it.

When the question was asked if Craven could shed any light on the matter, his answer was honest, forthright, and interesting. "No, I can't. No," he stated, adding, "I'm not denying anything, I really just don't remember some of this stuff."

In that camp is Cecere, who openly admits, "I don't recall any parts of Johnny Depp coming out of the bed."

Langenkamp, who was not in the scene, but was, peripherally, aware of the goings on, also cannot recall the moment. "I don't remember ever seeing him covered in blood or any of that, but it would've been a lot like *Carrie* (1976)," she says. "I'm sure people would've thought it looked too *Carrie*-ish."

Even editor Shaine can't give a complete answer. "If he did rise out of the bed, I guess it could've been the end of an outtake, because I can imagine that he would come back up and somebody might've poured blood on him in an outtake," he says, going on to clarify, "but it wasn't anything that we ever had in the film. And it wasn't anything that I ever would've considered using."

With director, stunt coordinator, actress, and editor unsure, it was seemingly left to others from the film to fill in the gaps—if, indeed, there are gaps to fill.

"There's some question that maybe there was a scene where Johnny came back out of the bed, but to my recollection, there was no such scene," Haitkin says, though he does offer a few possible explanations of why footage and images of the moment exist. "Sometimes the assistants will roll off footage because maybe they're slating. So if Johnny is coming in and out of the bed while we're rehearsing, that gets on the film. But there was no scripted scene of Glen coming from the dead and rising out of the bed."

Talalay is less sure of herself, offering, "I don't remember the details of Johnny coming out of the bed, but it sounds vaguely familiar."

That may be due to the fact that, as Haitkin mentions, there wasn't a specific scene scripted with Glen rising back out, but there was at least mention of something being spewed forth from the pit in the bed.

Early script pages make mention of "what's left of Glen is vomited up from the pit of the nightmare bed...a horrible mess of blood and bone and hair and wires... streaming out and over the bed."

Cook seems to recall some particulars, but, as seems to be the case, it's not entirely clear even to her. "I think they shot that scene with Johnny and the blood and guts, but everyone felt it was too gross to put in the movie," she says, adding cautiously, "but I can't swear to it. I may be remembering a conversation that went like that."

While no one may recall filming Glen rising out, effects men Miller and Belardinelli are clear in their memories of working to make some part of the aforementioned script portion come to life.

"I originally made a fake head of Johnny Depp," Miller reveals. "I guess his head was going to come up out of the bed after he was sucked down in there and it spits him back up. They canceled that, but I still have that cast. So it's nice seeing his young, twenty-year-old face and then looking at him now."

Taking it a step further, Belardinelli remembers the interesting moment he and Rideout were positioned under the bed and "throwing bones out of the hole from underneath, and it looked so stupid," he says. "It looked just like what it was, someone throwing bones from underneath. Wes was laughing his ass off."

Although Craven may not have had a clear recollection of the specifics, he offered, "I think it must have looked so ridiculous. It's one of those things where you think, 'We got what we need and anything else is just going to be silly.'"

It's an aspect that did, in some ways, permeate the show. "I remember doing hokey things like that all the time on that job," says Diers. "So it doesn't surprise me that, after the monster eats him and pours out his blood, a few bones would come out. That's kind of hokey, but it's also appropriate to the genre."

The big question then is: what did the man of the hour, Johnny Depp, ultimately think of his grand death scene, both filmed and mused upon? "Well, I got sucked into a bed. What kind of reviews can you get opposite Freddy Krueger? 'Johnny Depp was good as the boy who died,'" he states.

When asked if his career took off after his stint on *Elm Street*, Depp gamely replies, "No. Freddy's did."

FRED KRUEGER DID IT, DADDY...

With her friends gone at the hands of Freddy, Nancy understands that it's up to her to stop him before becoming his next victim. Fresh with the knowledge of what her own parents had done, she lets her father know she is well aware of who Krueger is and what she must do, even if she fears he won't understand.

"Well, yeah, my character was somebody who knew that Freddy might have been part of things, or he had seen or protected other people who had killed and burned Freddy Krueger in a furnace," Saxon says regarding his character's involvement and apparent unwillingness to completely believe, or even help, Nancy. "He was certainly somebody who wanted to deny the presence or the existence of Freddy, or that such a creature could have any continued bearing on everybody. That kind of thing. So he was saying, 'No, no, no, that's nonsense! He's dead!' You know, 'Forget it!' Like most of our parents would say."

Langenkamp concurs that the characterization of Nancy's father might have been well-intentioned, but that he was blinded by his inability to admit the truth of what he had done, what it had done to his daughter's friends and, now, to her. "All the parents are doing it in the best spirit of protecting their young and all of that," says the actress, "and I do think that the movie tries not to give a cynical portrayal of that, because a lot of movies do give that cynical portrayal. I think the nice thing about *Nightmare* is that there's kind of this pathetic depiction of the efforts that are going into protecting the kids."

It was a theme Craven hit on. "It's the kids who suffer, because one of the worst threats to them is the parents," he says. "The good intentions of the parents."

It was, however, those good intentions that started the vengeful wheel of Freddy turning, as Englund points out. "It's the disintegrating middle class. The single parents and alcoholic parents and neglectful parents. I think Freddy is the bad stepfather and he takes everything that the kids in the movies know and snits it back at them. He takes the culture that you all love. He takes your iPhone, and your MTV, and your boyfriends, and your sleepovers, and your hookups, and he just beats you with it. Freddy's punishing white-bread America," the actor says, adding, "I think Wes was the first guy to do that."

SHE'S INTO SURVIVAL

The fact remained, because Freddy was working to punish her, Nancy knew something must be done. Armed with the knowledge that, like the hat, she could pull Krueger from her nightmare and into the real world, she was hopeful that she could harm—or better yet, destroy—him. In order do to that, Nancy turns her current prison of 1428 Elm Street into a veritable warzone with the help of household items and the manual of antipersonnel devices.

"I believed it was the moment when Nancy becomes the most proactive and truly realizes her power in the scene. Until then she's following clues and trying to piece it together," Langenkamp says. "But she really takes very seriously her role in becoming a soldier in this battle against Freddy. She truly puts on a soldier's attitude that she can do it."

To do so, Craven gave Langenkamp's character the tools she would need to begin her fight.

"When she first got the handbook, the one Glen makes fun of her for having, she realizes as a kid, 'This is all I've got,'" Langenkamp states.

"I had read this Army manual called *Improvised Weapons*, and it was about how to make booby traps, and I think those booby traps were right out of that," Craven says, recalling that the things Nancy does were very real. "I was worried for years that some teenager was going to blow up his house."

From pendulous sledgehammers to exploding light bulbs, Carlucci remembers that "any booby traps that were set for Freddy were all set by the mechanical effects department. We'd go in there and help figure out what would work, and what would really nail Freddy once he came into contact with whatever it was we were rigging."

All prepared for Langenkamp to do what needed to be done. "Many of the booby trap elements were shot as inserts, but it's really me," the actress states proudly. "I remember filing down the light bulb glass and putting the gunpowder in, running the wire that would trip the light bulb to explode, and also hanging the sledgehammer, which was a lighter prop for me to lift."

Craven would know, as the sledgehammer was, at one point, hung above his studio door. "It weighs about two pounds," he admitted.

Langenkamp adds that, during filming, "Wes would tell me, 'Make it look heavier, Heather! Make it look heavier!'" she laughs.

Doyle concurs with the idea of making everything look as realistic as possible—because it was. "We just went to the books and said, 'Let's try this and let's try that,' like the swinging sledgehammer thing," he says.

To accomplish all of the separate moments, Doyle states, "I basically had one guy on that rig and one other prop guy for about a week. He would have something put together and we would run over and shoot it. Then the first company would go back to what they were doing and the guys would rig something else. And they were getting one or two rigs a day." He adds that everything was tested before the cameras rolled because they were real traps on an active, live set. "Every one of those little gags came out of one of the books on doing booby traps."

Picking approximately five or six insert shots of Nancy preparing the deadfalls in the house for her fight with Krueger, Langenkamp didn't just enjoy the preparations at the time of filming. "All of the traps laid out were so ingenious, and I'm gonna remember all of them in case I ever have to lay traps, because they all will work," she declares. "With very rudimentary knowledge of electricity and physics you can use them. I've kind of become a survivalist after reading that book, in my spare time, just sitting on the set. It's like how to be a spy and get out of a

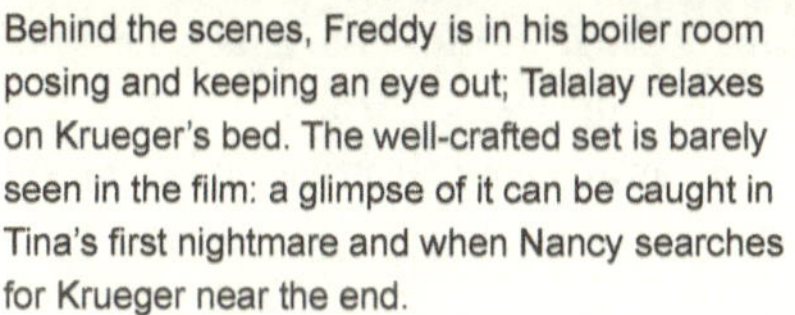

Behind the scenes, Freddy is in his boiler room posing and keeping an eye out; Talalay relaxes on Krueger's bed. The well-crafted set is barely seen in the film: a glimpse of it can be caught in Tina's first nightmare and when Nancy searches for Krueger near the end.

dangerous situation. I read a lot of them and it kind of took hold."

In terms of her character and the film, the actress comprehends Nancy's need to do what must be done, even though in the context of her situation, she admits, "It seems super naive and sweet that she thinks this little pamphlet of traps is gonna help her, but her commitment to it is one hundred percent, and that's what I love about it. There's no cynicism in it, it's really heartfelt. She lost so much and doesn't have much more to lose, and that's what's going through her head. At that point she's really saving herself and proving what she knew all along, that Freddy is real."

Craven felt it was right for Nancy to use those tools to fight her tormentor on her turf, but that perhaps he would soon have to take a break from the concept. "There were several films I did that had booby traps," laughed the writer and director. "Even on *The Hills Have Eyes* we had some rather elaborate booby traps, including one that used the mother as the bait. So I just thought they were fun. But after a while I said, 'You can't have any more booby traps, Craven, because it's like you always have those!'"

PREPARING FOR BATTLE

Having notified her father of her intentions, and with traps set, Nancy was finally ready to put her battle plan into motion. First she saw to Marge, the mother that should be protecting her, but instead is mothered by the child herself. It was yet another step in what would be an important part of Nancy's journey.

"Once Marge has disclosed that she and her cohorts, the other parents, have essentially caused the deaths of their own children," Craven states, "she starts drinking heavily to the point where, when Nancy is about to face her worst test, her mother isn't there and has to be kind of put to bed like a little child."

"You know, the society that we live in, unfortunately, requires kids to parent their parents sometimes. And that's the theme that people often talk about with *Nightmare on Elm Street*," Langenkamp proclaims, though she isn't entirely convinced Nancy was becoming the parent. "What I do believe, though, is that Nancy was becoming an adult, and becoming grown-up at a time when, you know, all parents don't wanna see that happen. And so that tension isn't so much Nancy parenting her parents, it's just her becoming an adult with them."

Blakley felt it was an interesting viewpoint, saying, "I think Marge is at her wits' end, but Nancy is maintaining her strength, and Nancy is not drunk, and Nancy is somehow managing to surmount every surreal, dreamlike, or real attack on her. So she maintains her strength and maturity, and her mother is losing hers in the process of her grief, and her sorrow, and her alcoholism."

Langenkamp feels it's an important occurrence in the film and, while Nancy doesn't take the bottle of alcohol from her mother, she "tucks her into bed that one night," says Langenkamp. "But for me, it was kind of her preparation for battle. She just needed to get her mother someplace safe, because she knew that she was about to go into this dream where the whole house was gonna become the battlefield."

It's a significant distinction for the actress who has always felt that both the house and her character's mother were not just iconic elements of the first film, but necessary ones. "How Nancy handles everything, and how she manages all of it is, I think, one of the most genius parts of Wes' script," Langenkamp declares.

"Nancy saw something happening based on a crime of their parents. The parents were in collusion to hide it," Craven says. "Her friends were in denial, taking all sorts of ways away from reality. Drinking, sex, drugs, whatever, and she was the only one that had the guts to say, 'I saw this, and I have to figure out how to confront it.' That's a real hero we can all relate to."

Englund looks at Nancy as "the woman warrior, that's what Wes intended. A woman always vanquishes Freddy," says Englund. "And Nancy specifically embodies that."

As an extension of her physical and psychological preparedness, Langenkamp believes that her clothing played a part. "My favorite piece of wardrobe that I wore is my pajamas. I think putting on the pajamas was almost like her putting on her battle armor," she proposes. "And when she gets ready to go to bed, it becomes more and more serious every time she goes to sleep."

Thinking of the garment, the actress calls out the details that have more meaning than one might think. "They're really simple Chinese pajamas made in Shanghai, I think it says, but the rosettes, to me, are so sweet. The rose bushes come back into the story at the rose trellis, so there's some thematic similarities. And then the blue piping I love because of my blue eyes," Langenkamp admits.

"I do remember pink roses on a cream background. They were piped and buttoned up the front, and they fit really well, but they were not body revealing at all," says Jensen. "And I totally agree that it was an armor."

"The physical scenes were the most satisfying scenes for me. They were really precise and the timing had to be just right." Heather Langenkamp

---

"They really were just great," says Langenkamp, citing that they were comfortable, she could run in them and they were flattering. "But not too flattering," she concedes. "And I don't think they consciously thought about all the ways that the pajamas were going to make Nancy more of a heroine. But in the twenty to twenty-five years that have gone by, I often think back to the pajamas and what a great costume they ended up being."

As Nancy prepares to close her eyes and enter the nightmare, she recites *Now I Lay Me Down to Sleep*, the classic children's bedtime prayer, whose earliest printed version seems to have appeared in 1711. "That was the first prayer I was ever taught," admits Craven.

Upon finishing the words, Nancy looks at her watch, setting the countdown for ten minutes. What many tend to recall, though, is that it was a digital timepiece, something not omnipresent in 1984. "It was all the rage to have anything electronic," points out Langenkamp.

"That was my watch," Craven reveals, "and it cost two hundred fifty dollars! I swear to God, that's how much they cost when they first came out."

Upon laying herself to sleep (a shot, viewers will notice, used for one poster of the film), Nancy is ready to enter Krueger's lair. "I always really enjoyed how they set dressed where he lived," says Langenkamp. "All these naked Barbies and strange little kid toys."

Huntley appreciates the actress' noticing the touches that were given to Krueger's boiler room abode. "The most fun was Freddy's lair, with the steam pipes and the steam room with his little bed and all his little things," she says. "You don't really see a lot of it, but there were all sorts of hanging little doodads, and little pieces of paper, and little chains and just his world. It's always fun to do real strange, unusual, character sets like that."

TACKLING A NIGHTMARE

"I really liked planning really serious fights," says Langenkamp. "I didn't want it to look feminine at all. I wanted Nancy to be the first young teenager who actually goes and jumps on the bad guy."

Indeed she did, after finding remnants of her friends while searching for Krueger in his boiler room during her final nightmare. And when Nancy is ready, Langenkamp says, "I turn around in front of the house and I just jump on Freddy, because I wanna pull him out of my dream. That's my whole plan."

A strategy that, according to the actress, had Nancy becoming a very active fighter, something she says is a rarity. "There's a lot of female heroines in film, but very rarely do they actually, without a gun or some really powerful weapon, just bodily go and attack. And that's what Nancy does. And I love those scenes," says Langenkamp.

Apparently so did Freddy, ostensibly welcoming Nancy with open arms when she rushes him, the two falling together on the broken rose trellis. ("And those were true roses and true thorns," clarifies Langenkamp.) The scuffle is short-lived as Nancy awakens in her own bed, seemingly out of the nightmare. "When [Nancy] wakes up in the bedroom on that set, we had the trellis and the roses on top, and then pulled them out of the shot and out of the set before we come back wide," Craven explains of the transition. "It's quite subliminal."

Langenkamp's stunt double prepares for a lengthy fall. It is the moment in the nightmare when Nancy jumps from a pipe in Krueger's boiler room, only to end up in her own front yard. In the final film, the fabric of the landing pad, surrounded by the dismantled rose trellis, can be seen billowing when the stunt is complete.

It would be a pre-cursor to what Craven deemed "a beautifully timed jump" when, after Nancy thinks her plan has failed, and that she is "crazy after all," Krueger makes a startling appearance. Upon his attacking Nancy, the penultimate showdown between heroine and villain—now in corporeal form—begins.

That physicality between the two characters was an aspect that lent to a more profound understanding of why Freddy might have appreciated Nancy. "She's smart, and beautiful, and strong," says Englund. "To Freddy, that is both reviled and enticing," adding that she, too, must be dealt with. "That's the punishment, to kill that child, or to make that child kill herself, or commit suicide, or die in her sleep. To punish those parents for what happened to him, if Freddy can just get in her little brain and turn it against her. That's why I think he considered Nancy such a worthy adversary."

"The physical scenes were really the most satisfying scenes for me. They were really precise and the timing had to be just right," says Langenkamp. "I was trained as a dancer and, to me, it was like a giant dance that we need to choreograph and do."

In charge of such planned action was Cecere, who had nothing but high marks not only for Langenkamp's ability to perform, but also her understanding of when it was time to step aside. "She would always listen," says Cecere. "She was always a perfectionist about what she wanted, and yet she would listen to all the safety things that you talked about. If you thought it was unsafe for her to do something, she would by all means say, 'Let someone else do it.'"

Langenkamp recalls the stunt doubles used for many of the scenes, including hers. "I remember Tony Cecere, when he was finding stunt people, he was always showing me the rear ends of all these stunt woman, saying, 'Okay, here's one for you,'" the actress recalls with a laugh.

HIT 'EM HARD!

As Nancy and Krueger play a carefully laid out game of cat and mouse, the heroine finds herself pleading with Sergeant Parker—tasked with keeping a watchful eye on the girl and the house—to get her father. Much to Nancy's dismay, but subsequently the audience's delight, he does not oblige quickly enough.

"It was a late night scene that took three or four days to do all of that. And that leads, of course, to my character going over and giving my famous line about, 'Don't worry, everything's going to be under control,'" laughs Whipp. "Nancy calls me an asshole, which is resoundingly applauded almost any time I've seen the movie with an audience. They enjoy me being stupid."

Langenkamp recalls that, in the original script, "Nancy cursed a lot more, and we ended up not having her curse quite as much," she states.

The reason for cutting the foul language back, Craven admits, was "I think when she finally does, it's very strong." He also mentioned the moment between Nancy and Parker "was a big audience favorite, I know."

As for his character and the moment, Whipp does believe that he should have gone back in to get Thompson, "but then, there wouldn't be that kind of tension in the film," he offers.

Unger not only enjoyed working with Whipp, but states the moment was much like the one his character had earlier with Nancy and Glen, reinforcing the notion of adults not heeding the cries of their children. "We were grown-ups, we weren't paying attention to these kids!" he exclaims. "The thought was, 'They should be home in bed,' or something. 'What are they doing out here?' And that was part of the tension that Wes created between younger people and older people."

The actor likens the concept (one seen in many a genre film) to the 1958 classic, *The Blob*, starring Steve McQueen. "The theme in that, too, as far as the adults and the high school kids goes, is there is a lack of trust," adds Unger.

Jensen fine tunes Englund's look for the camera; For continuity, Englund shows off the wounds his character suffers at the hands of Nancy's traps.

Such tension played well on screen, but there were also moments of uncertainty of another type going on behind the scenes. Craven revealed that while Langenkamp may have acquiesced to playing her more action-oriented scenes carefully, there were times when he questioned just how safe his stunt team actually was. "Tony Cecere, he did some really hard falls," admitted the writer and director. "There's a scene where Freddy gets knocked by the sledgehammer and falls backward over the railing. I thought [Cecere] had broken his neck for sure because his body rotated, and he turned his head sideways just for a split second and hit that thing like a ton of bricks."

Craven had always thought the stunt was dangerous, with Cecere landing on a mattress (on some releases of the film, vigilant eyes can see it at the bottom of the screen) on top of three-quarter-inch plywood. Why did Craven worry for his stuntman? "The plywood was cracked in half when we took it out," he says. "It was just hair-raising, the things he would do, and walk away from. I never saw him get hurt once."

True to form, the stunt was pulled off without any injuries and the climactic battle continued, this time moving to some more explosive moments.

"I walked Heather through and I did the shot where Freddy went by the light and it exploded," says Cecere. "I was there when Heather walked all the way through those things, because we had to show her how big the light bulb explosion was going to be."

Fortunately for Langenkamp, the explosion wasn't so great that they needed to replace her for the effect. "I remember running through the room, Freddy tripping on the wire and the effects team creating the explosion. A lot of it was really me," she reveals.

Not so lucky was Krueger, who by this time had been pummeled with a glass coffee pot and sledgehammer, crashed onto a flight of stairs, and was also the victim of a more-than-minor explosion. The real world wounds the character endured were subtly created by Miller. "We did a lot of blood stuff on his head, and then did some bruising and stuff, but it was all just makeup over his mask," he says. "It wasn't anything out of the ordinary like special prosthetics or anything like that. They didn't really have time for that kind of stuff."

KRUEGER: REKINDLED

Now that Nancy had proven to Krueger—and the audience—she was a force to be reckoned with, the time had come for her to enact the final piece of her plan, which was to destroy Krueger.

And she was going to vanquish Freddy the same way her parents had long ago: with fire. To do so, Craven and his team were ready to bring the heat.

"Oh, my gosh, everybody and their grandma from the fire department was there that day," jokes Woodrum, who was also present to watch the filming. "Such precaution was taken. It must have cost them a fortune, but the safety of the crew and the cast was paramount in Wes' mind, and it was just brilliant the way they did those effects."

"Nancy pre-loaded the lantern in the cellar with fuel, so when Freddy chased her down there she could throw it at him, and light him up," Doyle remembers.

The "him" in this instance would be Cecere, once again doubling Englund as Krueger.

"It was one of the best full burns I'd ever seen at that point," admits Doyle. "Wes knew Tony from his previous work and said, 'This guy will do body burns you won't believe.' The whole sequence of Freddy getting lit up in the cellar, turning, running up the stairs, falling down, rolling back down the stairs, was all one shot. That was one take."

Doyle was not alone in his amazement that anybody could burn that long, which created one of the most fantastic visuals of the independent feature. "It had never been done in a film before," reveals Craven. "It was a huge effect, and the heat from the fire was so intense that everybody on the crew was sort of backing away from the room."

Realizing the heat of the flames coupled with a small space could be a potential problem, Doyle made sure to fireproof the entire set. "The issue here was the body burn occurred in a closed room with an eight foot ceiling, so if he was going to do the type of burn he usually did, he was gonna light the set on fire," he says.

"Tony had studied it very carefully," Craven says. "The whole trick with fire gags is having a flame that is not as hot as other flames might be. For instance, if you were to douse yourself with gasoline or something, the flame would be, let's say, twenty-five hundred degrees. But if you put on rubber cement, which is what I believe Tony used, it burned at eight hundred degrees. There's quite drastic differences."

The trick, then, was for Cecere to find what he could put on himself that would burn, protect his body, but still look good. Ultimately, the stuntman experimented with a number of things before developing the final recipe. "He came up with a secret ingredient gel that he would put on his skin," Craven reveals. "And he practiced, he told me, before he got into the business, by putting various things on himself and setting himself on fire, and running around the family pool until it was too intense to stand. Then, he would dive into the pool. So he was a very ballsy guy."

"You smell the fire, and you smell the chemicals," says Englund. "And in real time, that stunt just seems to go on and on and on. Tony really went for it."

"I've done so much fire work in the movie industry that, as a stunt coordinator, I chose to do that particular burn myself. I actually fell down the flight of stairs on fire, and no one had ever done that before," Cecere says. "I told them that if we were going to do that we had to build the steps in a specific way so that rolling down the stairs on fire wouldn't tear the fire suit. So I actually had the stairs lined with rubber and then covered with black cloth in order to make it safe coming down."

After figuring out the logistics of how it could be done, the time came to make what would be the first, and only, attempt. "After we had done the shot where Heather hit me with the fuel, which was just water, I got set for the fire burn where we actually put fuel around my feet and poured fuel on me," Cecere remembers.

It was after Craven filmed an insert shot of Langenkamp lighting the matches and throwing them onto Freddy, played at that moment by Cecere, when the real heat began.

"He would just do so many crazy stunts, but the craziest one of all was the fire stunt," Langenkamp says. "He had the personality of one of those kids in school who would just eat anything, do anything, subject himself to anything for Wes. And they had a loyal friendship and partnership for a long, long time because of that. I lit the match, threw it down, and then ran. Then they had the stuntwoman running up the stairs. The timing and everything was critical because he was on fire. And you can't be anywhere near the fire."

Not able to tell how much fire was actually burning on him, "As the fire climbed up and over me, the safeties down below had to tell me when I was completely engulfed," says Cecere. "And that's when I would turn, and as I'd start to run, Heather's stunt double would jump in the shot right in front of me and run up the stairs. And I would go after her until I got to the door."

It was at the top of the stairs where a burning Freddy tugged at the door to get out, which was actually being pulled back on the other side not by Langenkamp, but by two stunt people. Those stunt performers were necessary, Cecere says, because, "I couldn't give a verbal command for the next bit of action to happen, which was Nancy pushing the door back in to knock Freddy down the stairs. So I gave them a count of three, and after I tug the door three times, they pushed it in, and I fell and rolled down the flight of stairs."

But the flames and scene did not end there. "Once I was at the bottom, I actually had time to start back up. And when I was halfway up the stairs, I realized that if I got all the way to the top landing again, I just didn't have anybody to put me out up there," states Cecere. Safety protocols had to come first and, he continues, "Though it might have made a better shot, I stopped halfway up the stairs."

Krueger finds himself engulfed in flames again. The full body burn was a memorable achievement for the low-budget film, ultimately earning body burn expert Cecere an award.

"I wouldn't have believed that anyone could burn that long, fall down, and then run back up the stairs again. We were just standing there in awe," Doyle recalls. "Waiting for this guy to give us the signal to put him out. But he just kept going, and I kept thinking the set was really gonna catch fire. Finally, he laid down and we put him out."

Cook was also surprised, if not a little shocked, at Cecere's work at that moment. "I remember asking Tony, who's a very sweet guy, 'Why are you doing this burn work?' He said, 'Because nobody else does it. It's a specialty gig and I've sort of cornered the market. I'm doing full-body burns and so it's a great way to make extra money,'" she says. "And, as I recall, he got two thousand dollars above and beyond a day's pay for doing that burn, which, to me, is not enough to set yourself on fire, but apparently that was the going rate!"

"I think he was a Marine in Vietnam, and he came back and he decided he was going to get into stunts, and he would specialize in fire," says Craven. "He had that burn down great."

The stunt, which lasted twenty-seven seconds on screen, won a Stuntman's Award for the Best Specialty Stunt.

"I actually attended the Stuntman's Awards to give the award to Tony that year," admits Englund. "It was at Warner Bros. I remember very distinctly because I had to help out when two of the presenters, David Carradine and Jan Michael Vincent, got drunk on tequila in their tuxedos and were unable to continue doing a lot of the narration and the presentation. I had to kind of run up and substitute, even though I was only there to present for Tony."

Looking back, Cecere brings to mind the notion of Englund not always enjoying the fact that he was doubled, something the stuntman understands. "I'm not built like Robert, but in a scene like the burn," he says, "my theory is, 'Hey, it happened so fast that nobody's gonna know the difference how tall the guy is, or how big the guy is. Just that he's on fire.'"

While that might discount the eagle eyes of some astute genre fans, Cecere is most confident when he says of the fire scene, "No, Robert didn't have any issues with me doing that!"

MARGE GETS BURNED

Though Nancy had done her best to send Krueger down in flames a second time, and her father did come to her—however late—rescue, the dream demon was out to prove that you can't keep a good killer down. In this case, that meant Freddy going after the next best victim, Nancy's mother.

Directly following the previous scene's heat, the fire work continued. This time, Nancy would follow Krueger's flaming footprints. "As Heather was going through the house looking at the flaming steps, I was there on set because she was running around all the fire," Cecere says. "We actually had those little tornadoes of fire that were being caused by the wind blowing."

It was a moment Craven remembered fondly. "It's one of my favorite shots. It's just one of those special effects and photography things that worked beautifully," he stated. It was also a one-take deal. "We were afraid [Heather] would catch on fire," the writer and director added with a laugh.

"It never occurred to me that it was dangerous or scary to do it!" confesses Langenkamp.

Tracking those licks of flame would lead Nancy to witness a still-on-fire Freddy, in the throes of murder atop her mother. (In very early drafts of the script, a much darker moment is revealed as Krueger is also "fucking the living daylights out of her" when Nancy and her father burst in.)

It's a sequence that Langenkamp feels lends a powerful and, perhaps, much-needed boost of pathos for Marge. "It ratchets the movie up to the final pitch because Nancy's already lost Glen, and now she's going to lose the next most important person in her life, which is her mom," she says. "So right at the time when you feel like there's really no place, emotionally, that the movie can go, suddenly we bring in the danger to the mother, which up until this point people don't love her that much. But Nancy loves her. It kind of saves Marge from being a caricature, because seeing Nancy's reaction to the fact that she might lose her mother suddenly makes all the bad things that Marge is, or represents, go away; because if Nancy loves her, that's enough."

But not for Freddy, who is hell-bent on exacting his revenge.

"Yes, that was me as Freddy on top of her," says Cecere. "We took the actress out and I did a complete burn. There was also a double for Heather to come in and hit me with the chair. And then another stunt man who doubled John Saxon came in and threw the blanket over me and put me out. That's when I was able to disappear from the shot."

Blakley was not used in the scene that made its way to the final cut of the film, but the actress does remember being present for her character's attack by Krueger. "I was there that day, yes. They used the fire close to me, but then I believe Wes did not use that take," she recalls.

"For the scene where my mom dies in a fiery blaze of light, it's the perfect end to her, because she burned Freddy and, therefore, she gets burned," muses Langenkamp.

Craven adds, "It's a poetic justice sort of thing. There was an element to the story that was very much about inheriting the wind. If you sow violence you will reap the wind."

Langenkamp feels that the scene is also one of the most fantastical. "It really is a no-holds-barred moment, because you have Freddy, you have my mother, you have my dad, you have me. And nothing really makes sense at that point," she says.

The actress (and audiences) may have found the sequence hallucinatory, but that wasn't the word that many on the crew, responsible for making the moment come to life, might have chosen.

"The end where charred Ronee Blakley disappears into the bed, I had a lot of trouble. Wes had a lot of trouble. Everyone had a lot of trouble trying to figure out how to end this movie, and how to exchange from the dream-space back to the real-space," Doyle says.

"I know they used a hydraulic lift of some kind that was rigged into the bed stand and it wasn't Ronee. It was a dummy," remembers Langenkamp.

Tasked to create the Blakley doppelgänger was Mark Shostrom, who, under the guidance of Miller, worked on it for a couple of days. "It was very influenced by Dick Smith's work in *Ghost Story* (1981), a big, rotted puppet with rotting breasts and whatnot. And for some reason, the sculpture ended up not being used and Dave had to throw something else together," Shostrom says. "Unfortunately, I don't have any photos of the sculpture I did. At the time, I had no idea it was going to be such a big film. I didn't bother to shoot photos."

"He worked on the skeleton and it had some kind of meat on it, a little bit of latex and polyfoam stuff, but they wanted it less skeletal and more her," states Miller. "So she came over for a face cast and we added her face on there. It was basically Mark's thing, and mine, and stuff that we added later after Mark had left."

Fleetwood recalls, "At that moment, I ran into the hair room and I grabbed a bunch of stuff and I started gluing hair on a stocking cap and putting it on this thing," she says. "And that's how we got the last of that going into the bed. It was one of those last-minute, 'Let's-make-something-and-shoot-it,' things."

To this day, the hair stylist recalls the moment as one of her best. "It was like the first time I was really able to help, and it was wonderful, and they liked what it was, and it worked," Fleetwood says. "It was one of my very first great, creative gigs where, in the split second, I made that. And as Wes was turning around, thinking, I handed it to him. I already had it done. So it was a good moment in my career."

Doyle, on the other hand, recalls that "even with the replacement dummy, to put a burnt Ronee Blakley on the bed and drop it into that thing, it was a shot I was never happy with. We didn't have enough time to properly work out with David how to animate that skeleton, or do the effects around the skeleton to cover the rig. The lighting wasn't good enough yet. The lighting effect wasn't set."

Haitkin reveals how they ultimately made it work. "We used an arc welder, instead of the lighting effect," he states.

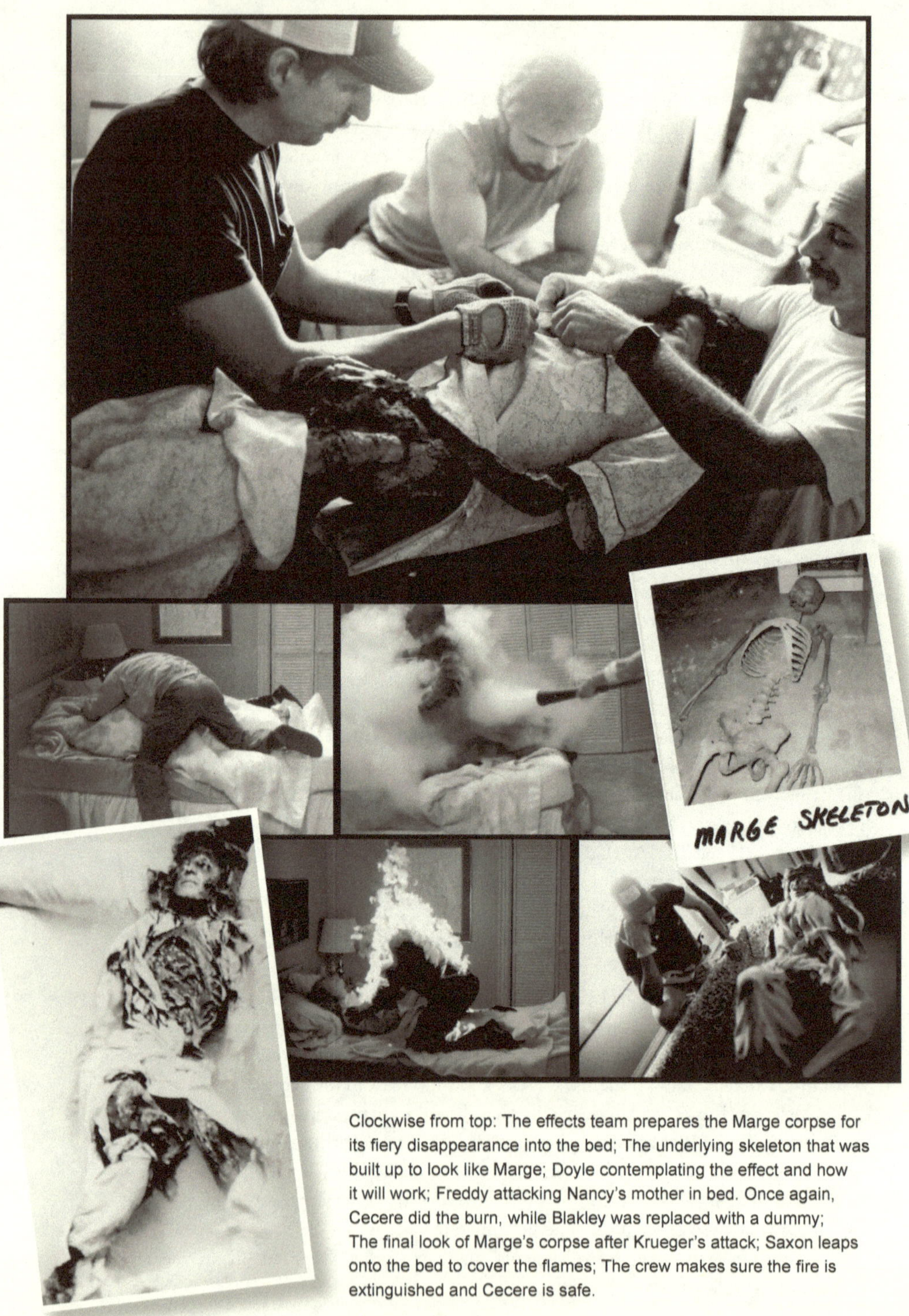

Clockwise from top: The effects team prepares the Marge corpse for its fiery disappearance into the bed; The underlying skeleton that was built up to look like Marge; Doyle contemplating the effect and how it will work; Freddy attacking Nancy's mother in bed. Once again, Cecere did the burn, while Blakley was replaced with a dummy; The final look of Marge's corpse after Krueger's attack; Saxon leaps onto the bed to cover the flames; The crew makes sure the fire is extinguished and Cecere is safe.

It is something Miller has not forgotten. "They didn't pass out sunglasses or anything like that," he says. "It was like looking into a welding light, which is dangerous. But I don't think anything bad happened."

Even with Haitkin pleased that it gave the moment a great look, Carlucci agrees with Doyle that it wasn't everything they had hoped for. "We used a liquid nitrogen effect, so that we'd have this white cloud effect that they would eventually dissolve into the sheet, and she would sink down into this cloud," he says. "It wasn't one of the best gags on the show, in terms of what I feel we could have done with it. Of course, today, they would have done a CGI effect."

Doyle agrees, saying, "Today I think a lot of stuff in *Nightmare* would have been done in CG. I think that would have taken some of the appeal out of it, especially with the horror fans, who sort of understand how this art is done. The fact that we do this stuff live, and we do it on camera, and we get it in one take or two takes, is part of the romance of the genre."

Without the benefit of CGI, the actors and the effects team did the best they could, especially under the limitations in which they found themselves. Doyle recalls the difficulties of trying to make happen all the things that were required on a short schedule, and on the first film he had ever coordinated. "We had eighty effects or shot sequences in a ninety-minute film that we were shooting in twenty-six days. There was just no way we could stuff it all in. And the most stressful thing for me was that there were no breaks," he says. "In most films you get some down time. The first company goes off and does this and you can catch up and do this. But I only had five guys on my crew. So just being able to supply the personnel and supply everything for everyday was really the biggest problem for me. Just the amount of stuff that had to be done."

Down to the last day or two, and needing to get the shot with Marge's corpse sinking into the bed, "that's what we were able to get," says Doyle. "If I had to go back and do it again, that is probably the one sequence that I'd really spend some more time on, and start much earlier in the process, and try to develop something that would be a better closing for what was really a great film."

"I remember it not being quite as gruesome or scary as Wes wanted it to be," Miller says.

Craven wasn't afraid to admit he felt it was "one of the least successful special effects in the movie," but kept his sense of humor about the whole thing by adding, "John's not upset that his wife just died, it was the special effects of the scene that tore him up!"

As an actress, Langenkamp understands that feeling. "I think that what we realized on *Nightmare on Elm Street* was that some of the effects might not play in our modern age as well as they did then," she says. "But the reality of it is, when you can actually be with the effect, or the monster, that just makes such a difference in an actor's performance."

Langenkamp is also aware that "sometimes your performance is kind of secondary to whether the special effects work, particularly in a horror film," she states. And if an actor isn't happy with a take that is printed, sometimes it's tough luck. "You didn't get to make everything precious, like, 'Oh, it's my scene and I'm going to do this,'" adds the actress. "It's, 'There's a guy running by you who's on fire and they're only gonna do that once.'"

TO: A Nightmare on Elm Street
All Production Personnel

DATE: July 17, 1984

FROM: Jim Doyle
Effects Contractor

Please accept my profound apology for the episode which occurred during the photography of Marge's corpse on Monday evening, July 16. Such an outburst is well outside the limits of professional behavior for anyone, especially those who handle noxious, dangerous materials while placing cast and crew in potentially dangerous situations as a daily part of the job. Any loss of control under any circumstance is absolutely unforgiveable and will not be repeated.

You may have every confidence that your safety is my first concern; therefore, pressure, exhaustion, and whatever else goes on will not be allowed to build again to such a level that I may not be expected to act prudently and quickly in any given situation, emergency or otherwise, during the remainder of this production.

Thank you,

Jim Doyle

A letter written by Doyle to apologize for an event on set during filming. A crew member had caused an issue and, says Doyle, "I fired him on the spot. He refused to leave. We are still friends."

Langenkamp credits Craven for knowing what he wants and how to get it, even if the talent wasn't always happy with their work in a particular moment. "Wes is such a great director that he can hide all the bad things you do with your performance," she laughs. Taking it further, she is emphatic in making a very salient point clear. "There was nothing fake in the first one. We were all there in the same room, we were all acting together, we were all doing it together, and that's why as a whole it still works today."

Even with that, the actress did find some difficulties playing the moment her mother disappears. "The part I have the most trouble with in that scene is that Nancy's watching for so long. I remember me and John would have to sit there for a minute and a half while the effects were taking place, and maintaining that look of horror for that long was just torture," Langenkamp concedes. "And I just wanted so much to have something to do, because Nancy is such an action character. But having to sit there, with John over my shoulder, and both of us staring into the bed, I found just agonizing."

SHE KNOWS THE SECRET NOW

Having handled the loss of her friends, and now her mother, Nancy is left alone to contemplate whether or not she was successful in her attempt to destroy Krueger.

"Even her father is dismissed as somebody who can't be with her," says Craven. "It's just one of those moments you realize it's something you have to face entirely alone. I think it's a great moment for a character in a film."

The question of whether or not Nancy had vanquished her tormentor would quickly be answered as Freddy makes a charred, angry encore right behind her, using an effect rigged moments ago for Marge's fiery comeuppance.

"When Freddy comes up out of the bed, we used the same rig that we had used to bring Marge down," says Doyle. "It was the opposite at that point so we could elevate Freddy and have him come up through the sheet and cut through it. It turned out to be a pretty good gag."

Krueger rising up and stretching the sheets before slicing through them was effective and, made possible Craven stated, "by more Spandex, if I'm not mistaken."

Once Freddy returns, Nancy is left to play her final card, finding strength from within. But to do that, Langenkamp felt she needed a little help on the outside. "There's the first action bits and then there's this interminable moment, with this crazy look on Nancy's face," she says. I remember really vividly trying to come up with a look for that scene with the makeup and hair. We just were like, 'Let's just go bags under the eyes, frizzed out hair, as frizzy as it can possibly go.'"

"We were selling the sad, distressed hair on that one because she had hit the wall at that point. Her character had had enough of Freddy," says Fleetwood. "He had pushed her to her limits and we really were trying to show that with her hair and makeup."

Taking about thirty minutes to create the final look, Fleetwood says, "We wanted it to be good because she's at the end of the movie, and she's facing Freddy. So you take time because that's the hero shot."

Langenkamp doesn't disagree, believing the look they achieved worked for the film. She does, however, joke, "It's not my best look. *Teen Vogue* is not knocking on the door for that one, either."

Now that the effect, hair, makeup, and performances were to the crew's liking, there did seem to be some thought as to how Nancy would, in fact, destroy Freddy. As he had in the past, Craven turned to the concept of understanding the truth so it can set one free. "I think the finest act of heroism in a film, let's just say in my films, is facing the truth," he says. "First of all, seeing the truth, which others often do, but then admitting to it and taking responsibility for it. Acting upon that truth no matter how painful or scary it is."

"What the ending of the original *Nightmare on Elm Street* means symbolically, with Nancy turning her back on Freddy, is 'I won't participate in fear,'" says Englund.

That fear, which Krueger engenders in all of his victims, whether they are the children of *Elm Street*, their relatives, or the very people who murdered him long ago, was something they unfortunately succumbed to, Englund believes. "The fear. They all got hooked on it, and Nancy finally realizes that at the end," he says. "She realizes to stop it, you must not surrender to it. And that's actually a very satisfying ending."

Nevertheless, Langenkamp feels its effectiveness may have ultimately been ambiguous. "I always find that scene hard to take, because it's such a simple solution. I just turn my back, and then it's supposed to be all gone," she states. "Freddy vanishes in a burst of light or energy."

Understanding the direction Craven was going in to resolve the whole story ("Turn your back on your fear and then it, or in this case Freddy, has no power left," states Langenkamp), the actress feels that the moment Nancy does turn away could have been the more appropriate ending. She doesn't deny her, and possibly audiences', bewilderment at what she deemed such a simple solution, but one that could be seen as a possible disappointment.

"It's a confusing scene because, with the ending that we now have, it doesn't quite make sense," Langenkamp says. "You know, if I turn my back, and that's supposed to be a successful resolution, then the fact that Freddy comes back means I failed. And so to me, I don't really like that Freddy comes back, because I think the original solution was actually really quite genius on Wes' part."

TRYING TO KEEP A GOOD MAN DOWN

With Freddy's power taken away and the horror seemingly over, Nancy opens the door to a bright new day, replete with both her mother and friends. The question nevertheless quickly became, did the ending work?

The answer to that, at least in one part, comes from Risher, who recalls, "There was never an ending in the script. The sky turned black. Lots of birds came out. It was apocalyptic," she states of early drafts of the screenplay before revisions were made.

The supposed day of reckoning Craven had envisioned had at least one issue that Talalay recalls. "I do remember that there was supposed to be this strange fog that came in at the end," she says. "Wes used the word 'tule.' A tule fog. I remember thinking, 'What is he talking about?' and 'What does he mean?' The fog was a big to-do."

Fog technicalities notwithstanding, it was that original ambiguity that led to what is, for many *Elm Street* and Craven aficionados, the much-talked-about dispute over what the film's ending was, should be, and eventually became.

The difference of opinion seemed to lie with Craven and Shaye. "It was our most contentious moment," admitted the writer and director. "He wanted to have a big hook to the picture so they could have a sequel. And I thought he was crazy. 'There'll never be a sequel.' Boy, was I stupid."

Even Langenkamp, who appreciated Craven's original concept, says she would be remiss in not acknowledging what Shaye was after. "I can understand both sides. But I do see that maybe they wanted to see Freddy keep going, and see the possibility for a sequel," the actress says. "But at the time, we never thought there was gonna be a sequel. It would just seem like the producer had wishful thinking. It seemed like to us, 'Ok, let's humor him.'"

Corri is firmly on Langenkamp's side with regard to talk of any concept of a follow up at the time they filmed. "The initial concept was not a franchise to begin with. It was one story," the actor states.

"I don't think there was talk of a sequel," offers Haitkin. "When we were debating the ending, though, that's when I realized that the sequel might be a possibility. And that's where those issues came into play between Wes and Bob. I think Bob's idea was to give it some kind of an ending that felt that it could go on, and Wes wasn't as concerned with that."

Shaye tends to look at the matter in a different light. "I've been accused of fighting for a movie that could have sequels, but that wasn't really the case," he reveals. "I just felt that the ending to the movie didn't send the audience out with any great

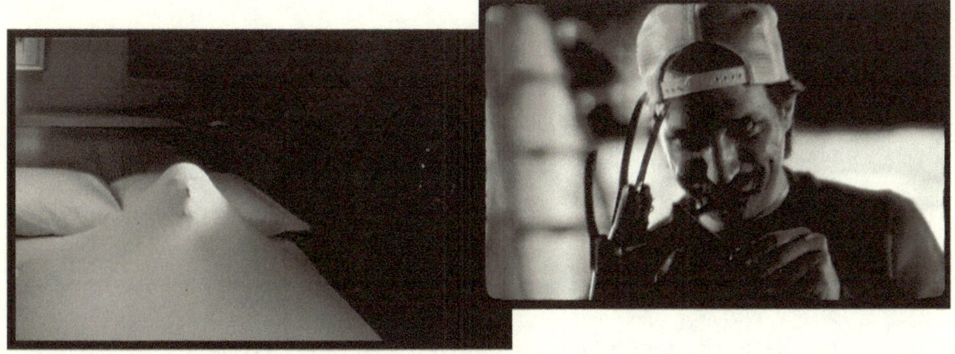

After his fiery encounter with Marge, Krueger comes up from the depths in order to destroy Nancy. Once again, the effect was achieved inexpensively. "By more Spandex, if I'm not mistaken," recalls Craven; Doyle works the weapon he helped bring to life, which would be used to slice through the stretching bedsheet.

excitement. And Wes wanted the ending to be that Heather woke up in the morning, and the sun was shining, and she walked away."

The producer certainly let Craven know his feelings. "We argued a lot about it. And Wes threw his hands up at one point, because we did have a pretty serious disagreement."

"It was definitely a difference between Bob and Wes," Risher admits. "Bob wanted the sort of shock ending."

Even with a differing opinion, Craven and Shaye understood that what they were both ultimately after was the best resolution for the film. As for the crew, they knew when to get involved, but also when to step back.

"Those kind of things I really didn't get involved in. When you have a producer and a director discussing those kinds of issues," Haitkin says, "you have big commercial issues at stake, you have Wes' artistic issue at stake. For a cinematographer, it's not a good idea to intervene and take sides."

Doyle also stayed on the periphery, ready to deliver whatever was needed, from whomever the edict came. "I don't remember specifically, but I think Wes was more for closure and for a comfortable end, and Bob was for leaving it a little more open, obviously thinking about the sequel possibilities and everything else," he says. "But Wes' argument was, if the film works, the sequel is already there. I think Bob was a little less confident that everything was gonna work out the way it did. So we shot a whole series of endings for that."

Craven believed that it was not necessary to have a hook on any picture. "If the picture is very popular, you can make up a sequel that'll make sense and you don't have to have some stupid hook on the end of it," he says.

THE GOOD, THE BAD, AND THE UGLY

The discussions and, some would say, arguments between director and producer led to "at least three different endings being shot," Risher recalls.

Deciding what those endings would be "was quick and rushed, and people were throwing ideas left and right to see how we could accomplish this, you know, existence of Freddy at the end," Langenkamp says.

Of the things they tried, many were spur-of-the-moment ideas ("There was a lot of talk. We all had our two cents worth," says Englund.), with one being deemed "the happy ending," where the kids simply "drove off in the car," Shaine remembers, with Risher adding, "We shot it without the top of the car slamming down."

Perhaps not surprisingly, that one is a favorite of Langenkamp's. "Even though there was a lot of 'Let's try this, let's try that,' in my heart, I really like the one where Nancy lives," she states, admitting that it might not be the one Shaye or Risher were happiest with because it "more definitively did not allow for sequels."

"What the ending of the original *A Nightmare on Elm Street* means symbolically, with Nancy turning her back on Freddy, is 'I won't participate in fear.'" Robert Englund

---

While Langenkamp has specific memories about the ending she prefers, as well as what it was like filming those she didn't, co-star Wyss' recollection of the filming of the end was less clear. "I remember driving away in the car, but I don't remember all the conversation about it. I don't have anything really to say about that because I don't know. Isn't that crazy?" she admits.

A second option more prominently showcased the car they were driving. "I really liked just the kids coming up, and the car mutating on them, because I think that made it a little clearer what I thought the movie was about," Englund says.

That notion dealt with the kids getting in the car and that "in one of the takes the convertible top kind of just closes on top of us, and it's obvious that he's taking us away," Langenkamp says. "There just seemed to be this sense that Freddy was the car."

To better illustrate the point, that convertible top would be painted in very distinct colors. "It wasn't just the idea of the car driving away, but that top slams down and it's the same color as Freddy's sweater," Risher says.

At least for Doyle, it was one effect he didn't have to worry about much. "The top came up and slammed closed, which it did anyway. We didn't even have to rig it. It was sort of goofy that way, but with the sweater painted on it," he says.

The silly aspect quickly gave way to real, if short-lived, shock as the actors were not expecting the top to smash down in such a forceful way. When it did, the looks of surprise and fear were very real for the talent inside the vehicle.

"Every gag was like that. There's usually one or two takes involved where they've never tried it out before, because we never had rehearsals," states Langenkamp. "But

Opposite page: Nancy finds herself in the final showdown with a flesh and blood Krueger. Though this particular moment is not seen in the final film, it represents the arc the young woman has gone through. "Her character had had enough of Freddy," says Fleetwood.

Cast and crew prepare to shoot the final scene of the film. It was one that created the most tension between Craven and Shaye as the biggest question of the shoot was posed: How would the movie end? Deciding that, Langenkamp remembers, "was quick and rushed, and people were throwing ideas left and right to see how we could accomplish this, you know, existence of Freddy at the end."

that was also the beauty of it. A lot of those reactions were real because we never had experienced these things. It's just so lucky that no one got hurt because that thing had a lot of force behind it, and it just snapped down over our heads. I think they had said, 'Keep your heads in,' but I don't think we had expected it to be that violent of a slam."

The third idea took the previous concept to a more literal end, and was the one in which Shaye got the conclusion for which he hoped.

"Bob, he did get his hook. We kind of compromised," Craven says, with Risher adding, "Wes did shoot the ending that Bob wanted, which was Freddy driving the car."

Langenkamp says the ending was meant to appear happy, but it becomes quite obvious that "it was Freddy, and not Glen, driving," she says.

It was a denouement that Englund quite liked. "Heather looks, sees her boyfriend driving, and looks away. When she looks back, it's me," he says. "And I smile this sickening grin."

Haitkin agrees with the on-screen villain. "In terms of the different endings that we had, my personal preference was the one of Freddy carrying the children away and being the evil driver," he says.

"I just remember we spent a long time doing those car scenes," Langenkamp says. "The driving away, the convertible top slamming, and then not slamming, and then it already being up when I get in the car. You know, those kinds of things always take a long time," she says.

While some of the cast and crew might have found that coda to be the most appropriate, Corri would disagree, though he is quick to reflect, "Then again, it's a franchise, so what do I know?"

A final option, and the one that caused the most interesting stir amongst the cast and crew, was where Marge waves goodbye to her daughter just before Freddy's clawed hand breaks through the front door window and pulls her through. Moviegoers were then left with a closing shot of the jump rope girls reciting their now-famous rhyme.

"The ending with my mother being squeezed through the door window was a complete surprise. I was in the makeup room when I was told they just pulled the doll, an effigy of Ronee, through the tiny window," Langenkamp says. "I think they originally did it for a blooper reel."

For laughs or not, Englund thinks the final effect worked on film, "but when we shot it, it was pretty silly shit. It looked kind of silly on the set," he says. "Of course, you try to imagine it sped up, or more violent, and the sound and the scream, and how quick they're gonna do it. But until you see it as an editorial rimshot, it was kind of funny on the set. I remember the day we did it, it was kind of, 'Is that gonna work?'"

That question was an appropriate one, and Englund was not alone in asking it. "I never thought it would work. I mean, we had this stupid, rubber woman and just pulled it through that tiny, little area," says Risher.

"She wasn't really supposed to die like that," says Fleetwood, "but it was the end and we needed to get rid of Ronee."

It was another time the hair, wardrobe, and effects worked together, under time and budget constraints, to craft something that would please Craven.

"We wanted to show a physical leaving of her. I remember Wes said, 'Can we make a dummy of her really quick?' So we said, 'Well, we'll give it a whirl.' And we all jumped in together. We stuffed pantyhose inside it. That's why when you see that movie, and that dummy that goes through the window, it's so god-awful because we made that in ten minutes so we could kill her and get her out of the movie," Fleetwood laughs. "I ain't lying."

Jensen recalls it wasn't always the smoothest of shots to accomplish. "I think when it went through a couple times, its head got caught, or its legs got caught. It wasn't the clean pull through on all the takes," she says. "I remember it really did look just like a foam rubber dummy a couple of times. I think a wig fell off once. It was kind of comedic in the process of shooting it."

One person who found the effect to be intriguing was Talalay who, instead of being caught up in whether or not the effect could work, simply wondered how it would be done. "I remember going to Sara and saying, 'How did they actually do that?' because this was pre-digital," she says.

"The dummy of Ronee Blakley going through the door was another one of those last-minute, improvised things," Miller says. "I made a copy of the dummy we had built for the scene where Freddy is on fire on top of her." This version of Marge, though, was different in that it had to be squishy because it had to go through a small window.

Haitkin admits to feeling the idea was "cheesy when we shot it," but goes on to say that the effects team "created a foam dummy that was like a cushion on a couch. But it was all painted with hair and everything, and you could just literally pull it through the door because it was made of foam. And that's why it looked so cheesy."

Blakley recalls the process well. "They made the dummy of me and cut that together with me standing at the door, then the dummy being pulled through the window," she says, recalling that Craven "said I was a good sport, because they had to break the fake glass, which is spun sugar, stick the hand through the window, grab me, and have me scream."

"Pulling the dummy of Ronee through the hole in the door was one of my guys who was six foot six and had long arms," Doyle says, noting that the effect was technically difficult due to chains that ran through the dummy to hold it together. "We tied a rope around the chains right at the back of her shoulder, and I had the key grip and another one of his burly guys grab hold of the rope. And when I said, 'Go!' they would run down the hallway as fast as possible, and the dummy was sucked through the window."

Doyle reveals that the door wasn't part of the actual house, but one that had already been built and used on the set. "We already had a duplicate for the chase scene with Nancy earlier, so we just took the window out of the door and braced the door so the only thing that could happen was that the dummy would collapse and come through the window."

Haitkin, for all his worry that it wouldn't technically work—or worse, not look good—did his part. "We also undercranked a little bit to help make her go faster through the door."

"It's a hokey dummy going through that glass. That's all we could do," says Fleetwood.

When all was said and done, the woman behind the character at the center of all the attention believes the effect, particularly for its time, worked just fine. "Today, the effect is not as impressive because we have so many advanced techniques since this movie was shot," remarks Blakley. "But at the time, it was a brilliant effect."

Still, there were a few cast and crew who weren't entirely sure of the ending's merit. "We didn't think it would make it in the film. It was just so comical-looking," Miller says.

Even Langenkamp admits to being "pretty shocked" when she saw the scene at the end of the film. "It just looked so fake and cheesy. It didn't live up to the rest of the movie. I don't know what happened in the editing, but whatever it was, that ending certainly confuses the audience."

While it wasn't necessarily crystal clear to Blakley, she does offer an interesting idea for her character. "Well, the way Wes wrote and directed the movie, you never know if Marge would be coming back. In other words, would that bit have been a dream?" she teases. "We assume that it's real that Marge died. So she died a couple of times, is what I'm saying. She burned up in the bed and she was yanked through the front door."

Confusing or not, Shaye is able to see all sides of the issue that he was involved in from the beginning, taking it all in stride. "It worked well enough, there was no question about that. But when you see it today, it's a little silly, but so what?"

Craven had a more philosophical, if not slightly humorous take on the character's demise. "I felt that since the mother never came to terms with reality, that she deserved to die."

AND THE WINNER IS...

"Though I seemed to be involved in so much, I was not privy to the questions of the ending, and when I saw the final version I was quite surprised by it," says Talalay.

> **"At the end, I didn't want the evil to have won, because Nancy had gone through that journey and dispelled Freddy by turning her back on him."**
>
> Wes Craven

That surprise would not just be due to the ending being different from what was in the script, or the fact that multiple versions were filmed. Instead, it was the decision to utilize a sort of amalgamation of the three options, something Langenkamp can understand with regard to the two creative forces who were, at least in that moment, at odds.

"There's a real dichotomy between producers and directors," states Langenkamp. "Directors are more concerned with the integrity of their ideas, while producers are more concerned with their audience. There are some producers who may care a little more about producing their art film. We can't kid ourselves, *Nightmare on Elm Street* isn't one of those. But Wes and the rest of us approached it with more seriousness other than thinking, 'This is just a role in a horror movie. We can just slouch.' I don't think anyone on the cast took it for granted."

"The irony is that the way the film finally was created, and this was Wes' decision after test screenings and stuff like that, we used all of the endings, just about," Shaye admits. "So it was good that we tried them."

Using portions of the ending as Craven saw it—with Nancy coming from her nightmare to the light of day to see her mother and friends—but also giving Shaye the shock and the sequel potential he was looking for, "It all worked," Risher says. "After it was finally put together, Wes was very happy with it."

Craven, though, revealed what seemed to be more melancholy. "Really, there was a spiritual side to this, believe it or not, that Nancy kind of represented the person, the soul, that is willing to look at the truth. And the truth is dangerous, and the truth is

Photos taken during one of the potential endings shot for the film. While ultimately not explicitly used, it was a concept Shaye championed: to see Freddy behind the wheel of the car, driving away with the kids.

Even with their characters' fates uncertain, the young cast is all smiles with their attacker (and his cassette player) behind the scenes; Langenkamp and Craven (inset) take some time to have a lighthearted conversation in between takes.

painful," he offered. "But the hero and heroine's journey is to look at what really is. And at the end, I didn't want the evil to have won, because Nancy had gone through that journey and dispelled Freddy by turning her back on him."

Looking back on the decision to film the different versions, Craven adds, "I felt, actually, very bad about doing that. But I also felt very much that Bob was the only person that was able to get this picture going, and championed it. So I gave him his hook."

That hook would, of course, leave the door open for a sequel, even though Craven revealed the mere notion of a sequel never crossed his mind. "It didn't. Not until Bob said he wanted a hook. Before the film opened, we had no idea. Maybe Bob did, but I didn't have any idea that it was going to work," he admitted. "And I had kind of a prejudice against sequels in general. Sort of the artiste. I felt it was better to leave the story as it was. It's the story in and of itself."

Shaye again admits the idea of a sequel was not something he had set out to do from the beginning. In fact, if it weren't for someone else, the notion might never have transpired. "I never thought about it," he states. "I absolutely never did, and it didn't even come to my feeble brain until somebody in our sales department said, 'You know, we've gotta make a sequel to this,' and that was what spawned the sequel. In truth, there was very little cynicism involved in the making of this movie."

The last thing audiences are treated to in Craven's story is a final appearance by the haunting jump rope girls, singing the *Elm Street* rhyme, though Adri-Anne and sister

Coye did not make a repeat appearance. "They didn't really give us any information as to why they went with different sets of kids for the opening and the ending," says Adri-Anne. "But we were really just excited to be able to be in that opening scene. We didn't know anything about another scene, with other girls at the end, at that time."

Rusoff, however, did return. "It was the same thing as the first scene in that there was very little direction," she recalls. "But what I remember the most was there was lots of the fog machine. They had to run through the streets with a fog machine, and they had to keep doing it over and over and over again for each shot. And I remember thinking that was cool."

Joining her would be Lauren Lepucki, another youngster who not only recalls very little direction, but believes any commands given might not have even come from Craven. "Honestly, I had little exposure to the industry so I wouldn't have really known who he was!" she admits. "But the other thing was there were no lead actors there. It was a second unit shot, so I'm not even sure if Wes was there for my scene."

The final image of *Elm Street*: the little jump rope girls, singing their haunting rhyme as the door is left open for Freddy to return.

Lepucki adds, "I think someone from the second unit crew was driving the car past us a few times on the street as we turned the rope. I don't remember the other kids being in the car."

Getting the role was a matter of Lepucki and her family being friends and neighbors with two crew members who had mentioned the film needed girls ages seven to nine, though she would eventually learn of another connection. "I knew it was a scary movie, because when we went to the production office they told us a little bit about the plot of the movie, and they showed a headshot of the actor who would be playing the villain. My mom said, 'Oh my goodness, that's one of my husband's very good friends!'" she remembers. "But that was just a coincidence because I got the role not through Robert, but the women in the office."

Lepucki is one of the girls turning the rope, "but you can't see my face in the actual movie. There's a cherry blossom in the way because it's hanging from the tree," she states.

Unintentional as Lepucki not being clearly visible might have been, the concept that the young girls were not always so front and center, yet strikingly memorable, might have been a slight addition to the mystery of the young characters.

Rusoff found the idea interesting. "Our characters were never fully explained. It was never said outright, but I believe we were children who had lost their lives, in one way or another, to Freddy Krueger," she says. "I think that we were ghosts or spirits of those innocent victims. I thought that was scary and cool."

Risher adds that with all that had happened up to that point, there was one thing of which she was certain. "It was always Wes' idea to pan to the little girls jumping rope, which is such an evocative ending. That's the real ending," she says. "And it's brilliant."

5

Post-Production

Five, Six, Grab Your Crucifix...

Now that the film had (in more ways than one) found its ending, the case could be made that it was time to decide what it all meant.

INTERPRETING NIGHTMARES

"I look at the entire film as a pre-cognitive nightmare of just Nancy," Englund proposes. "Everything in it will happen, but it hasn't really happened. She's just dreamt that it's going to happen, and she's trying to warn everybody, and then it begins at the very ending there, with the death of Ronee Blakley, the one thing she didn't dream."

If that were the case, then the end of the film is not a dream, but, in a sense, hyper-reality as a contrast to the nightmare sequences. "Freddy is gonna get everybody," continues Englund. "He's gonna get those kids, you know? Everybody that's died is in that car. They've all come to pick her up to go to school. It's a new day and you can hear the birds chirping on the soundtrack, and the colors are bright and nice. So that's my interpretation."

Blakley doesn't disagree with Englund's analysis, taking things further and stating that, while the movie does end, there are still questions. "What if they drive away and the convertible top

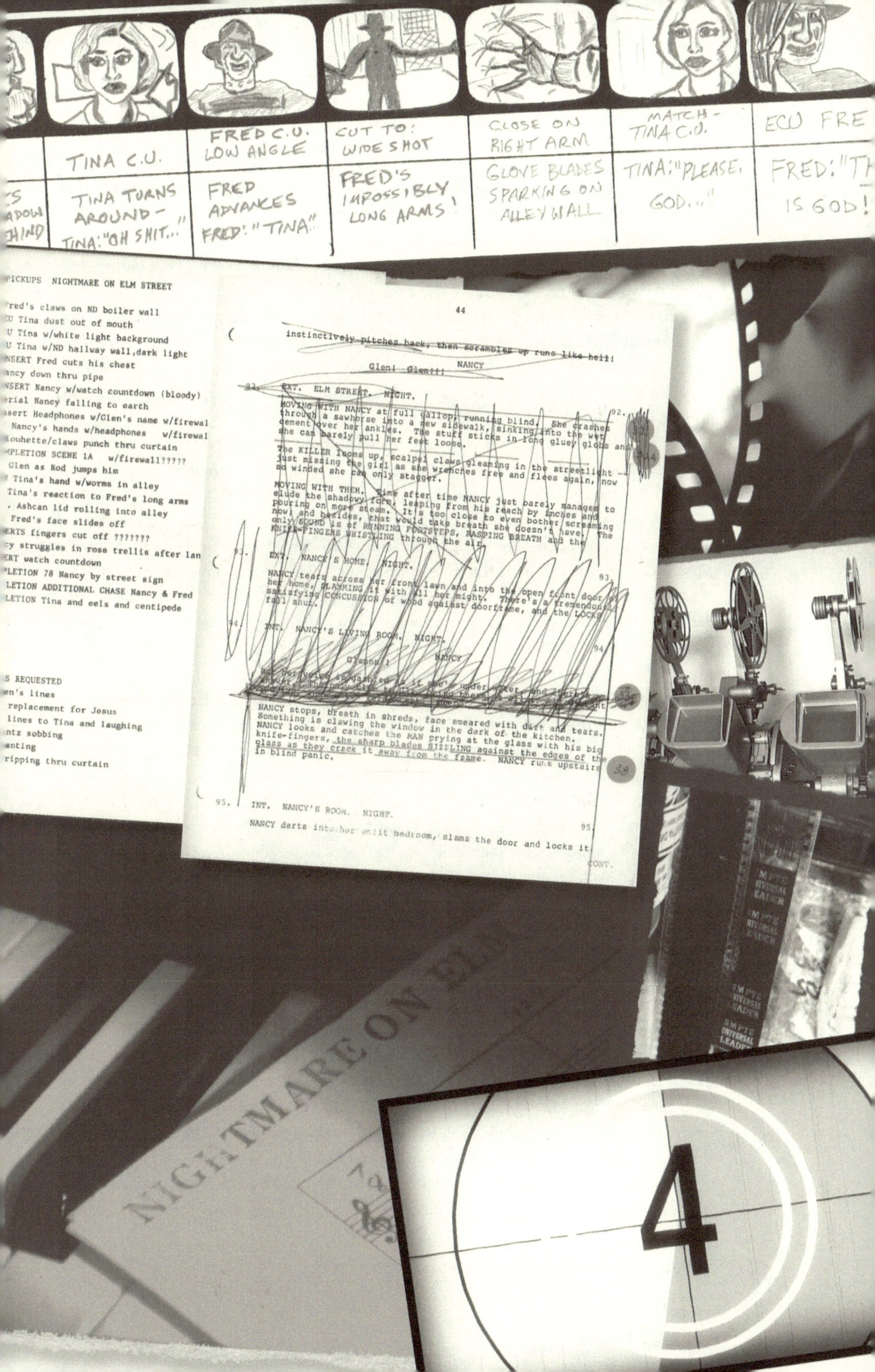

TINA C.U.
TINA TURNS AROUND – TINA: "OH SHIT..."
FRED C.U. LOW ANGLE
FRED ADVANCES FRED: "TINA"
CUT TO: WIDE SHOT
FRED'S IMPOSSIBLY LONG ARMS!
CLOSE ON RIGHT ARM
GLOVE BLADES SPARKING ON ALLEY WALL
MATCH – TINA C.U.
TINA: "PLEASE, GOD..."
ECU FRE
FRED: "TH IS GOD!
PICKUPS NIGHTMARE ON ELM STREET
red's claws on ND boiler wall
U Tina dust out of mouth
U Tina w/white light background
U Tina w/ND hallway wall,dark light
NSERT Fred cuts his chest
ancy down thru pipe
NSERT Nancy w/watch countdown (bloody)
erial Nancy falling to earth
sert Headphones w/Glen's name w/firewal
Nancy's hands w/headphones w/firewal
louhette/claws punch thru curtain
MPLETION SCENE 1A w/firewall?????
Glen as Rod jumps him
Tina's hand w/worms in alley
Tina's reaction to Fred's long arms
. Ashcan lid rolling into alley
Fred's face slides off
ERTS fingers cut off ???????
cy struggles in rose trellis after lan
ERT watch countdown
PLETION 78 Nancy by street sign
LETION ADDITIONAL CHASE Nancy & Fred
LETION Tina and eels and centipede
S REQUESTED
en's lines
replacement for Jesus
lines to Tina and laughing
ntz sobbing
anting
ripping thru curtain
44
instinctively pitches back, then scrambles up runs like hell!
NANCY
Glen! Glen!!!
92. EXT. ELM STREET. NIGHT.
MOVING WITH NANCY at full gallop, running blind. She crashes through a sawhorse into a new sidewalk, sinking into the wet cement over her ankles. The stuff sticks in long gluey globs and she can barely pull her feet loose.
The KILLER looms up, scalpel claws gleaming in the streetlight -- just missing the girl as she wrenches free and flees again, now so winded she can only stagger.
MOVING WITH THEM. Time after time NANCY just barely manages to elude the shadowy form, leaping from his reach by inches and pouring on more steam. It's too close to even bother screaming now, and besides, that would take breath she doesn't have. The only SOUND is of RUNNING FOOTSTEPS, RASPING BREATH and the KNIFE-FINGERS WHISTLING through the air.
93. EXT. NANCY'S HOME. NIGHT.
NANCY tears across her front lawn and into the open front door of her home, SLAMMING it with all her might. There's a tremendously satisfying CONCUSSION of wood against doorframe, and the LOCKS fall shut.
94. INT. NANCY'S LIVING ROOM. NIGHT.
NANCY
Glenn!
NANCY stops, breath in shreds, face smeared with dirt and tears. Something is clawing the window in the dark of the kitchen. NANCY looks and catches the MAN prying at the glass with his big knife-fingers, the sharp blades SIZZLING against the edges of the glass as they crack it away from the frame. NANCY runs upstairs in blind panic.
95. INT. NANCY'S ROOM. NIGHT.
NANCY darts into her unlit bedroom, slams the door and locks it
CONT.
SMPTE UNIVERSAL LEADER
NIGHTMARE ON ELM
4

was going up, and the girls are doing their little jump rope, and what if there was another scene and another hour and a half of movie there?" she asks. "Because once you're dealing with dreams and dream sequences, anything can be revealed later to have been just a dream."

"There are still some moments at the end where I don't know if it's the dream or if it's real, because it never finished," says Langenkamp. "You never got to the end of that particular dream. And I love that part of the movie."

In many early drafts of Craven's screenplay, the concept that the end of the movie was a dream might have been more pronounced had they filmed the jump rope girls and their haunting rhyme as he had written: "Music crossfades with this song, expanding the simple tune to symphonic, boundless dimensions as the little girls fade into thin air, and we fade to black."

Seeing the already ethereal jump ropers disappear would have certainly lent a clearer message that the coda was a dream, but the question of whether it would have stopped cast, crew, or audience members from positing theories may never be answered.

The ideas put forth, however, by Englund and Blakley—that Nancy has somehow foreseen the deaths of her friends and, perhaps, even herself—did resonate with Wyss. "I always felt like that's so scary that you can become so involved in a nightmare and have it seem so real, but then, as everybody drove away, it was like, 'But was it?'" the actress wonders. "That's how I felt about it. I always thought it was a great commentary on how scary a nightmare can be, and how much it would impact our waking life as well. But I just thought that was the psychology of it. Did it happen or didn't it? I think when we're left to our own devices we can scare ourselves more than anybody else can scare us."

"I showed the film to my father," recalls Shaye. "He looked at it and, after the screening, I said, 'What'd you think, Dad?' And he said, 'That was pretty good. Pretty scary.' And I said, 'Yeah, we're having a hell of a time with the ending. We can't figure out how to end the movie, so we actually decided to put all the endings in.' He said, 'You can't do that,' and I said, 'We did, Dad. The director said that's how he wants to do it and that's what we're doing.' He said, 'You can't do that. This is absolutely the wrong thing!'"

Shaye adds he remembers sitting at a bar with his father, who grabbed him by the shoulders, and that "he almost screamed at me, 'You're gonna fuck up this movie!' So I'm always amused when I hear people's theories about what the ending signifies. It signifies we had no clue what was the right way to end it," laughs the producer.

MAKING THE CUT

In order to ensure that everything Craven had shot could be culled together in a way that was both smart and scary, an editor with considerable skill and style was necessary. The task went to Rick Shaine, who had years of experience as an assistant editor on such films as *Night Moves* (1975), *The Godfather Saga* (1977), and *Apocalypse Now* (1979) before cutting films of his own. And in typical New Line Cinema fashion, he arrived at the position because of someone already in the family.

"I believe I had, at that point, cut a horror movie called *Eyes of a Stranger* (a 1981 film that was only the second role for a young Jennifer Jason Leigh [*Fast Times at Ridgemont*

High]), and I had also worked with Jack Sholder, who was based in New York," says Shaine. "He had worked with Bob and they were good friends, and I believe Jack recommended me, in addition to Bob having seen my work."

Editor Rick Shaine around the time he was chosen to edit *Elm Street.* He cut the film using two upright Moviola machines. The system, invented in 1924 by Iwan Serrurier, was the first for motion picture editing.

After Shaine expressed his enthusiasm, he and Shaye had a meeting where they hit it off, enough that the producer recommended him to Craven. "What I knew of Wes at the time was that I'd seen *Last House on the Left* and it just scared the bejesus out of me, which was rare, being a film editor, because I usually could see how they were doing things rather than get caught up in the film," says Shaine. "But I felt that he was able to kind of tap into my unconscious in a way that other horror movies hadn't been able to do."

Craven's vision and willingness to go wherever the material took him (no matter how dark a place) was something Shaine appreciated. "I think it's an amazing skill that he has. And on the basis of seeing *Last House* and reading the script for *Nightmare*, which I felt was an idea that plugged into this ability, I was very eager to do the job," states the editor.

It also didn't hurt that the post-production was going to be done in New York, where New Line Cinema, and Shaine, were located. Back on the West Coast, Craven had agreed to the necessity of hiring a New York editor. "Wes and I had a good phone interview and I was hired," Shaine recalls.

Craven offered a more humorous reason why the post-production process was handled in New York. "Bob Shaye wanted to be there to harass us," he says in jest.

EDITING A NIGHTMARE

Due to time constraints and the fact that many felt the future success of New Line Cinema was riding on the film, Shaine was encouraged by the company to begin making trims on the picture and its dialogue in order to keep things moving—even though Craven was not yet present.

"Since it was early in my career, I was a bit naive, and that's not really something that a director's editor should ever do without the director knowing about it," admits Shaine. "So when Wes first saw the film, I had already cut a bit of dialogue out and had tried to begin shaping it down, because we had so little time in the post process. And I think coming to New York on New Line Cinema's turf, so to speak, and seeing a film that already had some trims made in it, put him on alert. He was very annoyed that I had done this without waiting for him."

Craven matter-of-factly said, "I think that's the case with any rough cut that is done by an editor. They always want to do their cut first and, in some cases, it's almost a hundred percent the way you would do it. In some cases it's not, but there was nothing bad between me and Rick."

Shaine admits his goal was to tell the story and let the material breathe, but he didn't want to put a personal imprint on the film that would go against what Craven had shot. "I know there's a long dream sequence where Nancy ends up at the prison where Rod is incarcerated, and I remember that it was a very, very long trip for her to get there. I remember thinking it's wonderful to get into this kind of dreamy feeling, but there's a limit to it," he says. "I think that Wes had established that we don't know where we are, and she doesn't know where she is, but it was time to get somewhere to further this story and see something horrific happening."

As the editor, Shaine acknowledges it was his job to make a judgment about how long he thought the audience would be able to tolerate a journey where they didn't know where they were going.

"Wes had had a great understanding of the editing process, a lot of patience, and he would come up with inventive ideas of how to solve certain editing problems we had."

Rick Shaine

Craven did not disagree. "The film needed a lot of tightening up and kind of forming to work. And it was a tricky film, because it had that element that could very easily be just so unreal that it wouldn't be frightening," he admitted. "I just knew it was very much a film that could've died if it had not been edited properly."

"It should be enough to put everybody on edge so that you're anticipating, 'Oh my God, what's going to happen?' but not so much that you're going to get bored by it," states Shaine. "But once Wes and I started working together and relaxed around each other, we realized we were both on the same page and we could make a great movie together."

Collaborating with Craven to craft the cut of the film the writer and director wanted was something Shaine describes as "terrific." He continues, "Wes has a great understanding of the editing process, a lot of patience, a very good gift to communicate his ideas, and he would come up with inventive ideas of how to solve certain editing problems we had."

One of those problems, of course, was the ending, and it was something on which Shaine remembers spending an awful lot of time. "We kept trading off the three different endings they shot," he says. "I can't remember which ending was his favorite, but at some point, Wes said to me, 'Look, this ending's okay or that ending's okay, maybe either the convertible top or the mother getting yanked through the door. Play with those elements. I've gotta get back to California.'"

Tensions seemingly placed aside regarding the ending, Craven having to leave for other matters brought into play the one thing that nobody could control: time. "They started shooting in June and it was meant to be a Halloween release, so that's a very, very short amount of time to do everything properly," states Shaine. "And I know Bob was very nervous about making the dates."

Another problem the editor encountered was the question of just how much the audience should see of Freddy Krueger. Part of that answer came from the cinematography. "I think to some extent, in terms of lighting, we made sure we didn't see his face in the beginning, that he was just a form or graphic," admits Haitkin.

"Robert Englund was such a terrific actor, and he was doing things that were fun to watch, but we had to make sure that there was also the tension of, 'Okay, if you show too much of Freddy and make him too funny or too charming, that's going to eliminate the scare factor altogether,'" offers Shaine. "And so it finally came down to show enough to be scared and, in a way, entertained by him, but not so much that it seems overdone."

Englund did, however, feel that the trimming down of Krueger might have gone just a bit further than with what he was comfortable, potentially eliminating the spark of the character's personality that everyone had grown to love.

"During the filming, there was more of Krueger involved with Heather in an adversarial bond. Each time he'd chase her and she'd get away, he'd give her more of a nod to recognize her as a worthy opponent, and this nod became a sort of personality," explains Englund. "It was as if he began to enjoy this relationship and maybe even respect her a little bit. They left this in for Heather's performance, but cut it out of mine a little bit."

Englund also misses the cat-and-mouse improvisation that Craven allowed him and Langenkamp, but understands "there may have been a fear Freddy might have developed a little too much personality, but I would've liked to have seen the character as more than just a personification of abstract evil," he says. "I was still trying to find Freddy and imbue him with some kind of personality, which I felt Wes did want, because he exists not in reality. And that's a liberating thing for an actor to play, something that's really informed by other people's imaginations. That's what I was trying to figure out."

Particularly interesting is the fact that careful analysis reveals whether in the dream state, manipulating objects, or in any corporeal form, the presence of Freddy Krueger is only on screen for approximately a scant eight minutes out of the film's ninety-one-minute running time. The notion gives rise to Englund's assessment that there might have been more Freddy to show, though history has proven his diminutive screen time did not impact the character's ability to connect with audiences in a colossal way.

"I think you could say the same thing about the alien in *Alien*, too, if you really clocked it," Englund offers. "But Freddy, in that first film, they wanted to save seeing him."

Another reason to keep Krueger in the shadows could be attributed to the look of the character, and the worry of whether the makeup—which everyone had agreed was fantastic—would ultimately work on film. "I remember they would light for Johnny, and they would light for Heather, and I would walk into their lighting and it didn't work, because you'd see too much," says Englund, stating it had a tendency to look too pink

McMahon, who had worked with Shaine prior to *Elm Street*, was brought aboard the film as co-editor.

or too juvenile. "So at one point they started to light for me, and that took longer. And you'd wanna see just a little bit of light in my eye, or just half of my face. Sometimes we would oil just half of my face so that the other half wouldn't catch the light. And Bob was really worried. I think he and Wes wanted to reveal Freddy very slowly."

The result was the character seen mostly in shadow or in silhouette. In essence, saving the reveal of Freddy would garner more bang for their buck since his presence permeates the film even though he is seen only in intervals and, even then, sometimes only in glimpses.

"There were huge debates," admits Englund. "You almost have to plot that in the script if you wanna do it that way. And I don't remember the script being quite plotted that way. We didn't know when we'd finally reveal what Freddy looked like. And I'm sure, editorially, they went through a lot of arguments on that."

To help muddle through each issue, not to mention the time constraints the tight post-production schedule created, Shaine brought on Patrick McMahon, credited in the final film as co-editor. "I knew that we had a hard released date in the fall and, since they started shooting in June, that gave me very little time to get done what I needed to in the time we had. It was a very, very short schedule," Shaine recalls.

Making the decision to bring in help would assist Shaine in piecing the first cut together by the time Craven arrived in New York, which was just a few days after shooting wrapped. Choosing who to bring on board *Elm Street*'s editorial proved to be an easy decision.

"I thought of Pat because I admired his editing and we had collaborated together in the past," says Shaine.

That collaboration was on the CBS drama *Nurse* (1981-1982), in which McMahon, as supervising editor, brought Shaine on as an editor. Shortly after, McMahon went off to edit the Canadian comedy feature *Strange Brew* (1983) and, when complete, received a call from his former hire to work for him on Craven's horror film.

"Rick called me up and said he had been hired to do *A Nightmare on Elm Street* and that the schedule was way too tight," remembers McMahon. "He told me he asked Bob Shaye if he could have another editor, who said he could, and then he asked if I would like to edit with him. I said, 'Sure.'"

Coming on to the film after the end of the first week of shooting, McMahon says that the process went smoothly, with both he and Shaine working in New York while shooting continued in California. "At the end of each week, we would take our cut scenes and put them together in a video at Magno Sound in New York," McMahon recalls, "and send them out to California, where they would look at them and give the thumbs up, thumbs down, or any notes."

"Pat stayed through the end of the shoot and did excellent work in everything that he cut," Shaine states. "He was quite a help in getting that first cut together."

The ultimate test, however, would be when Craven and Shaye watched that first full cut. As McMahon recalls, "Rick and I were, of course, very nervous in terms of how it would be received by Bob and Wes."

"The first time we saw the film, Bob and Rick and I sat in a screening room and they rolled the film," remembers Craven. "The film finished, and the lights came up, and there was a long pause, and then Bob turned around, put his arm over the chair and, I'll never forget this, said, 'Do you think there's a film there at all?' I said, 'Yeah.' I think we then cut for four or five weeks and suddenly this terrific film emerged, though he was completely convinced that it was not working at all."

"Bob was so involved," states McMahon. "I do remember at that screening that there was a bit of tension in terms of how good it was. I thought it was fantastic, but I didn't know the genre. At the time it wasn't as ubiquitous as it is now."

Meyer-Craven recalls that one of Craven's biggest concerns was that he was going to be remembered as being "some sort of schlocky horror film director, but he treated every one of his movies like it was a child. It was a horror film, but he had integrity. He was always fighting for the film."

Craven notes the film was made as much in the editing room as anyplace else, something (as even Shaine pointed out) he had an eye for with his own editing background. "As somebody who taught me to edit said, 'You beat the shit out of it,'" the writer and director reveals. "You just don't stop trying to make it better."

Shaine remembers the first time they screened the film for an audience at the lab they were using, not sure exactly what they had on their hands. Utilizing Craven's thought that one must keep working the material to improve it, Shaine did. Because of that attitude, and the editors' hard work, the director and company were ultimately pleased with the finished product.

"I didn't know we had something that was so strong," Shaye admits.

"Rick did a terrific job cutting the film," adds Craven. "He was a very hard worker."

NOW YOU SEE THEM, NOW YOU DON'T

The film that ultimately did emerge certainly did not do so unscathed, as some moments (many being cast and crew favorites) ultimately wound up excised from the final released print.

"So much goes on film, and so much ends up on the cutting room floor in terms of takes that you do, and different styles," says Langenkamp. "We did shoot some scenes that never made it where I come into the house and there's a banquet that's all dead. I'm walking through the house and it's just these fly-ridden corpses, old food, and things like that," recalls the actress.

Haitkin agrees about shooting more than they were going to need. "Sometimes what you have doesn't work visually and contextually. So if you really need five things for the final cut, you'll shoot eight or ten," he says.

An example would be the material filmed as Nancy gets ready to battle Freddy. "I remember we shot all these shots of Nancy preparing in the living room, and in the basement, and all kinds of stuff," Haitkin recalls. "There were plenty of extra pieces with Nancy preparing to defeat Freddy, but they didn't make it, mostly because of timing. Some stuff will work and some stuff doesn't work. And for different reasons."

One scene excised for a specific reason was a moment when the coroner shows Saxon's character one of Krueger's blades at the scene of Glen's death. "The coroner finds it, and I think he was holding it up as a murder weapon, and then he talks to his deputy," says Doyle. "The interesting thing to me was that it indicated, and this may be why it was cut, that at that point John's character may have known who the guy was."

Jeffrey Levine, the man who portrayed the excised character (mentioned in the final cut of the film only when Lieutenant Thompson asks if the coroner has looked at the crime scene), understands. "There was a logic issue," he admits.

Also cut from those moments was when Craven asked Levine for a line to be delivered in a different way than what was scripted. "I thought it was funny when Wes asked me to do one of the lines for a television version," he remembers. "Instead of saying, 'Remember that fucker, Fred Krueger?' he asked me to replace the expletive. So, when we rolled, I said, 'Remember that ne'er-do-well, Fred Krueger?' and there was this moment when all the air went out of the room. I started to shrivel up and then everyone burst out laughing."

Ultimately, there would be no need to worry about the use of such a replacement, though Levine admits he didn't know his character had been removed. However, Craven remained thankful for his participation. "I wasn't aware the character had been cut until I was at a screening of the film, but Wes was one of the most gracious, lovely people you could ever meet," he declares. "He took the time from editorial in New York to hand write me a note thanking me, and flatteringly me a little bit. To this day it's one of the nicest gestures anyone has ever made to me."

Blakley, too, recalls that some moments were trimmed from the scene just after Rod's burial. "John and I were walking through the cemetery, and I'm smoking, and I just remember intensity, and I remember my character being angry," says the actress. The deleted conversation goes on with Marge remarking, "This reminds me too much of ten years ago." (An additional occurrence demonstrating that the parents in the film know more than they will admit to their troubled charges.)

Another instance in the script (draft dated April 30, 1984) that didn't make the final cut was Marge's telling Nancy of Krueger's demise in a much more elaborate way. In those pages, she explains that Krueger did not just burn to death quietly; instead, Marge states he "crashed out like a banshee, all on fire, swinging those finger knives every which direction and screaming he was going to get us by killing all our kids."

The character continues by saying what it actually took to put Krueger down, and that it was something no one, not even Nancy's policeman father, would do: take Lieutenant Thompson's gun and shoot the child killer dead.

Which is exactly what Marge did.

Also in the same scene, it is revealed that each of Nancy's friends had a brother or sister, presumably murdered by Krueger. Marge goes on to say to her daughter, "You too, Nancy. You weren't always an only child." It's a telling moment that punctuates why Marge and the parental mob did to Krueger what they felt was necessary so many years ago.

Blakley's thoughts on those moments and their being trimmed? "I think it was so meaningful that I was shocked when they excised a couple of those remarks."

Depp's character also had a moment removed, showcasing that it wasn't just his parents stopping their son from meeting Nancy to enact her plan of stopping Freddy. At one point Glen does put on his jacket, but when he sees no sign of Nancy outside her house, he tells himself, "Well, I'm not gonna risk sneaking out until she does."

Late in the film, a moment between Lieutenant Thompson and Glen's father further reveals that Krueger is on the minds of more than just their children. When Thompson asks who might have been responsible for Glen's death, Mr. Lantz quietly states, "He done it," going on to flatly name Krueger as the killer. (And strongly corroborating Marge's earlier admission.) When Thompson looks on with incredulity, Glen's father puts his head down and states, "God's punishing us all," a not-so-subtle reference to their violent act a decade ago.

Langenkamp points out a concept she found interesting was the notion of her

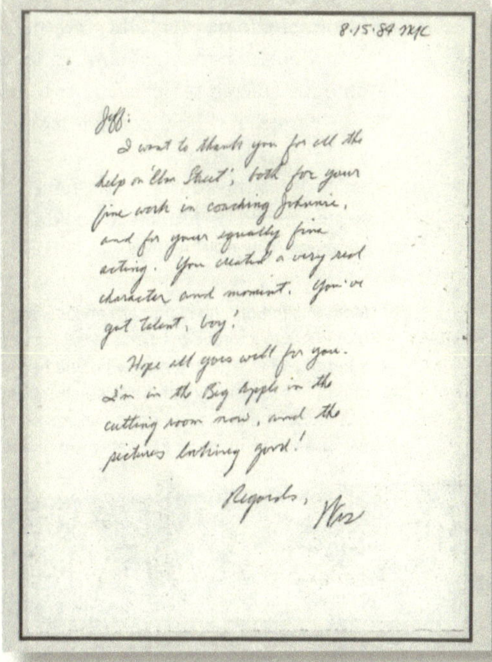

8.15.84 NYC

Jeff:

I want to thank you for all the help on 'Elm Street'; both for your fine work in coaching Johnnie, and for your equally fine acting. You created a very real character and moment. You've got talent, boy!

Hope all goes well for you. I'm in the Big Apple in the cutting room now, and the picture's looking good!

Regards,
Wes

During the post-production process Craven sent this handwritten note to Jeffrey Levine. Although the coroner character was cut from the final film, Craven praised the actor's work, both on screen and for helping Depp.

character going into the basement, or the boiler room, and how she "always liked this theme of descending, descending, descending," she says. "I do think that there was a lot of walking down stairways, when I'm going through the boiler room, making left turns and right turns."

In truth, the boiler location was only two levels, but, admits Craven, "We used every staircase they had."

As Craven marched the actress through as many paces as he could devise, Langenkamp says, "It was all good, interesting stuff that added to the tension, but Wes chose what he thought best, and it works."

The theme of traveling deeper and deeper into the depths harks back to one of Craven's early script drafts, which included a moment "at the end of the sequence when [Nancy falls] out of the boiler room, she was supposed to be falling from a great height," said the writer and director.

That deleted segment, which was filmed with the actress against a blue screen, can be seen in the May 5, 1984 draft of the script, stating, "Close on Nancy as she curves like a swan through her apogee," ultimately seeing the "glittering skein of light" from the San Fernando Valley. (An interesting notion, since the film was always meant to have a decidedly Midwest look and feel.)

"I remember that," says Langenkamp. "We were outside on location and Jim Doyle had this van, this very totally beat up van with tons of tools and things inside of it, and he just said, 'Come over here, I need to try something on you.' And he whipped out this harness, and I put it on, and it kind of fit. I do remember going up on the wire. At the Desilu Studio they had a big cavernous room where we just tried it out."

Unused in the final film, Nancy would, instead, simply leap from the boiler room onto the fallen rose trellis on her front lawn.

Something else that might have proved interesting, if only for the visual effect, was a shot from Tina's point of view as she is dragged across the ceiling in her final, deadly nightmare. "I do remember we used Jacques' wife for that sequence because Amanda couldn't operate the camera," remembers Englund. "Jacques' wife just took her pants off, and she had a pair of cut-

Moments in both the nightmare and waking world that were left on the cutting room floor to improve the pace of the film, clarify story, or both: Tina discovers a handful of worms in the alley behind her house before Krueger appears during her second nightmare; Lieutenant Thompson can't believe the coroner has found one of Freddy's razor knives at the scene of Glen's murder; Nancy prepares even more for her battle with the dream killer.

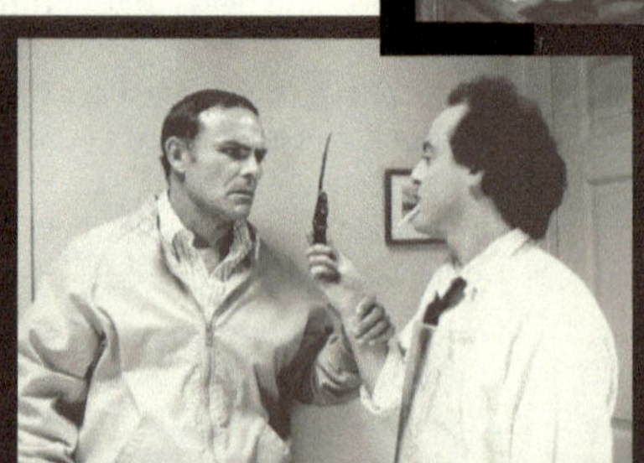

More deleted scenes: Glen makes a decision not to meet Nancy at midnight as they had planned; Late at night, Lieutenant Thompson visits the precinct to speak with Garcia.

offs on, or her own panties, and we put blood on her legs from the knees down. She took a handheld camera and I dragged her around the ceiling."

The shot would have been intercut with what Corri, as her boyfriend, saw as he watched Tina struggle. "Of course, when he looks up he just sees her, he doesn't see Freddy. Only Tina sees Freddy," Englund says, adding that the shot took several takes and ended with a rather chilling moment.

"It was tricky stuff, trying to keep me in the frame with the false ceiling and all that. And I remember improvising a kiss with my claws, like the kiss of death," says Englund. "And because I'd been holding onto the ankles of the camera operator, which were covered in stage blood, that stuff had gotten all over my hands and the false blades I was wearing on the glove. And when I blew a kiss I remember looking and seeing blood, like spiderwebs on the claws. And there was a little blood bubble. It never made the final cut, and I'm not sure if I saw it in dailies, or on a projector, or the actual being there that day, but I remember it being a weird, happy accident."

"We didn't know when we'd finally reveal what Freddy looked like. And I'm sure, editorially, they went through a lot of arguments on that."

Robert Englund

Englund has a notion on perhaps why the moment was ultimately left on the editing room floor, one that would bear out to be a considerable issue in both Craven's past, present, and future works. "Maybe Wes showed the censors that, knowing he'd never get it in the movie, because Wes used to always shoot things that were too violent, and show them to the censors, knowing they would never allow it in," he says.

The reason being that Craven could possibly get material in (whether for artistic purposes, to move the story forward, or both) that might otherwise have been cut—if the ratings board hadn't seen something deemed more inappropriate for him to remove. Either way, "The kiss of death moment, for me, was weird and wonderful and strange," states Englund.

"It was definitely a very scary, macabre moment," admits Wyss.

CRAVEN'S NIGHTMARE

Ratings battles are a subject that haunted Craven for decades, and at the heart of those conflicts is The Motion Picture Association of America.

Langenkamp is filmed against a blue screen for a moment where Nancy would be seen falling from a high point in the nighttime sky after jumping away from the boiler room; The script page detailing scene 124A, which was cut from the film.

Founded in 1922, the MPAA administers film ratings based on thematic and content suitability for certain audiences. Although MPAA ratings are voluntary (applied only to submitted films), and do not carry any force of local, state, or federal law, most theater owners agree to enforce the ratings as determined by the agency. Because of this, many theaters refuse to exhibit unrated films, which all but forces filmmakers (who hope for the widest, most publicized release possible), to submit their films to what many have called an arbitrary, monopolized, and closed-door practice.

For horror filmmakers like Craven, whose art might often rely on moments of unrestrained terror and violence, the argument between what a director wants his film to showcase—and what the MPAA will allow—can be maddening.

"It was quite common, and the whole system was so arbitrary. Because of the way the laws were written, they could only tell you that you had an R or you didn't," says Craven. "But they weren't allowed really to say why, because they weren't allowed to be censors, even though they were obviously being censors. They couldn't say, 'Cut that out,' so at best they would say, 'You know, between footages thirteen hundred and thirteen fifty, try to soften that a little.'"

The writer and director revealed that the process of not wanting to cut any moments and, specifically, not knowing what to cut, could be agony. "You didn't want to cut any more than you had to, so you would try a cut where you felt like, 'This is so painful, but I'll do this much,'" laments Craven. "You submit it, and sometimes you

Film rating system too secretive, doesn't work, says former rater

A headline about the MPAA's ratings process being somewhat secretive and less-than-effective. For Craven, one of *Elm Street*'s most painful cuts happened off screen when he was forced to trim Tina's dead body hitting the blood-soaked bed.

had to wait two weeks before they'd look at it, and then they'd say, 'No,' and you've lost two weeks, you're in your mix, you're already having to reconfigure all your tracks. It just becomes a real nightmare."

Prior to making the hard cuts, Craven's *Nightmare* was handed an X rating. (At the time, that particular rating was also used to signify pornographic content. It wasn't until September 1990 that it was replaced with NC-17, first given to the Oscar-nominated film *Henry & June*.) In his mind, those with the attitude that horror must be watered down or mitigated for public consumption might be throwing stones from a glass house. "Look at the violence perpetrated by our own government," he says. "We are the largest seller of arms to the world. For [the censors] to label art as threatening is something I find really ironic."

Craven also believed genre films serve a purpose to young viewers. "They're a mirror. They're a way kids have of coping with an extremely violent world," he offered. "I've always called horror films the boot camps of the psyche. They're a way kids have of toughening and testing themselves."

"It's so strange, censorship on all levels," expresses Englund, who, having gone on to direct projects of his own, is no stranger to the arduous ratings process. "I've talked to these people and they're all really nice. It's just, that's their job. They have these rules."

Unfortunately for Craven, it was those rules that forced his hand to make one of the hardest cuts in the film, one that he always regretted. "The cruelest cut to me, because of the censors of the film, was Amanda, when she falls off the ceiling and hits the bed. There was this beautiful, slow-motion sort of splash and sound, because we had the bed just loaded with blood," he remembers. "And the censors went after that whole scene. Once she started up the wall, they wanted it to be cut, and I fought and fought and fought and fought, and finally I got them to let her fall off. But as you can see in the film, it just looks like a bad edit, because as soon as she hit the bed, we were not allowed to show any kind of splash whatsoever."

In addition to Tina's falling into the blood being minimized, Craven knew the moment her chest was slashed open could present another problem. Perceptive viewers will observe that when Tina is cut, the model of Wyss' chest does not show any nipples. Craven was aware that showing both the blood and nipples in the same shot would have been an issue in gaining his desired R rating.

In another deleted scene, Marge and her ex-husband discuss their murderous secret of a decade earlier.

Another bloody segment that had the ratings board telling Craven he couldn't achieve an R if kept intact was the geyser of blood that erupts from Glen's bed after the boy's death. To successfully win that fight, Craven had to make clear an important point: it wasn't Glen's blood.

"I had to explain that to the MPAA ratings board. How could one hundred twenty gallons be the blood of one person?" Craven says. "In *Nightmare*, very little of the blood actually comes from the characters," going on to add that it is a symbol of life and humanity's essence, even pointing out its use as a religious symbol.

What disturbed Craven about the process is not only the lack of concrete guidelines ("There's nothing published," he stated. "Nothing."), but also that his work is often censored for intensity. "What they are saying is that it doesn't matter whether you have a bloody scene or not, it doesn't matter if there are lopped off limbs or not, what matters is that I'm simply too intense," he explained.

Having called the censors "the bane of my life," Craven often wondered how some other people get away with the things they did, while he was not so lucky.

He isn't alone; Englund, too, is perplexed.

"They're so arbitrary, but they're arbitrary because they started out as one thing, and people have hedged bets and tried to define them, and there's just no way to balance that," adds Englund. "You're either censorship or not."

In the end, Craven admits, "They ruined some incredible moments, and there was nothing I could do about it."

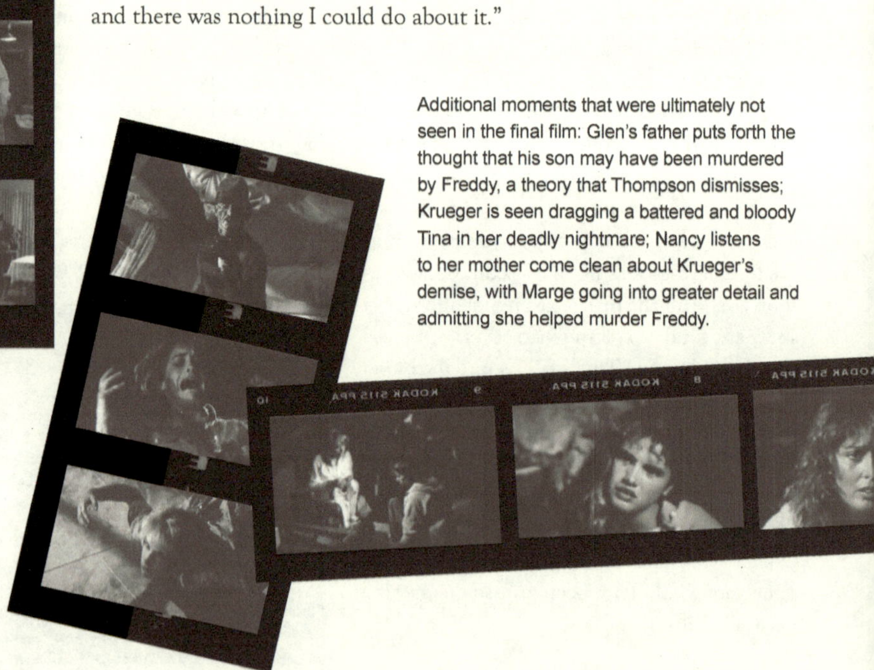

Additional moments that were ultimately not seen in the final film: Glen's father puts forth the thought that his son may have been murdered by Freddy, a theory that Thompson dismisses; Krueger is seen dragging a battered and bloody Tina in her deadly nightmare; Nancy listens to her mother come clean about Krueger's demise, with Marge going into greater detail and admitting she helped murder Freddy.

THE MUSIC OF THE NIGHT(MARE)

As Craven worked to mitigate the issues his film had with the MPAA, another important order of business at hand was the film's score. The task was to ensure that the music of *Elm Street* was balanced to be interesting, evocative and, of course, frightening. It would fall to Charles Bernstein, an accomplished composer who had nearly fifty credits to his name and was no stranger to genre film work (having previously created the scores for *The Entity* [1982] and *Cujo* [1983]) when Craven came his way.

"I was on vacation, and my agent called me and said, 'You know, there's a guy who does some horror movies. This is a small movie, and I don't know that anybody will ever see it, but it's a job. Do you wanna get involved in this?' And I said, 'Sure,'" Bernstein recalls.

After his agent described Craven as an intellectual who would be really fun to work with, Bernstein agreed to meet him, where the writer and director described his film to the would-be composer. "After that, I told Wes, 'Sure, let's do this,'" he says.

Interestingly, it wasn't getting Bernstein for the film that proved the most difficult task; it was making sure he stayed. "There's a great story," reveals Talalay, "about the fact that one of the music team stole money."

Risher remembers it well, stating, "Charles was such a nice guy to work with, and the way we got him was we had to first hire a music supervisor." It was that position's responsibility to pay Bernstein half the money upfront to compose all the music and, when the time came, Risher continues, "New Line would pay the second half to the supervisor who would take his fee and give the final payment to Bernstein."

As everyone would soon learn (including Risher, who had just had a baby and was still in the hospital), that would not be the case.

"That guy was involved in some sort of fatal car accident and he skipped town. He didn't want to go to court, and I suppose he might've been at fault, I don't know, but he ran out of town with our money," Risher says. "So I had to call Charles from my birthing bed and say, 'He left with the money, but we will get the money to you, we just can't do it right now.'"

After asking Bernstein to trust that they would come through, and to please ship them the music they needed to mix and finish the film, nobody was quite sure what the composer would do.

Until he agreed, much to the relief of everyone involved.

"He was one of the team players that helped the movie get made. And we are so grateful to him to this day," says Risher. "I ran into him not too long ago and we were talking about it and he said, 'Well, how could I say no? You'd just had a baby! What could I do? I didn't want to hear you cry!'"

Bernstein does recall the creative impact the missing funds had on his work. "The budget was already very, very small. And then twenty-five percent of the budget disappeared," he says. "At that point I thought, 'Oh my, I don't think there's enough money here to do this thing the way I'm hearing it,' and I had to reimagine the score on a smaller budget."

Craven was quick to call the work "wonderful," and revealed that Bernstein did it "for virtually nothing, but it came out very, very haunting."

A budgetary inadequacy wasn't the only thing with which the film's music had to contend. Once again, time (or lack thereof) was an issue, which affected Shaine. "I had no contact with Charles, and usually I get to have input, and usually there's a spotting session in the cutting room. But there was no time for that kind of thing," says the editor. "We actually got the reels of the score while we were already mixing. We would get FedEx packages of the cues for each reel the morning that we'd mix it!"

Essentially, Shaine was hearing the final music for the first time as he laid it into the film, but was happy to say that it all worked. "I've never been through anything like that before, and it was a tense mix, but Charles just got it. It's sort of one of those miracles of filmmaking that it worked so well."

In order to perform those minor musical wonders, Bernstein noted that the "severe monetary constraint," coupled with the fact that, at the time, he was unable to simulate an orchestra, led him to try different things than what he would normally do.

"I simulated orchestral elements because we couldn't replicate an orchestra, and a synthesized score was automatic," reveals Bernstein. "There were orchestral elements, but the flavor of the score was dictated somewhat by that budgetary limitation."

The composer admits to feeling emboldened by the fact that he might have been dealing with a little film that wouldn't be seen by many. "At the time, people said to me, 'Well, you know what? This may never see the light of day. This picture may never end up in the theaters,'" recalls Bernstein. It was a truism at the time that many lower-budgeted films either failed to get a release or were relegated to direct-to-video. "And I thought, 'Well, maybe I can stick my neck out here and do some really interesting and odd things.'"

His approach to the *Elm Street* score was not, Bernstein states, based on listening to other film scores. "When I approach a score musically, I'm more or less communing with the film, trying to really feel what the director's trying to do," he says.

In this case, a major component was fear and, specifically, fear of Freddy Krueger, a character that the composer was able to see well before the masses. "I was one of the first people to ever see Freddy Krueger, you know? And I thought, 'Razor-blade fingernails? This guy's weird-looking.' Because of that, my first thought was we had to scare people. And he was scary," Bernstein admits.

The composer is also careful to mention that it isn't just bringing scares to the surface. "Sometimes it's other kinds of unsettling emotions, and the music had a series of burdens to deal with," Bernstein explains. "It had to be scary, it had to perform certain emotional functions throughout the movie. We're dealing with dreams in this film, and we're dealing with relationships and with the family. The music had a lot of different things to touch."

Praising Craven for being wonderful at creating sequences that coax music out of a composer, Bernstein says, "The beginning was like that, the ending, the dream clinic, the scene on a bridge in Venice, California. There were just so many."

Declaring that oftentimes a composer must think practically when approaching a specific scene, Bernstein notes he was aware of how even the sound effects and design of a scene would affect his work. "The scene where Tina is being killed is a very noisy scene," he offers. "And I'm aware that the music has to do something that'll kind of

NEW LINE CINEMA

December 5, 1984

RETURN RECEIPT REQUESTED

Mr. Charles Bernstein
c/o Bart-Milander Associates
1488 North Kings Road
Los Angeles, CA 90069

Re: A NIGHTMARE ON ELM STREET

Dear Charlie:

Enclosed is the signed copy of the Composer's Agreement for A NIGHTMARE ON ELM STREET.

Kind regards,

Sara Risher
Co-Producer

SR/all
Encl.

cc: Ben Zinkin, Esq.

A letter from Risher to Bernstein about his agreement to score the film; Bernstein in his element around the time of *Elm Street*.

shoot through the sound effects. So in a scene like that, I'm aware that the music, in order to give it pulse and movement, has to avoid getting swallowed by the sound effects. So in that case I did something punchy and kind of edgy and gave tempo to the scene."

Sometimes, Bernstein points out, "You wanna go with the horror and sometimes you wanna give it a little pop edge. I wanted to create a kind of 'youth culture' element and still honor everything else. There's a religious element in there, there's a lot of dream elements and spiritual elements, and so I tried to hit all those bases."

Admittedly, he was lucky to have the ability to cover so many seemingly disparate ideas, and there are very few musical sequences in the film Bernstein is not happy with. "In fact," he states, "I won't even say there are any. I liked the way the music works in the film."

"It's one of the great things as a director, when something is totally in someone else's hands and it comes back and it's just terrific," Craven says. "You're almost holding your breath the whole time until it shows up."

He did, indeed, hold his breath, waiting to hear how the music would marry to his film.

And he was pleased. "It was just, 'Whoopee!' It was great," Craven exclaims.

MOTIF OPERANDI

Aside from the score in general, what many remember from the film's music is the incredibly haunting, and deceptively simple, main theme. The ten-note leitmotif, which is a musical term referring to a constantly recurring musical phrase associated with a particular person, place, or idea, was something Bernstein believed would really help create the flavor of *Elm Street*.

"I thought, 'Let's have a theme, let's get a melody involved here,' which would take me beyond what the picture's doing and beyond what I might normally do," says Bernstein. "I went to Wes and he wasn't closed to the idea, and when he heard it, he went, 'Yes!'"

Bernstein notes that unlike certain popular, memorable musical pieces (such as portions of Mike Oldfield's *Tubular Bells* used in *The Exorcist*), which you can't simply call out because they are more of a conceptual texture, he endeavored to create a melody for the film that one could not just remember, but whistle. "Something that had melodic contour," he describes, "like the great film scores. And I'm not saying that puts this in any class of that nature, but I've always loved films that had a melody which represented something important about the movie and that you could walk away with."

Craven agreed, remembering something he had been told when working early on in his career. "The secret to a good score is that you have one theme, and then you repeat it endlessly. You know, sometimes that is true," he says. "If you can get just the right musical phrase and then play it a million different ways—backwards, upside down and with different instrumentation—it unifies the entire film."

Another significant part of the music's composition was the use of voice. "There's the melodic element and then there was what sounds like a creepy female voice. And that was me," Bernstein reveals, admitting

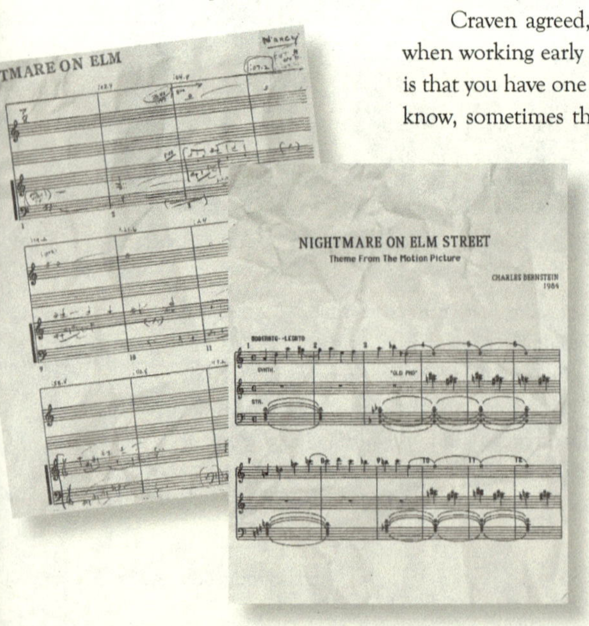

The sheet music from Bernstein's *Elm Street* compositions.

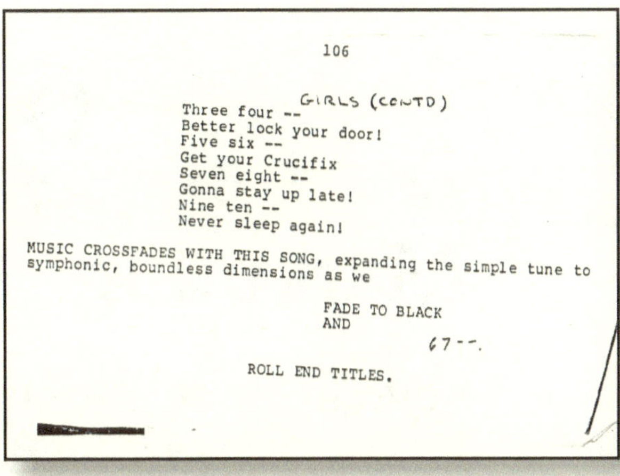
106

GIRLS (CONT'D)
Three four --
Better lock your door!
Five six --
Get your Crucifix
Seven eight --
Gonna stay up late!
Nine ten --
Never sleep again!

MUSIC CROSSFADES WITH THIS SONG, expanding the simple tune to symphonic, boundless dimensions as we

FADE TO BLACK
AND

ROLL END TITLES.

The last page of Craven's *Elm Street* script.

to singing falsetto into a Boss guitar pedal. "It just felt important to me in the title sequence that there be a human sound, and that would help enhance the horror. I wanted to be sure to touch the supernatural, which I think the voice helped with and, again, Wes gave the greenlight on that. There's not a voice or a sound in the picture that I didn't personally sing or play."

Voices were not only heard as part of the score, but in the nursery rhyme that has become synonymous with the film, something Craven used to evoke a sense of weirdness and dread. "I had written that little nursery rhyme, but I had no idea of how it could be set to music," confessed the writer and director.

Enter not Bernstein, who knew that the jump rope rhyme had already been worked out, but Langenkamp. "I think that her boyfriend came up with the melody and that little lilting thing," says Risher.

The actress' boyfriend at the time was Alan Pasqua, a musician who has gone on to be a jazz pianist, educator, and co-composer of the *CBS Evening News* theme. "We were just sitting around the piano one time, and I said, 'You know, they have this nursery rhyme that needs to be set to music, and I don't know how we're gonna sing it,'" remembers Langenkamp. "So he just kinda did this minor key thing. It was really short, but it helped me just think about those lines that I had to deliver. You know, the 'One, two, Freddy's coming for you.'"

"I kept that element and kind of worked it into the score in a few places because it seemed to be important in serving the film," Bernstein says.

And the little girls responsible for its singing?

"We did it at a little, tiny recording studio. They had one microphone and three sets of headphones," jump roper Rusoff recalls. "We just went and they gave us the rhyme, and we practiced it a few times. And then we did it. I was really sort of mystified by the whole thing and I didn't really think anything about the words or what I was actually saying."

Audiences did, making it a crucial portion of the film. "Everybody remembers it. Anybody who's seen the film can sing that to you," says Craven. "And ask people to sing a phrase to the score from most films and they go, 'Well, I can't remember. The music was kind of good, but I can't remember what it sounded like.' But that one, you could. It just captured the film."

The haunting rhyme also struck Shaye. "Iconic things kind of happen by their own grace," he offers. "Seeing little kids in pinafores jumping rope and singing it in the context of the movie is very eerie."

6

Marketing & Release

Seven, Eight, Gonna Stay Up Late...

With filming, scoring, editing, and mixing complete, and Craven receiving the R rating for which he and Shaye were hoping, the next task was to find a distributor.

HAWKING THE HORROR

Although New Line Cinema had begun in such a capacity (even having previous, minor successes with its first two original productions), the undertaking to find *A Nightmare on Elm Street* the best possible—and most lucrative—home was a task that almost seemed Herculean.

It was an aspect of the project that ostensibly started out as a dark cloud hanging over a director, a producer, and a company that had so much at stake, yet were never quite sure what would come back to them in return. Unbeknownst to anyone at the time, however, the end result of their efforts would ultimately prove to have something of an epic, unforgettable and, for New Line Cinema, company-changing silver lining.

"New Line's lawyer at that time, who subsequently became my partner, Michael Lynne, represented Sean Cunningham in selling *Friday the 13th* to Paramount. And he said, 'I think I can get

a couple million dollars for you for the film,'" says Shaye. "And we showed it to them. I vividly remember the screening one Saturday. In fact, we had the wrong ending on the film and we had the editor rushing out to the editing room to get the right ending."

With Craven having already gone back to California, the scramble was an event well remembered by Shaine. "Frank Mancuso showed up with a number of executives from Paramount. I had the ending without the mother yanked through the door and we started the screening," recalls the editor. "Bob called me in the course of the screening, probably around reel three or four of ten, and whispered into the phone, 'Which ending did we have in?' and I told him, and his reply was, 'No, no, no, I told Frank Mancuso about the other ending with the mother and he loved it! So what can we do?'"

The only thing that could be done was Shaine getting his assistant to take a cab to bring the correct footage to him so he could mix the ending while the screening continued, leaving him just shy of half an hour to do so. "I had to, from memory, reassemble the ending that he was talking about on the little synchronizer with the splicer that they had available. Meanwhile, it was like beat the clock, because the reels were unspooling and Bob was really nervous back there," Shaine states.

"We had to stop the film, actually, because he didn't manage to finish the process," Shaye explains, "so all of the executives, Frank Mancuso and all the marketing guys, were sitting in the screening room, and the screen went dark right at the ultimate moment."

Shaye went in to apologize and, eventually, the Paramount executives did get to see the end of the film. "Then they left, thanked me very much, and called me a few hours later and said, 'We don't want this film,'" laughs the producer.

Ironically, Paramount's issues with the project were similar to what their own *Friday the 13th* creator had mentioned when Craven first gave him the material. "They passed on the film because they didn't believe that films about dreams were scary enough," admits Shaye. There was also an additional reason. "Another film about dreams had just opened and flopped," he adds.

That project, as Craven knew all too well, was *Dreamscape*.

Ever the optimist, and in spite of the disappointment that Paramount (or any other major studio) wouldn't be taking *Elm Street* off his hands, Shaye decided to take the ultimate gamble: New Line Cinema would, as they had with so many other titles, release the film. But first, they would test the waters with international buyers in Milan.

"We had one screening, in one little screening room, and it was packed," says Shaye, "and the guy who put up the money, or some of the money, sent me a box of chocolates and I knew we were kind of on our way to something big."

THIS SEAT IS TAKEN

Now that New Line Cinema had decided to take the reins and get the picture out into the world, those who toiled on the project were eager to see the fruits of their labor. But what they might not have realized is that their first experience seeing the film would be slightly less glamorous than a lavish Hollywood studio debut, though it was no less exciting.

"There was no premiere," admits Langenkamp.

"In those days, it wasn't sophisticated," Corri explains, going on to relay another reason that had been a constant source of stress. "They didn't have any money, man. I think they were broke."

Broke or not, New Line Cinema did rent a little screening room at Warner Bros. to show the finished picture to cast and crew. "But the room was so small," recalls Langenkamp. "I mean, maybe it fit two hundred people. And when we got there, right on the money for it to start, there were no seats! So it was like, 'We'll just sit on the floor in the aisle.'"

It was a good plan, save for the fact that when more people showed up, such as Johnny Depp with friend Nicolas Cage, they, too, didn't have seats.

"Some people had to leave, and some people had to stand to be able to get away in a hurry. It was so weird and we were all laughing, but they wouldn't let us sit down."

John Burrows on the first screening of *A Nightmare on Elm Street*

"No one saved us any seats. So they called the fire department, and the fire department was gonna close it down unless they could get people to leave," Langenkamp remembers. "So seeing *Nightmare* the first night in the screening room made little or no impression on me. I remember more about getting kicked out by the fire department than what was shown on screen."

Burrows elaborates, "This gentlemen came walking by looking at everybody and we all thought, 'What's he doing here and who is he?' He finally got down to the front, turned around, and said, 'There are too many people here, I don't have any coverage, and this is not allowed.' Wes went over and talked to him and they finally let the screening happen, but some people had to leave, and some had to stand to able to get away in a hurry. It was so weird and we were all laughing, but they wouldn't let us sit down."

It was a moment Wyss also vividly recalls, except her experience began, and remained, outside. "The first time they screened *Nightmare on Elm Street*, it was at a studio. I got there right before it started," says Wyss, "and the fire marshal wouldn't let me in. I said, 'But I'm, like, the star of the movie!' And he said, 'I don't know who you are, but you're not coming in.' So I didn't get to go. I didn't see it that night."

"I mean, Hollywood's a different place than it was in 1984," muses Langenkamp, "and I remember walking into my agent's office and asking if he had seen the movie yet. And he looked at me, like, 'You're kidding, right?' And I know people don't ever believe me, but it was a low rent movie."

KRUEGER'S POSTER CHILD

Even though the first screening might not have fulfilled anybody's dreams of glitz and glamour, the more important question was whether or not the movie on the screen worked. For Craven, Shaye, and the cast and crew who labored and lived through it all, the answer would come when New Line Cinema unleashed the film to horror-hungry audiences.

One item used to draw viewers in was the picture's one-sheet poster, a tool that has been in use since the earliest exhibition of filmed entertainment. Beginning as placards used outside a theatre to simply list the program, usually short films, the first poster designed to actually promote an individual film belonged to *L'Arroseur arrosé* (1895), a short, French, black-and-white comedy also known as *Tables Turned on the Gardener* in the United States. It was an instrument in getting people into the theater and, though the concept of the one-sheet poster has evolved significantly, the end result was still the same: garner interest in the project. That fact was not lost on either Shaye or Craven, even if the early attempts left a less-than-spectacular impression.

As director and producer were mixing the film in New York, a concept had been prepared to advertise the film, which was a house on a street with a slash through it. Behind the slash, a woman could be seen screaming. It seemed, in theory, to be evocative of the film.

"I looked at it, and Wes looked at it, and I said, 'What do you think?' and he said, 'Well, I think it's okay. What do you think?' and I said, 'I think it's pretty much okay,'" recalls Shaye.

It wasn't really, though. As the young messenger with the material prepared to leave, Shaye, ever aware of youthful audience tastes, asked his opinion. "He said, 'I think it sucks. It's really a terrible ad,'" admits Shaye who, along with Craven, actually agreed. They then embarked on finding someone else to create the poster.

Enter Matthew Joseph Peak.

Son of famed artist and commercial illustrator Robert "Bob" M. Peak (1927-1992), whose work graced magazine covers, postage stamps, and over one hundred movie posters, including *West Side Story* (1961), *The Spy Who Loved Me* (1977), and *Excalibur* (1981), the young Peak carried on the artistic tradition. Born and raised in New England, he received his formal art training at the School of the Museum of Fine Arts in Boston, Art Center College of Design in California, School of Visual Arts in New York, and also apprenticed with his father. At the age of twenty-four he was commissioned to create the key art for *Elm Street*, his first movie poster.

"I just finished art school at the time that the first *Nightmare* was getting finished. I had shown an art director my portfolio and a day

Poster for *L'Arroseur arrosé*, which was the first time artwork was used explicitly to advertise a film.

Elm Street poster artist Matthew Peak's father, Bob Peak, who many call "The Father of the Modern Hollywood Movie Poster," surrounded by some of his imagery.

later I got a call," remembers Peak. The call was for a job to create "some girl sleeping, with monsters in her head," which was the direction Peak received. "It was not directly from the studio or Wes or anything like that. It was pretty random," he adds of the boutique movie poster studio who called him.

Once engaged, as was par for the course, the question became how quickly could Peak complete the job. Armed with only a few images and the basic plot, it was Krueger's gloved hand and the concept of nightmares that spoke to the artist. "When I saw the stills and read the synopsis, I was like, 'Whoa! The hand coming at you from a dead dream.'"

After presenting his own five or six sketches, the final design was decided upon and, coupled with the tagline, "If Nancy doesn't wake up screaming...she won't wake up at all," Peak was off and running.

"The poster was definitely based upon Heather and her character. It was basically her nightmare. That was it. Her nightmare on Elm Street," says Peak. "That was the core concept behind it. The choice of not depicting Freddy was intentional from my direction. I had no input from the studio of, 'Gee, we wanna show Freddy,' because he had not been established yet. So it was the nightmare on Elm Street and the horror and concept of it."

Once the art was approved and finished, Shaye was pleased. "It was a painting that really helped sell the movie," admits the producer.

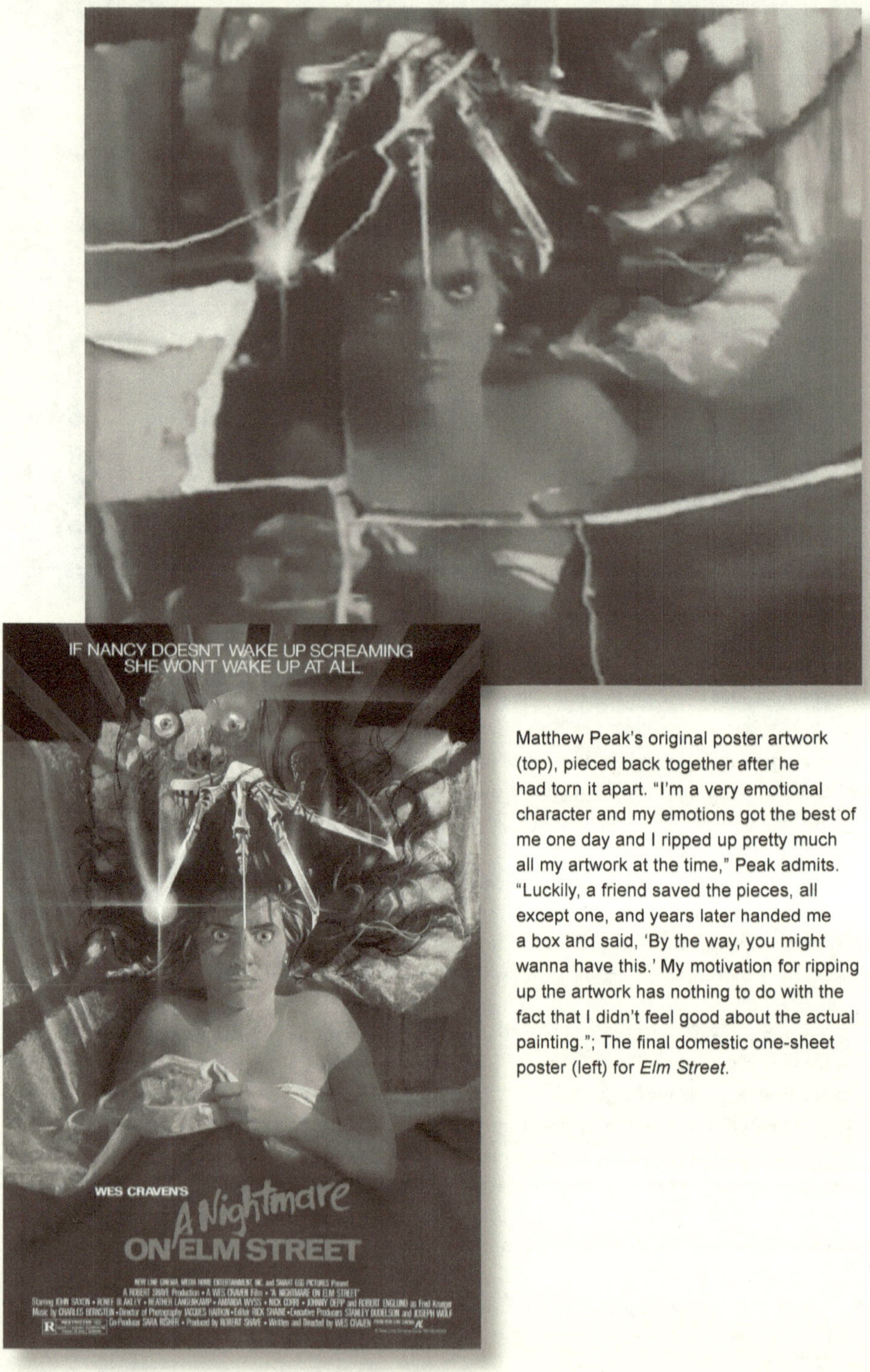

Matthew Peak's original poster artwork (top), pieced back together after he had torn it apart. "I'm a very emotional character and my emotions got the best of me one day and I ripped up pretty much all my artwork at the time," Peak admits. "Luckily, a friend saved the pieces, all except one, and years later handed me a box and said, 'By the way, you might wanna have this.' My motivation for ripping up the artwork has nothing to do with the fact that I didn't feel good about the actual painting."; The final domestic one-sheet poster (left) for *Elm Street*.

IT ALL (JUST BARELY) WORKS OUT IN THE END

On New Line Cinema's latest production, things seemed to be on track until, in what would appear to be another pull-up-their-bootstraps moment, Shaye and his company went to bat on what would hopefully be the last of their issues.

"Everything was together. We've got a release date. Publicity, TV spots, and everything had been done. It was a big deal for us," says Risher. "But the week before we were supposed to open, the lab we were using wouldn't release the negative because they hadn't been paid. We didn't have the money to pay them. Bob somehow worked out some kind of deal to pay the lab all of their costs."

Shaye remembers the issue—and its resolution—well. "We went to our laboratory, which was also a Mafia laboratory, I believe, because they used to process porno films at night, and we had a line of credit with them," he says. "And for some reason, which I never found out, when I went to order prints for the release of the film, we were told that they had foreclosed on our line of credit, for some technicality."

That left New Line Cinema with no money to pay for the prints. In order to release the negative, the lab demanded compensation for the outstanding balance, leaving Shaye stupefied. "After all this incredible story, here again they're after me. I went crazy trying to find money," he admits.

Eventually, Shaye asked a favor of one of their lenders, telling him that he found another lab that would take over the printing if he had the money. "This guy said, 'Fine,' and he loaned us the money we needed to pay off our bill and buy a letter of credit to secure the payment for the prints."

It was a good thing, particularly because of the earlier video rights deal Shaye had struck with Media Home Entertainment when the film needed its final financing. "We finally got the prints out, otherwise Joe Wolf would've seized the whole fucking thing and that would've been it," Shaye declares.

Through what might have felt like every conceivable up and down in the film business, the tenacity of Shaye and New Line Cinema paid off, much to the delight of cast and crew.

"Finally, the film was finished. I don't remember how long afterwards it was released, but I saw it in a theater and I took my son, who was twelve," Saxon remembers. "We sat and watched it, and my son nudged me, and said, 'Pop, this is really good.' And I said, 'Yeah, it is. I think it really is.' And I meant it."

Wyss felt the same, though she had to wait considerably longer to see the film for the first time. "It was opening in Westwood, California, and I went to go see it and it was sold out, and then I had to leave town," she says. "I was like, 'Wow, I got kicked out of the screening, it's sold out at the movies, and then I had to leave town. Someone tell me, how was it?'"

Eventually, the actress was able to watch the film on VHS. "You know what? I was completely terrified," states Wyss. "I got lost in the story and I found it to be incredibly scary, which was great."

"It was just another horror movie at the time, but I do remember seeing the film when it came out and knew it was something special," says Shostrom. "You could tell from the audience reaction that this thing was big."

Blakley also remembers her first time seeing the film in Times Square. "Everyone had bags of chicken that they were eating. And people were screaming, and it was a hit," she states, though does admit, "I couldn't watch a lot of it. I had to shut my eyes because I'm squeamish. It scared me. I couldn't watch the room turn with the blood in it. I couldn't watch Amanda in the bag go down the hall."

Miller had a similar reaction. "I was completely amazed. And even though I worked on the film, there were parts that scared me," he says. "And that's just amazing to me because I know how it's all done. It was a rollercoaster. I think that's what appealed to most people."

"I really loved it," admits Burrows. "The picture had a lot of things going for it: the acting was very good, the filming was very good, and Wes drove it all. He wanted the best of the best, and he got it. That's what made the picture, I think."

Benson recalls, "I thought it was really scary and really innovative. There were some scenes in there that shocked me and I thought, 'Wes is a really good director.' I enjoyed the movie."

Also captivated was Talalay. "I knew it was going to be a really successful film because when I saw it, I was scared. When you've been on set, and you've been involved in everything, and you know how everything's done, the fact is it was still so effective. It was just so powerful and scary," she says.

"With so little in the way of resources, and so many young actors who were untested," says Levine, "I was amazed at what a smart, scary, thoughtful film Wes had crafted."

Expressing a similar sentiment was Meyer-Craven. "I knew what the next scene was, the next moment was. I knew where 'the bodies were buried and who shot them' so to speak," she states. "And you know what? It still scared the crap out of me. I was mightily impressed. Scared to death and impressed beyond belief."

Theater marquee showing *A Nightmare on Elm Street*.

Lazzara's first time seeing the film was in a theater after being away on another job in Africa. "I was gone for a period of time and I just kind of forgot about it because I didn't think it was going to be anything special," he says. "But I remember it being very scary and it turned out amazing. I was shocked. Really shocked."

For Bernstein, *Elm Street* worked not just for what it was on its own, but in addition to being somewhat of a mirror to other classic works. "I was really taken with one aspect of it that

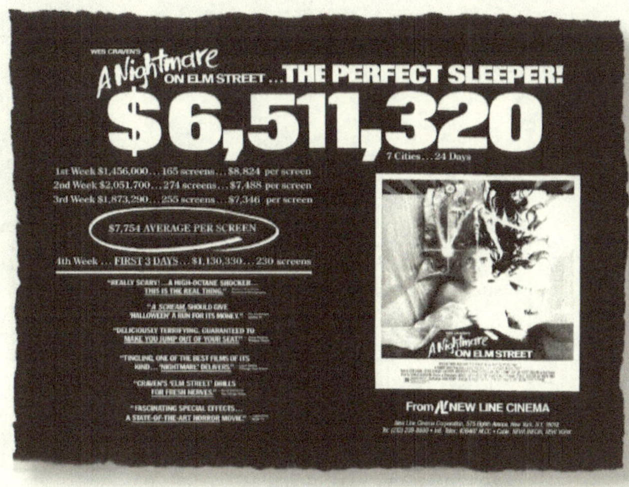

Trade paper announcements of *A Nightmare on Elm Street*'s release and subsequent smashing box office business.

reminded me of Fellini," he says. "Wes was playing with reality. 'Are we in a dream?' Sometimes a sequence starts and we think, 'Well, where are we?' And then suddenly things start happening that couldn't happen in reality and we say, 'Oh, we're in a dream.' So in a way, Wes was doing what Fellini was doing, which is manipulating the audience."

"We were just trying to get through it. We knew we had done a good job on a special project but none of us ever thought anybody would ever see it," Englund admits. "I think one of the great aspects of *Nightmare on Elm Street* is that it wasn't hyped. It wasn't jammed down your throat."

One cast member found herself unsure of what to think when she finally had the chance to digest the film in which she starred. "I had never seen a real 'horror' movie, certainly not a Wes Craven film. I couldn't see what other people were seeing," says Langenkamp. "Like a lot of teenagers, I relied upon the reactions of others to form opinions. Later, I saw the movie in Oakland, at a real theater, and I heard the audience talking to the screen, calling out to Marge as she took another swig of vodka. Right then, I learned what a scary movie was all about. It took ten more years before I was able to see the film for what it is."

If it took a decade for Langenkamp to appreciate the film on its own terms, Corri enjoyed the immediacy of seeing the film for the first time. "It was at The Dome theater in Hollywood. I sat behind some girls and I was kind of spying and checking it out," he says. "And then the girls were like, 'Oh, that's you. Cool!'" The actor recalls tempering that moment of excitement with the far more sobering truth faced by many actors. "I walked out, smoking a cigarette and trying to be cool, but then it was like, 'What is the next job?'"

Englund relates the time he saw the film and felt its true impact, which was at a theater near the University of Southern California. "Apparently, all the beautiful girlfriends of the football players had already seen the movie and they brought all these big, hulking guys," he recalls. Sitting in the back, the actor couldn't help but enjoy watching, as he says, "two-hundred-fifty-pound guys jumping out of their seats, screaming like girls and, of course, the women, the girlfriends, loved it, because they knew where all the scares were. They just loved watching their boyfriends jump. That was my first real sense of it. There was a bit of call and recall with the screen."

The formula was working. "From the very first time, we got very physical reactions, such as screams, people moving in their chairs, that sort of sense of excitement. And I realized, 'Boy, this is tapping into something I had no idea,'" Shaine states, recalling the time he saw the film on opening night in a movie house on Broadway. "It was like live theater. People were standing up, they were yelling at the screen, they were in the aisles. It was unlike anything I had ever experienced. I started to realize not only that it was working, but that it was tapping into something and hitting a nerve in the public that was more than I anticipated."

"It was so important to our lives at the time because our company could've gone under."

Sara Risher on *Elm Street*'s success

"It was a huge theater, like a thousand-seat theater, and it was mostly full," says McMahon of seeing the film for the first time with an audience. "The people just went nuts for the film. I'd never seen an audience like that, screaming at a film. 'Don't fall asleep! He's under the water'! They were doing stuff like that. It was the most interactive film experienced I'd seen. I think we all knew that night it was gonna be a hit."

But it wasn't just cast, crew, or random moviegoers who were enjoying the film. "It was opening day and John Waters had gone to one of the early showings in Baltimore," recalls Risher, "and afterward he called us up and told us that we had a hit. That's when I knew, because John knows. He knows what works and what doesn't."

Shaye admits to feeling a thrill when he thinks back to going to Times Square for the film's opening. Though it wasn't the first time a project he had released garnered audience interest, he says, "To see this huge line around the block on Broadway of people waiting to get into the theater, I knew then the fuse had been lit."

"My only memory of the release of *Nightmare* was that I was not sure how well it would do and I went away," Craven states. "I hadn't heard anything, and it opened and then came this call, I think on the third day, I think it was from Bob. You hear that tone, you know what's going to happen, your credibility goes way up, and you feel like you've connected with the audience. It's a great feeling."

THE VERDICT IS IN...

Risher remembers the first time there was an inkling they might have had a minor hit on their hands when, days before its official release, the film was screened at The Hof International Film Festival in Germany. "The film played at midnight and the head of the film festival called and said it was a standing ovation," recalls Risher. "It was absolutely a knockout. They had so many people who wanted to see this movie that it was a huge, huge hit at the festival."

The film seemed to please cast, crew, and an eager international festival audience, although upon its original debut in America there was a small, technical setback. The issue was that in some of the larger theaters, people began complaining the film was too dark.

"By that time my baby was a month old, I strapped him on me and I went to Times Square, which is not the Times Square of today. It was pretty rough," Risher states. Entering a theater that was, at the time, mainly attracting a genre crowd, she saw the film and agreed it "was very dark. You missed a lot of nuances."

Working to fix the issue, Risher went to the projection room and realized that it was not the film that was the problem. Instead, she learned that in order to save money, some projectionists were not using the full light. To ensure the film would be seen the way New Line Cinema had hoped, "We then lightened the prints because we knew this was gonna happen all over America," says Risher.

Even with the small hindrance, the film, which opened in limited release November 9, 1984 on one hundred sixty-five screens, had a weekend tally of $1,271,000. Rolling out the following weekend on an additional one hundred and nine screens, the film found its way in the top ten for three consecutive weeks, even with other genre fare such as *The Terminator*, *Night of the Comet*, *Silent Night, Deadly Night*, and the juggernaut *Ghostbusters* as its competition.

Playing in theaters over the course of three months, the film took in a final domestic box office gross of $25,504,513, which was no small feat for New Line Cinema and the risk they admittedly took on *Elm Street*.

"It was so important to our lives at the time because our company could've gone under. We were a small company, we believed in filmmaking, we wanted to make entertainment,

Shaye (with a faux beard) holds Risher's newborn son at the New Line Cinema holiday party. The festivities also included celebrating the success of *Elm Street*; A cake (with appropriate decoration) in honor of New Line's *Nightmare*.

we wanted to do the best work we could for the money that we had," Risher says. "But we were struggling, and there were times when the film could have literally destroyed the company. But the making of it was such a joy. And the fact that it worked, and was successful, was so fulfilling that it's obviously a sort of triumph of the underdog."

Shaye echoes the sentiment, adding, "Of course, I'm forever grateful to Wes for entrusting the project and material to us. And it certainly helped build New Line," he says, a nod to the oft-mentioned catchphrase that New Line Cinema is, "The House That Freddy Built."

"New Line Cinema was not the New Line Cinema we now know until *Nightmare*," adds Meyer-Craven. "But Bob is very smart. From the beginning he knew that this was somehow going to be a game-changing movie."

If *Nightmare* hadn't been the success it was, both Shaye and Risher realize, at the very least, it would have been much more difficult to make other films. "The entire success of New Line rested on that film. And our reputation really rested on it because it made us credible filmmakers," says Risher, "and all of a sudden we started getting good material, and we started getting the recognition that a film company needs in order to get anywhere."

Financial success wasn't the only boon to the company, or Craven's film. Critical reaction, despite the occasional less-than-stellar review that harped on the gore or, as some might have worried, the bizarre ending, was overwhelmingly positive.

The Los Angeles Times commented, "As skillful as it is sickening. Written and directed by maestro of ultragore Wes Craven, it has considerable style, some good performances and clever special effects."

On the east coast, Vincent Canby of *The New York Times* also picked up on the "special effects, which aren't all that bad."

The Village Voice was taken by the fact that, "Craven's movie drills for fresh nerves... because there's an implicit contract between a horror film director and his audience that dreams don't kill," ultimately hailing the film as a minor masterpiece.

L.A. Weekly stated in its review, "If achievement in this genre can be measured by the number of scares, then *Nightmare on Elm Street* is a rousing success."

Even Leonard Maltin credited Craven's film for having an "imaginative premise."

TV Guide, one of America's longest-running entertainment magazines, stated *Elm Street* is "one of the most intelligent and terrifying horror films of the 1980s," and that the "terror is almost nonstop."

The film continues to hold a rating in the ninetieth percentile on the critical aggregator site Rotten Tomatoes and has been considered by many to be one of the best genre films of 1984. In 2003, Freddy Krueger was named the fortieth greatest film villain on American Film Institute's "100 Years...100 Heroes and Villains" list, and ranked number seventeen on Bravo TV's *100 Scariest Movie Moments* (2004).

In 2008, *Empire Magazine* listed the film as number one hundred sixty-two on their list of "The 500 Greatest Movies of All Time."

The New York Times also selected *Elm Street* as one of "The Best 1000 Movies Ever Made."

ANOTHER CRAVEN FILM SOAKED IN BLOOD

"Nightmare on Elm Street" (citywide), which has a very hard R rating, is as skillful as it is sickening.

Written and directed by maestro of ultragore Wes Craven, it has considerable style, some good performances and clever special effects. It probably will attract a cult following, as did Craven's "The Last House on the Left" and "The Hills Have Eyes."

But when a film is designed to drench the screen in blood—with maximum violence directed, as usual, mainly toward women—rather than to give a good, fun fright, what does it finally matter how well it is made? There does come a point when form cannot sustain or justify content, and it arrives very early in this film when an unseen force slices up a high school girl (Amanda Wyss) as she sleeps and hurls her body around until the bedroom is covered with blood.

Craven envisions nightmares becoming real for Wyss and her friend, Heather Langenkamp. They dream of a hideous ghoul (Robert Englund) who attacks girls and boys in their sleep with a specially designed glove fitted with retractable knives in its fingers.

When Wyss dies so hideou[s]… Langenkamp realizes she's nex[t]… line and becomes determined… fight back. Naturally, she's ma… on her own, because no adu… including her increasingly c… cerned but perplexed mother, … nee Blakley, and tough-cop fat… John Saxon, are going to beli… her explanation of what's going o…

Both Langenkamp and Blak… have roles with more dimensi… than is usual in such films, and b… are impressive. Which only ma… you wish all the more that y… were seeing them in somethi… else.

—KEVIN THOM…

Various reviews of *A Nightmare on Elm Street*. A majority of critics found the film to be a worthwhile exercise in the genre, stating it was well-crafted, had interesting characterizations and, perhaps most importantly, was truly frightening.

Wed., Nov. 7, 1984

FILM REVIEWS

A Nightmare On Elm Street
(Horror — DeLuxe Color)

New York — "A Nightmare On Elm Street" is a highly imaginative horror film that provides the requisite shocks to keep fans of the genre happy. Absence of a powerful dramatic payoff will limit its breakout potential, however.

Unlike the Summer release "Dreamscape," which posed a nightmare vision within a far-fetched science fiction framework, "Elm Street" relies upon supernatural horror. Young teenagers in a Los Angeles neighborhood are sharing common nightmares about being chased and killed by a disfigured bum in a slouch hat who has knives for fingernails. It turns out that years ago, the neighborhood's parents took deadly vigilante action against a child murderer, who apparently is vengefully haunting their kids.

HOLLYWOOD REPORTER, THURSDAY, NOVEMBER 8, 1984

'Nightmare on Elm Street' may bring sweet dreams to Craven

By KIRK ELLIS

Wes Craven's "A Nightmare on Elm Street" won't do much for Sominex sales, but its insomnia-inducing chills are likely to prove sweet box-office dreams for distributor New Line Cinema. This latest bedtime story from the writer-director of such latter-day horror classics as "Last House on the Left" and "The Hills Have Eyes" is an exceedingly well-crafted, disturbing meditation on the subconscious guaranteed to set night-light electric bills skyrocketing nationwide.

Craven's penchant for discovering terror in everyday surroundings is well realized in his story of four ultranormal teenagers stalked in their dreams by a red-sweatered, facially disfigured ugly equipped with knifelike fingernails. When the kids start dying bloody deaths in their beds, it remains for the survivor (Heather Langenkamp) to confront the phantom in his own supernatural territory and thereby end his fatally rude awakenings.

Rarely has Craven so successfully blurred the line between the real and the imagined, allowing the scares to materialize — quite often literally — out of production designer Greg Fonseca's painfully observant middle-class settings. Harmless images become downright ghoulish: a lethal

A NIGHTMARE ON ELM STREET
New Line Cinema

Executive producers	Stanley Dudelson, Joseph Wolf
Producer	Robert Shaye
Writer-director	Wes Craven
Camera	Jacques Haitkin
Production design	Greg Fonseca
Special effects	Jim Doyle
Editor	Rick Shaine
Music	Charles Bernstein

Color 1.85/mono

Cast: John Saxon, Ronee Blakley, Heather Langenkamp, Amanda Wyss, Nick Corri, Johnny Depp, Robert Englund, Charles Fleisher, Joseph Whipp, Lin Shaye.

Running time — 93 minutes

MPAA Rating: R

— continued on page 6

FILMS IN FOCUS

'Nightmare' a haunting chill-seeker

"Nightmare on Elm Street," starring John Saxon, Ronee Blakley Heather Lagenkamp. A New Cinema film, rated R, opening today in Flagship theaters in Jersey.

RICHARD FREEDMAN

…really irksome thing about …res is that short of abstaining …m lobster thermidor and baked alaska as midnight snacks, there's no sure-fire method of preventing them.

This is the problem of a group of nice, only moderately promiscuous high-school kids in "A Nightmare on Elm Street," written and directed by Wes Craven, who made the cult horror classics "The Last House on The Left" and "The Hills Have Eyes."

His new one is the first really scary slasher flick in a long time.

In it, the kids seem …

Fantasy borders on reality in 'Nightmare'

By Glenn Lovell
Film Writer

ATTENTION, all fright fans: "A Nightmare on Elm Street" (opening today) is the year's most single-minded and ambitious horror outing. It is also, thanks to genre …

"Nightmare," which co-stars John Saxon and Ronee Blakley as Nancy's useless, separated parents, is at its best when Craven allows his macabre imagination full rein. As was abundantly clear after his overlooked "Deadly Blessings," Craven has an uncommon knack for blurring the lines between real-

Craven's stock-shock ending, wherein Nancy stalks Freddie on his own turf, is crawling with missed opportunities.

Still, if you're of stout heart, check this one out. It'll remind you of some of your most deliciously sinister dreams.

A NIGHTMARE ON ELM STREET. Written, directed by Wes Craven. R (gory effects). ★★★

"This year's best film!"

The ranking for Krueger's exploits fared even better in a 2013 experiment into the physiological effect of horror films and, more specifically, how genre movies affect viewers' heart rates. The outcome? *A Nightmare on Elm Street* was perceived to be the third scariest film of all time (behind *The Shining* and *The Exorcist*), while two scenes from the film—Tina's death and Glen's death—got audience hearts racing an average of twenty-six percent higher than normal.

Perhaps most important to Craven and New Line Cinema, however, were the industry reviews at the time, which did not disappoint. *Variety* said it was a "highly imaginative horror film that provides the requisite shocks to keep fans of the genre happy" and added, "Writer-director Wes Craven tantalizingly merges dreams with the ensuing wakeup reality."

The Hollywood Reporter ran a similar notice, saying, "Rarely has Craven so successfully blurred the line between the real and the imagined," and that the film was "an exceedingly well-crafted, disturbing meditation on the subconscious."

All told, it was a good day to be living on *Elm Street*.

COMING OUT OF THE DARK

"The first film was the real seminal movie," admits Shaye. "It still has some really genius scenes in it, not only in the context of genius scenes today, but historically. It really filled the bill."

That affection is not just offered by Shaye, the man who believed enough in Craven's script to take it on when no one else would, but shared by all who pooled their time, craft, and expertise to become a second family for a few months to create a *Nightmare* for moviegoers.

"It stands on its own as a real step forward in its genre," says Doyle. "Both from a story standpoint and the way the crew and cast really got together, and worked together, to realize Wes' somewhat twisted vision of how the dreamworld might be."

"I loved it," Haitkin declares. "I knew it was a commercial piece that on the surface of it would thrill and scare audiences. But I knew it went deeper than that. To this day, look how successful and popular horror films are. The appeal behind horror films is fear."

"Everyone loves the first film, almost out of loyalty, I think," Langenkamp says. "And they're right. It is special. It's where they got introduced to Freddy and Nancy and the battle that they wage. The film meant something and said something."

"Oh, Heather was this huge, big hero," adds Meyer-Craven. "You just didn't see girls doing that kind of stuff. Freddy was not to be trifled with, but she was the person that beat him and certainly gave him a run for his money."

Even Talalay understands that Craven wanted more from his film than just another teenaged gorefest. "Not to get preachy, but we wanted you to care about your teenagers, and we wanted you to learn how to confront your fears and to realize that you could confront your terrors," she says. "And I think that really worked for the audience. The film just stands on its own so brilliantly."

In addition to the characters, there was story, something that Corri realized early on. "If you don't have a great storyline, you don't have anything. That's why it goes deep," he says, adding that he and the cast wanted more from the film than the genre typically allowed. "We wanted to make it Shakespeare back then. We would have serious discussions with Wes about, 'Look, we don't want this to be another *Friday the 13th*, where we're camping, and the knife goes through the bed, and it's just gore and screaming. Let's make it psychologically damaging and real.' That's what the movie ultimately became."

Actress Shaye sums up the notion across many of their minds. "I don't think anybody had any idea how powerful this was going to be. It's about that timing thing where an audience is ready for something, and something delivers it, and then it all takes on a life of its own," she says. "We certainly did not know it was gonna be as big as it was."

Corri agrees the film's ultimate success was something unforeseen. "You kind of go, 'Wow,'" he admits. "Anybody that said that they calculated that this would happen is wrong. No one knew. Except we did it out of love. Love for the work. And we thought it was something really cool. And definitely Wes knew what he was doing. But you know, the ripples of what it did are still shocking to me."

"We wanted you to learn how to confront your fears and realize you could confront your terrors. And I think that really worked for the audience."

Rachel Talalay

Part of that power came from those behind the scenes who still recall what it was like bringing the horrors to life. "It's still gratifying to be part of the crew, one of the creative professionals who created the Freddy franchise, to have pulled the glove out of nowhere," admits Doyle. "David Miller pulled Freddy's face out of nowhere. These things just materialized for the first time in front of us. We were the first ones ever to see him, and in a fledgling business."

"Everyone seemed to have a lot of fun and, of course, nobody knew what it was to become," says Miller. "To most people, including myself, it was just another low, low, low-budget film, but it never seemed like it. The vibe was very good on that set."

Logan vividly remembers the fellowship amongst the crew. "There's a camaraderie on non-union pictures where everybody is just in there and helping everybody else," she proclaims.

"And everybody's door was open, too," admits Jensen. "The door to the special effects department, and the makeup department, and the hair department, and I could just walk in and watch the stuff happen when I had time. Everything was there and it was so communal. That was just great. Everybody was tired, but everybody was there with it. Everybody was just out there doing whatever they could to make it work. It was great."

Shaine likens his involvement to the job he performed. "Like any editing problem, it was lots and lots of hard work and problem solving," he says. "But there was a payoff to it."

"I thought it was really scary, and I think I looked at half of it through my fingers with my hands over my eyes," says Huntley. "But I was really proud of it. I know why it's become such a masterpiece, because it's so well-directed, and so well-crafted, and it just has a great story."

Also finding the film frightening was Diers, who was blown away when he saw it. "The image I remember sticking out in my mind is when Freddy's arms grow really long, because even though I'm involved in the behind-the-scenes of the film, it freaked me out," he says. "It was nightmare imagery. Literally, nightmare imagery. So I think at that point, I was like, 'This is one scary movie.' And I was impressed with Wes' work."

Ask almost anyone on the film, and while they'll agree the experience was enjoyable and memorable, few will admit it was something else: easy.

"Well, it wasn't fun when people would disappear for days on end. That was never fun," Rideout says. "Particularly if they happened to be on the effects crew, because it resulted in me trying to find them!"

When asked what might be the reason for sudden disappearances, Rideout isn't modest. "Drug use. They would crash and burn sometimes for days, and we were trying to make a film, and I had no authority, really, in terms of the crew," she reveals. "But I was just responsible for finding those people, and sometimes you just couldn't reach them because they were probably lying comatose in some other location."

Crew members such as Doyle and Talalay didn't condone the type of behavior that might have been occurring, but they do offer an explanation.

"There was a certain childlike naiveté about how we were making that movie," says Doyle. "Because we were just a bunch of young filmmakers running down the hall trying to get out of the door at the other end, with a product we would all be proud of and would satisfy our creative needs."

In order to do that, time was at a premium, something Talalay explains. "It was long hours. It was that business of there's no unions, so they can work us fifteen,

sixteen, seventeen hours. You're utterly exhausted and it was really, really hard work," she states. "There was some party atmosphere, at times, sort of when you go over the top with being that exhausted, but it's not like that anymore. But back then? It just wasn't as responsible a time. And no, it wasn't always like, 'Gee! Yay! We get to make a movie!' at all. It was really hard work."

The encumbrance of the long hours and low budget might have taken their toll, but for many, like Jensen, it worked because it had to. "It was just a production assistant and me, and I can't even conceive of how we did that, but we did," she laughs. "You just did it. And everybody was in such good spirits all the time, oddly enough, for all the hard work they were doing."

"It really was a wonderful time as far as the cast and crew," says Risher. "They were all pulling together, even when it was hardest, and we made it because we loved what we were doing."

Fans of the film did as well. "I really became aware of the *Nightmare on Elm Street* phenomenon while attending a science-fiction convention at the old Hotel Roosevelt in Manhattan," Englund remembers. "All of a sudden this line began to devolve into a lot of black leather. It started to look like the Ramones' roadies. And then there were a lot of punks, and then there were a lot of girls in black, leather vests, and not much else, and a lot of tattoos, and a lot of dog collars. And I was signing breasts, and they all wanted Freddy."

It was then that the actor knew something interesting had been stirred up among moviegoers. "It was really unusual that these rough, hardcore horror fans had turned out and stood in the rain for hours just to meet me. And very shortly after that it began to snowball," he says.

This page and **opposite page**: Proving every country can have an Elm Street, New Line Cinema's *Nightmare* went global. Shown (left to right) are foreign release film posters and ads from the United Kingdom, Germany, Belgium, France, and Italy.

Even Blakley is quick to say that the film and its success had a positive effect on her. "It never hurts to be in a hit. Yes, I did enjoy some perks from its success, and I still do," she says, adding, "It bought me my house. There are untold joys to working. And when you work on a fine project with great people, it's going to be a joy forever."

Langenkamp also saw the love for the film and its characters growing steadily over the course of years. "It was probably a good year or so after the movie came out that I realized more people had seen it. And I went to one of those horror conventions, and I saw that there were a lot of Freddy fans. And I actually was pleasantly surprised that they knew who Nancy was, too, at the time. And I've just seen that grow," she says. "And with regard to the success of the movie, I really think it has everything to do with home video and the way they can market things over and over and over again to new generations of people."

The actress acknowledges that fan appreciation for her, and the character she played, was a slower burn than Englund's seemingly instant recognition for essaying Krueger. "I felt it more ten years after the movie came out than I did the year after it came out," adds Langenkamp, admitting that at the time the film was released she didn't experience many "Look, it's that girl!" accolades.

"I wish I had," says Langenkamp. "That would have been a lot of fun. I went back to college, actually. And I remember sitting in my classes, and not one person the whole time I was at Stanford ever recognized me. And I remember telling one of my professors, 'Oh yeah, I was in a movie,' when asked why I wasn't in class the last semester. You know, I never really could just let it all hang out, because I just wanted people to think of me as someone who was taking their education seriously, and I think if I had mentioned that I was 'Freddy's Girl,' it might have taken something away from that."

Sympathetic to the notion that you want to be seen for who you are at a current moment in your life, Corri states, "It's annoying, because you want people to know your recent work, but you can't be a dick, either. You have to understand and accept, 'Hey, that fifteen-year-old girl or boy is moved.' Or, 'That weird guy in that clown suit's coming at me right now and I'd better smile because he's touched by you and what you're doing.' And that's our job. Our job is not to be running away from things like that. We put ourselves publicly out there. So ride the bull and don't be a pussy about it."

Never one to have shied away from the film's promotional whirlwind, Englund quickly saw how the *Elm Street* fan base had breached borders. "I was in Europe for an award show for *V*, and I literally got pulled out of my limousine, and separated from my date, and passed like I was in a mosh pit over the crowd," he recalls. "And they were all Freddy fans that couldn't get in to this ceremony, this award show. Then I knew. And I went, 'It's international.'"

Langenkamp credits much of the film's success and longevity to Englund's portrayal of the character. "Robert brought something so attractive to Freddy Krueger that people just can't get enough of him," says the actress. "People just like to identify with that evil. I don't know what it is."

"There were articles written about why people are so attracted to Freddy Krueger, about the psychology of it," says actress Shaye. "What is it that's appealing about this man to people? And I don't think anyone really understands it still, exactly. People were interested to see a horror film, and Robert really pulled it out. He did an extraordinary character that no one will ever match."

Englund notes his understanding that the fame and notoriety he was experiencing were coming from something that did have a stigma. "Back then it was still 'that low-budget horror movie,' but Wes did allow us to use the word 'slasher' on the set. There's no other verb to describe what Freddy would do. Freddy's not really a slasher character, but if Freddy goes to grab at you with that claw, he's slashing at you," he offers. "So unfortunately, Wes became 'horror-meister Wes Craven,' 'slasher-director Wes Craven,' and I became 'horror-star-slash-star Robert Englund.' And that gets attached to your name for a while."

It was an accessory to which Englund wasn't resolutely opposed, though he does admit it wasn't something he sought out at the time. "It was sort of a split for me because I didn't know whether I had made a wise decision. Obviously, I'm under all this makeup and I really had to trust Wes," the actor says, adding that Shaye having treated him well, and as an equal, was also nice. "I remember also realizing that Jacques Haitkin was very talented, and that Jim Doyle was special, and that the production design and the designers were really gifted, young people. I knew all that. But you have to understand, my first great success celebrity-wise was on *V* and I was on hiatus from that. While I was doing *Nightmare on Elm Street*, when I was working on it and was involved with it, I wasn't thinking, 'This is my big break.'"

Time would certainly agree that it might not have been Englund's big break, but it did thrust him into the horror spotlight more than ever before. The consolation was that at least the shining light came from working with a writer and director who was continually endeavoring to bring something fresh to the genre.

"I liked Wes so much, and I respected Wes so much, that that got me through it," admits Englund.

Blakley, too, credits three clear reasons why the film was a success and has stood the test of time. "Number one is Wes, number two is Wes, and number three is Wes," she states.

What Craven had dreamed up would, unbeknownst to him or anyone at the time of making the film, ultimately give birth to more than just a one-hit movie wonder. The exploits of Freddy Kruger would later be seen over the course of the next four decades in a wildly successful franchise consisting of six sequels, a matchup between Krueger and longtime competitor Jason Voorhees of the *Friday the 13th* franchise, a syndicated television show, and even a remake of Craven's classic.

What New Line Cinema realized, of course, was that there was more to monetize than just movie prints from the original film and those that followed. Over the years, merchandise related to the franchise would become bestsellers in an array of different fields as Freddy Krueger and A *Nightmare on Elm Street* were quickly attached to novels, comic books, video

A newspaper article states a fact about what *Elm Street* did for New Line Cinema.

Freddy Krueger makes studio's dreams come true

By ALJEAN HARMETZ
N.Y. Times News Service

HOLLYWOOD — On Aug. 11, Freddy Krueger will once again extend his razor-sharp fingers toward sleeping teen-agers, invading their dreams in 1,900 theaters.

With the regularity of a vampire awakening at sunset, each summer brings a new "Nightmare on Elm Street." And each new "Nightmare" is another sweet dream for New Line Cinema.

Small movie companies have been an endangered species in Hollywood for several years. Cannon, DeLaurentiis Entertainment

The "Nightmare on Elm Street" series of horror films

theme parks that want to create a Nightmare on Elm Street haunted house ride.

A syndicated television series called "Freddy's Nightmares" will return for a second year in September, and videos of the television programs are being sold in Britain.

No one could have predicted the success of Freddy Krueger, the illegitimate son of a hundred maniacs ("Nightmare 3: Dream Warriors") and a child killer who was burned to death and who takes revenge by entering the dreams of the children of his murderers and slaughtering them while they sleep ("Nightmare 1").

ran a wholesale grocery business in Detroit.

"I learned that product is everything," he said. "If you run out of Domino Sugar in the warehouse, you ask them to send you some more. The worst mistake an independent company can make is not having enough resources to assure itself of a product flow."

New Line assures itself of a product flow by making four or five reasonably low-budget films a year and serving as a distributor for independent producers.

Its $6 million "Hairspray" — the

Although small compani[...] New Line rarely compete [...] the powerful pictures distr[...] by the major studios duri[...] summer, New Line will [...] slugging it out when it dist[...] "Babar," a movie based [...] children's books about an el[...] king by Jean de Bru[...] "Babar" is to open in 400 t[...] on July 28.

SHAYE KNOWS he canno[...] on "Nightmare on Elm Str[...] support the 110 employees [...] Line Cinema forever.

"Unlike real estate, it's [...] resource," he said. He also [...]

A political satire using Freddy Krueger. The character and *A Nightmare on Elm Street* quickly became go-to euphemisms for politicians, policies, and ideologies that some wanted to scorn.

games, board games, toys, clothing, costumes, and more. Consumer products, however, weren't the film's only reach into mass culture. Freddy, the film's title, and even its concept would have wide-ranging usability, including mentions in television shows spanning *Cheers* to *30 Rock* (2006-2013), and movies like *Silent Night, Deadly Night* to *Transformers* (2007), as well as being part of comic strips and social or political satire. Craven's brainchild was even cited as a partisan wedge by Republican President Ronald Reagan. "Anything that's bad is a nightmare in the National League, a nightmare in the NFL, a nightmare in the NBA, a nightmare in Vietnam, it's a nightmare in Iraq, it's a nightmare in the Gulf. We were so part of the vernacular," says Englund. "It's become part of our culture."

Clearly, *A Nightmare on Elm Street* was here to stay. As for why, Englund nicely sums it up. "We only get so many great, classic stories. That's what separates us from the animals are the stories we tell," he offers. "And *A Nightmare on Elm Street* by Wes Craven is just a great goddamned story."

WHAT DREAMS MAY COME

Accolades from critics, cast, crew, and fans aside, the true measure of whether Craven's film had done what the writer and director had hoped would be seen in what lay ahead. "The fact that *Nightmare on Elm Street* was a critical and financial success helped me immensely," Craven admits. "When I started on the film, I was penniless. I was just in serious, terrible financial trouble because of three years of not being able to get a job. And I was looking for other jobs during that period, while working on this silly script at night."

The silly script, of course, turned everything around for the director who went on to the horror-thriller *Deadly Friend* (1986), though he confessed to being less than

enthusiastic. "It was the first film I got and that was something I didn't think was that good of a script, but my agent said, 'It's a major studio, go do it,'" Craven says. "It turned out to have producers who all had conflicting ideas as to what it should be. So it was quite a mess."

Interestingly, Craven also worked for the one studio that was rumored to have expressed some interest in *Elm Street*, Disney. The project was "Casebusters," an episode of *Walt Disney's Wonderful World of Color* (1954-1992), though it seems his getting work on the youth-oriented action-adventure might have lost him a subsequent, higher-profile project. "I don't know whether anybody knows this story, but in the course of making *Deadly Friend*, before that came out, I was offered *Beetlejuice* (1988)," reveals Craven. "And I was having meetings with the studio and everything else, but I had done [the Disney project] and they saw that and didn't think it was good, and so they called up and said, 'We don't want you anymore!'"

Merchandising Freddy Krueger and *A Nightmare on Elm Street* became a huge part of the characters', films', and New Line Cinema's success. From novels, comics, sticker books, albums, toys, figures, replica gloves, games, and even a weekly syndicated television series, *Elm Street* became a household name while Krueger was destined to be a character few would ever forget.

Craven eventually found out that, "The people from *Beetlejuice* got a call from Disney saying, 'Wes Craven can't do comedy,'" the director remembers. "That was it, bang, they were gone." Afterward, it was revealed the mysterious message came from none other than Jeffrey Katzenberg (Walt Disney Studios' head of production at the time). "I called him up and said, 'Why did you do that?' and he goes, 'You know, you're established in the genre and one of the great filmmakers, but I just was stating my honest opinion.'"

Another potential job lost, also perhaps due to his close association with the genre, could have been interesting. Had it come to pass, Craven might have had a hand in helping keep the "Man of Steel" up in the air for *Superman IV: The Quest for Peace* (1987). A meeting took place with star Christopher Reeve and, as Craven recalls, "I had the very

Domestic one-sheet posters for all of New Line Cinema's *Nightmare*s, films that spanned 1984 to 2010.

distinct feel, like a clique, that he was part of a very different world, kind of upper class. I think he took a look at me and said, 'Ehhh, I don't think so.'"

Despite the fact that Craven could look back on the time lightly, he admits, "It was a horrible year. Everything that you can imagine went wrong during that year. I was also being sued by some crackpot over *Nightmare on Elm Street*. That went on forever."

The case involved an Indian man who claimed Craven had rewritten his script about a mother being terrorized by a snake cult living in caverns underneath their plantation. The case was, Craven states, "really spurious," and he named the events "an extraordinarily difficult period in my life."

There would be a break in the clouds, though, in the form of his next feature project. "After all that," Craven says, "*Serpent and the Rainbow* (1988) came along, and that was really a fascinating and interesting project, and I kind of got to the next notch."

How did Craven feel about the fact that, even after moderate financial and critical successes already under his belt, it took a trip down a suburban street full of secrets, nightmares, and a child killer to get massive appreciation? "Well, I think *Nightmare on Elm Street* put me into the big time, so to speak. It really gave me recognition because I wrote it as well as directed it. I think I was seen as somebody that was a bit of a visionary," he says. "It's never made me feel ashamed. I've always been proud of that work. I think I did some things that were really innovative. And I had the chance to work with some enormously talented and wonderfully spirited people. If you get something that makes people a lot of money, and also you can look at it and say, 'That artistically is interesting to me and you did good work,' and you were glad to have an opportunity to work with those actors, then it's wonderful. There's a lot of friendships that came out of it and it's been great. It's been really great."

And of the one who believed enough to stake his name, company, and career to make sure Craven could see his vision come to life? "I think more than anything else, Bob Shaye is a very, very smart guy who was willing to gamble on something he really believed in," reveals the writer and director. "And that's what a filmmaker needs."

"What it shows is that if you have an adventurous spirit, and you are willing to risk some money and some time, then you could have this incredible upside. And I think that's the whole spirit behind independent films," expresses Langenkamp. "If you're willing to risk your blood, sweat, and tears, you kind of just have to have that spirit. And Bob, I think he epitomizes that spirit."

In terms of Shaye being a gambler who was willing to do all that and more, Langenkamp adds, "He played his cards right."

"I always did think that producers had something to offer besides raising money," contemplates Shaye. "And I didn't get into this business because I wanted to make a lot of money. I got into the business because I wanted to entertain people. In my heart and soul, mostly from my father, even though he was a supermarket owner in the wholesale grocery business, I've always kind of had an instinct about marketing. Sometimes you don't get it right and sometimes you do."

Regarding the latter, did he ever. For Shaye, New Line Cinema, and even Craven, Freddy Krueger proved, above all, you can never keep a good villain down.

7

Legacy of a *Nightmare*

Nine, Ten, Never Sleep Again...

To say *A Nightmare on Elm Street* was an unqualified success might seem to be a bit of an understatement. What began as a script nobody wanted turned out to be a jackpot-winning gamble for many involved. The saying that "one man's trash is another man's treasure" could have been proven singlehandedly the moment Shaye took a chance on Craven's material.

Those pages were crafted into a film that ultimately helped move Shaye and New Line Cinema to successes they may never have thought possible. Craven's career received not just another jump-start, but a full-throttle propulsion into accomplishments both on and off the screen. The cast found success in professional and personal ways, with the film even starting the career of Hollywood star Depp. Behind the scenes, crew members took all they had achieved on this one small film and parlayed that into exciting work on hundreds of other motion picture and television projects.

All told, each and every person who decided to take a walk down *Elm Street* came away with something that can never be seized back from them—

Memories beyond their wildest dreams.

"It really is a super-original and strong idea, because you can control lots of your fears in your life. You can go to therapy, you can have rational ideas that there's no one under the bed, but the idea that as soon as you go to sleep, which we all need so we don't go nuts, becoming the thing that triggers the monster that can get you is a genius idea," states Diers. "And I'm sure that's why it's had a lasting effect on so many people: we all are afraid. If someone told you that you couldn't go to sleep, it would be petrifying. I would say for such a funny, little, low-budget horror film with such a strong idea, I'm proud to have had some part of it."

"I was totally surprised that such a small film became such a great hit," admits Huntley. "There are so many films made, and I was lucky enough to be a part of this team. It was really an honor. We all knew there was something special about it when we were making it, but I think when it's all put together, it's more wonderful. I'm just really proud when I tell people that I worked on it. They're always so amazed. And I'm amazed, too, and very proud that I got to be a part of it. It's a great film."

"It was a seminal moment in life and time, for me, personally. And it was wonderful in so many ways, and it was fantastic in all of the ways it was hard," offers Rideout. "It was a grand thing. I will always be grateful for *A Nightmare on Elm Street*, not just because my marriage came out of it, and my three sons came out of it, but it just taught me a lot of really fantastic life lessons and gave me an opportunity that I'll always treasure."

"I list Wes Craven as one of my top two favorite directors to work with, the other one being David Lynch," says Cook. "It was a great time to be working in L.A., and that movie was sort of the epitome of what it was like to have a lot of young, energetic people pushing the envelope in the time when there wasn't sort of a digital out for doing all this stuff. I've been teaching at the University of Central Florida for fourteen years, and when my students, who are literally young enough to be my children, find out I worked on *A Nightmare on Elm Street*, they just think that's the bomb. They can't believe it. They're so excited. I'm like, 'Really? Do you really even watch that movie? It's so old!' But they love it. It was one of the highlights of a twenty-year career of working in film and television."

"Being part of the filmmaking team that made *Nightmare*, it was more of a dream than a nightmare. It was a fabulous dream come true working with everybody," Jensen says. "And the dream was just all the teamwork, which really set a standard. There are only a few movies in my career that I can say really made me feel truly happy during the process of making them. And I think *Nightmare* was really that."

"I remember watching *Psycho* and I couldn't take a shower in a house if I was all by myself for the longest time. And that was in black and white. So I think Wes opened the door for a different kind of horror genre," expresses Logan. "I think that's why people are still talking about it. It was just a great experience."

"Looking back, who knew that the little movie that Wes was writing while I was upstairs healing in the attic was gonna still be going strong today?" Fleetwood ponders. "I think it was a real blessing that I got to be a part of that. And part of film history. It's a good blessing. It was a great shoot, an all-around good gig, and I had a lot of fun. I think the most fun were those moments where I got to create things that were desperately needed."

"People tell me, 'You're my hero! Oh, man, you worked on that movie?! What was it like?!' And then when I tell them I was the hands in the front credits, they can't believe it. They're awestruck," says Belardinelli. "And that's been so nice for me because it's been that way for twenty-five years. Any time I speak to people who ask about it, they are so thrilled because it has such a great following. I think that's been some of the most fun. People, still to this day, are in awe of that movie. It's wonderful to have been a part of that."

"It's humbling to be considered one of the, sort of, formative parts of the movie. That's an honor," says Craven's daughter, Jessica. "The movie is a cultural icon, so to feel like I had any part in it at all is, of course, very humbling. But on the other hand, I didn't really do anything. My father used elements of his life, and he used me, but I think there's something nice in knowing that this film has become part of the cultural landscape, and that I contributed to it through strength of character that at the time I was completely unaware of. Honestly, I could not have felt less strong. But that my dad saw something in me that he used to create a character who was strong, and has inspired other women, I suppose, is wonderful. So in a very personal, selfish way, I can say that it's moving and inspiring for me. And as for the movie, it's a great work of art. It's a great work of horror. I can't watch that film objectively, to a certain extent. There's a little bit of family history in that film. So for me, my father is in there and I'm in there in ways that other people can never understand. But I still find it just a frightening and wonderful piece of art. I feel everything from confusion to incredible awe and joy that I had anything to do with that film."

"Standing in Dave Miller's garage, working that one single week on *A Nightmare on Elm Street*, making the Freddy pieces, looking at the molds crumbling in my hands and re-gluing them every day, I had no clue that I was working on a project that would become a legendary horror film," says Shostrom. "A huge box office success. And I never even went to set or got to meet Wes Craven. Amazing. It was incredible."

"It's iconic," states Lazzara. "It's definitely a classic. What Wes did and put together, how he made the scares, and how Robert is incredible in the film. Heather is wonderful. In fact, the cast is good all around. It was a great experience and I loved working on it. We had a great time and I made a lot of friends that I still have. At the time, I didn't think it was going to be anything special. And it is. It truly is."

"It's great to have been involved with it. Looking back at doing the original, what a pleasure it is to be involved with something like that," states Carlucci. "It wasn't a one night stand, it's a film that just keeps on going. And there's a lot of gratification in this business when you're part of it. I am absolutely glad I have been part of it."

"It was a pleasure creating Freddy for the first film," reveals Miller. "If I had to do it all over again I would do things a little differently, plan ahead, and try not to lose sleep. Overall it's been just a pleasure working on it and talking to people about it. Living it. I think the main thing I'll always remember is even though it was a low-budget film and there wasn't a lot of money to do everything, everyone was very professional about everything. Wes made everyone feel like he was their uncle. He's just one of the nicest people in the world. That was the best experience

Don Diers

Lisa Jensen

Kathy Logan

Annette Benson

Anne Huntley

David Miller

Louis Lazzara (with Arnold Schw

Rachel Talalay

Jeffrey Levine

Lou Carlucci

Mark Shostrom

RaMona Fleetwood

Lisa Cook

Tony Cecere

I could have as a young, up-and-coming makeup effects artist. Everyone thought that *A Nightmare on Elm Street* was just another low-budget horror film, and to have it escalate the way it did, I think it just made it the best, most rewarding thing I've ever worked on, really."

"What I enjoyed the most about it was working with Wes and working with someone who allowed us to use our own imagination on how to do things," declares Cecere. "Wes is probably the best director I've ever worked with, and that's probably the most enjoyable part of that whole picture was working with him."

"I am incredibly grateful for having been part of this iconic project," Talalay says. "I am thankful to Wes Craven for teaching me the essence of horror, and to Bob Shaye for showing me true creativity, for expanding my life in horror, and for inviting me on the ride. I feel the utmost admiration for Wes and the film—the elemental understanding of the need for the audience to root for Nancy, for her to be smart and innovative, and the importance of the psychosexual content. In other words, it completely holds up, in spite of the clothes and haircuts! It's incredible to me how it changed my life and how important it still is to people. But never in my life, when I went to do *Nightmare*, did I ever believe it would be a life-changer and that it would be something that's a bible in my life. I learned so much about production from those experiences. I learned about innovation and being creative in the film business. Everybody should have those opportunities to be that creative."

"*Elm Street* was an amazing, scary film and casting it was an honor," says Benson. "Wes Craven created a film that, to this day, is revered as a great horror movie and still scares new generations of young people. It opened the door to a longtime relationship with New Line Cinema, Bob Shaye, and Sara Risher, which was one of the best experiences of my life."

"*A Nightmare on Elm Street*, for me, came around at the right point in my career. It was working with Wes and working with Jacques that allowed me to expand, open up, and try things," admits Doyle. "I developed an awful lot of confidence during the film, and the arc of my career has a lot to do with *Nightmare on Elm Street*. And it's still gratifying. People still remember that I'm the guy that did the original glove, and I'm the guy that did the original *Nightmare*."

"At the time, it was the best picture I made," offers Burrows. "It had great humor, it had great fright, it had everything a person would like that wants to come in and see a movie that scares you right out of your chair. I ran it I don't know how many times, looking at it with the editors, and I never got tired of seeing it. Everything was good in the picture. We all enjoyed making the picture so much."

"I'm honored to be a part of *A Nightmare on Elm Street* because of the integrity of the film itself," says McMahon. "I'm also honored to be a part of it because it was the main building block for New Line, which has gone on to do so many wonderful things over the years. Every step along the way the film seemed to grow and grow in terms of how good it would be. It just got better and better, stronger and stronger. I always was, and continue to be, proud to be a part of it."

"It was a huge thrill," acknowledges Shaine, "that lots of little decisions and details had an effect on kind of a national psyche. It was great to be part of that."

"It's a very complete and satisfying little picture," says Bernstein. "And it happens to be in the horror genre, but it works as a story and as a movie. I'm just very, very happy to have been a part of it and that I was able to contribute the musical sound."

"Wes had the depth. His own character had the depth, and his artistic sense had that kind of depth and understanding that audiences want. They need resonance in the stories," offers Haitkin. "It wasn't superficial. That's one of the things that makes great horror films great is that at the heart of it there's something really deep, very human. Part of the grand argument of the story is the battle between good and evil in decent folk."

"If there is a power to *Nightmare on Elm Street*, as far as affecting our lives as the people involved in the project, I think it's all on a very uplifting, positive thing," states Peak. "There's no way I can say, 'Gee, I'm not a big part of *A Nightmare on Elm Street*.' I'm pretty proud of helping launch it, helping create it. And that feels great. I don't do all that much movie poster work. I've done a handful of different projects, so it's a big deal to me."

"It's great to be able to say you were around when something cool happened in this business," says Levine. "Something that is memorable enough to keep talking about so many years later. And, to have worked with Wes Craven, who was such a brilliant, warm, generous man."

"Being in the original *Nightmare on Elm Street*, for an eight-year-old girl, it was probably one of the coolest things that I could ever do in the world," confesses Adri-Anne. "I think probably until the day I die I will remember 'One, two, Freddy's coming for you' and the entire saying all the way through. I think that's something that I'll probably take with me to the grave."

"It's a great feeling in the sense that a lot of people know us as 'the scary girls,' which I find very funny," states Coye. "When I train people at work a lot of them will talk about their favorite movies, and it's funny when someone says *Elm Street*. 'Yeah, that scary song and those creepy girls,' and I chuckle because, well, that was me! I was one of those 'creepy girls.' It's neat to know that the history is still there. I was happy to have been part of it. Even if I didn't comprehend everything it was definitely fun, absolutely."

"I would say it was a really fun experience for a little girl. I feel pretty special to have been a part of it, and people still think that it's the coolest thing when I tell them that I'm a jump rope girl," Rusoff admits. "And they all want me to sing the song! It's cool that people are still talking about it and still know who we are. That I have left an impression on people that still remains today is pretty fun. It's really great that people are still fascinated. I'm a little bashful about it sometimes, but when I do tell people they just think it's the coolest thing in the world."

"It was a great experience because it was such a well-known and talked about film," says Lepucki. "And, for me, when people ask what was it like to grow up in L.A., I tell them the story of how I ended up in *A Nightmare on Elm Street*. It sort of sums up what it's like to be a child in Los Angeles: you never know, you just might end up as an extra in a movie that people are still talking about decades later! I am definitely happy

Jim Doyle

Rick Shaine

Charles Bernstein

Adri-Anne Cecere (l) and **Coye Cecere**

Leslie Hoffman

Don Hannah

Patrick McMahon

Mimi Meyer-Craven

Annie Rusoff

Matthew Peak

Jacques Haitkin

Joe Unger

Lin Shaye

Sandy Lipton

Nick Corri (with John-Roger and Jaime King)

Amanda Wyss

Joseph Whipp

Ronee Blakley (with Anders Eriksen)

Heather Langenkamp

John Saxon

Robert Englund

Sara Risher

Robert Shaye

Wes Craven

that I was part of something that became so big. Forever I have this story to tell about being part of something that was so great and people still love talking about."

"What I take away from it is gratitude," offers Meyer-Craven. "I'm proud to have been a part of it. I think of myself as Freddy's mom, because I watched him be born. To see that go from a little idea embryo to Freddy now, who's twelve feet tall and bulletproof, that was Wes' baby. He did it all. He saw it. He had the vision. He made everybody follow his dream, his 'nightmare' dream, and I think it changed the way horror films are seen and the expectations people have of a horror film. It raised the bar. So thankful is what I am. I'm so thankful."

"For someone like me, whose career has been as an educator and I continue to work as an actor and director, it's something I am proud to have been a part of," says Shea. "*Elm Street* has had tremendous staying power over the years and I run into a lot of people, and they Google my name and they go, 'Oh my God, you're in *A Nightmare on Elm Street!*' and I go, 'Yeah, it was a small part.' Of all the few things I did in film, this is the one thing that has had that kind of staying power. That's a testament to Wes and it turned out to be one of the best movies of the genre. It's very nice to have been part of something like that."

"I'm very proud that I was in that film. I love that film," Woodrum states. "I enjoyed working with every one of those people. I think Wes Craven is an icon in the film industry. I cherish the experience with all my heart. It really was wonderful, and I loved it."

"Every time I talk to anyone about my past as a Hollywood actress, I always use the fact that I played Johnny Depp's mother in the first *Nightmare on Elm Street* to identify myself," Lipton admits. "That was an important role to play, an important movie to be in, and I am so proud of the fact that Wes decided to put me in it with so little experience. I had been an actress in Chicago for several years and had very little on-screen experience at the time. He gave me the ability to work for fifteen years in L.A., so I owe a lot of gratitude to Wes Craven."

"It was an excellent experience working with Wes, the cast, and the entire crew for the one scene that I was fortunate enough to be a part of," says Hannah. "I was thrilled, I was nervous, I was excited, and I rehearsed my butt off for my little tiny part. It got me into reading Shakespeare, which became a big part of me after the film. 'A dream itself is but a shadow' was Hamlet's next line, and I think that pretty perfectly sums up *Elm Street*."

"When I was working on *Scream 2* with Wes, he was telling me in *Scream* he actually filmed himself as the janitor, and he actually said the line, 'Where's your pass?'" Hoffman says. "It ended up on the cutting room floor, but for some reason the line is as iconic as, 'Hey Nancy, no running in the hallway.' That is such a memorable part of the movie. I will be remembered!"

"Thank you Bob and Wes for creating a powerful, iconic piece of work that's audience-friendly, audience-scary, smart, and has some universal reach, I think. This was filmmaking at its best," states Lin. "I think this film has its place firmly, firmly planted in film history."

"I'm very proud to have been cast by Wes Craven and to work with as many good people as I did," says Unger. "Just as a professional, that's a delight. That's what your goal is: to work on good projects, with good people, and work well. To me, the thing that made it successful is that concept of sleep. You're tired. You're stressed. You want to go to sleep, but can't. It's a terrific concept and I am glad that I was a part of it."

"I am just very happy to be involved with one of the movies that is continually listed as one of the ten best horror movies, the ten scariest movies," Whipp says. "It was a tremendous experience all the way through. I think the only regret I have, is that I didn't get Johnny Depp's signature on a call sheet!"

"I am very proud to have been a part of something that became such an iconic film of its era, and that it was really intelligent storytelling in the genre of horror," offers Wyss. "It also forged long-lasting friendships for me. I really am very proud to have been a part of Wes' vision."

"We're blessed to be a part of it. To be serving and to be entertainers. We're artists," admits Corri. "I want to thank all the fans, because out of all my jobs and movies, this thing keeps transcending. And if the film is something that gives them happiness, I don't have anything to say except thank you. And I'm glad that I was part of something. It's cultural here in the USA. Hot dogs, hamburgers, apple pie, and *Nightmare on Elm Street*. It's really good to know."

"I was very happy to be in it," Blakley says. "I believe that it is a classic that fits right in with *Dracula* and *Frankenstein*. I believe it's one for the ages."

"I'm appreciative for all the success," states Saxon. "Even at the end I was a little skeptical, but that it was a big few weeks at the box office around the country was a very, very pleasing feeling for me. I got into a big, big film and I'm appreciative of that."

"As I get older, and I look back at the movie that we made, I appreciate how fortunate you have to be to be able to be an actor that is working in a movie that people actually like. It's so rare," explains Langenkamp. "And so I always say to myself, 'If I never, ever work in Hollywood again, I would not have a single regret.' That's because I've already been able to achieve what thousands and thousands and thousands of other actors never have the opportunity to see or feel. Being Nancy was enough. It really was. It was enough. I also cannot overemphasize how important Wes Craven is in my life. I think back to the fact that he's given me this role of a lifetime. If I never work again, I can kind of die happy that I played a role that is so important in American cinema."

"For me, in hindsight now, the great gift that Wes gave me, the great, great gift, aside from teaching me to respect the genre, and to look to the art within the genre, is that it's as equal an ingredient to the history of cinema as the Japanese film or the Western or the action film or the romantic comedy or anything else," Englund says. "The horror film is as significant in the history of Hollywood and film as cinematic literature. I'm still working in Europe because of Wes Craven and *Nightmare*, which was so embraced internationally. That's just this great bonus to a career that I'm sure has been extended because the film has given me a worldwide audience, and worldwide fans. It's incredible."

The cast and crew of *A Nightmare on Elm Street.*

"I'm very fond of the work we did, and I love looking back. I'm very proud," Risher admits. "It was so important to us at the time, and the making of it was such a joy. The fact that it worked and was successful was so fulfilling. It's obviously a sort of triumph of the underdog. We owe a lot to Freddy Krueger."

"What I say to the fans is, 'Thank you.' And I also say that to everybody who's participated," Shaye declares. "I know everybody broke their neck or broke their back to do the best that they possibly could. And it was a fantastic experience in that way. Not because of the amount of money it made, but the fact that we were able to do what I always liked to do: really entertain people."

"I think it was the first film that I'd made that really had a broad audience, that had a universal audience. It wasn't just a slasher film or something like that, and it didn't have a rape scene. It was more palatable to a broader audience," explains Craven. "I built into it a sort of philosophical basis that got some interviewers interested in it as something more than just a slasher film. And the fact that it did so well and it kept generating sequels gave me leverage as a director. It got me the offers of more and more interesting films. And it still is the first question anybody asks me about if I'm in an interview for directing a film. It's like, 'What was it like to make *A Nightmare on Elm Street?*' So it became kind of the hallmark of my career. For *Nightmare*, it was something I thought of and wrote, and it was very, very personal. I think to me it's probably one of the signal films of my career. I think I did some things that were really innovative, and I had the chance to work with some enormously talented and wonderfully spirited people. It doesn't get much better than that in the business."

The Gifts of Elm Street

by Robert Englund

You know, when I look back at the *Elm Street* franchise's success, there are so many gifts that came to me as a result of that phenomenon.

I find it hard to pinpoint any one takeaway from the experience. Of course, there were the friendships both in front of and behind the camera. Wes Craven, our fearless leader. Bob Shaye. Rachel Talalay. My leading ladies Heather Langenkamp, Lisa Wilcox, Lisa Zane, and Monica Keena, and my gal pal, Amanda Wyss. I remember sharing old Hollywood stories and gossip at lunch with the wonderful John Saxon. Hanging out with the multitalented Ronee Blakley at airport-adjacent steakhouses. Ronee playing the piano in the bar, singing Bob Dylan. My makeup effects bros David Miller, Kevin Yagher, and KNB: Kurtzman, Nicotero, Berger. And directors like the foodie Jack Sholder, and Renny Harlin, who hired me several times.

There are so many others, but I neglect them here, and I'm sorry. But to be honest, the most fulfilling, I think, and longest-lasting bonus to my career is the international success of the *Nightmare* films. It has enabled me a parallel career as an actor and a personality. I'm able to work abroad at film festivals all over the world and with the continued fan interest at conventions. I performed in films worldwide in Great Britain, Italy, Sicily, Madrid, Barcelona, Budapest, Romania, Bulgaria, St. Petersburg, Tel Aviv, Johannesburg, Zagreb, Puerto Vallarta, Montreal, and Oahu.

All that travel and adventure is due to Wes Craven's little film that's become this juggernaut of horror.

Freddy's been very good to me. I'm glad I sat through all those countless makeup sessions, pulled on that stinky sweater, donned my dirty fedora, and lurked in the shadows all those years.

Sweet dreams.

Memories of Elm Street

by Heather Langenkamp

Forty years later, it is perhaps the one thing that haunts me. My only regret. The gnawing feeling of something I'll never have. Like red hair or dark skin. There are a few things in life that you can endlessly wish for but know, with fatalistic certainty, that you will never enjoy. It's a deep-pitted, dark feeling—akin to jealousy—that has visited me for many years.

It is usually triggered when I watch the faces of Elm Street fans discussing the cataclysmic moment in their lives when they saw the film for the first time. Their eyes give way to a vibrant, childlike animation when they talk about where they were, whom they were with, whose rules they were defying by seeing the film. In their mind, seeing *A Nightmare on Elm Street* is an important moment in their personal history: whether they were hiding behind the couch at their cousin's house, quaking next to their best friend at the movie theater, or sneaking into a matinee alone. Sometimes I see a very young child proudly announce that her mother let her watch it last year like she had won a trophy for bravery.

The thrilling nostalgia with which people remember this "first time" is positively rapturous, and I'm left with my dark feeling again. Like an alien that visits a planet filled with scrumptious flavors she will never understand because she has no mouth. Looking through this amazing book, I enjoy remembering the work, my co-stars, and the crew. But I don't have what you have: a memory of sitting in the dark, experiencing Freddy's terror, and rooting for Nancy as she fights him.

Nothing can change the fact that I will never have the opportunity to watch *A Nightmare on Elm Street* for "the first time." I will never enjoy the unrelenting parade of shocks, diabolical acts, plot twists, and unfathomable fear that Freddy brought to you: thrilled beyond measure, sitting expectantly in the audience together, enduring that unbearable tension with no idea how all that was going to turn out for Nancy, Glen, Tina, and Rod. Tell me again about that spine-tingling, edge-of-your-seat thrill ride! How loud did you scream? Whose arm were you digging your fingernails into? What did you shout at the screen? I truly live vicariously through your telling of that experience. I wish it were mine!

How thrilling was that moment when Freddy's glove raises itself from beneath the surface of the water while Nancy takes a bath? How shocked were you when Freddy drags Tina onto the ceiling and eviscerates her in what is perhaps the scariest scene of all time? Or when Glen gets sucked into his bed and thrown up again in a fountain of blood? At any moment did you think that Nancy's booby traps might work? And would Lieutenant Thompson be there to help Nancy after she goes to sleep that last time? All of it is so wonderful. The originality is relentless. The story is magnificent. The movie is a masterpiece.

Of course, I have a different relationship with this film. Nostalgic and loving. Filled with warmth and pride and the kind of feelings you'd feel at the birth of a child. How fortunate for all of us to be able to access this compilation of stories in one place between the covers of a lovely book. For me, this carefully crafted account encompasses these memories with a beauty and depth that makes my experience even more vibrant in my memory.

I read Wes Craven's words on the page before a single frame of film was shot and tried to imagine how such words come alive on screen. I knew the punchline to the twisted joke of Freddy Krueger before I knew exactly what his sweater looked like. And of course, Robert Englund, your Freddy Krueger, was and always will be my friend, which has naturally ruined the film for me.

Over the six weeks of shooting I ate my lunch during "dailies" (the showing of the previous day's footage) and marveled at the beauty of the film, the color and richness of the settings, the wardrobe, the textures. I saw the story come alive out of sequence and in bits and pieces. I saw all of the takes. I saw Wes and his team of artists—Jacques Haitkin, the director of photography, Greg Fonseca, the production designer, Jim Doyle, the mechanical special effects designer—make hundreds of decisions a day, but I didn't understand the process of crafting horror or the potential result. In dailies, we watched all of the terrifying takes of Tina's death scene.

We watched as Robert Englund crafted the role of Freddy Krueger, day by day and scene by scene, settling into a character who personifies evil, and finding all the expressions for that by using a glove with knives for fingernails. In dailies you get to see the actor just before "Action!" is called and just after Wes says, "Cut": Robert fiddles with his hat, Ronee switches the hold on her vodka bottle, Johnny adjusts his earphones, Amanda bravely endures a body bag with an offhand joke, Nick pretends to sleep without moving his eyelashes. There is a touching ordinariness to watching the actor prepare in that moment just before "Action!" And no amount of gore or scary music washes my memory clean of those tiny, endearing moments. Yes, I appreciate the movie so much for its artistry and skill.

But I will never be scared by it. Hence, my dark jealousy persists.

I suppose the next questions that follow from this meditation are, "Would I trade one for the other? Would I trade the opportunity to be Nancy Thompson for the ability to watch *A Nightmare on Elm Street* with the fresh eyes of a young horror fan?"

Reading through this chronicle, I've never been more sure: the answer is "No."

Just know, that for the rest of time, you have one up on me.

Acknowledgments

Gratitude. Recognition. Credit. Praise. Gramercy.

I could keep going with ways to voice the two simple words I must say, to so many, who were invaluable to me over the course of writing this book. What is ultimately in your hands is the culmination of years of research, interviews, telephone calls, emails, asking, persuading and, when necessary, pleading. All of what is contained within this book would never have been possible were it not for a multitude of people who, either directly or indirectly, assisted not only in the creation of this book, but made sure my dream of writing it did not turn into, well, you guessed it: a nightmare.

While the below list is not—and probably could never be—exhaustive, I am absolutely indebted to the many people with whom I crossed paths on this project:

Wes Craven, who I, and so many others, will miss greatly. He was as incredible a writer, director, and producer as he was a kind, funny, and whip-smart human being. I am so incredibly fortunate to have had the chance to get to know him more than I would have ever hoped. He and his work will always be an inspiration to me. I must also mention it was Wes who helped me identify the little visitor outside my window as I work: a Western Scrub-Jay. Every time I see him, I think of Wes.

Bob Shaye, for believing in Wes and so many others, and for taking the time to share with me so much about his life (and with such candor). He has proven that if you set out to entertain the world, you can not only do it, but enjoy the process. I know I have.

Sara Risher, for the wonderful support and words of encouragement, which were indispensable to me. I am indebted to her constant kindness and sincerity. She also went above and beyond to find fantastic materials and impart interesting information that makes this project so special.

Robert Englund, who terrified audiences on screen, but is the most gentle, caring, giving, and funny person off screen. Nobody can spin a yarn quite like him, and I am lucky he pulled out some new threads for this book. His resolute support of me and my work over the years is astounding and appreciated more than he'll ever know.

Heather Langenkamp, who is a stream of positivity, always offering words of wisdom and steering me in the right direction. She never wavers in her belief in me, even when I do. She has been a traveling companion, sounding board, teaser, confidant and, above all, friend who has shown both the world and me that good can defeat evil.

All those interviewed in these pages, for their time, memories, and sincerity in explaining to me everything I could ask about Wes Craven, Bob Shaye, New Line Cinema, and *A Nightmare on Elm Street*. This is their story, and I am honored they allowed me to take a walk to the past with them so that I could tell it.

Michael Aloisi and everyone at Dark Ink. Their belief in this book and in me has been incredible.

Peter Bracke for his keen eye, fantastic design aesthetic, and patience in finding a way to make this book look incredible. (And for not going crazy in handling all of my questions and concerns.)

Michael Perez and Lito Velasco, who assisted me in putting together the first two editions of this book, whether it was more reading, more research, more interviews or, in general, more everything.

Daniel Farrands, who originally said I should write this book. And for always letting me make him laugh. Dino's forever.

Each and every agent, manager, publicist, attorney, friend, or acquaintance of the cast and crew that offered their help in securing interviews, images, and materials. When I say that every little bit helps, it's proven in this book.

The crew involved in the making of the documentary *Never Sleep Again: The Elm Street Legacy*, because they endured long production days, sleepless nights, crazy dreams, and, for those who lived it, a sing-along of "Reproduction" from *Grease 2*. (Yes, you can commence jealousy for that last part.)

The many journalists and filmmakers who had previously crafted material on Wes Craven, Bob Shaye, New Line Cinema, Freddy Krueger, and Elm Street. You led the charge when it first started and continue the fight to keep the genre dream alive.

My parents, who never dismissed any of my crazy ideas or notions, either as a child or now as an adult. You've loved me no matter what (and there were a lot of "what's!?"). For that, and so much more, I did, do, and always will love you, too.

My family, for taking the time to nurture and support my every endeavor. I couldn't have done this without you, and I love you.

The following for everything they did to assist in the creation of this book. It is appreciated more than you know: Susan Allenback, Clive Barker, Steve Barton and DreadCentral.com, Justin Beahm, Harlan Boll, Anthony Brownlee, Chris Carbaugh, Galena Cecere, Aimee Chaouch, David Chaskin, Sean Clark, Jessica Craven, Jonathan Craven, Mimi Craven, Crash Cunningham, Izzy Donnelly and The Grosse Pointe Historical Society, Jim Doyle, Nancy Englund, Anders & Asia Eriksen, Carly Feingold, Michael Felsher, Stacy Fountain, Roy Frumkes, Mike Fulop, Lee Gambin, Mick Garris, Ted Gerdes, Michael P. Griffin and Clarkson University, Jacques Haitkin, Philip Hallman, Michelle Hanson, Kathleen Dow and University of Michigan, Special Collections Library, Maria Hernandez, Robert Hornsby and Columbia University, Del & Sue Howison and Dark Delicacies, Thomas Hummel, Laurence Keane, Tuesday Knight, Iya Labunka, Diandra Lazor, Kara Lindstrom, Elvira Lount, Adam Lovell, Derek Spinei and The Detroit Historical Society, Robert Lucas, Gloria Martel, Brenna McCormick-Thompson and The New York Historical Society Department of Prints, Photographs & Architectural Collections, Mark Alan Miller, Brad Miska and BloodyDisgusting.com, Tim Noakes and Special Collections, Stanford University, Dorothea Paschalidou, Michael Benni Pierce, Richard Reimer and ASCAP, Zade Rosenthal, Jeffrey Schwarz, Lin Shaye, Steve Sévigny, Jack Sholder, Society for Cinema & Media Studies, Jonna Smith, Ashley Swinnerton and The Film Study Center at The Museum of Modern Art, Nina Tarnawsky, Rachel Talalay, April A. Taylor, Ryan Turek, Jennifer Velasco, Fred Vogel, Christine Walther and Internationale Hofer Filmtage, Penny White and The Department of Special Collections and Archives, Libraries and Media Services at Kent State University, Will Watson and NightmareOnElmStreetFilms.com, Amanda Wyss, Valeria Yaros, Molly Youker, Terri Zaneski, and Larry Zerner.

Finally, you, the reader. I hope you have enjoyed this tome as much as I have enjoyed creating it. It was done because, like so many of you, the movie struck a chord in me. I believe this was a story worth telling. I hope you agree.

And I haven't forgotten those two simple words that must be stated explicitly to everybody who has helped me with this project.

They might seem to be as old as time, but can actually be traced back to c. 1000, where the saying began to form its current meaning. The root of the expression came from the word "think" and originally connoted, "I will remember what you did for me." While that isn't quite how the phrase is construed today, I certainly cannot deny it is how I feel. For the sake of clarity, I'll go ahead and say it in layman's terms—

Thank you.

Thommy Hutson

Bibliography

The material for this book is drawn from over fifty new and exclusive interviews with the cast and crew of *A Nightmare on Elm Street* and other films involving Wes Craven and Robert Shaye. It also includes content from dozens of exclusive interview transcripts—both published and unpublished—from the definitive documentary Never Sleep Again: The Elm Street Legacy.' Additional quoted material, facts, and historical data are sourced from various print publications, books, filmed productions, television programs, and online sources.

INTERVIEWS

Adrienne Barbeau, Charles Belardinelli, Ronee Blakley, Janus Blythe, John Burrows, Joanna Cassidy, Adri-Anne Cecere, Anthony Cecere, Coye Cecere, David Chaskin, Lisa Cook, Nick Corri, Jessica Craven, Wes Craven, Don Diers, Jim Doyle, Robert Englund, RaMona Fleetwood, Roy Frumkes, Jacques Haitkin, Don Hannah, Anne Huntley, Lisa Jensen, Heather Langenkamp, Louis Lazzara, Lauren Lepucki, Sandy Lipton, Peter Locke, Kathy Logan, David Miller, William Munns, Gerald Olson, Lee Purcell, Christina Rideout, Sara Risher, Annie Rusoff, John Saxon, Rick Shaine, Lin Shaye, Robert Shaye, Charlie Sheen, Marc Sheffler, Jack Sholder, Mark Shostrom, Rachel Talalay, Joe Unger, Dee Wallace, David Warner, Joseph Whipp, Donna Woodrum, Amanda Wyss

IN PRINT

Anderson, John. "Horror Revisits the Neighborhood," The New York Times, March 12, 2009.

Canby, Vincent. "Swamp Thing Fun and Fright," The New York Times, July 30, 1982.

Canby, Vincent. "Screen: Nemec's 'Martyrs of Love'," The New York Times, February 4, 1969.

Clarke, Frederick S. "New Line Cinema on Working with Wes Craven," Cinefantastique, Volume 18, Number 5, July 1988.

Collins, Keith. "Showmen 2004: A Brief History," Variety, August 22, 2004.

Cosford, Bill. "Johnny Depp Turns Street Smart," US Magazine, June 13, 1998.

Crowther, Bosley. "The Screen: Czechoslovak Showcase: Center, Museum Join in Festival Project," The New York Times, June 19, 1967.

Cziraky, Dan and Szebin, Frederick C. & Linaweaver, Brad. "Heather Langenkamp: Freddy's Babe," Femme Fatales, Vol 8, No 7, November 1999.

D'Angelo, Carr. "My Breakfast with Freddy," The Bloody Best of Fangoria #6, 1987.

Ebert, Roger. "Last House on the Left," Chicago Sun-Times, January 1, 1972.

Farrell, Mary H.J. and Alexander, Michael. "After A Nightmare on Elm Street, Director Wes Craven Dreams Up Shocker's Maniacal Killer," People Magazine, November 13, 1989

Ferrante, Tim. "Meet Freddie Krueger!," Fangoria #47, August 1985.

Finn, Robin. "Despite Its Charms, Horror Can Pale," The New York Times, January 2, 1997.

Gambin, Lee. "They Are Still His Children, Part One," Fangoria #293, May 2010.

Garcia, Chris. "One Last Scream," Fangoria #16, March 1997.

Georgiades, William. "An American in Paris," Detour, December/January 2000.

Gire, Dann. "Bye, Bye Freddy! Elm Street Creator Wes Craven Quits Series," Cinefantastique, Volume 18, Number 5, July 1988.

Heath, Chris. "Johnny Depp: Portrait of the Oddest as a Young Man," Details, May 1993.

Kutzera, Dale. "Wes Craven's New Nightmare," Imagi-Movies, Volume 2, Number 1, Fall 1994.

Lofficier, Randy and Jean-Marc. "Wes Craven's Deadly Friend: Building a Better Monster," Fangoria #56, Aug 1986

Lupton, Aaron. "Freddy Vs Freddy," Rue Morgue #99, April 2010.

Martin, R.H. "Wes Craven's Triple Play," Fangoria #38, October 1984.

Martin, R.H. "David Miller: Fred Krueger's Main Man!", Fangoria #44, May 1985.

Maslin, Janet. "Movie Review: Deadly Blessing," The New York Times, August 15, 1981.

Maslin, Janet. "Movie Review: Alone in the Dark," The New York Times, November 19, 1982.

McDonagh, Maitland. "Still Giving Us Nightmares," Fangoria #284, June 2009.

McKeown, Matthew. "Nightmare on Our Street?", Publication Unknown, Undated.
Oppenheimer, Jean. "Welcome to His Nightmare," LA Village View, October 28-November 3, 1994.
Pond, Steve. "Depp Perception," US Magazine, June 26, 1989.
Rickey, Carrie. "Movie Review: Deadly Blessing," Village Voice, Aug 20, 1981.
Scapperotti, Dan. "Film Ratings: "The Hills Have Eyes II," Cinefantastique, Volume 16, Number 1, March 1986.
Schilling, Mary Kay. "Johnny Depp Rocks," YM Magazine, March 1988.
Unknown. "Johnny Depp: The Secret of His Success!", 16 Magazine, September 1998.
Variety Staff. "Review: 'Stunts,'" Variety, December 31, 1976.
Variety Staff. "Variety Reviews: The Hills Have Eyes," Variety, Dec 31, 1977.
Waters, John. "Johnny Depp, by John Waters," Interview Magazine, April 1990.
BOOKS
Bracke, Peter. Crystal Lake Memories: The Complete History of Friday the 13th. Sparkplug Press, 2005.
Film Critics of The New York Times. The New York Times Guide to the Best 1,000 Movies Ever Made. St. Martin's Griffin, 2004.
Lamberson, Gregory. Cheap Scares!: Low Budget Horror Filmmakers Share Their Secrets. McFarland, 2008.
Muir, John Kenneth. Wes Craven: The Art of Horror. McFarland & Company, Inc., 1998.
Robb, Brian J. Screams & Nightmares: The Films of Wes Craven. The Overlook Press, 1998.
Szulkin, David A. Wes Craven's Last House on the Left: The Making of a Cult Classic. FAB Press, 2000.
Schoell, William and Spencer, James. The Nightmare Never Ends: The Official History of Freddy Krueger and the "Nightmare on Elm Street" Films. Carol Publishing Group, 1992.
Wooley, John. Wes Craven: The Man and His Nightmares Wiley, 2011.

TV, DVD & VIDEO

1986 Fangoria's Weekend of Horrors (D: Mike Hadley, Kerry O'Quinn; Media Home Entertainment)
1989 This is Horror (D: Rick Marchesano; Atlantic Releasing Corporation)
1999 The Directors: The Films of Wes Craven (D: Robert J. Emery; Fox Lorber)
—— Commentary on A Nightmare on Elm Street (New Line Home Video)
2002 Forbidden Footage: "Last House on the Left" (D: David A. Szulkin; MGM)
——The Making of "Last House on the Left" (D: David A. Szulkin; MGM)
2006 Looking Back at "The Hills Have Eyes" (D: Perry Martin; Anchor Bay)
—— Never Sleep Again: The Making of "A Nightmare on Elm Street" (D: Jeffrey Schwarz; New Line Home Video)
2007 Charlie Rose: A Discussion About the 40th Anniversary of New Line Cinema (D: Mike Jay; PBS)
ONLINE
Abrams, Simon. "Wes Craven: I Always Encouraged Robert Englund to Make Freddy Krueger His Own," RiverFrontTimes.com, January 17, 2014.
"AFI's 100 Years...100 Heroes & Villains," Afi.com, June 2003.
"A Nightmare on Elm Street (1984)," RottenTomatoes.com, Undated.
Erickson, Hal. "Kent State (1981) Review" NewYorkTimes.com, Undated.
"The 500 Greatest Movie of All Time," EmpireOnline.com, September 2008.
GeekChicDaily. "Scream Engine: Wes Craven Talks Ghostface Origins, and the Challenges of the Fourth Film," NerdistNews.com, April 13, 2011.
Laukhuf, Adam. "Q&A with Sam Raimi," Esquire.com, August 1, 2005.
Marc, David. "Katzenberg, Jeffrey 1950–," Encyclopedia.com, 2005.
Meetbrandon. "Is Freddy Krueger Real? The True Story Which Inspired A Nightmare Before Elm Street," MeetBrandon.Hubwpages.com, April 17, 2010.
Murray, Rebecca. "George Romero Talks About 'Land of the Dead'" Movies.About.com, June 21, 2005.
Pardy, Robert. "Summer of Fear: Review," TVGuide.com, Undated.
Primalroot. "Don't Fall Asleep: A Nightmare on Elm Street Revisited," FromDuskTilCon.com, April 6, 2010.
Shaye, Robert. "Some Tools I've Taken Away," Law.Columbia.edu, May 22, 2003.
Tina. "Wes Craven Says Johnny Depp Owes His Success To Daughter Jessica," AllielsWired.com, October 17, 2007.
Tobias, Scott. "Interview: Wes Craven," AVclub.com, March 11, 2009.
Weiner, Robert. "Johnny Depp's '21 Jump Street' Days," Etonline.com, March 16, 2012.
Wikipedia, the Free Encyclopedia. "The McMartin Preschool Trial," Wikipedia.org, August, 2004.
xxnapoleonsolo. "Robert Englund Exclusive interview Part One – Star Wars, Willie and V, a Role in New V and Listening to Monty Python with Mark Hamill," ScyFiLove.com, November 2009.

IMAGE CREDITS

© 1428 Films: 283; 308 top/© ABC Entertainment: 127 left/Courtesy Anne Ahrens: 93 top right/Courtesy ASCAP: 54 bottom left/© Baby Fat, Inc. & Woodacres, Inc.: 32 top left/Courtesy Ryan Baxter|Wikimedia Commons|CC-BY-SA-2.0: 283/Courtesy Charles Belardinelli: 98 top left; 159 left/ Courtesy Annette Benson: 100; 330 first row fourth image/ Courtesy Charles Bernstein: 299 top; 299 middle; 333 first row third image/Courtesy Peter Bracke: 1/ Courtesy Anthony Brownlee: 327 second row third image/ Courtesy John Burrows: 95 bottom third image; 157 bottom left; 283/Courtesy Chris Carbaugh and Stacy Fountain: 168 left; 193; 333 fourth row third image; 334 first row second image/Courtesy Lou Carlucci: 147 bottom left; 147 bottom left; 147 top right; 187 top left; 276 all images/Courtesy Joanna Cassidy : 67 middle left/ Courtesy Adri-Anne and Coye Cecere: 333 second row first image/Courtesy Anthony Cecere: 43 bottom right; 43 top left; 43 bottom middle; 46 top left; 46 top right; 46 bottom left; 48 top right; 48 bottom left; 98 top middle; 164 left; 187 middle left; 265 bottom; 268 bottom middle; 268 middle left; 268 middle center; 301; 330 fourth row third image/© Chevy Chase Films Limited Partnership: 85/ Courtesy of David Chaskin: 70/Courtesy Clarkson University Archives: all images/© Cleveland Plain Dealer: 21 bottom/© Comic Images: 323 top middle/Courtesy Lisa Cook: 93 middle right; 337/Courtesy Jessica Craven: 21 top right, bottom left, bottom middle, middle right, bottom right, 25/Courtesy Wes Craven: 11; 21 middle right; 22;

23 top left; 75 middle right; 114 middle/© Crystal Lake Entertainment: 84 bottom right; 84 bottom left/Courtesy Crash Cunningham: 51 top; 69; 310/Courtesy Detroit Historical Society: 51 bottom; 51 middle left/© Dallas Morning News: 81 top right/Courtesy Don Diers: 330 first row first image; 92 top right; 93 bottom right; 93 top left; 93 bottom left; 229 left; 270/Courtesy Jim Doyle: 94 bottom second image; 147 top left; 157 second row left; 159 right; 172; 176 all images; 183 all images; 187 middle right; 188; 202 left; 205 all images; 227 top right;; 227 bottom left; 249; 260; 268 top; 268 bottom right; 273 right; 273 left; 279 left; 283; 292 bottom right; 315 middle left; 333 first row first image/Courtesy dpade1337 / Wikimedia Commons|CC-BY-SA-2.0: 283/© Elektra: 127 middle/ Courtesy Nancy Englund: 334 third row third image/ Courtesy Robert Englund: 103 top left; 103 bottom right; 103 bottom middle; 103 top right/Courtesy Anders Eriksen: 327 third row second image; 327 top right; 334 second row second image/Courtesy Anders and Asia Eriksen: 330 third row third image/Courtesy RaMona Fleetwood: 45 bottom right; 94 bottom right; 95 bottom left; 95 bottom second image; 103 bottom left; 151 top left; 151 bottom left; 157 third row left; 157 third row middle; 157 top left; 214 all images; 235 top left; 235 top right; 330 fourth row first image/Courtesy The Roy Frumkes Archives: 26 top left; 27 bottom left; 27 bottom middle; 30; 31; 33; 39 middle right; 39 bottom right/© Film Funding: 124 bottom left/Courtesy Mike Fulop: 327 fourth row second image; 327 top left/Courtesy Jsu Garcia: 334 first row fourth image; 121 left; Courtesy David Greenstone: 77/Courtesy The Grosse Pointe Historical Society: 37 middle right/Courtesy Jacques Haitkin: 95 bottom right; 227 top left; 333 fourth row second image/© Handmade Film Partnership: 101/Courtesy Don Hannah: 194 all images; 333 second row third image/Courtesy Michelle Hanson: 327 bottom row third image; 327 third row third image; 327middle right/© Hills Two Corporation: 32 top right; 45 middle right; 46 bottom right/Courtesy Leslie Hoffman: 196; 333 second row second image/ Courtesy Anne Huntley: 330 second row first image/© Thommy Hutson: 330 third row second image/Courtesy Lisa Jensen: 94 bottom third image; 98 top right; 151 right; 157 second row middle; 168 right; 177; 252; 257 left; 262 left; 330 first row second image/Courtesy Karl Josker: 16/© Laurence Keane, Courtesy of Utopia Pictures Ltd.: 71 top/ Courtesy Heather Langenkamp: 19; 107; 110 top; 110 left; 110 middle right; 110 lower right; 110 bottom right; 114 left; 197; 206; 235 bottom left; 235 bottom right; 236; 240 bottom left; 280 bottom; 327 third row first image; 334 third row second image; 341/© Carlos Latuff: 322/© Lawrence Journal-World: 321/Courtesy Diandra Lazor: 327 second row first image; 327 bottom right/Courtesy Louis Lazzara, Louis: 218 left third image; 268 bottom left; 330 second row third image/Courtesy Jeffrey Levine: 291; Courtesy Sandy Lipton: 334 first row third image; 253 all images/Courtesy Kathy Logan: 330 first row third image/© The Los Angeles Times: 315 top left/Courtesy Gloria Martel: 334 third row first image/© Marty Toy, Inc.: 323 top right/Courtesy Patrick McMahon: 288; 333 third row first image/Courtesy Mimi Meyer-Craven: 13; 333 third row second image/© MGM-UA Entertainment Company: 121 right/Courtesy David Miller: 94 bottom left; 114 right; 134; 135 all images; 139 all images; 140 all images; 141 all images; 142 all images; 143; 145 all images; 157 top right; 157 middle right; 157 middle top; 175 all images; 179 all images; 185 top right; 185 top; 185 bottom right; 198; 198 all images; 210 background; 210 left third image; 210 left fourth image; 210 left second image; 217 all images; 218 left fourth image; 218 left first image; 218 top; 222 left; 234; 245 top left; 245 right; 251 all images; 262 middle right; 262 bottom right; 262 top right; 268 middle right; 279 right/© Courtesy Nathan Thomas Milliner: 240 background/© Milwaukee Journal Sentinel: 295 top/© Moonlight Productions II: 36; 37 top right/Courtesy Mumford High School: 51 bottom right; 53; 37 middle left and top right/© New Line Cinema: 58 top right/© New Line Cinema Corporation, New Line Distribution, Inc. & New Line Productions, Inc. and Chemical Bank, as agent: 58 top left/© New Line Productions, Inc.: 93 middle; 122; 164 right; 165; 174 right; 174 left; 185 middle right; 210 left first image; 229 right; 233; 265 top; 281; 292 middle right; 292 lower right; 292 right filmstrip; 292 middle filmstrip; 292 left filmstrip; 293 all images; 296 all images; 300 all images; 308 bottom; 318 right; 318 left; 319 left; 319 middle; 319 right; 324 top middle; 324 top right; 324 middle left; 324 middle center; 324 middle right; 324 bottom left; 324 bottom middle; 324 bottom right; 324 first row left/© The Night Company: 26 top right; 27 bottom right/© NMD Film Distributing Co, Inc.: 29 middle right/© the Passions Joint Venture: 110 center/Courtesy Matthew Peak: 303; 307; 330 fourth row first image/Courtesy Lisa Peterson: 330 fourth row second image/Courtesy John Poer: 48 top left; 48 bottom right/© PolyGram Pictures, Ltd.: 39 bottom left/Courtesy Geoffrey Rayle, Geoffrey: 43 top middle; 43 top right; 43 bottom left/© Ric Records: 323 top left/Courtesy Sara Risher: 73; 87 top right; 88; 227 bottom right; 240 bottom right; 257 top right; 257 bottom right; 294 left; 313 left; 313 right; 334 fourth row first image/Courtesy Joe Robinett: 330 second row second image/© Nicole Rivelli, Courtesy of Wes Craven: 334 fourth row third image/Photo by Joyce Rudolph. Courtesy of Alan and Joyce Rudolph Archive, University of Michigan, Special Collections Library: 154; 157 bottom right; 161 middle left; 161 bottom; 187 top right; 190; 202 right; 222 right; 230; 275; 294 top; 295 bottom/Courtesy Annie Rusoff: 164 middle; 333 third row third image/ Courtesy John Russo: 64 middle right; 64 middle left; 64 top/Courtesy Doug Saquic: 131 all images/Courtesy Saxon, John: 124 right; 124 top left/Courtesy Steve Sevigny: 18/Courtesy Rick Shaine: 285; 333 first row second image/Courtesy Lin Shaye: 334 first row first image/Courtesy Robert Shaye: 9; 54 bottom right; 59; 87 top left; 334 fourth row second image/Courtesy Jack Sholder: 68 top; 68 middle left/Courtesy Mark Shostrom: 330 third row fourth image/© David Slade, Courtesy Iya Labunka and Nina Tarnawsky/SqueakyMarmot|Wikimedia Commons|CC-BY-SA-2.0: 52/Courtesy Amy Steel: 75 top right/© St. Martin's Press: 323 bottom right/© Stunts Film Partnership: 37 top left; 67 top/Courtesy Rachel Talalay: 92 middle right; 132; 330 third row first image; 92 top left; 245 bottom left; 280 top/© April A. Taylor: 327 bottom row second image/Uncredited: 113; 2; 60 top left; 60 top right; 60 top middle; 78 top left; 78 top right; 81 top left; 127 right; 239; 306; 17; 21 top left; 29 top right; 79; 311 right; 311 left; 315 bottom left; 315 bottom right/Courtesy Utopia Pictures Ltd.: 71 middle right/© Variety: 315 top right/ Courtesy Lito Velasco: 283; 327 bottom row first image; 327 second row second image; 327 third row third image/© Video University: 283/Courtesy Videvo: 283/ Courtesy Amanda Wyss: 119 top right; 119 bottom right; 119 left; 334 second row first image/Photo by Steve Yeager, © Charm City Productions: 63/© Molly Youker: 57

Index

In Loving Memory

Wes Craven

1939-2015

www.ingramcontent.com/pod-product-compliance
Lightning Source LLC
LaVergne TN
LVHW050926080826
845145LV00001B/231